93-1323

MOR   Y,
RATI   LITY,
AND   CIENCY

Studies in Socio-Economics

SOCIO-ECONOMICS
TOWARD A NEW SYNTHESIS
Amitai Etzioni and Paul R. Lawrence, editors

MORALITY, RATIONALITY, AND EFFICIENCY
NEW PERSPECTIVES ON SOCIO-ECONOMICS
Richard M. Coughlin, editor

MORALITY, RATIONALITY, AND EFFICIENCY

New Perspectives on Socio-Economics

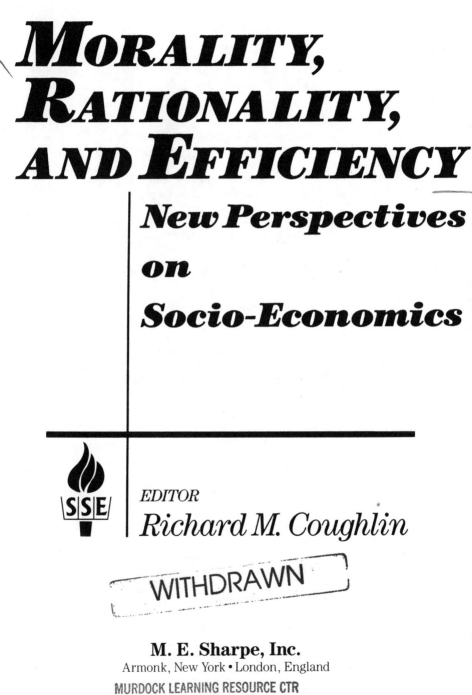

EDITOR

Richard M. Coughlin

M. E. Sharpe, Inc.

Armonk, New York • London, England

Copyright © 1991 by M. E. Sharpe, Inc.
80 Business Park Drive, Armonk, New York 10504

Available in the United Kingdom and Europe from M. E. Sharpe, Publishers,
3 Henrietta Street, London WC2E 8LU.

Library of Congress Cataloging-in-Publication Data

Morality, rationality, and efficiency:
new perspectives on socio-economics / Richard M. Coughlin, editor.
p.   cm.—(Studies in socio-economics)
Includes bibliographical references and index.
ISBN 0-87332-821-3 (hardcover)   ISBN 0-87332-822-1 (paper)
1. Economics—Moral and ethical aspects.
2. Economic man.
I. Coughlin, Richard M.
II. Series.
HB72.M57   1991
330—dc20
90-19137
CIP

Printed in the United States of America

The paper used in this publication meets the minimum
requirements of American National Standard for
Information Sciences—Permanence of Paper
for Printed Library Materials, ANSI Z 39.48-1984.

⊗∞

MV   10   9   8   7   6   5   4   3   2   1

Contents

List of Figures

List of Tables

Preface

The papers in this volume were presented at the Second Annual International Conference on Socio-Economics, held at George Washington University, Washington, D.C. in March 1990. One measure of the great interest that socio-economics has inspired over the past few years is the remarkable growth in the field since the First Annual Conference held at the Harvard Business School in 1989. More than 800 people attended the Second Annual Conference, and nearly 200 papers were presented at some 50 sessions. The atmosphere of the Washington, D.C. conference reflected the growing excitement and enthusiasm in socio-economics. The prospect of liberating the study of economic phenomena from the straightjacket of the neoclassical approach inspired a good deal of lively discussion, just as it had at the Harvard conference. But there was more to the Second Annual Conference than "neoclassical bashing"; the conference marked important progress toward identifying and drawing together innovative theoretical insights and empirical analyses from a wide range of social science and associated disciplines. The conference brought together psychologists, sociologists, political scientists, philosophers, economists, and students of management and business administration. More importantly, the conference encouraged scholars from these diverse backgrounds to begin to talk to one another, to share ideas, and to develop cross-disciplinary analyses of the economic realm. Such opportunities to communicate across the frontiers of established disciplines and address enduring questions with a fresh eye are as rare as they are precious.

No editor of a volume of conference papers ever had an easier or more enviable task than I did in preparing this book. The papers included in this volume are the *crème de la crème*—the very best selected from a large number of excellent papers presented at the conference. In addition, the papers included here are broadly representative of major themes and debates currently addressed under the rubric of socio-economics. A major goal of this book is to provide a snapshot of the current state of socio-economic research being pursued across a range of established academic disciplines.

My first debt of gratitude is to the contributors for providing papers of such fine quality and for meeting the tight deadlines that I ruthlessly imposed on them. I would also like to thank the members of the conference Empirical Paper

Award Committee: James Burk, Jerald Hage, Fred van Raaij, and Charles Lockhart. The committee's deliberations helped to hone my editorial sense of which papers would be most appropriate for inclusion in this volume. Finally, I would like to offer special thanks to Amitai Etzioni on two counts: first, for all that he has done for socio-economics, from launching the intellectual movement, to founding its professional organization, to contributing many of its central theoretical insights; and second, for suggesting that I serve as editor of this book. The book, and indeed socio-economics as a whole, owes its existence to Amitai's extraordinary dedication and service.

Richard M. Coughlin
January 1991

1

Introduction

Richard M. Coughlin

Introduction:
Toward an Agenda
for Socio-Economics

Political Economy is inseparably intertwined with many other branches of social philosophy. Except on matters of mere detail, there are perhaps no practical questions, even among those which approach nearest to the character of purely economical questions, which admit of being decided on economical premises alone.

> —John Stuart Mill, *Principles of Political Economy with Some of Their Applications to Social Philosophy* (1848)

Socio-economics assumes that economics is embedded in society, polity and culture, and is not a self-contained system. It assumes that individual choices are shaped by values, emotions, social bonds, and judgements—rather than by a precise calculation of self-interest.

> —Society for the Advancement of Socio-Economics, "What is Socio-Economics?: A Brief Platform" (1990)

In name only, socio-economics is of recent ancestry. Amitai Etzioni's book, *The Moral Dimension*, published in 1988, launched the current socio-economics movement, but the intellectual roots of socio-economics reach back to the very beginnings of the social sciences.[1] Before disciplines had names, before they differentiated themselves by laying claim to distinctive theories and methodologies, the idea that behavior in the economic realm could or should be separated from the study of other aspects of human behavior would have been regarded as an anomaly, if not an abomination. Consider the terms used to describe the early stages in the development of the science of economics in the eighteenth and nineteenth centuries—*moral* philosophy and *political* economy—although these terms subsequently took on meanings quite different from their original denotations. The classic theorists of the social sciences, from Adam Smith through Max Weber, Emile Durkheim, Alfred Marshall, and of course Karl Marx and

Friedrich Engels, each in his own way attempted to locate the study of economic phenomena within the context of society, politics, history, and philosophy. So, too, do the papers in this volume, each in its own way, attempt to improve the understanding of economic behavior, drawing upon the insights and methods of the contemporary disciplines of sociology, psychology, political science, philosophy, economics, and management.

Of Paradigms and Disciplines

To appreciate the contributions these perspectives offer, it is important to understand both what socio-economics is and what it is not. It is not, at this stage at least, either a radically new paradigm or an academic discipline, at least in the sense that these terms are now widely understood. Here I use "paradigm" in the sense Thomas Kuhn used the term in his classic study, *The Study of Scientific Revolutions* (1962). A paradigm suggests a relatively closed system of assumptions and propositions that delimit the range of scientific inquiry. A paradigm, in *this sense, determines which questions are appropriate and useful to explore and which are not. Clearly, neoclassical economics has developed into a paradigm according to this definition. Paradigms impose constraints, as Kuhn demonstrates, but they also confer advantages. They help to guide and order inquiry; they lead to development of parsimonious models of explanation and prediction (albeit at the cost of reductionism); and they are conducive to the legitimation of particular approaches as intellectual disciplines in their own right.

If we apply these restrictive criteria to socio-economics in its current state, it is not a paradigm. Not everyone would agree with this contention. Lutz (1990), for example, argues that *The Moral Dimension* presents a "visionary hope of creating some new (and more encompassing) . . . Kuhnian paradigm, replete with positions on ethics, methodology, and epistemology" (pp. 4–5). It is certainly true that socio-economics presents a fundamental challenge to the dominant neoclassical paradigm, and may signal the start of a "paradigm shift" (Swedberg, 1990), and while there are paradigmatic elements in Etzioni's outline of socio-economics (for example, the propositional inventory found on pp. 253–57 of *The Moral Dimension*), these elements do not even come close to the closed system of theoretical propositions or methodological assumptions that mark a full-blown paradigm. Etzioni's exposition of socio-economics contains some fundamental propositions (e.g., the rejection of a mono-utility conception of behavior; the recognition of the mediation of economic behavior by social and political processes and structures), but these are relatively few in number and, more important, are treated as working hypotheses rather than as axioms. Along the same lines, the platform of the Society for the Advancement of Socio-Economics (1990) emphasizes the open character of socio-economic inquiry:

> Socio-economics is an evolving discipline that seeks to draw on a variety of social sciences. . . . [S]ocio-economic propositions contain at least one independent variable of economics and one of another social science. Collections of new data and inductive studies are co-equal in methodological status to deduction and manipulation of existing data. [p. 1]

Contrasting this new approach to the "economic imperialism" of the current dominant paradigm, Swedberg (1990) succinctly sums up the situation as follows: "Socioeconomics . . . tries to keep the door open" (p. 151).

At its present state of development, socio-economics is a locus of convergence, from multiple and often quite diverse perspectives, on a set of central and relatively enduring questions about the nature of human behavior in the economic realm. Even in its core questions and concerns, much of the intellectual terrain of socio-economics remains to be explored and charted. The elements of a paradigm are still developing, growing, and adapting themselves to new theoretical propositions and empirical findings.

Nonetheless, although the boundaries of socio-economic inquiry are not yet firmly etched out, certain general features of the field can be discerned, particularly with regard to such core concerns as the moral underpinnings of economic behavior; the complex nature of rationality, self-interest, motivation, and preference formation; the importance of organizational culture, political institutions, and other elements of social structure as mediators of economic activity of both individuals and business firms. Although there are numerous interconnections among these concerns, as the papers in this volume amply demonstrate, there is as yet no overarching socio-economic framework that specifies *a priori* how intellectual inquiry should proceed. This kind of openness of inquiry is probably possible only in the absence of an entrenched, dominant paradigm.

Carried to an extreme, of course, a lack of a tight paradigmatic structure runs the risk of intellectual chaos: each analysis begins anew with no antecedents or descendants; theory disintegrates into countless fragments; hypotheses remain unconfirmed; knowledge fails to accumulate. This is a real danger, one that socio-economics cannot ignore, but on balance I do not regard it as a serious problem at the present time because the very questions that are at the center of socio-economic inquiry are also central to the established scholarly disciplines from which the ranks of current "socio-economists" are drawn.

This observation leads to a second point about the organization and production of knowledge: namely, the state of socio-economics as an academic discipline. Let me introduce this point with an anecdote. At the First Annual International Conference on Socio-Economics, held at the Harvard Business School in 1989, the distinguished economist Amartya Sen was one of three individuals honored as a "founding father" of socio-economics. (Lest this nomenclature be interpreted as evidence of a sexist bias in socio-economics, it should be noted that anthropologist Mary Douglas was similarly honored at the

1990 conference.)[2] In accepting the award, Sen commented humorously that being named a founding father of the discipline was a little like being unexpectedly served with a paternity suit—the "father" is unaware of the child's existence, and even unsure of his part in the conception. To anyone familiar with Sen's central contributions to the study of rationality and social welfare economics, the appropriateness of the award was self-evident. But Sen's academic appointments are in economics and philosophy, and it was *in these fields* doing the work *identified with these disciplines*, that he made his important contributions to socio-economics. The emphases in the preceding sentence are critical to understanding how socio-economics has related thus far, and at least for the time being should continue to relate, to existing academic disciplines in the social and behavioral sciences.

Academic disciplines serve primarily as vehicles of social organization. First, disciplines are the main means for organizing the production and dissemination of knowledge among scholars of kindred interests. Considered in this broad sense, socio-economics is no less a discipline than its older, more established counterparts in the social and behavioral sciences. Second, in the bureaucratic setting of the contemporary university disciplines are the principal institutional mechanism for organizing and supporting the activities of individual scholars. With few exceptions, scholarly disciplines *qua* academic departments offer opportunities for employment, make collective claims on institutional resources, and enable the training of new graduates. These mundane aspects of disciplines take on critical importance mainly when they are absent, a hard fact of life that many well-intentioned "interdisciplinary" efforts have discovered on the road to oblivion. New intellectual disciplines are in a meaningful sense analogous to small business enterprises—the risks are high, the chances of long-term success are slim, and experience teaches that most fail in a relatively short time. Certainly there are few incentives for individual scholars to renounce their current disciplinary identities to join up with a new intellectual movement—at least not if the latter requires foregoing all the practical advantages offered by an existing disciplinary niche. The good news, however, is that such choices do not have to be of an either/or type. For socio-economics, the best chances for success appear to lie in a dual strategy: building on the foundation of scholarship in existing disciplines, while at the same time reaching out to forge new and stronger links across disciplinary boundaries. In time socio-economics may evolve into a "discipline" in the sense of establishing academic departments, offering degrees, and the like—but it need not do so to survive, even flourish, as an intellectual enterprise. At the moment, what is essential to the continued growth of socio-economics is the definition of research agenda that makes sense for scholars to pursue within their current disciplines. If successful, this approach will likely lead to development of a research agenda that is more distinctively socio-economic. In the next section I attempt to sketch out, in a preliminary way, what such an agenda might look like.

Central Questions, Enduring Concerns, and Points of Convergence

To reiterate, my general argument is that socio-economics comprises a set of shared substantive and theoretical concerns through which scholars from a variety of backgrounds are fruitfully exploring a set of interconnected questions about economic behavior. These concerns are, for the most part, not in themselves new, having been identified in one form or another within existing scholarly disciplines as important to the development of sound social theory. What sets socio-economics apart, and gives it a distinctive character, is the convergence on these questions from multiple directions, but with an identifiable communality of purpose. Taken separately and together, these questions form the framework for socio-economic research.

Rationality

One of the most enduring problems in the social sciences concerns rationality as the basis of human behavior. As incorporated into neoclassical economics, cognitive theory in psychology, exchange theory in sociology, and public choice theory in political science, rational choice has become the dominant paradigm (Etzioni, 1988; Coleman, 1989). Within the rational choice paradigm, however, rationality is typically taken for granted—at least in the narrow terms in which it is defined—and being taken for granted, it has ceased to be studied as a problematic concept. It is only *outside* of the dominant paradigm of rational choice that interest in rationality as a phenomenon to be studied in its own right has remained active.

In rational choice models, rationality is commonly treated as a simple expression of self-interest. Indeed, the term "rational behavior" has taken the connotation "narrowly self-interested" in many contemporary contexts—not only with respect to economic activity but across a broad range of behavior. Alternatively, "rational behavior" is conceptualized as the manifestation of individual preferences, allowing "altruistic" impulses some latitude. The latter usage is problematic, however, since it easily slides into the tautology that "people do what they do because they want to do it." Commenting on the tautological nature of rational choice models, two sociologists write, "Shiite martyrs who die charging machine guns are no less rational than Wall Street stockbrokers; they just have different utilities" (Evans and Stephens, 1988, p. 733). Only by specifying where preferences come from, they add, can the revealed preferences conception of rational choice be saved. Such a specification is precisely what rational choice theorists are reluctant to do.

The possible approaches to developing a more complete understanding of rationality are numerous. For a start, we can recognize that behavior can be understood as rational only by reference to a particular set of contextual conditions—historical, political, or sociocultural. Only by placing actors in the context of such variables can we begin to make sense out of what is otherwise strange or incomprehensible behaviors: for example, the odd wagering patterns of the Balinese cockfight, which Geertz (1973) describes, or the apparently irrational purchasing decisions of Japanese consumers (*The Economist*, 1987). Sen (1977) has provided us with the *reductio ad absurdum* of rational choice in his famous depiction of the "rational fool." Operating in a mode of relentlessly rational self-interest, no individual could function for very long in the real world; a society organized along these lines is equally unthinkable, as Thomas Hobbes correctly recognized long ago.

Another objection to rational choice is that it does not accurately describe how people process information, rank alternatives, and make decisions. Nearly forty years ago Milton Friedman attempted to answer this objection by offering a clever counterargument. Conceding that the conception of rationality found in neoclassical economics is not true to life, Friedman (1953) suggested that it nonetheless serves a useful purpose in generating accurate explanations and predictions of behavior. Comparing individual rationality to leaves on a tree, he argued that one need not actually believe that individual leaves position themselves on branches in such a way as to maximize their exposure to sunlight in order to explain how leaves in trees are actually distributed. The measure of the model is not in its faithfulness to nature, Friedman contended, but in its usefulness as a heuristic tool. The problem with Friedman's argument, however, is precisely the fact that predictions of rational choice theory are often simply wrong (see Coughlin, 1986).

For those who are unprepared to accept the narrow or tautological definitions, rationality remains a phenomenon for study—more elusive, yet richer and more suggestive. For example, while few contemporary social theorists would reject the notion that most human behavior is intentional, calculated, and goal directed, the question of how to go about conceptualizing and understanding "intentionality," "calculation," and "goal direction" remains fiercely contested. Posing these questions immediately raises a host of related questions: Where do intentions (or preferences) come from? Once formed, how do preferences change? How do preferences and other internal states translate into behavior in actual social settings? How do the cognitive limitations of the individual's capacity to process information affect both the formation of preferences and attempts to realize them? Such questions, which have been largely assumed away in the dominant rational choice paradigm, are key concerns in socio-economics.

Morality

Related to the idea of rationality is the place occupied by moral values as determinants of behavior. Like rationality, morality has not been regarded as an important object of study in neoclassical economics and related schools of thought in the social sciences. Morality has either been defined *a priori* as outside the scope of economic theory (see the reference to Robbins in chapter 12 by John Oliver Wilson) or it has been treated as just another individual preference. These positions can be challenged on several grounds. First, the disjunction of morality from scientific inquiry is a recent and rather aberrant development—a curious combination of naivete and arrogance. Second, ignoring the moral dimension distorts the basic model of human behavior which lies at the heart of the neoclassical paradigm's "methodological individualism." For one thing, as noted above, methodological individualism has little to say about where preferences come from, including the fundamental values to which humans turn in the attempt to find meaning in their lives. Moreover, in taking preferences for granted, methodological individualism pays little or no heed to what is perhaps the most interesting aspect of morality: the competition among values that is found in all modern, pluralist societies that leads to multiple conceptions of what is moral. Individual freedom to pursue one's own happiness is one such value, to be sure, but so is the right to some minimum share of the material and other benefits of society (see Lockhart, 1989 for a discussion of these competing rights). It is precisely because moral values are in constant competition with one another and with other values in a complex socio-cultural matrix that morality cannot be neatly reduced to individual-level motivation. As Etzioni (1988) emphasizes, the very existence of a free market presumes a moral order that encapsulates competition, prohibiting, for example, one business firm from firebombing its competitor's factories or threatening the lives of its employees. Those who would deny the implicit and often taken-for-granted principles that protect private property and the rights of individuals in market economy democracies might take a look at *The Godfather* or the activities of contemporary Colombian drug cartels for a glimpse of what a system based on unrestrained, amoral competition could look like.

Arriving at a better understanding of how moral factors shape preference formation and constrain expressions of self-interest is at the heart of the research agenda of socio-economics.

Efficiency

In the neoclassical paradigm economic efficiency is usually understood in straightforward terms of market dynamics; indeed, in some usages "efficiency" and "free market outcomes" are treated as one and the same thing. This view of efficiency assumes that individuals, whether acting alone or corporately as firms, possessed with complete information, freely seek to maximize their utilities (self-interest or profit) in market transactions. In this scheme of things, attempts to effect a more equitable distribution of goods or services are regarded as a "trade off" with pure efficiency considerations (see Okun, 1975). The implication here is that interference with market mechanisms necessarily reduces efficiency. This idea has been challenged both by economists and those outside the discipline. For example, Geiger (1978) points out that interventions to produce more "equity" can be either "positive-sum" or "negative-sum" in terms of economic efficiency. Improvements in nutrition, public health, education, housing, and other conditions of life obviously increase a nation's productive capacity; other public goods such as old age pensions, disability, and family allowances, coupled with macroeconomic management policies, can also serve beneficial purposes by increasing aggregate demand during periods of underutilization of productive capacities. "Negative-sum" outcomes are possible too, of course, as in the case where government intervention undercuts individual motivation or incentives to work.

Other market outcomes that militate against "pure" efficiency include monopolistic pricing and other "market failures" (including destructive competitive practices and the instability toward which completely unregulated markets seem to be prone), and vast disparities in income, wealth, and life chances—especially when these result in the immiseration of some segments of the population.

Within a socio-economic perspective, efficiency is viewed as problematic both conceptually and in empirical terms. Consequently, from a socio-economic point of view questions such as "Efficient for what purposes?" and "Efficient for which segments of the population?" remain open for investigation. These questions underscore the basic socio-economic position that economic activity is embedded in society, politics, and culture, and is not reducible to a pure market model.[3]

Social and Political Context of Economic Behavior

Socio-economics' renewed emphasis on the social and political forces impinging on economic behavior follows an intellectual tradition with a long and distinguished history.[4] The narrow parsing out of social reality as the object of scientific study is a relatively recent development. The intellectual monopoly of established disciplines is increasingly being questioned. Increasingly, social scientists are recognizing the need to expand their models to include more variables and wider fields of action; the result is less parsimony but better social science. In the study of economic behavior, a major theme of criticism focuses on the artificial disjunction of economic behavior from social reality. Granovetter (1985), for example, points out the central role that social networks play in organizing various kinds of economic activity. Block (1990) notes that the dominant concepts of "pure markets" and "individual choice" in neoclassical economics have been developed in isolation from any reference to social or political reality—as if the socio-political context did not exist.

Concern with the socio-political context of economic activity introduces a wide and diverse array of structures and forces into models of economic behavior. The inevitable result is a loss of parsimony and elegance in theoretical models, and the need to do a great deal of empirical research to test hypotheses and build theory.[5] It also requires a broad-based approach drawing upon the contributions of other disciplines. Important work along these lines is already ongoing in, for example, economic sociology and institutional economics. While exploration of the socio-political context will remain a major part of the socio-economic agenda, the scope of the task facing the social sciences here is too large to be claimed by any single intellectual enterprise. The myriad of questions concerning the effects of unequal power relations, organizational characteristics of firms, group affiliation and commitment, and the many other factors that shape economic activity will continue to be pursued across a broad front, engaging many different points of theory and methods of investigation. In this immense undertaking, socio-economics can help to draw together work being done across disciplines and offer new opportunities for communication and collaboration among researchers.

Policy Analysis

Socio-economics holds great potential for improving policy analysis in both public and private arenas. The reason for this is obvious, and derives directly from socio-economics' central concern with replacing conceptions of narrow rationality and market efficiency with models of individual motivation and collective action that capture the interplay of logical-empirical and normative-affective factors (Etzioni, 1988). To ask whether a policy works or not is rarely as simple costing out its inputs and outputs in logical-empirical terms. While this fact has long been recognized, policy analysis based on conventional economic models has tended to shunt aside nearly all factors that cannot be quantified in straightforward cost-benefit terms, in effect saying that if something cannot be included in the analytical framework, it does not really exist. Locked into an approach that assumes fixed preferences and strict utility maximization, the most conventional policy analysts have been able to do is note in passing the factors they recognize as having been left out of their analyses. The problem with this approach is twofold: first, there is the ever-present temptation to place too much credence in the model — to be seduced by the numbers, as it were — however much reality is ignored in the process; second, because there is no place in conventional policy analysis for such things as complex rationality, mixed motivations, or socially-mediated preferences, it is not clear how conventional policy analysts can adequately identify what their models "leave out."

Socio-economic policy analysis is still in its infancy, but it is clear that it offers potential solutions to both problems. First, compared to conventional policy analysis socio-economic models will tend to contain more variables providing a more realistic representation of reality. Although these gains will come at the expense of parsimony and loss of quantitative "precision," socio-economic policy analysis will be less likely to go catastrophically awry due to the omission of some critical, but difficult to quantify, factor. Moreover, socio-economics already provides many clues about normative-affective variables (e.g., moral values, social contexts) are likely to be important determinants of policy outcomes. As socio-economic theory develops, the criteria it suggests for evaluating policy will almost certainly improve.

Conclusion

The socio-economic agenda is still evolving; indeed, the work has just begun. Undoubtedly, the list of central questions and points of convergence I have identified above will need to be modified as more work is done in socio-economics and as the debate among its practitioners progresses. Some items may be dropped from the list, and others added, as the process of establishing a new discipline unfolds. One thing is certain: if the current level of energy and interest in socio-economics can be sustained, and there is good reason to think that it can, the potential benefits to be reaped are enormous.

Notes

1. Swedberg (1990) summarizes the intellectual history of socio-economics, leading up to the current *methodenstreit,* or paradigmatic struggle. Kaish (1986) outlines the main elements of behavioral economics, a close relative of the present socio-economics.

2. A complete listing the honorary fellows ("founders") of socio-economics reveals the multiple directions from which seminal contributions to the field have come: Mary Douglas (anthropology), Neil Smelser (sociology), Herbert Simon (decision sciences and economics), Amartya Sen (philosophy and economics), and Albert Hirschman, Harvey Leibenstein, and Kenneth Boulding (economics).

3. In chapter 7, Lester C. Thurow's provides an excellent illustration of how the conventional notion of market efficiency fails to account for the behavior of firms who seek strategic conquest of markets. In chapter 6, Peter Doeringer explores the concept of labor efficiency in terms social harmony as well as economic incentives.

4. In the twentieth century, Joseph Schumpeter and Karl Polanyi are examples of towering intellectual figures in economics whose writings were significantly concerned with the socio-political context of economics.

5. As Albert Hirschman (cited in chapter 20 by Amitai Etzioni) has suggested, there is such a thing as too much parsimony.

References

Block, Fred. 1990. *Postindustrial Possibilities: A Critique of Economic Discourse.* Berkeley: University of California Press.

Coleman, James S. 1989. "Editor's Introduction." *Rationality and Society* 1:5–9.

Coughlin, Richard M. 1986. "Understanding (and Misunderstanding) Social Security: A Behavioral Perspective on Public Policy." In Stanley Kaish and Benjamin Gilad, eds., *Handbook of Behavioral Economics*, vol. B. Greenwich, CT: JAI Press.

The Economist. 1987. "A Critique of Pure Irrationality about Japan." (December, 12):39–43.

Etzioni, Amitai. 1988. *The Moral Dimension: Toward a New Economics*. New York: The Free Press.

Evans, Peter B. and John D. Stephens. 1988. "Studying Development since the Sixties: The Emergence of a New Comparative Political Economy." *Theory and Society* 17:713–45.

Friedman, Milton. 1953. *Essays in Positive Economics.* Chicago: University of Chicago Press.

Geertz, Clifford. 1973. *The Interpretation of Cultures.* New York: Basic Books.

Geiger, Theodore. 1978. *Welfare and Efficiency: Their Interactions in Western Europe and Implications for International Economic Relations.* Washington, DC: National Planning Association.

Granovetter, Mark. 1985. "Economic Action and Social Structure: The Problem of Embeddedness." *American Journal of Sociology* 91:481–510.

Kaish, Stanley. 1986. "Introduction." In Stanley Kaish and Benjamin Gilad, eds., *Handbook of Behavioral Economics,* vol. B. Greenwich, CT: JAI Press.

Kuhn, Thomas S. 1962. *The Structure of Scientific Revolutions.* Chicago: University of Chicago Press.

Lockhart, Charles. 1989. *Gaining Ground: Tailoring Social Programs to American Values.* Berkeley: University of California Press.

Lutz, Mark A. 1990. "Emphasizing the Social: Social Economics and Socio-Economics." Paper presented at the Second Annual International Conference on Socio-Economics, March 16–18, Washington, D.C.

Okun, Arthur. 1975. *Equality and Efficiency: The Big Tradeoff.* Washington, DC: Brookings.

Sen, Amartya K. 1977. "Rational Fools: A Critique of the Behavioral Foundations of Economic Theory." *Philosophy and Public Affairs* 6:317–44.

Society for the Advancement of Socio-Economics. 1990. "What is Socio-Economics?: A Brief Platform." Unpublished.

Swedberg, Richard. 1990. "Socioeconomics and the New 'Battle of the Methods': Towards a Paradigm Shift?" *Journal of Behavioral Economics* 19:141–54.

2

Rationality, Motivation, and Preferences

Robyn M. Dawes

Social Dilemmas, Economic Self-Interest, and Evolutionary Theory

Social dilemmas are collective situations in which egoistic incentives yield individually dominating strategies that converge on deficient equilibria—that is, on outcomes that are less preferred by the choosers than are alternative outcomes. (The best-known example is the two-person prisoner's dilemma.) The widespread existence of such situations in contexts of interacting individuals provides normative and descriptive challenges to both classical (Western) economic/political theory and to evolutionary theory based on sociobiological assumptions. The normative challenge arises because both theories maintain that beneficent consequences (e.g., economic growth and evolutionary change) follow from responding wholly to egoistic incentives. The descriptive challenge arises because people (and other organisms) often refrain from choosing what appear to be dominating strategies in social dilemma contexts, instead opting for strategies that have more benign collective consequences.

The standard response to these challenges by both classic economic/political theories and sociobiological ones has been to postulate side-payments that make otherwise dominating strategies in social dilemma situations no longer dominating. Governmental sanctions (through Leviathan), reputational harm (from breaking contractual promises) and norms of reciprocal altruism are postulated by various economic/political theories to be the mechanisms for changing otherwise dominating strategies; sociobiologically oriented evolutionary theorists have proposed the mechanism to be "the selfish gene" (in contrast to the selfish individual), and other evolutionary theorists have proposed a "social evolution" that counters exclusive attention to external incentives by instilling—through

Reprinted with permission from *Frontiers of Mathematical Psychology: Essays in Honor of Clyde Coombs*. Edited by Donald R. Brown and J.E. Keith Smith. Copyright © 1990, Springer-Verlag.

upbringing—internal incentives to avoid guilt and enhance self-esteem. Both types of theories maintain the assumption that if a strategy were "really" dominating, it would be chosen.

Such side-payments are often found in natural settings. Support for postulating them as the mechanisms to avoid deficient outcomes in social dilemma situations has been claimed to follow from the observation that when they are introduced (experimentally or naturally), otherwise dominating strategies are chosen less often. The logical flaw in such reasoning is that postulating the necessity of side-payments does not imply that their introduction will change behavior (*of course* organisms respond to side-payments), but rather that their *removal* will change behavior. A series of experiments over a ten-year period demonstrates that their removal does not necessarily change behavior, specifically that subjects will eschew otherwise dominating strategies in the absence of such side-payments when factors eliciting group identity are present. (These factors may interact with others.) Rates of choosing the strategy that enhances group—as opposed to individual—payoff change radically as these factors are manipulated in the absence of the standard side-payments; consequently, these choices cannot be ascribed to generalization from other situations in which such side-payments are present. Moreover, group identity is parochial; it can produce social dilemma situations between groups in which individuals choose strategies that are dominating from the group perspective—leading to outcomes far more pernicious than those that could result from individuals choosing on the basis only of individually egoistic incentives.

Automatic group-regarding behavior can be both economically and evolutionarily efficient, even though it occasionally leads to individual disaster, and to disasters involving competition between groups. If the requirement that behavior be optimal in order to be retained is dropped in favor of the requirement that it be satisfactory, the type of behavior observed experimentally makes both economic and evolutionary sense. A careful analysis of the postulates of classic economic and sociobiological theory suggests that the optimality assumption is indeed unnecessary. Both economic/social development and evolution are probabilistic processes in which the requirement for retaining behavior is not that it be optimal ("fitt*est*") compared to potentially competing behaviors (in a given environment) but that it be fitt*er*; moreover, while the nonoptimality of a superior behavior always entails the possibility that an even more superior one will displace it, such a possibility does not guarantee the existence of this still-fitter behavior; granted physical and cognitive limits, many highly superior behaviors may exist only hypothetically on theoretical evolutionary and social hills that have never been climbed.

Adam Smith's "invisible hand" passage is one of the most quoted in social theory:

> As every individual, therefore, endeavors as much as he can both to employ
> his capital in the support of domestic industry, and so to direct that industry

that its produce may be of greatest value; every individual necessarily labors to render the annual revenue of the society as great as he can. He generally, indeed, neither intends to promote the public interest, nor knows how much he is promoting it. By preferring the support of domestic to that of foreign industry, he intends only his own security; and by directing that industry in such a manner as its produce may be of greatest value, he intends only his own gain, and he is in this, as in many other cases, led by an invisible hand to promote an end which was no part of his intention. [Smith, 1976, Book 4, p. 477]

The argument is simple: by pursuing self-interests, individuals promote collective interests. There is no need to respond to collective incentives; egoistic incentives are sufficient.

Smith's argument, which is often interpreted as the basic rationale for capitalism, is partly one about human motivation, but also partly one about the *social structure* of a capitalist society. In economic terms, selfish people responding to the positive *internalities* associated with industry create positive *externalities* for others (the "public interest"). In game theory terms it is possible to do away with the interpersonal comparison that places internalities and externalities on a common scale (i.e., to individual actors and to others who are affected by their acts) by analyzing the situation as one in which strategies that are beneficial to the individual converge on outcomes that are beneficial to others as well. The assumed motive is selfishness. The situation is benign.

Often, however, situations arise in which strategies beneficial to the individual result in outcomes that are detrimental to society. Consider, for example, the "Tragedy of the Commons" (Hardin, 1968), in which herdsmen must share a common pasture. Each may direct "that industry in such a manner as its produce may be of the greatest value" by increasing the size of his personal herd. But when all do so, the commons is overgrazed (beyond its "carrying capacity")— which can bring ruin to all. Here, in economic terms the negative externalities associated with selfish pursuits are larger than the positive internalities; here, in game theory terms the individually beneficial strategies of increasing herd size converge on a collectively undesirable outcome.

The extreme of such a pernicious situation is found in *social dilemmas*. Such dilemmas are defined (Dawes, 1980) as structures involving individually *dominating strategies* that converge on a *deficient equilibrium*. A strategy is dominating if its personal payoffs are superior to those of all other strategies no matter what others do; an outcome is "deficient" when that outcome is less preferred by *all* choosers to some other outcome; such an outcome in a social dilemma will, however, be in equilibrium because no individual chooser has an egoistic incentive to depart from selecting a dominating strategy.

Examples of social dilemmas abound; the most common is the well-known two-person prisoners dilemma shown in Table 2.1. Here, choice of the dominating strategy (*D*) for row player yields a payoff of one unit if column player likewise chooses the dominating strategy (*D*), while row player's choice of the

Table 2.1

The Two-Person Prisoner Dilemma

		Player #2	
		Choice D	Choice C
Player #1	Choice D	1.1	3.0
	Choice C	0.3	2.2

The first entry indicates the payoff to the row player for each combination of choices, the second the payoff to the column player.

nondominating strategy (C) would yield a payoff of zero units; if column player were to choose the nondominating strategy (C), role player's choice of the dominating strategy would yield three units and choice of the nondominating one would yield two. The situation is symmetric. Both dominating strategies are indeed dominating, yet the resulting (1, 1) outcome is deficient because both players would prefer the (2, 2) outcome.

Such social dilemmas are common outside simple two-person games as well. Consider, for example, the choice of someone who is asked to give "a fair share" to public broadcasting. Unless that person is unusually wealthy, the nature of public broadcasting will be unaffected by her or his choice of whether or not to contribute; the success of the appeal depends upon the number of *others* who contribute. Thus, even if a "fair share" is defined as an amount *less* than the public broadcasting is worth to each potential contributor, the choice is between having public broadcasting available in a form determined by the amount of others' contributions—and keeping the potential contribution for private use—versus having that same quality of public broadcasting and relinquishing that amount of money. Keeping the money is a dominating strategy. Yet the result of the simultaneous decision of all potential contributors to keep potential contributions for private use would be the demise of public broadcasting. Given the assumption that such broadcasting is worth more to each individual than the contribution requested, that equilibrium is deficient. Moreover, no distinction can be made between "long-term" versus "short-term" interests in the decision involving contribution, because the success of public broadcasting depends upon the contributions of others in both "terms."

Or consider the decision of people who are asked to ride their bicycles to work during a pollution alert. Once again, the extent of the pollution will be determined primarily by the number of other people who drive their cars, and from the individual-payoff perspective, the period of a pollution alert is the *worst* time to ride a bicycle. Yet if everyone drives their cars during such alerts, the results are worse than if everyone who could ride a bicycle decided to do so. Or consider the decision of whether to publish yet another mediocre article. Because academic deans do not have time to read articles, publishing as many of them as possible tends to be a dominating strategy. The result, however, is journal pollution *and* a change in the adaptation level of deans about what constitutes a reasonably extensive publication list. These collective results are clearly deficient. Finally, consider the choice of whether to take a deadline for a handbook chapter seriously. Clearly, the later a chapter is supplied to the editors, then more current it is. Yet, uniformly practiced delaying tactics on the part of the contributors can yield an outcome that is less preferred by all than would result if all met the initial deadline.[1]

In fact, many current social thinkers such as Hardin had speculated that modern technology and medicine have created worldwide social dilemmas involving energy use, pollution, and—most importantly—overpopulation, which have led humans to exploit the earth beyond its "carrying capacity." It is clearly to the advantage of each individual, family, group, or nation to extract as much food and energy as possible from the earth and to diffuse the negative effects of such extraction as broadly as possible across space and time (e.g., dumping toxic wastes in the ocean and letting future generations worry about eroded topsoil). The results are deficient equilibria, such as global warming. Thus, the widespread depletion and contamination of the earth's resources are conceptualized as a result of a multitude of actors choosing in their best interests, thereby creating worldwide dilemmas; moreover, to the degree to which they are successful—aided in simply staying alive by modern medical techniques—that multitude increases.

These examples are, of course, oversimplifications. Consequences are often sufficiently uncertain that it is hard to find strategies that are strictly dominating no matter what others choose; likewise, it is difficult to find outcomes that are strictly deficient for every chooser involved in a social interaction. Clearly, there are some collectively harmful strategies that come close to being dominating, without leading to equilibria that are deficient for every single chooser. The theoretical aspects of this essay, however, are addressed to the structure of social dilemmas, which will therefore be considered in their purest form. Moreover, the experiments to be described later will present subjects with choices in pure dilemma situations.

The existence of social dilemmas, and especially global ones, proposes a serious normative challenge to economic and economic/political theories based on the premise that individual pursuit of self-interests through reponse to egoistic incentives has beneficial results for society as a whole. In effect, Adam Smith's butcher and brewer can end up poisoning not only the rest of us but themselves as well. I will return to this challenge later—after a discussion of sociobiology, which faces the same challenge.

According to most generally accepted views of evolution, the degree to which an individual's genes are transmitted to future generations depends on the *fitness* these genes provide, where "inclusive fitness" means that these genes *per se* will survive. Because there are not enough resources in a given environment for all organisms to accomplish this feat, a "struggle for existence" arises, and on a probabilistic basis, the genes of more inclusively fit organisms eventually displace those of less fit ones. (This "struggle" need not have dramatic connotations commonly ascribed to that term in culture and literature, although many popularizers of evolutionary theory stress these connotations—in contrast, for example, to the survival value of successful symbiosis.) To survive, genes must therefore provide characteristics that are adaptive within a single generation, where the adaptiveness of such characteristics is a function of the environmental demands and opportunities, which include those resulting from the characteristics of other competing organisms. Evolution is thus a "hill climbing procedure" (Simon, 1983), with hills situated on the shifting sands of environmental change. An apparent implication is that an organism must respond to egoistic incentives and maximize immediate payoffs if it is to survive and its genes are to propagate and become predominant in future generations. While this immediacy may be tempered by qualifications such as "enlightened" or "long-term," successful organisms cannot respond to collective payoffs beyond those that influence their own and their offspring's ability to reproduce (or—in "inclusive fitness" terms—the survival of other organisms with the same genes). Thus, they should generally choose dominating strategies in social dilemma situations, and the result should be deficient equilibria.

Evolutionary theory *per se* is, of course, value-free. Nevertheless, the most cursory reading of the sociobiological literature reveals an implicit belief that organisms that propagate their genes are "superior" in more than a tautological sense, which is not surprising given that the literature was written by members of a recently evolved species that has come to dominate the resources of the earth. Only to destroy it through the dilemma situations this species itself has created? (Even nuclear war and destruction can easily follow from responding to egoistic incentives in a dilemma situation in which "attack" is the dominating strategy; see Rapoport, 1960.) Thus, sociobiological theory faces the same normative problem as does the classic Adam Smith economic theory. Behavior that the theory normatively mandates can easily lead to the destruction of the individual and species that follow this mandate.

Both classic economic theory and sociobiological theory also face a descriptive challenge. Humans (and other organisms) often appear to forego choosing dominating strategies in favor of those that have more benign collective results. People do not rip off their neighbors whenever they know they can avoid being caught; airplane squadrons in war fly in formation even though the planes at the periphery are most likely to be shot down, and some soldiers even fall on hand grenades to save their comrades. Female birds often behave in ways that simulate injury likely to draw a predator's attention to them and away from their chicks; many animals make "calls" that warn others of imminent danger, even though such a call may draw attention to the caller and thereby enhance its personal danger.

One response of economists to this descriptive challenge is to evoke the concept of "revealed preference." Literally, whenever an organism does "reveal" its true preferences (utilities), and so long as the organism does not make self-contradictory choices (e.g., by violating general tenets of rationality or more specific ones found in such systems as the axioms of von Neumann and Morganstern), these preferences are simply inferred from overt behavior. Or they may not be inferred at all, but are simply assumed to exist, at least as hypothetical constructs (MacCorqudale and Meehl, 1948). Thus, by definition, a dominating strategy cannot avoid being chosen; and if some strategy other than the apparently dominating one is chosen, this apparently dominating one cannot by definition be dominating. The problem with this approach is that it simply moves a normative problem "one step back" to the utilities themselves. Individual actors are saved by definition from irrationality only to become "rational fools" (Sen, 1977) if their revealed egoistic preferences are collectively self-defeating. Sociobiologists as well could fall back on a "revealed evolution" principle ("whatever evolved evolved"), but many have instead regarded the existence of behavior that apparently benefits others to the detriment of the organism choosing that behavior to present a problem. They search for *what* it is that is revealed—i.e., for the mechanism by which apparently nonegoistic choice can be explained as involving egoistic payoffs in the form of reproductive success—so that, for example, what "appears" to be altruistic is "really" selfish (not just in the tautological sense that organisms do what they choose to do). Thus, at the very beginning of *Sociobiology: The New Synthesis,* E.O. Wilson (1975, p. 3) defines the "central problems" of sociobiology as being to explain how altruism is possible.

The mechanism most proposed by both classic economic and social/psychological theory and by sociobiology to meet with these normative and descriptive challenges is that of the *side-payment.* Such payments involve additional payoffs, either positive or negative, that make strategies that appear to be dominating no longer dominating. Certain types of side-payments are postulated, with the result that it is no longer normatively compelling to choose the apparently dominating strategy; nor is it descriptively problematic that organisms do not do so. Because theorists proposing side-payment mechanisms actually postulate what these payments consist of, their approach is different from that of the revealed-preference approach. In what follows, I will list well-known examples of such side-payments.

1. *Sanctions and rewards from a powerful central authority ("Leviathan").* In 1651 Hobbes (1947) proposed that without some central governing mechanism, people are engaged in a "warre of alle against alle." However it is established, a powerful structure of authority mandates that people cooperate with each other by choosing strategies with collectively beneficial outcomes; it creates this mandate by enforcing side-payments of punishment for choosing dominating strategies that lead to socially deficient results, and sometimes rewards for

choosing more beneficient choices. (Hobbes himself emphasized the punishing role of Leviathan.) Thus, people will often accept a central authority even if it consists of a hated minority using the mandated cooperation of others primarily for its own benefit. The authority makes life safe and predictable. The way in which the central authority came about and the nature of the people maintaining it (whether Royalists or Roundheads, in Hobbes's time) are of minor importance compared to its viability. Without it, people face a most vicious dilemma of unrestrained competition that leads life to be "cruel, brutish, nasty and short." Its ability to provide side-payments of rewards and punishment is what keeps life from being that way.

Much in the spirit of Hobbes, Hardin (1968) has proposed that sanctions need not come from an authoritarian state structure but may arise as the result of "mutual coercion mutually agreed upon." The logic, however, is basically the same. Some (agreed-upon) mechanism must be set up to provide side-payments in the forms of sanctions delivered with sufficient certainty that people tempted to choose otherwise egoistically desirable strategies with socially pernicious results (e.g., overexploiting, overpopulating) will not make such choices.

2. *Reciprocal altruism* (Axelrod and Hamilton, 1981). Through some mechanism—perhaps biological (Trivers, 1971)—choice of the nondominating collectively beneficial strategy on the part of one individual in a dilemma situation enhances the probability that others will make the same choice later in that same situation or in similar ones, thereby creating a side-payment that benefits the original chooser. Thus, an individual's long-term self-interest may be served by such a choice. In computer tournaments of iterated prisoners dilemma games, Axelrod (1984) has studied the success of Anatol Rapoport's TIT-FOR-TAT strategy (Rapoport and Chammah, 1965: cooperate on trial 1 and then make the same choice that the other interacting individual did on the previous trial), and demonstrated that it garners more profits for itself in prolonged interaction than do any competing strategies; moreover, Axelrod has demonstrated that in an evolutionary context in which strategies' payoffs are positively related to their survival, TIT-FOR-TAT can become predominant.

While this work demonstrates that reciprocity can be an important side-payment in two-person interactions, its generalization to social dilemma situations involving more actors is dubious. First, situations involving more people may permit anonymous choice, which is clearly not a possibility in an iterated two-person dilemma. Second, the collective harm resulting from a single collectively harmful choice may not be evident, because it is generally spread out among many people. Third, and most important, it is impossible to reciprocate a set of choices made by many other individuals, some of whom may choose the collectively harmful dominating strategy and others of whom may not. Yet another problem arises because the TIT-FOR-TAT strategy may be described in terms that have nothing to do with reciprocity. When payoffs are symmetric, it is *exactly equivalent* to the strategy "defect only if behind the other player"—a strategy based wholly on a concept of social equality independent of any attempts to influence the other player's choices.

3. *Inclusive fitness* (Hamilton, 1964). A "selfish gene" (Dawkins, 1976) would be concerned with kin altruism (Alexander, 1987), in which the inclusive fitness of an offspring or sibling would have one-half the genetic value of the inclusive fitness of the self, of a niece or nephew one-fourth, and so on. Since evolution is a matter of genetic survival, genes that were truly "selfish" would take account of the expected payoffs for helping such close relatives, and for helping more distant ones. Thus the collective outcomes of relatives could benefit genes, and the transformation of payoffs from individual ones to genetic ones could make apparently dominating strategies that lead to collective problems no longer dominating. The side-payment to the gene overwhelms the egoistic payment to the individual carrying it. A number of mathematical models have been developed to demonstrate the conditions under which genes leading the individual who carries them to respond to genetic rather than egoistic incentives in social dilemma situations would indeed have an evolutionary advantage. The problem is that the "selfish gene" is more a metaphor of personification than a hypothetical construct, because there are as yet no tests for checking the consistency of the hypothesis—as there are, for example, for checking the consistency of hypothesized utilities inferred from the revealed preference assumption. Altruistic behavior is simply observed in particular dilemma situations, and sensitivity to genetic payoffs is hypothesized; there is a paucity of empirical data, or even speculation, about the implications of the selfish gene hypothesis for a series of choices.

4. *Socially instilled conscience and self-esteem* (Campbell, 1975). Although externally provided payoffs may define a social dilemma, social training can lead to a side-payment of such a "bad conscience" for choosing a dominating but collectively harmful strategy—or such heightened self-esteem for eschewing this strategy—that the individual is better off not choosing it, irrespective of external consequences. This solution, which was suggested to psychologists in Campbell's presidential address to the American Psychological Association, aroused controversy—in part because it supported traditional morality in contrast to urging people to "do your own thing." According to Campbell, "social evolution," through moral teachings, the evolution of norms, and the development of social structures, reinforces collectively beneficial behavior, thereby keeping "biological evolution" from running amuck only to drain into a sink of universal competition.

These four approaches all have one characteristic in common. They turn an apparent dilemma into a nondilemma by automatic or planned manipulation of the consequences accruing to the individual for strategic choice. Whether the side-payments come from a central authority, from the later reaction of others to the individual chooser, from benefit to the chooser's genes, or from internal feelings, they change the choice situation sufficiently so that an individual no

longer faces an unambiguously dominating strategy leading to collectively deficient results. Manipulation of behavior through the egoistic payoffs resulting
from such side-payments is compatible with: (i) psychoanalytic beliefs in the
preeminence of primitive drives; (ii) behavioristic beliefs in the automatic and
omnipotent effects of reward and punishment ("reinforcement"); (iii) capitalist
economic theory; (iv) social exchange theory; (v) a view of evolution as dramatic "struggle"; and (vi) the obvious success in U.S. politics of appeals to
personal payoffs (e.g., "read my lips" about no new taxes, or "are *you* better off
than you were four years ago"?). All these approaches imply that if a social
dilemma situation were *really* a social dilemma, people (and other organisms)
would choose a dominating strategy. It is that implication I wish to challenge.

My basic claim here is not that any or all of the side-payments postulated
above do not encourage collectively beneficial behavior; certainly, for example,
beliefs that one will go to jail or be tortured by guilt for hurting others will
enhance the tendency to avoid hurting them, as will the social rewards accruing
to an individual with a reputation for being cooperative and trustworthy (Taylor,
1976; Axelrod, 1984). My claim is that a series of studies conducted over the
past ten years by my colleagues John Orbell and Alphons van de Kragt, and me
has led us, somewhat reluctantly at first, to conclude that none of these side-
payments is *necessary* to promote collectively beneficial behavior—in particular,
to promote it above a base rate that can be ascribed to the habit of engaging in
such behavior outside our experiments in situations similar to those within them.
And if side-payments are unnecessary, they cannot be the mechanism that saves
the theories outlined above from being normatively and descriptively deficient.

Our experiments led us to conclude that rates of foregoing dominating but
collectively harmful choices can be radically affected by one particular factor
that is independent of the consequences for the choosing individual. That
factor is group identity. Such identity can be established and consequently
enhance collectively beneficial choice in the absence of any expectation of individual side-payments.

The problem with much previous research is that while it demonstrates that
side-payments work, social dilemmas have not generally been studied *in the
absence of side-payments*. The clearest example of this lack can be found in
experimentation on two-person prisoners dilemmas (estimated to consist of at
least 2,000 studies). In almost all of these, play has been *iterated*. In fact, my
colleagues and I have been able to find only a few instances in the literature prior
to our own work in which players make a single choice (e.g., Deutsch, 1960;
Wrightsman, 1966). The hypothesis supposedly supported by numerous results is
that choosing the cooperative response in prisoners dilemma situations is *due to*
the successful establishment, or the attempt to establish, reciprocal altruism
through engaging in such strategies as TIT-FOR-TAT. But in the absence of any
evidence that people do *not* cooperate in the games that are *not* iterated, this
interpretation is dubious. Moreover, the claim that choosing collectively benefi-

cial strategies results from egoistic rewards approaches vacuity given the standard instructions that subjects are "to get as many points for yourself as you can." Experimental subjects tend to be cooperative—with the experimenter at least—and solve the problem the experimenter presents to them in the best manner they can. It follows that behavior given such instructions is in large part determined by the egoistic consequences for the subjects. (The claim that egoism is responsible for experimental results is saved from complete vacuity by the empirical fact that experimental manipulations often don't work at all.)

In contrast, in our own experiments, we (e.g., Dawes, van de Kragt, and Orbell, 1988) make self-conscious use of the "subtractive procedure" by systematically comparing the presence of factors with their absence. We eliminate all side-payments of a concrete nature by simply prohibiting them; we eliminate concern with reputation by having all choices be anonymous; and we eliminate the possibility of reciprocal altruism by having our subjects make a choice in our dilemma situations only once. Moreover, the fact that our subjects chose strategies having socially beneficial results cannot be accounted for by the existence of side-payments outside our experiments in situations similar to those within them, because we can manipulate the group identity variable in a way that will yield rates of choosing collectively beneficial strategies— given the same egoistic payoffs—ranging from 25% to 100%. I will describe here conditions from three recent series of experiments, in which group identity is manipulated; for a fuller discussion of these experiments, see Dawes, van de Kragt, and Orbell (1988) or Orbell, van de Kragt, and Dawes (1988).

Our standard manipulation is to allow groups of strangers to talk for ten minutes about the dilemma with which they are experimentally presented; of course, in line with our "subtractive" philosophy, such groups are compared with those who cannot communicate. We do *not* allow our subjects in the discussion condition to make deals, agreements to meet later, or even agreements to tell each other what they chose; moreover, we make every effort to insure that our groups really do consist of strangers. We are not claiming that our discussion manipulation is the only way to create group identity, or that discussion automatically leads to group identity, or that other factors may not be confounded with discussion—but that discussion works *in the absence of side-payments*. Our group identity interpretation is the same as that of Kramer and Brewer (1986) and Wit (1989), who have shown that simply having the magnitude of subjects' payoffs determined by the same coin toss (as opposed to using different tosses to determine whether each subject receives a high or low payoff) enhances collectively beneficial choice.

All our experiments concern monetary contributions to a public good. In the first series of studies presented here (van de Kragt, Dawes, Orbell, Braver, and Wilson, 1986), we discovered that discussion between group members not only enhanced contribution when people had at least a mild egoistic incentive to contribute but also enhanced cooperation when people *did not*. Specifically, we found that allowing discussion in an assurance game—where all receive $10 if all contribute $5—enhances contribution. But we later discovered that discussion enhanced contribution when the subject's own contribution had only a probabilistic relationship to the subject's outcome. Later, we found the same pattern of the beneficial effects of discussion when a subject's own contribution had no effect on the subject's own outcome—that is, in *noncontingent* games in which subjects received or didn't receive a bonus only on the basis of others' rates of contribution.

First Set of Experiments

Let us explain the method used in these studies in some detail. First, subjects were recruited for a one-hour "group decision-making experiment" from advertisements in local student and town newspapers promising "from $4 to $19 depending upon what you and the other group members decide." Only those responding who were over eighteen years of age (by self-report and judgment of telephone voice) were invited to participate. Subjects who called to participate as groups were scheduled for separate experimental sessions, and a list was maintained to make sure that all subjects participated in only one session.

Upon arrival, subjects were run in experimental groups of nine people. All were paid $4 for "showing up," including any extra subjects we had scheduled to make sure that we would have nine participants in each group. At the beginning of the experiment itself, all were given a "promissory note" for $5, which was theirs to keep if they chose. They were also told that there was the possibility of receiving a $10 bonus depending upon how many people chose to "give away" their $5 to the group. Subjects were told that the choice of whether or not to give away the $5 was anonymous; to assure anonymity, they would make their choice by placing a check mark on one of two lines in a response form that others couldn't see, and we would pay each subject one at a time, making certain that the previous subject had left the area before the next was paid—which we did.

One factor in our design was defined by the rule according to which each subject received or did not receive the $10 bonus.

Contingent rule: If five or more subjects including the choosing subject him or herself gave away the $5, all received the $10 bonus.

Noncontingent rule: If four or more of the *remaining* subjects gave away the $5, the subject received the $10 bonus.

According to both rules, a subject who gave away the $5 lost it. Such a subject received $10 according to both rules if four or more of the remaining subjects gave the $5 away, and otherwise received nothing (except for the flat $4 for attending the experiment). A subject who kept the $5 received either $15 or

$5, depending on whether enough of the remaining subjects gave away the $5. The crucial difference between the two rules was that in the contingent condition subjects could "help themselves" by giving away the money; for if exactly four others did, a subject who gave away the $5 received $10 rather than $5. In the noncontingent condition, a subject always received $5 more for keeping the money than for giving it away—$15 rather than $10 if four or more others gave it away, and $5 rather than zero if not. Thus, the noncontingent condition confronted subjects with a strict social dilemma (all would receive $10 if all gave away, $5 if none did, yet not giving away was a dominating strategy). In contrast, exactly five subjects' giving away the money was an equilibrium outcome in the contingent rule condition (in which case, those who gave it away received $10 and those who didn't $15).

In half of the groups in each rule condition we let the subjects discuss the choice for up to 10 minutes, and in half they had to remain silent. Our previous research (van de Kragt, Orbell, and Dawes, 1983) demonstrated that subjects develop an awareness of the equilibrium in the contingent condition, and when allowed to discuss will determine—by a combination of volunteering and lot— exactly *which* five should give away the $5 (thereby creating an 'assurance game' for these five individuals; see Sen, 1967). To prevent subjects in the discussion condition from designating such a minimal contributing set, we told them how many give-away choices were required for the bonus only after they had completed their discussion. Many groups hit upon the idea of numbering themselves and requiring people numbered 1 through k to give away the $5 after the experimenter announced the number k necessary to provide the bonus. The experimenters simply told subjects in such groups that "you can't do that," and being thus prohibited they were unable to implement the idea.[2]

Experimental Results: I

Figure 2.1 shows the percent contributing in each of the four conditions defined by the contingent versus noncontingent rule and discussion versus silence. Both effects of the rule and of discussion are significant ($p < 0.04$ and $p < 0.001$ respective; for more details, see the original paper). What is striking, however, is that the effect of discussion *per se* is the stronger of the two. While the results show an effect of self-interest (the contingent rule elicits higher cooperation rates), such interest cannot explain the relatively high rates of giving away the $5 in the noncontingent condition after discussion, a condition in which subjects *always* receive the higher payoff for keeping the $5.

Second Set of Experiments

In a subsequent series of studies (Orbell, van de Kragt, and Dawes, 1988), we addressed the question of whether the discussion effects we had previously found

Figure 2.1. **Results from First Set of Experiments**

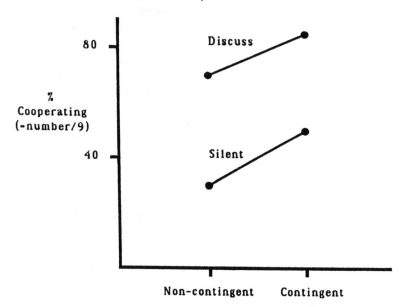

to be important may have served to arouse "conscience" and its associated payoffs, or whether the results can be better accounted for by concern with others' actual outcomes—and if so, how that concern relates to group identity.

To pit conscience against personalized caring, we varied the identity of the beneficiaries of cooperation: other group members versus strangers. If discussion triggers conscience, and our contributing subjects are acting to satisfy its demands, then discussion should enhance contribution to strangers. If, however, discussion elicits group identity, then it should enhance contributions only to people in the group with whom one interacts.

Our basic condition was a *give-away* dilemma game involving seven people. Subjects began with promissory notes for $6, which they could either keep or give away (anonymously, again) for the group benefit. Each $6 given away was augmented to $12 by the experimenters, with a $2 bonus going to each of the other six group members. The situation is a dilemma, because each subject is $6 better off keeping the money, but if all give it away all receive $12, while all receive $6 if all keep.

Using the same recruitment methods as in the previous experiment, we formed groups of fourteen subjects who were then randomly divided into groups of seven that met in separate rooms. Again, we crossed discussion with no discussion. We varied the games, however, by telling half the groups that the $12 would go to the other six members of their own group and half that it would go to six comparable members of the other group—with subjects' own potential bonuses being dependent, respectively, upon what members of their own or the other group did. In all conditions, the $6 was kept by the subjects themselves if they chose not to give it away.

Finally, three minutes before the final choice, we switched the group membership of the relevant others in half the conditions. For example, in a switch condition, a subject discussed the choice believing the $12 would go to the subjects in his or her own group and that he or she might receive money from them, but was subsequently told that it would go to subjects in the other group—and that money would come from "give" choices in this other group. In an equal number of instances subjects believed that the relevant subjects were in the other group, and were then told that they were their own group members. Half the time we made no such switch. No further discussion in the discussion conditions was allowed after the switch.

Experimental Results: II

We thus crossed three factors: the initially understood locus of relevant others (own group versus other group); interaction (discussion versus no discussion); and actual locus of relevant others (own group versus other group). We ran eight groups in each of the resulting eight conditions (number of groups = 64; number of subjects = 448). The results are presented in Figure 2.2.

With group cooperation rate as the unit of analysis, all main effects are significant beyond the .001 level. Of greatest importance, however, is the interaction (also $p < .001$) of discussion with belief about locus of benefit. With discussion, cooperation rate averaged 69% when people first believed that relevant others would be in their own group, but only 31% when they believed they would be in the other. The comparable figures for the no discussion conditions were 34% and 33%. Thus, discussion does not enhance contribution when beneficiaries are strangers, which runs counter to the clear conscience hypothesis. Moreover, there is *no* ingroup-outgroup effect in the absence of discussion. Also, the believed locus of relevant others when the subjects first considered their choices was more important than the actual (subsequent) locus; $\omega^2 = 30\%$ versus 10%).

Because discussion does promote cooperation vis-à-vis the parochial group but not the group with which there was no contact, we concluded that group identity was the most important factor. (Recall, again, that choices were single ones made in total anonymity.) Also, however, we noted a great deal of promising to give the money away in the high cooperation condition, and it *appeared* to be effective. Slightly over 11% of coded subject-predicate utterances across all conditions were commitments to give (as opposed to 3.1% commitments to keep, which most often occurred when the beneficiaries of giving were believed to be in the other group), and the product moment correlation between number of commitments to give and cooperation rate in the group was 0.59 (p < 0.01; using

Figure 2.2. **Results from Second Set of Experiments**

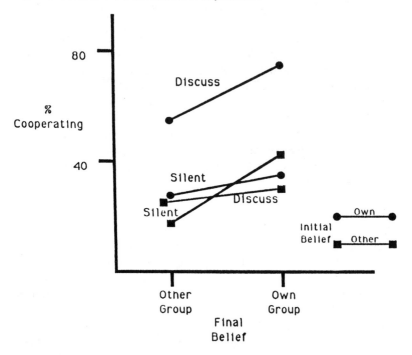

groups as the unit of measurement). True to our own commitment to subject anonymity, however, we were not able to link individual promising with subsequent choice. Thus, we were led in a subsequent experiment to investigate the importance of the following three other factors.

(1) *Group identity.* Research in the "minimal group" paradigm (e.g., Tajfel and Turner, 1979; Tajfel, 1974, 1978; Turner, 1975; and the papers contained in Turner and Giles, 1981) has repeatedly demonstrated that allocative decisions can be sharply altered by manipulations substantially weaker than ten minutes of discussion. For example, as mentioned previously, a "common fate" group identity—amount of payoff dependent on the same coin toss—can lead subjects to attempt to "compensate" for defecting people in their own group by increasing cooperation, while simultaneously decreasing cooperation when the defecting people are believed to be in the other group, even when the identities of all people are unknown (Kramer and Brewer, 1986; Wit, 1989).

(2) *The desirable and binding nature of promising.* Even though subjects' choices are anonymous, similar choices in the world outside our experiments typically are not. In general, it is to a promiser's long-term best interests to develop a reputation for cooperation and reliability (Axelrod, 1984; Taylor, 1976). Thus, while there are no reputational effects of not promising or reneging

on promises made in our particular experimental situation, it may be psychologically similar to situations in which there are such effects—similar enough that it does not elicit clearly distinct behavior. Alternatively, subjects may adopt cooperative promising and fulfillment of promises as a good "rule of thumb" ("heuristic"), given that in most situations such behavior is desirable from the perspective of future consequences. Irrationalities in a particular situation may appear less irrational when the situation is viewed as one of a class of situations that might require too much "mental accounting" to distinguish among (Thaler, 1985).

(3) *Expectations derived from others' promises.* A single individual who keeps the $6 while all others give away $12 receives $18; if that individual likewise gives away the $6, his or her payoff is $12. In contrast, an individual who keeps the $6 when no others give their money away receives only that $6, while the payoff for giving away the $6 under these circumstances is zero. Perhaps, consistent with Fechner's law, the difference between $18 and $12 is psychologically less than the difference between $6 and zero. And in general, while there is a constant $6 incentive to defect, this incentive may become less psychologically dominant as more others are expected to give away the $12. But other incentives—for example, "desire to do the right thing"—may simultaneously remain constant. Perhaps, as Dawes (1980, p. 191) has speculated: "if others contribute, then the expected payoff for cooperation will not be too low, even though—in a uniform game [as this one was], for example—the *difference* between the payoff for cooperation and that for defection is still quite large. People may be greedy, may prefer more to less, but their greed is not 'insatiable' when other utilities are involved." The more other people expected to contribute, according to this hypothesis, the less important the $6 incentive. Promises may, then, perform the self-exacerbating role of leading to expectations that a sufficient number of others will contribute that the choosers themselves are motivated to contribute. The 0.59 correlation between promises made and cooperation appears to support this interpretation, but it is important to note that these promises are not equivalent to the number of *people* who promised, because we did not identify individuals.

Third Set of Experiments

A third series of experiments (Orbell, van de Kragt, and Dawes, 1988) assessed the impact of these factors. (It also concerned others not relevant here, which is why it is quite complex.) Subjects meeting in groups of fourteen were informed that they would be subsequently divided at random into two subgroups of seven and then faced with a *trinary* choice: (i) keep $5 for themselves; (ii) give away $12, with $2 going to each of the other people in their seven-person subgroup; (iii) give away $21, with $3 going to each of the people in the other seven-person subgroup. After being told that both subgroups would either be allowed to discuss the choice or would have to remain silent, all fourteen-person groups were given up to ten minutes to discuss the problem. This fourteen-person discussion was monitored by two experimenters who coded whether or not *each subject* in that initial discussion made at least one promise—or otherwise indicated a commitment—to give away the $21 to the members of the other subgroup once the groups were divided.

Experimental Results: III

What is of importance for our purposes here is that in about half (13 of 24) of the fourteen-person groups all subjects made a verbal commitment to give away the $21 to the other subgroup members. Eighty-four percent of the subjects in these *universal promising* groups actually did so. In contrast, only 58% of the subjects from the other eleven groups gave away the $21. The difference (again using groups as the unit of analysis) was highly significant, $p < 0.01$.

That finding was not surprising, because it follows from all three factors listed above. In contrast, the relationship between promising and actual choice in the eleven groups without universal promising was striking. There wasn't any. First, the correlation across groups between the number of people who promised to give away the $21 and the number who subsequently did was only 0.09. Second, the contingency at the individual level between promising to give away the $21 and actually doing so was only 0.03. Finally, the correlation between each individual's choice to give away the $21 or not and the number of others in the group who promised to give away the $21 was, again, 0.03. The hypothesis that promises *per se* are binding implies a positive correlation between commitment and choice. The hypothesis that cooperation is due to expectations of a "reasonable" payoff if others are expected to contribute implies a positive correlation between choice and the number of commitments made by others in the group. Neither correlation occurs in the data.

While the actual choice of the promisers was unknown to the other group members, the experimenters were aware of it. This partial lack of anonymity might have led those who promised to give away to do so in fact, and the data analyses might have had to test whether the contingency was greater in the groups where everyone promised than in the other groups. In addition, the similarity of the experimental situation to situations without choice anonymity outside might have led to the same contingency. What happened, however, was that there was no contingency at all in the groups in which not everyone promised to give away the money.

We are left with two hypotheses. First, unanimous promising may reflect group identity, which is the important variable in eliciting the contributions to others. Second, the efficacy of promising may interact with group identity, or at least unanimity. Atiyah (1981) has argued that in a bilateral situation promises are binding only in the presence of reciprocity, and if our latter interpretation is correct, subjects in our experiments may be treating the entire remainder of the group as a single entity. It is difficult to differentiate between these hypotheses because if promises are to have impact, they must be freely given (Dawes, McTavish, and Shaklee, 1977), and consequently in a freely interacting group, unanimity and identity will be confounded—perhaps even having a reciprocally augmenting (Maruyama, 1963) relationship across the ten minutes of discussion. According to either hypothesis, however, it is group unanimity that leads to an increase in contribution rate, not the payoffs to the individual chooser.

This finding also calls into question the analysis of eighteenth-century philosopher David Hume (1928) of why promises are binding. Hume argues that the ability to make a promise (contract) is very useful to individuals who engage in joint social ventures; the reputation for reneging on promises, however, leads to the loss of this ability, and hence to harm to the person who reneges. The implication is that there would be no need to keep promises on anonymous conditions, or that doing so would simply result from the similarity of such conditions to those in which the subsequent behavior of the promiser was known. Again, the data do not support these implications.

How can these experimental results be consistent with the almost tautological principles that people need to receive personal benefits in order to prosper economically, and must be fit in order to their genetic characteristics to be propagated? A possible solution to this conflict (Caporael, Dawes, Orbell, and van de Kragt, 1990) is that given the group living and interdependence conditions of the human race throughout its existence, group effort is in general beneficial to individuals in the group—even though it may lead to less than optimal outcomes in a true dilemma situation (where egoistic payoffs are defined as including all side-payments of sanctions, reciprocity, and so on). *Automatic* concern for the welfare of a group of which one is a member will in general provide personal benefits. Moreover, to the degree to which attentional and physical efforts are limited—and they are—not having to figure out in each choice context exactly what constitutes the individually optimal strategy frees energy for other tasks, in particular for achieving the group goal. It is not necessary to postulate a benefit to group *qua* groups (or in evolutionary terms "group selection") to hypothesize that across a wide variety of contexts what is good for the group is good for the individuals in it.

The objection to this argument we most often encounter is based on the hypothetical "perfect hypocrite." This is the individual who selectively supports group goals when no dilemma exists but deviates from them in dilemma situations without simultaneously losing the benefits of group membership—a "cheater" who "never gets caught." Such a person in our experiments would be one who fakes great concern with group outcome, persuades others to give away the money, and then does not do so herself or himself. In fact, we have observed such subjects (e.g., "having lived on a commune, I know how very important it is . . ."). The problem is, however, whether such a person could prosper. First, there is the possibility of exposure resulting from each act, and consequent ostracism (Campbell, 1983) and loss of group benefits or worse (e.g., being the recipient of "moralistic aggression"). As, for example, White (1973) observed about the Nixon administration, the sequence of events leading to the arrest of the burglars at Watergate may have seemed extraordinarily improbable in retrospect, but the administration policy of endorsing unethical or illegal acts made the probability that *at least one* of these acts would be exposed quite high. (It is tempting to make reference to "the long run" in this argument, but the point is that the possibly low probability of exposure must be considered in determining the expected value of each act.) Hypothetically, individuals can exist who would never get caught. The question is whether actual people could in fact be such hypocrites within the constraints of reality—which involves limited foresight. Moreover, as pointed out earlier, "computational capacity" and energy are limited, and to the degree they are addressed to the problems of avoiding detection, they will—even if *that* problem is successfully resolved—not be available to be devoted to other problems. As, for example, the late Senator Ervin pointed out—again in connection with Watergate—the practical problem of lying is that it is a lot more difficult to remember exactly what you said than it is to remember what happened. Overcoming this difficulty requires the use of intellectual resources; intellectual resources are limited. As Frank (1988) points out, the *easiest* way to be perceived as an altruist is to be one; likewise, the easiest way to be perceived as a person devoted to group goals is to be devoted.

If automatic identification with group goals benefits—on a probabilistic basis—the person who is consequently willing to forego dominating strategies for those with greater collective benefits, then there is neither a descriptive nor a normative problem for economic and sociobiological theories. People will naturally opt for collectively beneficial strategies (*some* of the time), and the potential disasters that follow from mutual choice of dominating ones will be averted (*some* of the time). Would such benefit be just another side-payment? No. First, the individual may have no awareness of this benefit, but instead be simply *motivated by* concern for the group. Second, the personal benefit for many self-sacrificial but group-regarding acts—such as falling on a hand grenade—may be entirely negative; thus, personal benefit cannot "explain" such acts. Third, an extension of the domain of "side-payments" beyond those commonly hypothesized to acts that are commonly termed "altruistic" dilutes the concept to the point of meaningless tautology. To make these points clear, consider the contrast between the hypothesis proposed here and that proposed by Alexander (1987). He proposes five "rules of giving": (1) give to genetic relative; (2) give when the recipient is likely to give you back more than received; (3) give if sanctions for failure to give are likely; (4) give if observers of the giving are likely to provide you with benefits in the future; and (5) "in all other situations do not give." First, of course, our subjects gave money away, in direct contradiction to rule 5 because none of the former conditions was satisfied. It is possible, of course, that their behavior was somehow abhorrent from a biological evolutionary perspective—perhaps, for example, supporting Campbell's idea of a "social evolution" that acts counter to biological evolution. According to our hypothesis it isn't. The question, then, arises of where the flaw might have arisen in Alexander's derivation of these rules.

The flaw is that of trying to make a direct motivational and behavioral inference from the principle of fitness, or inclusive fitness. As Cosmides (1989) points out, this principle constrains what behaviors (and morphologies) can exist, but does not determine what they are. That is, we can certainly hypothesize that a characteristic that would decrease inclusive fitness would not evolve—provided, of course, that our analysis leading us to believe it would decrease such fitness is correct. But that does not imply what will evolve, either in a particular environmental context (which again includes other organisms) or in the "long run." Again, as Simon (1983) has pointed out, evolution is a "hill climbing" procedure, because to be successful change must result in an increase in progeny who themselves reproduce in a single generation. There are many hypothetical evolutionary hills that have not been climbed. (Earthworms living in cities would do better to sprout wings and fly to the nearest ground than to crawl out on the pavement to avoid spring flooding, but they don't.) The logic leading to rules such as Alexander's appears to be based primarily on an analysis of what hypothetically would optimize inclusive fitness and then concludes that such behaviors necessarily exist. The logic then follows a "revealed preference" path; if giving is observed, for example, then Alexander's side-payments 1 through 4 must be there, because an optimally fit strategy would require them. Such side-payments must be there, whether or not they are evident to the observer, especially if they can be hypothesized to exist for some totally dissimilar organism (e.g., a wasp)—on the basis of an analysis of observed behavior that does not include subjecting the resulting hypotheses to the traditional test of experimental manipulation (which sociobiologists tend to eschew). The extreme form of this approach is found in the discussion of an evolutionarily stable strategy, or ESS (Maynard-Smith, 1984): An ESS is a strategy that by logical analysis can be shown to be superior to all competing strategies, hence it is "stable" in an evolutionary sense. Also, not surprisingly, since evolutionary analysis is based on expected utility, the von Neumann and Morgenstern axioms can be derived from the hypothesis assumption that a decision maker's choices constitute an ESS.

Automatic identification with the collective goals of a parochial group is *not* an ESS. Does that mean that it must decrease inclusive fitness, or even that it does not increase inclusive fitness? No. First, hypothesizing an "ESS" does not establish its existence, any more than Thomas Aquinas's conception of the perfect being established the existence of God (in his "ontological proof"). In fact, extensive evidence that current humans do *not* satisfy the von Neumann and Morgenstern axioms in their choice behavior (cf. Dawes, 1988) contradicts the hypothesis that human behaviors could be explained by such logic—given that our ancestors were by definition inclusively fit. Second, the superior human who always chose dominating strategies whenever it was in his or her best interests (again considering side-payments in their choice), the "perfect hypocrite," would have had to appear on the human scene with great suddenness. Given the consistency of group living arrangements in human evolution, an individual who climbed only part-way up the hill to the pinnacle of pure selfishness, one who had sufficient foresight to avoid the pitfalls of such a strategy only *much* of the time, would *not* be inclusively fit. The automatic concern for group welfare by those with whom the person interacted would lead that person to be an evolutionary failure.

It should, finally, be pointed out that group-regarding behavior is not equivalent to morality. For example, many people who publicly presented themselves as "good Nazis" (and may have privately regarded themselves as such) stated that they did so for the benefit of their group; specifically, Rudolph Hoess, the commandant of Auschwitz, claimed that he exerted great effort to "stifle all softer emotion"—which many regard as moral feelings—as part of a "war," fighting on the side of those with whom he had ethnic and national identification (Hoess, 1959).

It should also be pointed out that the type of group identity hypothesized to account for our experimental results cannot resolve the worldwide dilemmas involving overexploitation, pollution, and overpopulation. In fact, behavior chosen to benefit a parochial group can make such dilemmas worse. Even within a country, as pointed out by Olson (1982), self-negating behavior that benefits an "interest group" can lead to nationally deficient outcomes. Recall that we find precisely such behavior in our second experiment—in the interaction effect between discussion (presumed to be crucial in the formation of group identity) and belief in the locus of the beneficiaries of individuals' contributions. What was particularly striking in these experiments was that there were no social differentiations between the members of each group a few minutes earlier, prior to their randomly determined separation into different rooms. Yet we immediately observed statements such as "wouldn't it be great if we all kept our money and they all gave theirs away to us." Such observations are relevant to the earlier point about morality as well.

Notes

1. Having received the "suckers payoff" for actually meeting an initial deadline for the latest Handbook of Social Psychology, I promised its editors that I would use this example whenever possible. The deadline was June 1980; the handbook was published in April 1985. While a small part of the delay was due to change of publishers, the importance of the dilemma structure was clear to me when I observed several colleagues working on first drafts of their chapters roughly three years after the initial deadline.

2. The actual experiments involved four additional conditions not presented here.

References

Alexander, R.D. 1987. *"The Biology of Moral Systems."* New York: Aldine de Gruyter.
Atiyah, P. 1981. *Promises, Morals and Law.* New York: Oxford University Press.
Axelrod, R. 1984. *The Evolution of Cooperation.* New York: Basic Books.
Axelrod, R., and W.D. Hamilton. 1981. "The Evolution of Cooperation." *Science* 211:1390–96.
Blaney, P.H. 1976. "Comment." *American Psychologist* 31, 358:19.
Campbell, D.T. 1975. "On the Conflicts between Biological and Social Evolution and between Psychology and the Moral Tradition." *American Psychologist* 30:1103–26.
———. 1983. "The Two Distinct Routes beyond Kin Selection to Ultrasociality: Implications for the Humanities and Social Sciences." In D. Bridgman, ed., *The Nature of Prosocial Development: Interdisciplinary Theories and Strategies.* New York: Academic Press.
Caporael, L., R.M. Dawes, J.M. Orbell, and A.J.C. van de Kragt. 1990. "Selfishness Examined: Cooperation in the Absence of Egoistic Incentives." *Behavioral and Brain Sciences* 12, 4:683–99.
Cosmides, L. 1989. "The Logic of Social Exchange: Has Natural Selection Shaped How Humans Reason? Studies with the Wason Selection Task." *Cognition* 31:187–276.
Dawes, R.M. 1980. "Social Dilemmas." *Annual Review of Psychology* 31:169–93.
———. 1988. *Rational Choice in an Uncertain World.* San Diego: Harcourt Brace Jovanovich.
Dawes, R.M., J. McTavish, and H. Shaklee. 1977. "Behavior, Communication and Assumptions about Other People's Behavior in a Common Dilemma Situation." *Journal of Personality and Social Psychology* 35:1–11.
Dawes, R.M., A.J.C. van de Kragt, and J.M. Orbell. 1988. "Not Me or Thee but We: The Importance of Group Identity in Eliciting Cooperation in Dilemma Situations: Experimental Manipulations." *Acta Psychologica* 68:83–97.
Dawkins, R. 1976. *The Selfish Gene.* New York: Oxford University Press.
Deutsch, M. 1960. "The Effect of Motivational Orientation upon Trust and Suspicion." *Human Relations* 13:123–39.
Frank, R.H. 1988. *Passions within Reason.* New York: W.W. Norton.
Hamilton, W.D. 1964. "The Genetical Evolution of Social Behavior, I-II." *Journal of Theoretical Biology* 7:1–52.
Hardin, G.R. 1968. "The Tragedy of the Commons." *Science* 162:1243–48.
Hobbes, T. 1947. *Leviathan.* London: J.M. Dent.
Hoess, Rudolph. 1959. *Commandant at Auschwitz: Autobiography.* London: Weidenfeld and Nicholson.
Hume, D. 1928. *Treatise on Human Nature.* Oxford: Clarendon Press. Reprinted from the original edition and edited by L. A. Selby-Bigge.
Kramer, R.M., and M.B. Brewer. 1986. "Social Group Identity and the Emergence of Cooperation in Resource Conservation Dilemmas." In H. Wilke, D. Messick, and C. Rutte, eds., *Psychology of Decisions and Conflict, 3, Experimental Social Dilemmas.* Frankfurt am Main: Verlag Peter Lang.
MacCorquodale, K., and P.E. Meehl. 1948. "On a Distinction between Hypothetical Constructs and Intervening Variables." *Psychological Review* 55:95–107.
Maruyama, M. 1963. "The Second Cybernetics: Deviation Amplifying Mutual Causal Processes." *American Scientist* 51:164–79.
Maynard-Smith, J. 1984. "Game Theory and the Evolution of Behaviour." *Behavioral and Brain Sciences* 7:95–125.

Olson, M. 1982. *The Rise and Decline of Nations: Economic Growth, Stagnation, and Social Rigidities.* New Haven, CT: Yale University Press.

Orbell, J.M., A.J.C. van de Kragt, and R.M. Dawes. 1988. "Explaining Discussion-Induced Cooperation." *Journal of Personality and Social Psychology* 54, 5:811–19.

Rapoport, Anatol. 1960. *Fights, Games, and Debates.* Ann Arbor: University of Michigan Press.

Rapoport, A., and A.M. Chammah. 1965. *Prisoner's Dilemma.* Ann Arbor: University of Michigan Press.

Sen, A.K. 1967. "Isolation, Assurance and the Social Rate of Discount." *Quarterly Journal of Economics* 80:112–24.

———. 1977. "Rational Fools: A Critique of the Behavioral Foundations of Economics." *Philosophy and Public Affairs* 6:317–44.

Simon, H.A. 1983. *Reason in Human Affairs.* Stanford, CA: Stanford University Press.

Smith, A. 1976. *The Theory of Moral Sentiments.* Indianapolis: Liberty Classics.

Tajfel, H. 1974. "Social Identity and Intergroup Behavior." *Social Science Information* 13:65–93.

———, ed., 1978. *Differentiation between Social Groups: Studies in the Social Psychology of Intergroup Relations.* London: Academic Press.

Tajfel, H., and J. Turner. 1979. "An Integrative Theory of Intergroup Conflict." In W. Austin and S. Worchel, eds., *The Social Psychology of Intergroup Relations.* Monterey, CA: Brooks/Cole.

Taylor, M. 1976. *Anarchy and Cooperation.* New York: John Wiley & Sons.

Thaler, R. 1985. "Mental Accounting and Consumer Choice." *Marketing Science* 4:199–214.

Trivers, R.L. 1971. "The Evolution of Reciprocal Altruism." *Quarterly Review of Biology* 46:35–57.

Turner, J. 1975. "Social Comparison and Social Identity: Some Prospects for Intergroup Behavior." *European Journal of Social Psychology* 5:5–34.

Turner, J., and H. Giles. 1981. *Intergroup Behavior.* Chicago: University of Chicago Press.

van de Kragt, A.J.C., R.M. Dawes, J.M. Orbell, S.R. Braver, and L.A. Wilson II. 1986. "Doing Well and Doing Good as Ways of Resolving Social Dilemmas." In H. Wilke, D. Messick, and C. Rutte, eds., *Experimental Social Dilemmas.* Frankfurt am Main, Verlag Peter Lang.

van de Kragt, A.J.C., J.M. Orbell, and R.M. Dawes. 1983. "The Minimal Contributing Set as a Solution to Public Goods Problems." *American Political Science Review* 77:112–22.

White, T.H. 1973. *The Making of the President—1972.* New York: Atheneum.

Wilson, E.O. 1975. *Sociobiology: The New Synthesis.* Cambridge, MA: Harvard University Press.

Wit, A. 1989. *Group Efficiency and Fairness in Social Dilemmas: An Experimental Gaming Effect.* Doctoral dissertation, Rijksuniversiteit, Groningen.

Wrightsman, L.S. 1966. "Personality and Attitudinal Correlates of Trusting and Trustworthiness in a Two-Person Game." *Journal of Personality and Social Psychology* 4:328–32.

3

KENNETH G. DAU-SCHMIDT

Opportunity Shaping, Preference Shaping, and the Theory of Criminal Law

The economic model of individual behavior is predicated on the assumption that people choose rationally among their opportunities to achieve the maximum satisfaction according to their individual preferences. In accordance with this model, if a person's opportunities or preferences change, the opportunity the person chooses to satisfy his or her preferences will also change. Thus the economic model suggests at least two methods by which society can promote desired individual behavior: (1) shaping the individual's opportunities to give incentive for desired behavior, or (2) shaping the individual's preferences to increase his or her taste for desired behavior.

To date, economists have primarily examined the criminal law as an opportunity-shaping policy. Beginning with the work of Gary Becker (1968), the role of criminal punishment has been largely limited to reducing the attractiveness of criminal opportunities in order to induce optimal compliance with criminal law. Although this analysis has proven fruitful, some scholars have recently expressed misgivings about the adequacy of the current model (Klevorick, 1985; Coleman, 1985; Etzioni, 1988, p. 241). The critics contend that the model has trouble explaining fundamental characteristics of the criminal law, including the importance of intent to criminal liability, the relative lack of importance of actual harm to criminal liability, the treatment of imprisonment and fines as incommensurate punishments, and the variation of punishment based on the characteristics of individual offenders. Perhaps the most troubling shortcoming of the current economic model is its failure to yield a satisfactory distinction between criminal and

This chapter is adapted from Kenneth Dau-Schmidt, "An Economic Analysis of Criminal Law as a Preference Shaping Policy." *The Duke Law Journal* 1990: 1–38. Used with permission.

tort law (Klevorick, 1985, p. 295). Economists have assigned to both tort and criminal law the role of providing incentives for efficient behavior. What, then, explains the distinction between torts and crimes in legal doctrine?

In this article I provide an economic analysis of criminal law as a preference-shaping policy. I argue that, in addition to creating disincentives for criminal activity, criminal punishment is intended to promote social norms for individual behavior by shaping the preferences of criminals and the population at large. By taking account of this preference-shaping function, I explain many of the characteristics of criminal law that have heretofore escaped the logic of the economic model. It is also the preference-shaping function and the prerequisite ordering of preferences that distinguishes criminal law from tort law. My analysis suggests that society will make an activity a crime whenever the social benefits of changing individual preferences through criminal punishment outweigh the social costs. However, since this weighing of social costs and benefits is conducted through the political process on the basis of ethical standards, and requires estimates of the costs of changing opportunities and preferences, I conclude that the economic model of criminal law can be usefully informed by other disciplines.

The Economic Analysis of Crime

The Problem of Crime as an Externality

In economic analysis, crime can be characterized as an externality. An externality is an action or activity by which a person realizes his or her preferences, despite the fact that other people have incompatible preferences, and this incompatibility is not accommodated through the market (Varian, 1984, p. 259). Because of the incompatibility in preferences, the person who undertakes the activity imposes costs on the people he or she affects who have incompatible preferences. These costs may be distributional in terms of the frustration of the affected people's preferences, or allocational in terms of the cost of the precautionary measures they undertake to avoid the effects of the activity (Skogh, 1973). Because there is no market in which the losers can charge the winner for the costs they suffer, these costs are "external" to the winner's decision of whether or not to engage in the activity. As a result, the winner may decide to undertake the activity even though the benefits he or she derives are less than the costs he or she imposes on other people. This state is clearly not Pareto-optimal since the losers could be made better off without making the winner worse off merely by bribing the winner to yield to their preferences. To curtail the externality through a bribe would also increase social welfare, assuming society valued the increase in utility to either the winner or the losers. The externality persists because there is no market in which the winner is charged the costs of his or her activity and transaction costs prevent the losers from making an effective bribe.

To give this analysis meaning for the problem of crime, imagine a society in which crime is not discouraged by a criminal justice system. Every person runs the risk of theft and, in turn, is free to steal from other people. Assuming that there is incompatibility of preferences in that some people desire to consume the fruits of their labor rather than give them away, while other people desire to take and consume those same fruits, and that there is sufficient opportunity for the other people to take and consume those fruits, theft will occur. Assuming that the benefits the thief obtains from the stolen good are less than the costs he or she imposes on the victim and potential victims in the form of the loss of the good and the precautions taken to avoid theft, this situation is not Pareto-optimal. Theoretically, potential victims could bribe the thief to end his or her life of crime for some amount greater than the benefits the thief derives from theft but less than the amount that theft costs the potential victims. The potential victims would retain more of the fruits of their labor, making themselves better off without making the thief worse off. The increase in utility to the potential victims from achieving such an agreement to end crime would increase social welfare. However, with the exception of some "protection" contracts sold by criminal organizations, transactions costs in bringing potential victims together with all potential thieves prevent the use of such bribes to limit crime.

The Traditional Solution: Shaping Opportunities

Traditionally, economists treat preferences as exogenous and immutable and only examine changes in opportunities. When viewed from this perspective, the problem of externalities becomes one of a missing market. An externality presents an efficiency and social welfare problem because there is no market in which the person who undertakes the activity is charged the costs the activity imposes on other people.

The traditional solution to this problem is to impose a tax on the externality equal to its external costs. This solution was first proposed by Arthur Pigou (1920) and accordingly is called a "Pigouvian tax." The Pigouvian tax, in essence, creates a "market" in which the person who undertakes the externality is charged the external costs of his or her activity. The person is thus forced to take into account—or "internalize"—these costs in deciding whether to engage in the activity, and will decide to engage in the activity only if the benefits he or she receives exceed the external costs. As a result, the costs of the activity no longer exceed its benefits, theoretical opportunities for bribes to improve someone's position no longer exist, and society achieves Pareto optimality and increases social welfare.

This traditional solution is the one analyzed by Gary Becker (1968) in his economic model of crime. Becker envisioned the criminal sanction as a "tax" or "price" that society imposes on crime to make criminal opportunities less remunerative. In the Pigouvian tradition, Becker argued that society could reduce criminal activity to the Pareto-optimal level by setting the criminal penalty so that its *ex ante* expected value is equal to the external costs of the crime. With such a sanction, a person would commit a crime only if his or her benefits from the crime exceeded the costs of the crime to society. Because criminals are not always caught and convicted, the actual penalty imposed on a convicted criminal would have to exceed the external costs of the crime so that the expected value of the penalty equaled the external costs. Moreover, because the optimal criminal sanction depends only on the external costs of the crime and the probability the criminal will be caught and convicted, the criminal sanction for a given crime should be the same for everyone with a similar probability of being caught. Finally, because in Becker's model the only purpose of criminal penalties is to give incentives for efficient behavior, the objective of criminal punishment can be met equally well by imposing a jail term or its monetary equivalent in a fine. Becker argued that, to minimize the costs of our criminal justice system, we should rely first on monetary fines and resort to more costly imprisonment only for criminals who cannot afford to pay an appropriate fine.

Becker did not confine himself, however, to analyzing the problem of crime from an efficiency perspective. Instead he extended his analysis to a social welfare perspective, arguing that an appropriate Pigouvian tax would minimize the "social costs" of crime (Becker, 1968, p. 181). The problem with this extension of the argument is that although a Pigouvian tax may ensure a Pareto-optimal result, there is no *a priori* reason to assume that in choosing among Pareto-optimal states to maximize social welfare, society will choose the Pareto-optimal state resulting from the current distribution of initial assets and preferences. A Pigouvian tax balances the benefits of crime to the criminal against the costs of crime to society in determining the Pareto-optimal level of crime. To elevate this analysis to a social welfare argument implicitly assumes that society values the benefits of crime to criminals and includes those benefits in the social welfare function.

There seems good reason to doubt that criminal benefits are included in the social welfare function. First, including criminal benefits in the concept of social welfare defies common sense. My own anecdotal observation is that, unless they are thoroughly steeped in efficiency theory, people are generally shocked to find that some economists argue that the benefits of crime to the criminal should be balanced against the costs of crime to society to determine the optimal level of crime. Even among economists, there is a growing consensus that criminal benefits carry no weight in the social welfare function (Stigler, 1970, p. 527; Dau-Schmidt, 1984, p. 90; Shavell, 1985, p. 1234; Klevorick, 1985, p. 293).

Second, the examples of socially beneficial crimes that are given to support or explain Becker's social welfare analysis are unconvincing. The two most common examples are parking violations and the "Goldilocks parable" of a person who steals food to survive (Posner, 1986, p. 206; Polinsky, 1989, p. 75). Crimes such as parking violations carry no moral stigma and are merely *malum prohibitum*. Such crimes are basically torts that are enforced by the state because the social costs of the externality are too dispersed to allow efficient private prosecution. The social welfare analysis of such crimes varies greatly from that of the core of criminal acts such as theft, rape, and murder which are *malum in se*.[1] In the case of the Goldilocks parable, the person's decision to commit the crime is dictated by his or her opportunity set—either the person commits the crime or the person dies. The fact that we find such actions justified does not mean that society in general values the benefits criminals derive from crime.

Finally, certain practices under our criminal justice system suggest that we do not value the benefit of crime to the criminal. First, we punish repeat offenders more severely than first-time offenders to ensure that future decisions to violate the law are not made on the same cost-benefit analysis as past infractions (Mann, Wheeler, and Sarat, 1980, p. 498). This practice suggests that we do not accept the idea of a socially beneficial crime, since repeating the same offense is met with increasing penalties even though the external costs of the later crimes may be the same. Second, we exclude certain serious offenders from the political determination of what maximizes social welfare by revoking their right to vote and hold office. This exclusion helps ensure that criminal utility is valued in the social welfare function, or at least is underrepresented.

If, in fact, society gives no weight to criminal benefits in the social welfare function, what implications does this have for the use of criminal penalties to shape opportunities and promote behavior that maximizes social welfare? The only author to deal seriously with this question to date is Steven Shavell (1985). The simple answer is that if criminal acts have no social value, criminal penalties should be set so high that the potential criminal's benefits never exceed his or her expected costs and crimes are never committed. This solution would have the additional benefit that, because crimes are never committed, society would never have to spend resources actually punishing criminals. However, Shavell has pointed out that in the real world such an ideal solution is impossible (Shavell, 1985, p. 1243). Due to imperfect information and mistake, increasing penalties to prevent crime imposes costs on society in the form of the punishment of people who mistakenly commit crimes, the mistaken punishment of innocent people, the deterrence of beneficial but marginally lawful activity, and the destruction of marginal incentives for good behavior. Shavell concludes that, for opportunity-shaping purposes, the expected value of the criminal penalty for a crime should be set so that the social benefits of the penalty in preventing crime equal the social costs of the penalty listed above. The optimal expected value of the criminal penalty may well exceed the external costs of the crime, but it cannot be set arbitrarily high to maximize social welfare.

However, the prospect that society gives no value to criminal benefits in the social welfare function suggests another mode of affecting individual behavior and preventing crime: the shaping of individual preferences.

An Alternative Solution: Shaping Preferences

If we treat opportunities as fixed and examine only changes in preferences, we can view the problem of externalities as one of incompatible preferences. The realization of one person's preferences imposes costs on people with incompatible preferences in the form of the direct frustration of their preferences and the resources they expend to protect themselves from the externality.

The obvious solution to the problem is to shape people's preferences so that they are compatible. If the people's preferences are compatible, no one's preferences will be frustrated, and there will be no need to expend resources on precautionary measures.

Economists have been slow to examine this preference-shaping solution for several reasons. First, changes in preferences are less readily observable than the changes in taxes, prices, and wages that make up changes in opportunities. Moreover, if opportunities change at the same time that preferences change, it is difficult to separate their simultaneous effects on behavior. Second, a complete model of a societal preference-shaping policy requires specification of the preference-shaping technology and the process by which society gives some people's preferences preeminence over others' in the social welfare function. Economists have little expertise in these areas, and have traditionally left them to other disciplines (Dau-Schmidt, 1990, p. 16, n.76). Finally, the Pareto-optimal and social welfare criteria are both based on individual preferences. Allowing individual preferences to change undermines the basis for these criteria. The social welfare criterion can be salvaged by assuming intertaste comparability of the intensity of preferences as well as the traditional interpersonal comparability of the intensity of preferences (McManus, 1978, p. 103). The Pareto-optimal criterion, however, is largely useless in evaluating the desirability of changes in preferences within the context of a model of single order individual preferences (Dau-Schmidt, 1990, p. 16, n.78).

It is becoming increasingly apparent that the failure to address the malleability of preferences seriously limits the explanatory power of economic analysis (Etzioni 1988, p. 10). Preference shaping, on an individual, organizational and societal level, is an important human endeavor. It has been identified as a primary or secondary goal of: childrearing, education, religion, advertising, public service announcements, legislation, and, as I argue, criminal punishment.[2] Although economists might usefully assume that these preference-shaping processes are exogenous to their analysis of traditional markets, when economists expand their analysis to social institutions that are intimately related to the preference-shaping processes, either affecting or being affected by them, this assumption should be relaxed. Certainly when one is analyzing a possible preference-shaping policy, such as the criminal law, one must explore the possible implications of endogenous preferences. Although it complicates empirical tests and introduces greater subjectivity via the social welfare analysis, relaxing the assumption that preferences are exogenous promises greater understanding of many social phenomena.

Based on consideration of the identified preference-shaping processes, one might assume the following general outline for the preference-shaping technology. The first requirement is that the person or group of people who are endeavoring to affect another's preferences have some legitimate claim to authority over the person, or at least have the confidence of the person. An untrusting and defiant person is probably a poor candidate for preference modification. The authority figure then characterizes a behavior as either "good" or "bad" and reinforces this characterization with rewards, punishment, and/or education as to why the behavior is good or bad. By characterizing a behavior as good or bad rather than just inexpensive or expensive, the authority figure indicates the need for a fundamental change in the basis upon which the affected person makes decisions. Different types of punishments, rewards, and methods of education may vary in their cost and effectiveness in shaping preferences. For example, corporal punishment in which the person experiences physical pain or isolation is more costly, but also more effective in shaping preferences than charging a fine. Education that shapes preferences should not merely supply more complete information—although this may also shape preferences—but should fundamentally change the way the person views the behavior, for example by asking the person to empathize with the victim. Finally, either positive or negative examples can shape people's preferences. Witnessing someone else's reward or punishment for a behavior can affect a person's preferences towards that behavior.

Families, friends, and associates will engage in the most preference-shaping activity because they have the greatest incentives and abilities to shape preferences. The external costs of a person's behavior are visited largely on his or her family, friends, and associates. Also, the existence of interdependent preferences within these relationships gives rise to strong paternalistic incentives to shape other people's preferences. Family members, friends, and associates, with their shared confidence, time, and experiences, have the best opportunity to shape each others' preferences. Hierarchies within these relationships determine which of incompatible preferences prevail. Parents, in particular, have a strong incentive and ability to shape the preferences of their children to modify their behavior in ways the parent deems desirable. Because of their superior incentives and ability to shape preferences, families, friends, and associates will prescribe a set of desired preferences broader than that prescribed by society at large. This broader set of desired preferences can be understood as the economic description of morality.

To the extent that the preference-shaping efforts of family, friends, and associates coincide with the preferences desired by society as a whole, society can rely on these subgroups to promote its interests. However, these subgroups may sometimes fail to promote society's interests adequately. An individual may have: particularly resistant preferences; inept family, friends, and associates; or family, friends, and associates who do not share and promote the same preferences for behavior as society as a whole. Even if these failures do not occur, society will play a role in reinforcing the preference-shaping activities of the subgroups and ensuring that the preferences learned in these relationships are applied to people outside them. Accordingly, society will have to develop a policy for the shaping of individual preferences. But how should society formulate and evaluate this policy? Which preferences should be changed and to what extent should society expend resources to change preferences? As previously discussed, the Pareto optimal criterion is inappropriate for such determinations. Thus, we must proceed directly to the criterion of maximizing social welfare.

In order to specify a preference-shaping policy that maximizes social welfare, society must first determine what constitutes social welfare. This determination occurs through the political process. Through the votes of the populace and their elected representatives, society determines whose utility and what activities will be valued. The utility derived from some activities and their associated preferences may be highly valued, while utility derived from other activities and their associated preferences may not be valued at all. This ordering of utilities and preferences may be made on the basis of efficiency, ethical, or political considerations. The ordering can never be unanimous. By definition, people desire the activities they prefer and will dissent from the subjugation of their preferences to other people's preferences. Accordingly, the social welfare function and the optimal preference-shaping policy that it specifies must be formulated by one group of people imposing their desires on another group of people through society's political structure.

Once society has specified its social welfare function, it can then proceed to construct a preference-shaping policy to maximize that function. The optimal preference-shaping policy would be one in which society changed those preferences for which the social benefits of the change exceed the social costs. The social benefits consist of the value society places on the utility derived by the people whose preferences would escape frustration with the change in preferences, the value society places on the utility derived from the newly formed compatible preferences, and the savings in resources spent to avoid the externality. The social costs consist of the value society places on the utility derived from the preferences that would be modified and lost, the value society places on the loss of individual autonomy that accompanies the change in preferences, and the resources spent on shaping preferences. Society could use this social welfare maximizing rule of balancing social benefits and costs to specify an optimal set of social norms for behavior to which it would attempt to conform individual preferences.

Of course, the social welfare function is a theoretical construct not subject to precise definition. Scholars could argue endlessly about its form, as well as whose utility and what activities are included. Given this indeterminacy in the model, what can "objectively" be said about the optimal preference-shaping policy?

One observation that can be made is that, assuming that the cost technology of changing preferences is similar for all preferences, the preferences subject to the most extensive efforts of modification will be those whose realization is assigned no value in the social welfare function and that interfere with preferences whose realization is highly valued in the social welfare function. It is from changing such preferences that society would derive the greatest net social benefit because society highly values the realization of the preferences that are saved from frustration, and there is no countervailing social cost from the loss of the realization of the preferences that are changed. This characterization of preferences whose realization is not valued and that interfere with preferences whose realization is highly valued seems to describe the preferences that give rise to criminal activity. As discussed in the last section, there is good reason to believe that the benefits of crime receive no value in the social welfare function. Moreover, the preferences with which crime interferes—the desire for the integrity of one's body and property—are among our most cherished preferences. Thus it seems reasonable to examine criminal law as a preference-shaping policy.

Accommodation of the Two Solutions in an Optimal Policy on Crime

Society employs both opportunity- and preference-shaping methods to treat the problem of externalities. Indeed, the two can be viewed as complements in producing desired behavior. A society that relied solely on incentives, without some underlying basis of morality or social norms, would soon grind to a halt. The costs of policing externalities to ensure optimal behavior in an amoral society would prove prohibitive. Similarly, a society that relied solely on morality to promote desired behavior would soon find itself disappointed by people's baser instincts. Almost anyone could be induced to commit an immoral act, given sufficient opportunity. This complementary relationship is apparent even in less extreme examples. It is cheaper to provide adequate incentives for good behavior if people's preferences are roughly compatible, and there is less need for society to engage in preference shaping for good behavior if significant incentives exist for such behavior.

To maximize social welfare, society will employ both opportunity- and preference-shaping methods to the extent that their social benefits exceed their social costs. The exact mixture of the two methods used and the precise techniques used to shape opportunities and preferences will depend on the technology of behavior control. Although this technology is very complex, it seems safe to assume that shaping opportunities is less costly than shaping preferences. This is true because opportunity-shaping policies, such as damages, taxes, and subsidies, are cheaper to administer than preference-shaping policies, such as criminal fines, probation, and imprisonment.[3] Moreover, shaping opportunities for desired behavior does not involve the same loss of individual autonomy as does shaping people's preferences. Accordingly, it is predictable that society will rely first on the cheaper solution of opportunity shaping to control the problem of externalities. To this end, and to the end of compensating the victims of externalities, tort law was invented. This solution will be the only one employed for externalities in which the net social benefit of changing preferences is negative because society values the utility obtained from both sides of the incompatible preferences about the same. The more costly solution of preference shaping will be reserved for externalities in which there are substantial benefits from preference shaping that exceed the higher social costs because there is a significant disparity in the value society assigns to the utility derived from each side of the incompatible preferences. To this end, criminal law was created and superimposed on the structure of tort law.

Society's efforts to shape opportunities and preferences to prevent crime are evident from the damages and punishments for which criminals are liable under the law. First, almost all crimes are also torts. Accordingly, the criminal is liable for monetary damages—assuming he or she is able to pay—that create a disincentive for criminal behavior. Second, the criminal is subject to criminal punishment in the form of condemnation, fines, probation, and imprisonment. Criminal punishment creates a disincentive for criminal behavior by imposing costs on the criminal in the form of a fine or the pain and lost wages of imprisonment. Moreover, the moral condemnation and punishment of a criminal sentence is also intended to eradicate preferences for the prohibited activity from the criminal and the rest of society.

To follow the social welfare maximizing rule in criminal punishment, society should employ both opportunity- and preference-shaping methods to the extent that their social benefits exceed their social costs. Because criminal punishment results in both opportunity and preference shaping, it should be used to the extent that its *combined* social benefits from both these means of controlling crime exceed its social costs. Accordingly, in setting the optimal amount and form of the criminal sanction, society should consider the potential social benefits and costs of each possible punishment, given the likely disincentive effects of tort law. For a crime that causes small social costs and thus presents the opportunity for small increases in social benefits from opportunity and preference shaping, society should assign a small penalty and use a less expensive and effective preference-shaping method—for example, condemnation with a small fine and probation. For a crime that causes large social costs and thus presents the opportunity for large increases in social benefits from opportunity and preference shaping, society should assign a large penalty and use a more expensive and effective preference-shaping method—for example, a long prison term. Individual characteristics of the criminal may also be relevant to the optimal amount and form of punishment since different individuals may need more or less preference modification, or be more or less susceptible to different methods of preference modification.

Criminal Law as a Preference-Shaping Policy

There is considerable ambiguity in the criminal law between applications of the opportunity- and preference-shaping theories. Both methods of controlling behavior are used in preventing crime and find representation in the doctrine of criminal law. Moreover, the two methods coincide in purpose, observable effect, and often in their means. As a result, policies to decrease crime can be justified by either theory, and the success of these policies can be attributed to a change in either opportunities or preferences. Despite this ambiguity, it does appear that some of the fundamental characteristics of criminal law are best explained by a preference-shaping theory.

The Importance of Intent to Criminal Liability

The concept of intent is central to criminal law. Generally, the government must show that the defendant intended the proscribed harm in order to prove his or her guilt in the crime and liability for criminal punishment (LaFave and Scott, 1986, p. 212). A person is not guilty of criminal battery (striking another) for a blow inadvertently or negligently delivered. Similarly, a person is not guilty of theft (taking another's property) for appropriating property he or she mistakenly believes to be his or her own.

This requirement of intent is puzzling under the opportunity-shaping theory. If a person imposes external costs on someone, that person should be assessed the Pigouvian tax regardless of whether he or she intended the harm. Certainly under tort law, intent is not required for liability (Keeton, 1984, p. 4).

Posner (1985, pp. 1221–22) and Shavell (1985, p. 1248) have argued that intent is relevant to punishment under the opportunity-shaping theory because it is positively related to the probability of harm and negatively related to the probability of apprehension. A person who intends to harm someone is more likely to achieve that harm and to plan a way to escape. Accordingly, these authors argue that a person who intends harm and is caught should receive a larger Pigouvian tax than someone who unintentionally causes the same harm. However, why probable, rather than actual harm, is relevant has not been adequately explained, especially since actual harm is the relevant concept under tort law. Moreover, even if probable harm is relevant, there are other facts that are related to the probabilities of harm and escape that have no similar exalted position (or indeed any relevance) in criminal law. If the owner of a railroad decides to operate for another year without crossing gates, knowing several people will be killed crossing his or her tracks, should the owner be guilty of murder when some are killed because this omission involved a high probability of harm? If a person commits a murder in a brightly lit restaurant with many witnesses after leaving his or her name for a reservation, should that person receive a lighter sentence because he or she will be easily caught?

The preference-shaping theory of criminal law offers a ready explanation of the importance of intent. Under this theory, one of the purposes of criminal punishment is to shape people's preferences when they deviate from established social norms. A court can tell that a person's preferences deviate from the prescribed social norms when his or her actions indicate that the person intended or *desired* to bring about the proscribed harm. If the person does not intend the proscribed harm, but causes it out of negligence or mistake, the person's acts do not indicate deviant preferences. From a preference-shaping perspective, it does no good to punish a person who does not have deviant preferences, either to shape the person's preferences or as an example for the general population. This interpretation comports well with legal theorists' understanding of why the criminal law generally requires proof of intent for criminal liability. The establishment of the requisite *mens rea,* or "guilty mind," is necessary to show the defendant's blame-worthiness or culpability in the committed acts (LaFave and Scott, 1986, p. 212).

The "Irrelevance" of Actual Harm to Criminal Liability

Under the criminal law the actual harm to the victim is of secondary importance in the determination of criminal liability (LaFave and Scott, 1986, pp. 404, 495). This is true even if the person acts with the requisite intent. A person who attempts a crime but fails to do any actual harm is subject to criminal punishment. On the other hand, a person who actually commits a crime and causes harm may not be subject to criminal punishment if the act was justified by self-defense, duress, or necessity. Although it is something of an exaggeration, Richard Epstein (1977, p. 248) has argued that the harm to the victim is irrelevant to criminal law.[4]

The opportunity-shaping theory of the criminal law has difficulty explaining this lack of connection between actual harm and liability. In simple terms, if criminal punishment is the "price" of a criminal act, the obligation to pay that price should be associated with the receipt of the "good" and the realization of the harm it entails. Under tort law, the general rule is that the obligation to pay is associated with the realization of actual harm (Keeton, 1984, p. 6).

Two arguments have been put forward to justify the punishment of attempts within the context of the opportunity-shaping model. First, Posner (1985, p. 1217) and Shavell (1985, p. 1250) have argued that we punish criminal attempts to raise the *ex ante* expected value of criminal punishment without increasing the punishment for the completed crime. They argue that it is cheaper to raise the *ex ante* expected value of criminal punishment by punishing attempts rather than increasing the punishment for the completed crime because the latter involves greater social costs in the mistaken punishment of innocent people, the deterrence of beneficial but marginally lawful activity, and the destruction of marginal incentives for good behavior. However, they fail adequately to explain why a similar assessment of damages for activity with a high probability of harm would not be optimal under tort law. Second, Posner (1985, p. 1217) has argued that the occurrence of a criminal attempt indicates a person with a high probability of committing a crime who should have his or her criminal opportunities reduced to zero by incapacitation. Why such a drastic and costly restriction of the person's opportunity set is optimal when the less expensive alternative of increasing sanctions is available is never explained.

The preference-shaping theory of criminal law offers a more convincing explanation of the punishment of attempts. The commission of significant acts toward the completion of a crime evidences deviant preferences that should be punished for the purpose of shaping preferences, even if no harm actually comes from the acts. This rationale seems to agree with the purpose of punishing attempts discerned by legal theorists. The application of corrective action to those who have sufficiently manifested their dangerousness has been identified as the primary purpose (LaFave and Scott, 1986, p. 499). The deterrence of the commission of completed crimes has been identified as merely a secondary purpose.

The defense of necessity is often put forth by proponents of the opportunity-shaping theory of criminal law as an example of a socially beneficial crime. The example commonly used is the "Goldilocks parable" of a person who, lost in the woods, steals food from a cabin to survive (Posner, 1985, p. 1205). Such an act would be justified under the necessity defense and therefore would not be subject to criminal punishment. This result is explained by proponents of the opportunity-shaping theory as a case in which the social benefits of the crime outweigh its social costs, and therefore the crime should be committed to maximize social welfare. It is argued that we don't actually punish the person who commits a crime out of necessity because it is wasteful to punish undeterrable crimes. This explanation seems plausible. Although society does not value the benefits of crime, in some cases the commission of a crime may avoid a greater social harm and therefore maximize social welfare. Some legal commentators have identified this "lesser of evils" rationale for the necessity defense (LaFave and Scott, 1986, pp. 441–43).

The preference-shaping theory of the criminal law offers an additional explanation of the necessity defense. Nothing can be inferred about the deviation of a person's preferences from the social norm against theft from the fact that the person steals to survive. Given a choice between stealing food to survive and not stealing but dying, even a person with a very strong preference for honesty would obtain a corner solution and choose to steal. Since in the case of necessity the criminal act indicates nothing about the person's preferences, it is not an occasion for criminal punishment to modify preferences. This rationale for the necessity defense also seems plausible and, indeed, has been identified by legal commentators (Brett, 1963, p. 155).

It seems that on the issue of the necessity defense, the two models happily coalesce.

The Amount and Form of Criminal Punishment

Under legal theory, the amount and form of criminal punishment is based on individual culpability (Flynn, 1967, p. 1308): judges determine an offender's culpability by assessing the offender's responsibility for the offense and the seriousness of the crime. The judge then levies an appropriate punishment that may consist of condemnation, fines, probation, imprisonment, or death. Legislative guidelines aid in the determination of the appropriate sentence. Excluding death, imprisonment is viewed as the strongest form of punishment, appropriate for only the most culpable offenders (Mann, Wheeler, and Sarat, 1980, p. 483). Fines are treated as incommensurate with imprisonment and appropriate for less culpable offenders. Criminal punishment may vary in amount and form with characteristics of the individual offender. For example, an offender's punishment may be lighter and of a more rehabilitative bent if he or she is young or has marketable skills (LaFave and Scott, 1986, p. 28). Finally, courts generally try to ensure that the incidence of criminal punishment falls on the culpable individual. If a person commits a crime on behalf of a corporation, it is generally the individual and not the corporation that is held criminally liable (Dau-Schmidt, 1984, p. 79).

These aspects of criminal punishment are curious from the perspective of the opportunity-shaping theory of criminal law. If criminal punishment is the "tax" or "price" levied to discourage criminal activity, then it should make little difference whether that tax is paid in dollars or the pain and foregone earnings of imprisonment. In fact, as Becker (1968, p. 193) has argued, society should prefer fines to imprisonment in punishing criminals, since fines are cheaper to administer. Moreover, if criminal punishment is a tax or price that optimally should be set equal to the social costs of the crime divided by the probability of apprehension and conviction, the sentence for a given crime should vary only according to the person's probability of apprehension and conviction, and his or her opportunity costs of imprisonment. On this basis, Becker (pp. 179–80) has even argued that rich people should receive shorter prison terms than poor people because of their greater wage losses during imprisonment. Finally, Posner (1976, p. 226) has argued that corporations, not individuals, should be held liable for antitrust offenses since the corporation can weigh the costs and benefits of the criminal act and fire the perpetrator if the crime's benefits do not outweigh its costs.

Under the preference-shaping theory of criminal law, criminal punishment is used to shape people's preferences as well as their opportunities. The technology of shaping preferences in part determines what is the optimal amount and form of punishment. Society may not view fines and imprisonment as equivalent for purposes of preference modification. Moreover, the optimal amount and form of preference modification, and therefore punishment, may vary with personal characteristics that indicate more or less deviant preferences and more or less susceptibility to different methods of preference modification. For example, it makes sense to use rehabilitative methods on younger criminals who are not yet "hardened" and committed to a criminal lifestyle. Indeed, under a preference-shaping theory of criminal law, we may want to punish rich people more for a given crime because, given their greater legal opportunities, their commission of the crime indicates more deviant preferences. Finally, it makes sense under the preference-shaping theory of criminal law that the incidence of punishment should fall on the individual. Organizations, such as corporations, have no preferences independent of their officers and agents that society can hope to modify.

Explanation of the Criminal Category

The very existence of the criminal category has posed a puzzle for economists. If externalities are subject to private actions for damages under the tort law, why are some externalities designated crimes and subject to state prosecution for condemnation and fines or imprisonment?

Several opportunity-shaping explanations of the existence of the criminal category have been put forward. Becker (1968) has argued that an externality is designated a crime when a significant number of the perpetrators of the externality will not be caught. In such a case the penalty imposed on the perpetrator will have to exceed actual damages so that the *ex ante* expected cost of the externality to the perpetrator will equal its social costs. Calabresi and Melamed (1972) have hypothesized that we characterize certain acts as crimes and impose criminal sanctions to prevent individuals from undermining property, liability, and inalienability rules which society has established based on efficiency, distributional, and "other justice" considerations. Posner (1985, pp. 1195–96) has taken a similar but narrower approach, arguing that expected criminal penalties must exceed damages to "channel" activities into efficient voluntary transactions and discourage people from resorting to inefficient involuntary transactions.

Yet there are problems with all of these explanations. The fact that not all criminals are caught has never seemed convincing as an explanation of the criminal category. If all criminals were caught, would that really end the distinction between torts and crimes? Although a better explanation, the primacy of voluntary transactions based on efficiency considerations does not fully explain the existence of criminal law. Criminal law is sometimes used to frustrate efficient voluntary transactions—for example, vote selling, prostitution, drug sales, and blackmail. Calabresi and Melamed's explanation is not subject to the same criticism since these aberrations from the rule of efficiency could be explained by distributional or other justice considerations. Coleman (1985, pp. 323, 326), however, has argued that despite its inclusion of these nonefficiency considerations, Calabresi and Melamed's explanation of the criminal category does not adequately account for the moral aspect of the criminal law.

The preference-shaping theory of criminal law provides an economic explanation of the distinction between tort and criminal law. In controlling externalities, society will rely first on the cheaper opportunity-shaping methods of the tort law. The prosecution of torts is left to private parties for reasons of administrative efficiency. The prospect of tort damages simultaneously creates incentives for good behavior and provides a means to compensate the victims of externalities for their losses. Society can use the opportunity-shaping properties of tort law to reduce an externality to the efficient level by limiting tort damages to compensation, or to reduce an externality below the efficient level by allowing punitive damages.[5] Tort law will be the only legal remedy for externalities in which there are negative net social benefits from preference shaping through the criminal law because society values the utility derived from both sides of the incompatible preferences almost the same.

The more costly preference-shaping methods of the criminal law will be reserved for externalities in which there are substantial social benefits from preference shaping through criminal punishment that exceed its higher social costs. The prosecution of crimes is conducted by the government because it facilitates the preference-shaping process and no single individual has sufficient interest in society's preference-shaping policy to undertake the task. As previously discussed, the criminal law's reliance on condemnation and imprisonment is also dictated by the preference-shaping technology. Of course, criminal penalties shape opportunities as well as preferences, and these social benefits should be taken into account in setting the optimal criminal penalty. However, the characteristic that distinguishes crime from other externalities is that society has determined that in these instances, the social benefits of preference shaping through the criminal justice system outweigh the social costs because society values the utility derived from only one side of the incompatible preferences.

It should be noted that although the preference-shaping theory of the criminal law provides an economic explanation of the criminal category, it by no means provides a determinative economic answer to the question of which activities society will designate as crimes. The analysis depends on the technology of shaping opportunities and preferences and society's determination as to whose utility from what activities should be valued in the social welfare function. My simple treatment of these concepts in this paper masks a myriad of important questions. How are preferences formulated and shaped? How is the social welfare function produced in the political process? Why are certain preferences or values placed above others to become social norms enforced by criminal laws? These questions are traditionally the domain of other disciplines, including sociology, psychology, political science, philosophy, theology, criminology, and jurisprudence. Although economics can add further insight into these questions, it would seem that economists can be usefully informed by other disciplines on the subject of crime.

Conclusion

To address the problem of externalities, society uses both opportunity- and preference-shaping methods. The optimal social policy for using such methods will depend on society's valuation of the utility derived from the realization of the various preferences of the members of society, and the cost technologies of shaping opportunities and preferences. In general, shaping opportunities will be cheaper than shaping preferences because it requires fewer resources and involves less infringement of individual autonomy. Accordingly, opportunity shaping will enjoy wide use by society and may be exclusively employed where society values the utility derived from both sides of incompatible preferences. However, society will also use preference-shaping methods where the social benefits of such methods exceed their social costs. In particular, preference-shaping methods will be used where society values the utility derived from only one side of incompatible preferences.

Criminal law can be usefully treated as a preference-shaping policy. The preference-shaping theory of the criminal law provides an explanation of the importance of intent to criminal liability since the intentional infliction of proscribed harms indicates deviant preferences in need of modification. The evidence of such deviant preferences by sufficient acts is the true test of criminal liability, whether or not harm is actually visited on a victim. Moreover, the optimal amount and form of criminal punishment will depend on the technology of preference shaping and will vary with individual characteristics of the criminal that indicate more or less deviance from societal norms and more or less susceptibility to different methods of preference modification. Finally, the preference-shaping theory of the criminal law provides an economic explanation of the criminal category. An externality is designated as a crime when, because of a grave disparity in the value society assigns to the utility derived from each side of the incompatible preferences, the social benefits of shaping preferences through criminal punishment exceed its social costs.

Notes

1. The distinction between crimes that are merely *malum prohibitum* (wrong only because the act is prohibited by law) and crimes that are *malum in se* (inherently wrong) is longstanding in the law (Perkins and Boyce, 1982, p. 880). It has also been long recognized that crimes that are merely *malum prohibitum* are not really crimes, but are torts enforced by the state (ibid., p. 886).

2. Galbraith, 1967, pp. 211–18 (advertising); McKenzie, 1977, pp. 214–17 (families, education, friends, religion); Weisbrod, 1977, p. 944 (childrearing); Marschak, 1978, p. 386 (public policies, advertising, education); McManus, 1978, p. 104 (education, advertising, public service announcements); Kelman, 1981, p. 45 (criminal punishment); McKean and Keller, 1983, p. 29 (families, friends, government policies); Etzioni, 1988, p. 241 (criminal punishment). See also, McPherson, 1983, p. 100, and Etzioni, 1988, p. 10. But see Stigler and Becker (1977) arguing that all preferences are innate and immut-

able and that apparent changes in preferences can be explained as people learning how to better satisfy their innate preferences.

3. Even a criminal fine has higher administrative costs than a commensurate tax because the government must meet a higher burden of proof to establish liability.

4. Actual harm does play some role in criminal law: more harmful crimes tend to have more severe punishments, successful crimes are punished more severely than attempts, and under an optimal law enforcement policy, police and prosecutors will spend more resources to catch and prosecute the perpetrators of the most harmful crimes.

5. Punitive damages may also serve two other purposes. First, they may be used to raise the expected cost of the tort to the tortfeasor so that it equals the social cost of the tort in instances in which not all tortfeasers are successfully prosecuted. Second, punitive damages may be used for preference shaping in instances in which the activity is not a crime, but society has determined that lesser preference-shaping methods are appropriate. Examples of the latter case include punitive damages for slander or libel where society has determined that some preference shaping is warranted, but because of the greater interest in individual autonomy in First-Amendment-related issues, criminal punishment is not appropriate.

References

Becker, Gary S. 1968. "Crime and Punishment: An Economic Approach." *The Journal of Political Economy* 76:169–217.

Brett, Peter. 1963. *An Inquiry into Criminal Guilt.* Sydney: The Law Book Co. of Australasia.

Calabresi, Guido, and A. Douglas Melamed. 1972. "Property Rules, Liability Rules, and Inalienability: One View of the Cathedral." *The Harvard Law Review* 85:1089–1128.

Coleman, Jules L. 1985. "Crime, Kickers, and Transaction Structures." In J. Roland Pennock and John Chapman, eds., *Nomos XXVII: Criminal Justice,* pp. 313–28. New York: New York University Press.

Dau-Schmidt, Kenneth G. 1984. "Sentencing Antitrust Offenders: Reconciling Economic Theory with Legal Theory." *The William Mitchell Law Review* 9:75–100.

———. 1990. "An Economic Analysis of the Criminal Law as a Preference Shaping Policy." *The Duke Law Journal* 1990: 1–38.

Epstein, Richard A. 1977. "Crime and Tort: Old Wine in Old Bottles." In Randy Barnett and John Hagel, eds., *Assessing the Criminal: Restitution, Retribution, and the Legal Process,* pp. 231–58. Cambridge, MA: Ballinger Pub. Co.

Etzioni, Amitai. 1988. *The Moral Dimension: Toward a New Economics.* New York: The Free Press.

Flynn, John J. 1967. "Criminal Sanctions under State and Federal Antitrust Laws." *The Texas Law Review* 45:1301–46.

Galbraith, John K. 1967. *The New Industrial State.* Boston: Houghton Mifflin.

Keeton, W. Page. 1984. *Prosser and Keeton on Torts,* 5th ed. Minneapolis, MN: West Publishing.

Kelman, Steven. 1981. *What Price Incentives? Economists and the Environment.* Boston: Auburn House.

Klevorick, Alvin K. 1985. "On the Economic Theory of Crime." In J. Roland Pennock and John Chapman, eds., *Nomos XXVII: Criminal Justice,* pp. 289–309. New York: New York University Press.

LaFave, Wayne R., and Austin W. Scott. 1986. *Criminal Law,* 2nd ed. Minneapolis, MN: West Publishing.

Mann, Kenneth, Stanton Wheeler, and Austin Sarat. 1980. "Sentencing the White Collar

Offender." *The American Criminal Law Review* 17:479–500.

Marschak, T.A. 1978. "On the Study of Taste Changing Policies." *The American Economic Review Papers and Proceedings* 68, 2:386–91.

McKean, John R., and Robert R. Keller. 1983. "The Shaping of Tastes, Pareto Efficiency and Economic Policy." *The Journal of Behavioral Economics* 12, 1:23–41.

McKenzie, Richard B. 1977. "The Economic Dimensions of Ethical Behavior." *Ethics* 87:208–21.

McManus, M. 1978. "Social Welfare Optimization with Tastes as Variables." *Weltwirtschaftliches Archive* 114, 1:101–22.

McPherson, Michael S. 1983. "Want Information, Morality and Some 'Interpretive' Aspects of Economic Inquiry." In Norma Haan, *Social Science as Moral Inquiry,* pp. 96–124. New York: Columbia University Press.

Perkins, Rollin M., and Ronald N. Boyce. 1982. *Criminal Law,* 3rd ed. Mineola, NY: The Foundation Press.

Pigou, Arthur C. 1920. *The Economics of Welfare,* 2nd ed. London: MacMillan.

Polinsky, A. Mitchell. 1989. *An Introduction to Law and Economics,* 2nd ed. Boston: Little, Brown.

Posner, Richard A. 1976. *Antitrust Law: An Economic Perspective.* Chicago: University of Chicago Press.

———. 1985. "An Economic Theory of the Criminal Law." *The Columbia Law Review* 85:1193–1231.

———. 1986. *Economic Analysis of Law,* 3rd ed. Boston: Little, Brown.

Shavell, Steven. 1985. "Criminal Law and the Optimal Use of Nonmonetary Sanctions as a Deterrent." *The Columbia Law Review* 85:1232–62.

Skogh, Göran. 1973. "A Note on Gary Becker's 'Crime and Punishment: An Economic Approach.' " *The Swedish Journal of Economics* 75:305–11.

Stigler, George J. 1970. "The Optimum Enforcement of Laws." *The Journal of Political Economy* 78:526–54.

Stigler, George J., and Gary S. Becker. 1977. "De Gustibus Non Est Disputandum." *The American Economic Review* 67, 2:79–90.

Varian, Hal R. 1984. *Microeconomic Analysis,* 2nd ed. New York: W. W. Norton.

Weisbrod, Burton A. 1977. "Comparing Utility Functions in Efficiency Terms of What Kind of Utility Functions Do We Want?" *The American Economic Review* 67, 5:991–95.

4

Chris de Neubourg

Job Libido and the Culture of Unemployment: An Essay in Sociological Economics

It is often suggested that high levels of aggregate unemployment can be blamed in part on the attitudes of the jobless. Empirical studies, however, found that the unemployed want only one thing: a job. This paper explores the explanations for this "job libido" and concludes that high levels of (long-term) unemployment may cause important changes in the attitudes of the unemployed, rather than vice versa. More precisely, it is argued that the chance that work-shy attitudes arise is positively correlated with the level of unemployment, the mean duration of unemployment, and the concentration of unemployment among specific groups of the labor force. This positive correlation can be attributed to the fact that higher levels of unemployment, longer durations of unemployment, and more concentrated unemployment change the relation between aggregate unemployment and unemployment insurance benefits via changes in the attitudes towards paid work. The analysis is based on the discussion of a behavioral model of complex rationality.

The first section elaborates the traditional view and the underlying theory and confronts them with the results of empirical studies. The alternative complex rationality framework and its application to the problem at hand, are discussed in the second and third sections. The fourth section briefly explores the empirical relevance of the model. A theoretical note is added in the final section.

Work-Shy Unemployed?

High unemployment rates are often assumed to be partly caused by work-shy attitudes on the part of the jobless. Passive searching behavior, reluctance to

I am indebted to Maarten Vendrik, Joan Muysken, Jacques Siegers, and Frits Tazelaar for helpful comments on earlier drafts of this paper. Parts of the framework presented in this paper are also elaborated in de Neubourg and Vendrik (1989). Used with permission.

mobility, and excessive reservation wages are said to be characteristic for an important part of the unemployed. In line with this argument, the existence of an unemployment insurance system and the generosity of the related benefits are indicated as the major sources of increase of the actual levels of unemployment (especially in Europe).

Unemployment insurance benefits are assumed to provide a major work disincentive and to raise aggregate unemployment in three distinct ways: first, they may cause an increase in the unemployment incidence; second, they tend to lengthen the duration of unemployment; and third, they induce persons to stay in the labor force (eligibility for unemployment benefits may stimulate persons to postpone withdrawal from the labor force until exhaustion of the benefits).

The hypotheses, consistent with recent theoretical developments, fit in the framework of what Feldstein (1973) calls "a New View of Unemployment." This "new view" states that most unemployment consists of flows of persons who are unemployed for short periods rather than stocks of persons who are unemployed for a long period. The instability of employment, the brevity of unemployment spells, and the large flows into and out of unemployment have been emphasized.[1] Although three mechanisms are distinguished to explain why unemployment insurance benefits exert a significant upward pressure on actual unemployment, the one that is most often referred to and that is most relevant in this context relates to the individual duration of unemployment (a complete discussion of the arguments is found in de Neubourg, 1986).

According to the theory, the length of time a person tends to stay unemployed is inversely correlated with the economic hardship experienced by the unemployed. It is clear that unemployment insurance benefits reduce the money costs of being out of work. Consequently, prolongation of the individual duration of unemployment is consistent with rational economic behavior under the existence of an unemployment insurance scheme.

The greater part of the empirical evidence, however, does not sustain the hypothesis that a significant part of current unemployment is induced by the unemployment insurance system. There is a positive interrelation between the magnitude of unemployment benefits and the number of beneficiaries but it is smaller than might be expected on the grounds of microeconomic theory (search theory).

Empirically, the relation between the duration of unemployment and the level and existence of social insurance benefits can be studied either on a macro or a micro level. The majority of macro studies found a substantial and significant effect of the raise in the unemployment benefits upon measured unemployment.[2] The most pronounced results have been found for Canada, the United Kingdom, and the United States (Grubel, Maki, and Sax, 1975; Maki and Spindler, 1975; Grubel and Maki, 1976; Holen and Horowitz, 1974; and Komisar, 1968). Evidence suggests that the effect is much smaller (although still significant) in other countries (Claasen and Lane, 1979; Koning and Franz, 1978). These macro studies, however, have been seriously criticized and discredited on methodological and statistical grounds. Extrapolation beyond the range of observations (Hamermesh, 1978), serious specification errors (Hart, 1982), and careless interpretation of the available data (Cubin and Foley, 1977) are the most convincing arguments.

Micro studies seem to be more appropriate for studying the described mechanism. Almost all investigations based on micro cross-section data find that unemployment insurance does cause a significant but small increase in the mean duration of unemployment (see Chapin, 1971; Ehrenberg and Oaxaca, 1976; Marston, 1975; Nickell, 1979; Mackay and Reid, 1972; Lancaster, 1978; Hamermesh, 1978). The noneconometric results of Clark and Summer (1979) are consistent with this result.

More recent studies for the Netherlands—a country still facing an unemployment rate of nearly 10 percent and where 60 percent of the unemployed are jobless for more than twelve months—show basically the same results: 85 percent of the persons unemployed for more than two years had looked actively for a job, and 71 percent had interviews during the observation period. Although the majority of the long-term unemployed were pessimistic about their chances of finding a job, and although the intensity of their search diminished over time, the great majority of them never stopped looking for a job, followed courses, and were prepared to invest in training (Kloosterman, 1987; Harmonisatieraad Welzijnsbeleid, 1986). A number of studies have concluded that willingness to find work, rather than reservation wage- or income-related considerations, determines search intensity and employment probabilities (Kapteyn and Woittiez, 1985; Ultee et al., 1987; Vissers et al., 1986; Theeuwes, 1989).

In other words, from the empirical studies it may be safely concluded that most unemployed are not work-shy. It is interesting to investigate the sources for the discrepancy between the theoretical expectations and actual economic behavior. Three types of arguments enter the discussion: the first has to do with the type of rationality implied in the behavior of workers, unemployed, and employers; the second concerns the aggregation of individual decisions; and the third centers in the indirect macroeconomic (welfare) impact of social insurance. The first argument is elaborated in the next section.[3]

A Complex Rationality Model with Social Norms

Economic theory, governed by the Pigouvian (Marshallian) tradition of individual labor market behavior analysis, emphasizes the rationality of the choice in favor of receiving a benefit instead of gaining a wage, when the difference between the two becomes smaller. More specifically, a rationally behaving individual will choose to become or stay unemployed (and to cease working or stop actively looking for a job) when the utility of the increase in leisure exceeds the utility of the difference between the (expected) wage and the received social insurance benefit. Moreover, standard economic theory states that unemployment benefits subsidize job search and contribute to the mistaken real wage expectations, and hence induce the unemployed to hold out for more (thus, their reservation wage tends to exceed the market clearing wage, making them voluntary unemployed).

The theory, however, ignores the fact that it would be irrational for job seekers to choose to remain out of work for an extended period, first, because they violate a powerful social custom (norm), and second, because their skills, morale, and physical and mental capabilities are liable to deteriorate to the point where employers would be most reluctant to hire or rehire them.[4]

Notwithstanding the existence of an elaborated system of social security providing transfer incomes of different types, the dominant norm in Western societies is that "in principle," one should work in order to gain income. This norm is sustained and reinforced by the fact that not only the money income but also status, prestige, and power are distributed among the population according to whether or not a person works and the type of work he or she does. Disobedience of an accepted social custom, despite any pecuniary advantage for the individual, leads to loss of reputation or, more extremely, to the exclusion of the individual from the group that accepts the norm. In this case disobedience has a price that may be judged larger than its pecuniary advantage. Applying the theory of social custom developed by Akerlof (1980) in order to explain wage inflexibility accompanied by considerable aggregate unemployment leads to a plausible explanation of the fact that most individuals do not choose to become or stay unemployed, even if the economic costs would be zero. The social costs (loss of reputation, prestige, status, power) and sanctions (exclusion from the group and stigmatization) are incorporated in the utility function of the individual and will shift the decision towards conformity with the social custom. This explains why the rationality of the search theory is not found in its pure form in actual behavior.

The complex rationality model adds arguments to the traditional utility function. Essential to the theoretical framework is the existence of social norms, with a fraction of the population subscribing to the norm. The second major assumption concerns the role of reputations in preferences. "It is assumed," says Akerlof, "that persons care about their reputations . . . in addition to caring about their consumption of goods and services and, for believers in the community's norm, in addition to caring about the agreement of their actions with that norm" (1980, p. 753). It is also assumed that persons care about the agreement of their actions with the norm, if they themselves subscribe the norm. The internal costs of disobedience of the norm are also incorporated in the utility function.

The standard neoclassical model includes primarily pecuniary variables in the equations. Stripped down to its essentials, the model may be summarized as:

$$\text{Max } U\,(Y, L) \qquad\qquad [1]$$
$$Y, L$$

given the restrictions:

$$Y = Y_G - T = wH + Y_{GO} - T(wH, Y_{GO}) \qquad [2]$$
$$H + L = L_o \qquad [3]$$

where Y = net total income; L = unpaid time; Y_G = gross total income; Y_{GO} = other (i.e., nonlabor) gross total income; T = total taxes; W = gross hourly wage; H = paid (labor) time; and L_o = total time. The complex rationality model can be written as:

$$U = U(Y, L, R, A, d^c, \varepsilon) \qquad [4]$$

where R = the individual's reputation in the community; A = obedience or disobedience of the norm by the individual; d^c = belief or disbelief in the norm by the individual; and ε = personal tastes; D^c and ε are parameters, the other four arguments are choice variables.

Utility is maximized under the restrictions [2] and [3] as well as:

$$R = R(A, \mu) \text{ with } \frac{\partial R}{\partial A} > 0, \frac{\partial R}{\partial \mu} < 0, \qquad [5]$$
$$A = A(H), \qquad [6]$$

where μ = the fraction of the population that believes in the norm.
Assuming $Y_{GO} = 0$, equation [2] may be further specified as:

$$Y \begin{array}{ll} = wH - T(wH) & \text{if } wH \geq Y_m \text{ or } H \geq (Y_m/w) \\ = Y_m & \text{if } wH \leq Y_m \text{ or } H \leq (Y_m/w) \end{array} \qquad [7]$$

Here Y_m is a minimum social security transfer income.

Equation [5] can be seen as a social restriction. It states that the (loss of) reputation of an individual depends on whether the norm has been obeyed or not (A), on the one hand, and on the size of the part of the population that endorses the norm (μ), on the other hand. Restriction [5] thus models the effects of social control. To make these more explicit, [5] can, for example, be specified (as in Akerlof, 1980) as:

$$R = -\overline{R} \mu (1 - A), \qquad [8]$$

where $\overline{R}$ is a positive constant.
Assuming also a linear specification for the utility function [4], i.e.,

$$U = a + bY + cL + d\varepsilon R - \overline{C} d^c (1 - A), \qquad [9]$$

Substituting [8] into this specification yields:

$$U = a + bY + cL - d\varepsilon\overline{R}\,\mu\,(1 - A) - \overline{C}d^c\,(1 - A)\,. \qquad [10]$$

Let A and d^c be specified as dummy variables being $A = 1$, if the individual obeys the norm, and $A = 0$, if the individual disobeys the norm, and $d^c = 1$, if the individual believes in the norm, and $d^c = 0$, if the individual does not believe in the norm. Disobedience of the norm then leads to a loss of utility specified by the fourth and the fifth terms of equation [10]. The term $- d\,\varepsilon R\,\mu\,(1 - A)$ specifies the loss of utility due to the negative impact of the social control, i.e., due to the loss of reputation; the term $-Cd^c(1 - A)$ specifies the loss of utility due to the fact that the individual disobeys the norm while being a believer in (the underlying social values of) the norm (while having the norm internalized). An individual who has adopted (internalized) a norm but behaves in contradiction with the content of the norm loses utility because of what can be described as "cognitive dissonance" (Festinger, 1957). The utility loss can take the form of a loss of self-esteem, personal identity, and self-confidence.

The threat of the loss of reputation and the threat of cognitive dissonance introduce elements, respectively, of social-psychological and individual-psychological inertia into the behavior of individuals. The former inertia is specified in equation [8] by the reputation parameter R, whereas the latter inertia is related to the cognitive dissonance parameter C in equation [9].

Equation [6] states that obedience or disobedience of the norm is a function of the total number of hours of paid work H. The question is how many hours should be worked in order to fulfill the requirements of the norm or how large (or small) should H be in order to make $A = 1$ ($A = 0$). The simplest solution is to define A as a dummy equal to zero if $H = 0$ and $A = 1$ if $H > 0$. Other specifications are more interesting and more realistic. The basic model can now be summarized referring to the utility function [4] and the restrictions [3], [7], [6], and [8]. From these equations it is clear that individual labor supply is not only determined by leisure and the pecuniary gains and losses stemming from paid work, but also by utility gained or lost stemming from reputation and cognitive dissonance (or harmony), which is in turn due to either obedience or disobedience of a norm. According to specification [10], an individual who believes in the norm and disobeys it loses utility both by the loss of reputation $[-d\,\varepsilon R\,\mu\,(1 - A)]$ and by cognitive dissonance $[-Cdc\,(1 - A)]$. For persons who do not endorse the norm, disobedience of the norm implies a loss of utility due to the loss of reputation among the believers of the norm (μ). A person who obeys the norm does not lose utility (the third and fourth terms on the right-hand side of [10] are both zero).

By means of the equations specified above and some additional assumptions, the conditions of a short-run equilibrium may now be established (see Akerlof, 1980, for more details). The most important outcome is that the existence of a norm prevents trades that would occur in a "normless" society, because individuals involved in the trade believe in the norm and do not wish to disobey it. Even an individual who does not endorse the norm may nevertheless be inhibited from making choices that he or she may consider economically advantageous because of the loss of reputation among the rest of the community. Thus, social customs may act as a constraint on economic activity, preventing choices that would occur in the absence of such norms. The existence of social norms and their significance for the members of a community thus act as a constraint on simple rational economic behavior.[5]

Norms and Work

Among the norms related to paid work there is what we will call the "dominant work norm," which states that a person should work in order to gain an income. It goes back as far as biblical wisdom telling Adam "Thou shalt work in order to live." It is clear, however, that the dominant work norm does not apply equally to the entire population. The norm recognizes legitimate reasons for nonapplication. The most obvious groups within the population for which the dominant work norm is believed to be irrelevant are the very young members of the population, the older members, those who are ill or unable to work, and those engaged full-time in their education. Since the norm is said not to apply to the members of these groups, they are not expected to obey the norm and their "disobedience" is not interpreted as potentially undermining the system's social values underlying the norm. For simplicity's sake, these groups are left out from the rest of the analysis.

Crudely stated, the rest of the population can be described as the individuals aged between sixteen and sixty-four, except those who are ill or pursuing education full-time. The norm that an individual should work to gain an income, or that one should work in general, applies in full vigor to the male members of the population. This means that they will tend to obey the norm, regardless of whether they endorse it or not, because of their utility-maximizing behavior which guarantees the avoidance of the disutility connected with loss of reputation when they disobey the norm.

The most simple specification of the "work norm" is the one discussed above. In terms of equation [6] (the norm restriction), the norm then states that ("one should work") H should be positive, while A is specified as a dichotomous variable being $= 1$ when $H > 0$, and otherwise $= 0$. This is, however, only a very rudimentary version of the "work norm." A first step in refining the analysis is to specify that the work norm for males states not only that "one should work," but that "one should work enough hours to earn one's own income," i.e., one should earn enough to make "a decent living." We call this the "bread and butter norm." A_B may still be a dummy $= 1$ if Y_G (gross income) is at least equal to the social minimum. So:

$$A_B = 1 \text{ if } Y_G = wH \ge Y_{sm} \ (Y_{GO} = 0) \text{ or } H \ge (Y_{sm}/w)$$

$$A_B = 0 \text{ if } Y_G < Y_{sm} \text{ or } H < (Y_{sm}/w) \tag{11}$$

where Y_{sm} = social minimum income; A_B = bread and butter norm variable.

It is, however, more adequate to specify A_B as a continuous variable with values in the range [0,1], modeling the extent to which an individual is obeying the bread norm. For example:

$$A_B = \frac{Y_G{}^{\alpha_B}}{Y_{sm}} = \frac{wH{}^{\alpha_B}}{Y_{sm}}, \text{ if } H \le (Y_{sm}/w)$$

$$A_B = 1 \text{ , if } H \ge (Y_{sm}/w) \tag{12}$$

where α_B is an elasticity parameter being a function of the perception of the norm.

If $A_B < 1$, an individual suffers from a loss of reputation according to the "bread and butter norm" or the norm that an individual should be able to cover his or her sustenance. It can now be seen that the dominant work norm reformulated as the "bread and butter norm" applies not only to men but to all members of society who are supposed to earn enough to make a decent living. A lot more sophistication can be introduced in the analysis, allowing it to account for various norm configurations. It is possible, for example, to introduce a "good husband norm," a "macho norm," or a "kitchen norm." The discussion of these kinds of complications, however, falls outside the scope of this paper (see de Neubourg and Vendrik, 1989).

Job Libido

The insights stemming from the complex rationality framework can now be applied to the problem at hand: the framework can be used to explain why individuals are involved in paid work despite the fact that the pecuniary gains are small or even absent compared to the situation wherein they would stay unemployed and receive a social security benefit. It is clear that when the dominant work norm and the role of reputations and cognitive dissonance are introduced into the analysis, it may be completely rational for individuals to work even when there are no pecuniary gains. Moreover, the analysis result sustains the hypothesis that an individual is more likely to become or to stay unemployed when the chance that he or she knows someone in his or her surrounding who is already unemployed relative to the chance that he or she knows someone who is employed. In other words, an individual is less reluctant to break the work-ethic norm when social sanctions are likely to be less severe and are likely to be shared by a larger number of peers.

The Culture of Unemployment

The fact that it is a dominant norm in Western societies that an individual is expected to work in order to gain an income does not exclude the possibility that this norm is not obeyed by some persons or even some subgroups within the population. Individuals may be prone to more disobedience, either by taste or when forced by the situation. This breaking of the norm may, at least to some extent, undermine the beliefs responsible for its observance. This can also be seen from equations [5] and [10], where μ (the fraction of the population that believes in the social values underlying the norm) plays an important role; this fraction is a major determinant of the loss of reputation from disobeying the norm. In order to analyze the long-run equilibrium, Akerlof (1980) introduces an additional equation:

$$\mu_{t+1} = g\ (\mu_t\ , x)$$

where μ_{t+1} = the fraction of the population that endorse the norm in the next period; and x = the fraction of the population that obeys the norm.

If $\mu_t > x$, g is negative; if $\mu_t < x$, g is positive.

Let $g(\mu_t, x)$ have the special form $g(\mu_t, x) = \beta\ (x - \mu_t)$, then:

$$\mu_{t+1} = \beta\ (x - \mu_t)$$

According to equation [12], if more people obey the norm than believe in it, the number of believers will rise. Conversely, if fewer people obey the norm than believe in it, the number of believers will fall. Since, according to equations [4] and [9], "nonbelievers" may also obey the norm due to fear of loss of reputation among the rest of the community, the presence of a (small) number of disbelievers does not necessarily set in motion a process that cumulatively undermines the system's social values. Akerlof (1980) analyzed the long-run properties of the system mathematically, and came to the conclusion that "under normal conditions" social norms persist, despite the fact that they may lead to "irrational" economic behavior.[6]

Social norms, however, are neither unassailable nor immutable. Their existence and their preservation are highly dependent on the behavior of the members of a community, which in turn is a function of every possibility to obey the norm. What happens if it becomes impossible for a significant part of the population to obey the norm? This is the situation in the case of mass unemployment: individuals would like to obey the norm that one should work in order to gain an income, but are confronted with the quantitative shortage of jobs.[7] On this level of analysis, the theory of cognitive dissonance enters the discussion again (Festinger, 1957).

According to this theory, an individual tries to reduce dissonance originating in the lack of agreement between an accepted (by the individual) social norm and his or her knowledge that he or she fails to obey the norm. There are three possible ways to reduce the dissonance: first, the source of dissonance may be removed; second, the knowledge concerning the failure may be denied; or third, the social norm may be rejected or perceived as (temporarily) inapplicable.

Translated into the terms of an unemployed person who wishes to obey the relevant norm but knows he or she does not, the person may react in three distinct ways. It is clear that the first—accepting a job—removes the dissonance. Second, the unemployed may try to deny that he or she is out of work by stating that although he or she holds no regular job, he or she does do some work (e.g., by working in the household, taking care of children, or engaging in illegal or black market activities), and thus the social norm is obeyed. It should be noted that this is a hard way to react since both the very dependence on social security benefits and the relative "abnormality" of the everyday behavior will reinforce the dissonance. The third possible reaction, to reject the dominant norm, is not easy either, but is of particular interest in this context. An individual may decide to disobey the social norm in order to reduce his or her cognitive dissonance. This decision, however, is a function of the number of persons endorsing the norm (μ) and the number of persons obeying the norm (x), according to equation [12].

From the analysis in this and the previous section, it should be clear that the likelihood of an individual disobeying the norm is negatively correlated with μ and x; i.e., an individual is more inclined to reject and disobey the norm when the norm is accepted and obeyed by fewer people, since in that case his or her loss of reputation (and the related disutility) is smaller than if the norm is accepted and obeyed by more individuals. The fractions of the population that endorse (μ) and obey (x) the norm, in turn, are a function of the number of people who are able to obey the norm. In terms of the labor market problem, μ and x are a function of the volume of unemployment. As more people become unemployed and thus are unable to obey the norm, μ and x will diminish, hence more unemployed will be inclined to disobey the norm. As more people disobey the norm, the beliefs responsible for its observance will be undermined, which will, in turn, lead to an increase of μ and x, etc.

It can now be understood that as the number of unemployed increases, the dominant work norm will erode. Together with the erosion of the existing norm, a new norm concerning the accepted attitude towards paid work may emerge. The diffusion process of the new norm (provided that those who reject the prevailing norm reach consensus about a new code of behavior) may be analyzed by an analogous mechanism.

If that happens, "a culture of unemployment" may emerge; this is to say, a large number of unemployed may adjust their behavior according to the rejection of the old norm and the acceptance of the new code of behavior, i.e. they adjust their values and norms, in the first instance to reduce cognitive dissonance and later on because the loss of reputation diminishes. As a result, a new culture may arise and may lead on the aggregate level to more unemployment.

This process of cumulative change may mathematically and statistically be described by models adopted from epidemiology. In these models, the number of persons who catch a contagious disease is among other things proportional to the number of persons who are infectious. Baily (1957) has done pioneering work in this area (see also Monin et al., 1973). The model is applied in the social sciences mainly to study the diffusion of innovations (both social and economic)[8] and is described theoretically by Coleman and Katz (1957) and Schelling (1978). It is impossible and unnecessary to discuss the models in depth here. One element, however, should be explained because it adds important variables to the study of our problem.

So far, we have treated the population as homogeneous: no group structure is observed and all individuals are assumed to react in the same way. Let there be two groups, A and B, with more intragroup contact then intergroup contact. It is easy to understand that the spread of an "infection" is a function of the frequency of contact within a population. It can be shown that the rate of change of the proportion of the population that is infected (m_a in group A and m_b in group B) can be expressed in a pair of nonlinear differential equations, [13] and [14] (one equation for each group) (for details, see Coleman, 1964):

$$\frac{dm_a}{dt} = k\,[(1 - P_{ab})m_a + P_{ab}m_b](1 - m_a) \tag{13}$$

$$\frac{dm_a}{dt} = k\,[\frac{n_a}{nb}\,P_{ab}m_a + (1 - \frac{n_a}{nb}\,P_{ab}m_b)](1 - m_b) \tag{14}$$

where m_a, m_b = the proportion of the population that is infected in group A and B respectively; k = the coefficient of contagion; n_a, n_b = the number of individuals in groups A and B, respectively; and P_{ab} = the relative frequency of contact between members of A and B.

Equations [13] and [14] show that besides the number of persons already infected (m; $1 - \mu$ in the previous equations), two other variables determine the speed of contagion: the number of contacts between the infected and the noninfected, and the relative size of the groups.[9] Parameter studies can now be used to investigate the effects of different values of P_{ab} and the relative group sizes n_a/n_b. Assume, for simplicity's sake, that the "disease" starts off in group B. As the groups are more and more isolated from each other (i.e., as $P_{ab} \to 0$), and if something starts off in group B, it will grow there very rapidly until it is nearly universal in B, before it catches on in group A. The effects of changes in the relative group size can also be studied: let B equal the minority group and let the disease start in the same group; then the infection will diffuse through this group before it goes far in the larger one.[10] This rather simple exercise by means of a deterministic model without constraints (everybody is infected sooner or later)[11] demonstrates that the spread of a disease—i.e., the spread of disobedience of the work norm—is a function of the number of individuals already infected $(1 - \mu; m)$, the number of contacts between "haves" and "havenots" related to the frequency of contact between the groups if we assume two groups (P_{ab}) and the relative group size (n_a/n_b). Moreover, we know that with fewer intergroup contacts and a smaller group size of the group where the infection starts off, the infection will spread first and almost exclusively among that group before it catches up with the other group.

To summarize, we can apply our analytic framework to the relationship between aggregate unemployment and work attitudes. The dominant norm in Western societies is that one should work to gain income. As a consequence, workers are reluctant to break this code of behavior and take into account the disutility of the loss of reputation that results from disobeying the norm. The outcome of empirical investigations suggests that the majority of the (employed and unemployed) workers choose to conform their behavior with the norm despite the pecuniary advantage they may gain when an alternative source of income (e.g., a social insurance benefit) is provided. The majority of individuals judge that obeying the norm yields more utility in terms of reputation than the utility derived from the social security income and the related enormous increase in leisure.

As more people become unemployed and are unable to obey the norm due to the shortage of jobs, the fraction of "nonbelievers" is bound to increase. Individual unemployed abandon the norm as a guideline for their behavior to reduce the cognitive dissonance that originates in the lack of agreement between the (initially) accepted code of behavior and the knowledge that the individual fails to obey it. An increase in the share of individuals who reject and disobey the norm undermines the beliefs responsible for its observance, which, in turn, may induce a cumulative process of erosion of the norm.

It is safe to assume that this process will proceed faster when individuals are unemployed for longer periods since cognitive dissonance grows and the need for its reduction becomes more pressing when the expected duration of unemployment increases. The erosion of the dominant norm is therefore positively correlated with the duration of unemployment.

Unemployment, however, is not stochastically distributed among the labor force and is concentrated in certain age and sex groups and geographical areas. To the extent that age, region, and gender are relevant variables for individuals in defining their respective reference group,[12] the concentration of unemployment leads to different rates in the erosion of the norm. If large numbers of individuals reject and disobey the norm, a culture of unemployment may arise. The concentration of these individuals in distinct groups with relatively few intergroup contacts, but with a high frequency of intragroup contacts, may give rise to a subculture of unemployment. In these parts of the community where the subculture is relevant, the dominant work norm is no longer accepted and new norms may be established, leading to another equilibrium.[13] In this context, the emergence of a subculture of unemployment among two specific groups will also lead to a faster erosion of the norm among all other individuals. The groups are particular in this respect since they consist of the persons to whom the traditional norm applies most explicitly, i.e., those persons who are, more than other members of the community, expected to obey the norm, namely prime-age males. If, therefore the number of nonbelievers among them becomes larger, the acceptance of the norm among the other individuals will be influenced negatively. If unemployment and the number of nonbelievers are high among the younger age groups, the same effect will occur. Moreover, the future observance of the norm will be undermined since the younger cohorts of today become the older, norm-setting cohorts of tomorrow. Although a cumulative process that undermines the dominant norm may emerge, it is very unlikely that the norm will disappear completely for two reasons: first, there will always be a group (μ) that accepts and obeys the norm because the members of that group hold a job; in order to avoid cognitive dissonance, they are bound to accept the traditional norm. Second, the number of unemployed, although relatively large, is but a fraction of the number of job holders. Given the theory of cumulative change and its properties, it is more likely that a subculture of unemployment will arise while the majority of the population accepts and obeys the work norm.

The Subculture of Unemployment

No evidence could be found in empirical studies that the culture of unemployment and its consequences were quantitatively very important during the past decade. The previous section, however, argued that the emergence of the culture may be accelerated when unemployment rates increase (hence, the ratio of potential nonbelievers to potential believers grows), when the mean duration of unemployment becomes longer, when unemployment is concentrated in specific groups, and if the concentration of unemployment is particularly high among prime-age males and young workers. Descriptive studies and empirical analyses indicate that some forces may undermine the long-term belief in the norm. Unemployment rose dramatically and the spells of unemployment became significantly longer during the 1980s, especially in Europe (de Neubourg, 1990a). The distribution of unemployment is far from equal; younger workers experience unemployment more often. The unemployment rate for prime-age males, however, is relatively low; this may act as a countervailing force against the other factors. The Netherlands seems to take a special position in the context of this paper: aggregate unemployment is still close to 10 percent of the registered labor force, more than half of the unemployed stay without a job for more than a year, and a fourth of the youth labor that entered the labor market between 1980 and 1985 are looking for a job.

Recent empirical studies lend support to the hypothesis that a subculture of unemployment is emerging in the Netherlands, although the finding that the largest majority of the unemployed are still looking for jobs and are eager to accept the first job offer, is again confirmed. About 10 percent of the Dutch long-term unemployed appear to have abandoned the dominant work norm. The people belonging to this group are concentrated in big cities and among certain age groups. A discussion of all the important relevant mechanisms, however, falls outside the scope of this paper (but see Kroft, Engbersen, Schuyt, and van Waarden, 1989; Kerckhoffs, de Neubourg, and Palm, 1990; and de Neubourg, 1990b, for details).

The analysis presented in this paper is far too superficial to allow any firm conclusion. It may be said that the circumstances are present to lead to an erosion of a central norm in Western societies and that this situation is unmatched by anything in postwar history. It is unlikely that an erosion would take place on a societywide level, but the emergence of a subculture of unemployment is not impossible. The fact that, relatively and absolutely, a lot of young workers suffer from long-lasting unemployment may have far-reaching consequences for the long-term observance of the work norm we have been discussing.

A Theoretical Note

Let us leave the merely speculative analysis of the last two sections, and consider some final remarks concerning the relation between the theoretical framework presented in this paper and orthodox economic theory and sociology. While this framework differs from the traditional neoclassical theory, it is compatible with its basic assumptions about rational (maximizing) and purposive behavior. The labor market problems themselves induce us to take "noneconomic" variables into account. The theoretical framework subscribes to Solow's contention that "the labor market is a little different from other markets, in the sense that the objectives of the participants are not always the ones we normally impute to economic agents, and some of the constraints by which they feel themselves bound are not always the conventional constraints" (Solow, 1980, p. 3).

The theoretical framework presented here uses important elements of orthodox sociological analysis. The study of the impact of social norms and values belongs to the very heart of the sociological discipline and goes back as far as Durkheim and Weber. The mathematical analysis of social change through the diffusion of ideas and innovations can be found in the work of many early anthropologists. Its empirical application marks the beginning of the mathematical sociology. The moderate utilitarian perspective underlying the present framework is also found in the recent sociological work of Boudon (1979), who emphasizes the social constraints for a rationally behaving individual.

The complex rationality model is also consistent with some new developments in economic theory. The role of attitudes in labor market behavior and the self-reproducing mechanisms are also found in the dual labor market theory. The basis of complex rationality is especially consistent with Heiner's (1983) intriguing contribution concerning "The origin of predictable behavior," and with the corridor idea of Leijonhufvud (1981).

It should be repeated that the analytical framework presented here has to be developed further and studied empirically. Its plausibility, however, raises serious doubts about the impact of work-shy attitudes upon the level of unemployment.

Notes

1. See Walch (1981) for a detailed survey.

2. The latter argument is not developed in this paper. It relates to the recruitment behavior of employers and emphasizes unemployment as a screening device. For an elaboration, see de Neubourg 1990a and 1991.

3. Although the standard neoclassical model cannot account for the mechanisms described above, the phenomenon is well known among economists. The persistence of racial discrimination on the labor market is extensively studied by Becker (1957) and by Arrow (1972). Akerlof (1980) himself uses his model to explain the coexistence of mass unemployment and downward wage inflexibility due to the fact that both employers and unemployed abstain from undercutting actual real wages even though they both would gain by acting that way.

4. Early work in this area is found in Coleman and Katz (1957), and Rapoport (1953).

5. If it begins in the larger group, it will catch on very quickly in the smaller group, so that the groups rapidly become more nearly in the proportion of "haves."

6. In particular, "membership-reference group." Reference group is an important theoretical construct in sociology elaborated by Runciman (1966); the membership reference group is the group that is recognized by an individual as the one to which he or she belongs.

7. Although the reasons for the concentration of unemployment among specific groups are not crucially important in this context, some explanation is in order. If no plausible explanation for the phenomenon could be given, it would be possible that unemployment is higher in one group than in another, because the unemployed of the first group are more prone to work-shy attitudes than the members of the second group. Without elaborating all the possible reasons, it is possible to refer to the explanations provided by the queue theory, the theory of internal labor markets and the use of on-the-job-experience as a screening device (especially if the wage structure falls to adjust to changing skill structure).

8. See Feldstein (1973, 1975); Hall (1972); Perry (1972); and Salant (1977).

9. It may also be argued that, clearly, "paid work" itself has a positive utility. The utility derived from having a job is not only to be attributed to the wage, since this can be replaced by a benefit; it is also derived from conforming to the actual system of social values within the community and the status and prestige gained by this conformity. This is another formulation of the reputation variable presented above.

10. It may be possible for an individual to find a job; the aggregate effect, however, would be that another person would be displaced and become unemployed (given the demand for labor and the wage level).

11. Evidently, this variable is also important when a homogeneous population is studied; this can be interpreted as the special case for which P_{ab} is equal to chance.

12. The next step would be to expand the number of groups beyond two. The general equation analogous to [13] and [14] can be written:

$$\frac{dm_i}{dt} = \sum_{j=1}^{k} P_{ij} m_j (1 - m_i)$$

References

Akerlof, G.A. 1980. "A Theory of Social Custom, of which Unemployment may be One Consequence." *Quarterly Journal of Economics* 92(2): 749–55.

Arrow, K.J. 1972. "Models of Job Discrimination." In A.H. Pascal, ed., *Racial Discrimination in Economic Life.* Lexington, MA: D.C. Heath.

Bailey, N.T.S. 1957. *The Mathematical Theory of Epidemics.* London: Griffin.

Becker, G.S. 1957. *The Economics of Discrimination.* Chicago: University of Chicago Press.

———. 1965. "A Theory of the Allocation of Time," in *The Economic Journal* 75:493–517.

Boudon, R. 1979. *La Logique du Sociale.* 1979. Paris: Hachette.

Chapin, G. 1971. Unemployment Insurance, Job Search and the Demand for Leisure. *Western Economic Journal* 9(4): 102–7.

Claasen, E.M., and G. Lane. 1978. "The Effects of Unemployment Benefits on the Unemployment Rate in France." In H.G. Grubel and N.A. Walker, eds., *Unemployment Insurance: Global Evidence of Its Effect on Unemployment.* Vancouver, BC: The Fraser Institute.

Clark, K.B., and L.H. Summer. 1979. "Labor Market Dynamics and Unemployment: A Reconsideration." *Brookings Papers on Economic Activity* 1:13–72.

Coleman, J.S. 1964. *Introduction to Mathematical Sociology,* London: The Free Press of Glencoe.

Coleman, J.S., and E. Katz. 1957. "The Diffusion of an Innovation among Physicians." *Sociometry* 20:253–70.

Cubin, J.S., and K. Foley. 1977. "The Extent of Benefit-Produced Unemployment in Great Britain: Some New Evidence, *Oxford Economic Papers* 29 (March): 128–40.

Ehrenberg, R.L., and R.L. Oaxaca. 1976. "Unemployment Insurance, Duration of Unemployment and Subsequent Wage Gain." *American Economic Review* 66, 5 (December): 754–66.

Feldstein, M.S. 1973. "The Economics of New Unemployment." *Public Interest* 33 (Fall): 3–42.

———. 1975. "The Importance of Temporary Layoffs: An Empirical Analysis," *Brookings Papers on Economic Activity* 3:725–45.

Festinger, L. 1957. *A Theory of Cognitive Disonance.* Evanston, IL: Row, Peterson and Company.

Grubel, H.G., and D.R. Maki. 1976. "The Effects of Unemployment Benefits on U.S. Unemployment Rates." *Weltwirtschaftlisches Archiv* 112, 2:274–99.

Grubel, H.G., D.A. Maki, and R. Sax. 1975. "Real and Insured-Induced Unemployment in Canada." *Canadian Journal of Economics* 8, 2 (May): 174–91.

Hall, R.E. 1972. "Turnover in the Labor Force." *Brookings Papers on Economic Activity* 3:369–402.

Hamermesh, D.S. 1978. "Unemployment Insurance and Unemployment in the United States." In H.G. Grubel and M.A. Walker, eds., *Unemployment Insurance: Global Evidence of Its Effect on Unemployment.* Vancouver, BC: The Fraser Institute

Harmonisatieraad Welzijnsbeleid [Council for Welfare Policy]. 1986. "Perspectief voor Langdurig Werklozen" [Perspectives for the long-term unemployed]. *Advies,* No. 46. The Hague. Mimeo.

Hart, R.A. 1982. "Unemployment Insurance and the Firm's Employment Strategy: A European and United States Comparison." *Kyklos* 35:648–72.

Hartog, J. 1980. *Tussen Vraag en Aanbod.* Leiden: Stenfert Kroese.

Heiner, R.A. 1983. "The Origin of Predictible Behavior." *American Economic Review* 83, 4:541–59.

Holen, A., and S. Horowitz. 1974. "The Effect of Unemployment Insurance and Eligibility Enforcement on Unemployment." *Journal of Law and Economics* 17 (October): 403–32.

Kapteyn, A., and J. Woittiez. 1985. "Arbeidsaanbod en voorkeursvorming" [Labor supply and preference formulation]. Tilburg: Economic Institute. Mimeo.

Kerckhoffs, K., C. de Neubourg, and F. Palm. 1990. "The Determinants of Individual Unemployment Duration," Maastricht: University of Limburg, Faculty of Economics. Research memorandum.

Kloosterman, R.C. 1987. *"Achteraan in de rij"* [Closing the queue]. OSA-Voorstudie no. 20. The Hague: Government Publishing Office.

Komisar, J.B. 1968. "Social Legislation Policies and Labor Force Behavior." *Journal of Economic Issues* 2 (June): 187–99.

Koning, H., and W. Franz. 1978. "Unemployment Compensation and the Rate of Unemployment in the Federal Republic of Germany." In H.G. Grubel and N.A. Walker, eds., *Unemployment Insurance: Global Evidence of its Effects on Unemployment.* Vancouver, BC: The Fraser Institute.

Kroft, H., G. Engbersen, K. Schuyt, and F. van Waarden. 1989. *Een Tijd zonder Werk; een Onderzoek naar de Levenswereld van langdurig Werklozen.* Leiden: Stenfert Kroese.

Lancaster, T. 1978. "Econometric Methods for the Duration of Unemployment." *Econometrics* 47 (4).

Leijonhufvud, A. 1981. *Information and Coordination.* New York: Oxford University Press.

MacKay, D.J., and G.L. Reid. 1972. "Redundancy, Unemployment and Manpower Policy." *Economic Journal* 82 (December): 1256–72.

Maki, D., and Z.A. Spindler. 1975. "The Effect of Unemployment Compensation on the Rate of Unemployment in Great Britain." *Oxford Economic Papers* 27:440–54.

Marston, S.T. 1975. "The Impact of Unemployment Insurance on Job Search." *Brookings Papers on Economic Activity* 6 (1): 13–60.

Monin, J.P., R. Benayoun, and B. Sert. 1973. *Initation aux Mathématiques des Processus de Diffusion, Contagion et Propagation.* Paris: Mouton/Gauthier-Villar.

de Neubourg, C. 1985. "The World According to Jantje van Leiden or the Culture of Unemployment." Working Paper 85–007, Faculty of Economics, Limburg University, Maastricht.

———. 1986a. "Jantje van Leiden of de Cultuur van Werkloosheid." In *Tijdschrift voor Arbeidsvraagstukken,* pp. 26–40.

———. 1986b. "Social Security, Unemployment and the Utilisation of Labor Resources: A Complex Interrelation Internationally Compared." In W. Albeda, ed., *The Future of the Welfare State: Comparative Analysis.* Maastricht: Maastricht University Press.

———. 1987. "Naar een Theorie van Arbeidsaanbod Gebaseerd op Complexe Rationaliteit." In P. Keizer and S. Soeters, eds., *Economie en de Gedrags- en Maatschappijwetenschappen.* Assen: van Gorcum.

————. 1988. *Unemployment and Labour Slack: Theory and Evidence in Labour Market Accounting*. Amsterdam-New York: North-Holland.

————. 1990a. "The Dynamics of Hyperunemployment." In C. de Neubourg, ed., *The Art of Full Employment*. Amsterdam-New York: North Holland: 1990.

————. 1990b. "The Socio-Economics of Unemployment Duration." Maastricht: University of Limburg, Faculty of Economics. Research memorandum.

————. 1990c. *Unemployment and Labour Market Flexibility, The Netherlands*. Geneva: International Labour Organization.

————. 1991. "The Socio-Economics of Unemployment Duration." Research memorandum. Maastricht, Faculty of Economics, Limburg University.

de Neuborg, C., and L. Kok. 1986. *Projecting Labour Supply: Theory, Methods and Research. An International Comparison*. The Hague. OSA, Government Printing Office.

de Neuborg, C., and M.C.M. Vendrik. 1989. "Endogenous Social Norm Changes." Working Paper. Maastricht, Faculty of Economics, Limburg University.

Nickell, S.J. 1979. "The Effect of Unemployment and Related Benefits on the Duration of Unemployment." *Economic Journal* 89 (March): 34–49.

Perry, G.L. 1972. "Unemployment Flows in the U.S. Labor Market." *Brookings Papers on Economic Activities* 2:245–78.

Rapoport, A. 1953. "Spread of Information through a Population with Sociostructural Bias." *Bulletin of Mathematical Biophysics* 15:523–33.

Robbins, L. 1930. "On the Elasticity of Demand for Income in Terms of Effort." *Economicas* (June).

Runciman, D. 1966. *Relative Deprivation and Social Justice*. Harmondsworth, U.K.: Penguin.

Salant, S.W. 1977. "Search Theory and Duration Data: A Theory of Sorts." *Quarterly Journal of Economics* 91 (February): 44–45.

Schelling, T.C. 1978. *Micromotives and Macrobehavior*. New York: Norton.

Solow, R.M. 1980. "On Theories of Unemployment." *American Economic Review* 70, 1:1–11.

Stigler, G.J., and G.S. Becker. 1977. "De Gustibus Non Est Disputandum." *American Economic Review* 67, 2:76–90.

Theeuwes, J. 1989. "Unemployment and Labour Market Transition Probabilities." In J. Muysken and C. de Neubourg, eds., *Unemployment in Europe*. London: Macmillan.

Ultee, W.C., et al. 1987. "From Unemployment to Unemployment—From Employment to Employment: A Comparison of Short- and Long-Period Intragenerational (Un)employment Mobility Tables for Sixteen Western Industrial Nations at the End of the Seventies and in the Early Eighties." Paper presented at the Meeting of the Research Committee on Social Stratification and Mobility of the International Sociological Association, Nuremberg, April.

Vendrik, M.C.M. 1988. "Preference Drifts in Labor Supply: Towards an Integration of Economic and Psychological Motivation Theories." In P. van den Abeele, ed., *Psychology in Micro & Macroeconomics*. Leuven: Proceedings of the 13th Annual Colloquium of the International Association for Research in Economic Psychology, vol. 3.

Vissers, A.M.C., et al. 1986. "Arbeidsmarktgedrag ten tijde van massale Werkloosheid" [Labor market behavior in times of massive unemployment]. OSA-Voorstudie no. 12. The Hague: Government Publishing Office, 1986.

Walch, B.M. 1981. Unemployment Insurance and Labor Market: A Review of Research Related to Policy. OECD, MAS/WP5: 1 (1), Paris, 1981.

5

Robert E. Lane

Money Symbolism and Economic Rationality

The purpose of this chapter is to show how the symbolization of money alters economic calculations and distorts economic rationality. First I will provide a suitable, if unconventional, definition of rationality as a standard against which to measure the effects of money symbolism. After a brief discussion of the common idea of money as a neutral sign, whose only function is to facilitate transactions, I will review studies of popular attitudes towards and beliefs about money that reveal eleven ways whereby the symbolization of money influences economic rationality. A concluding section will analyze the more general influence of money symbolism on economic thinking and behavior.

Criteria for Individual Rationality

The first criterion for rational preference formation, we will say, requires that four conditions be met: (i) In accordance with accepted doctrine, preferences must be framed so that they are consistent and transitive,[1] but also flexible enough to accommodate learning. (ii) Preferences must be made in the light of alternatives, that is, utility maximization implies rejecting some preferences as well as choosing some others. This condition is important because it implies that rational decision making must be informed; it is not satisfied by habit (unless that is itself a conscious decision), and takes into account decision making and information costs. (iii) The preferences or values pursued must be "ego-syntonic," that is, they must be such that if they are achieved or consummated, they yield genuine satisfaction. Elster (1983) has pointed out one way in which

This paper is adapted from a chapter in my forthcoming book, *The Market Experience* (New York: Cambridge University Press, 1991.) Used with permission. I wish to thank Yale's Institution for Social and Policy Studies and Nuffield College, Oxford, for logistical and intellectual support.

stated preferences are misleading: if those preferences are conditioned on the belief that certain otherwise desirable objects are unattainable ("sour grapes"), or alternatively, that only the unattained and unattainable is preferable ("the pastures are greener on the other side of the fence"), they are not an adequate guide to satisfaction. The grapes would and the pastures would not yield satisfaction. Similarly, it would be absurd to accept as rational a schedule of preferences whose purpose was to maximize the economic equivalent of what the psychiatrist calls "neurotic gain" at the cost of some greater satisfactions which, with more insight, an individual would welcome. (iv) A fourth condition for accepting a schedule of preferences as rational reflects an important requirement for maximizing satisfaction: a person's aspirations must be within the bounds of his potential achievements. Studies of people's satisfaction with their housing, for example, reveal that satisfaction depends heavily on the relationship among aspirations, expectations, and achievement. The objective character of the housing is much less important than the relation of achievement to aspirations (Campbell, Converse, and Rodgers, 1976, chap. 6). One reason why the more mature members of the population are more satisfied with their lives than the younger members is that they have brought their aspirations into closer line with their achievements—but everyone has, and generally uses, a subjective upgrading of "achievements" to help this process of reconciling the desired with the achieved (Campbell, Converse, and Rodgers, 1976, pp. 171–98). This condition also rules out the insatiability of appetites that Durkheim said led to anomie. Thus, we cannot be content with the simple criterion of stable and transitive preferences, and of course neither can we be satisfied with the tautology implied by the doctrine of "revealed preferences," that is, the pattern of purchases is, *ipso facto,* evidence of utility maximization within a given budget.[2]

A second criterion for procedural rationality is ends-means rationality, a criterion that has two parts. (i) Within the information reasonably available (available within the time and effort budget dictated by some satisficing criteria) the selected means must be chosen efficiently to bring about the preferred ends. In more formal terms, the selection of means within a payoff matrix must match the preferences in the matrix of utilities. But this is insufficient, especially in a market economy where consumer pleasures tend to dominate considerations of what Juster (1985) calls "process benefits," for it seems to ignore the intrinsic satisfaction of the means. As Charles Fried (1970) reminds us, all means have some intrinsic satisfactions or dissatisfactions that are, therefore, proximate ends in themselves. Thus, rational calculation must not only account for the effectiveness of the means, but also (ii) their intrinsic hedonic qualities. Our intention is to be sure to include work satisfaction in the rational calculus, but with a little extension, this consideration might also include the satisfaction of conscience in the process of acquisition.

When discussing economic rationality one must consider whether rationality implies exclusive attention to self-interest. We reject this, partly on the grounds that it is ambiguous: for example, David Gauthier (1975, p. 93) distinguishes between "self-interest" and "self-directed aims," and the extended self may incorporate not only family and friends but also the nation, thus blending with altruism. But more importantly, we reject it on the grounds that from the individual point of view it is as rational to follow the Kantian imperative or to follow the line of reasoning in Justice as Fairness as it is to be solely selfish. No one would say that altruism is irrational unless he accepted a self-interest premise, thus begging the question. It is better to leave unspecified the beneficiaries of the utilities a person seeks to maximize. The rationality of the market accommodates all altruism mediated by purchases (for it does not matter whether a person buys flowers for his own enjoyment or for a gift) but it is disturbed by altruism expressed in the satisfaction a person receives from other people's income and welfare (e.g., interdependent utilities) when they are achieved without any economic act of the altruistic individual (see Koopmans, 1957, p. 41).

The Neutrality of Money

What we wish to explore is the way attitudes towards money, what we will call the symbolization of money, affect these various criteria for economic rationality. Most economists, and even their critics, hold that the meaning of money is exhausted by its command over goods and services. After rehearsing the various materials used in primitive society as money and the period when money was "backed" by precious metals, the economist, Walter C. Neale, says: "Today . . . the paper and the tokens 'stand for' nothing except what they can do for their owners: make payments to payees who will accept the paper and tokens in payment" (Neale, 1976, pp. 16–17).[4]

Georg Simmel (1978), too, claims that the value of money is relative to its command over goods and services; therefore "money is nothing but the symbol of this relativity; . . . it expresses the relativity of objects of demand through which they have economic value." As time passes, "money becomes more and more a mere symbol [sic], neutral as regards its intrinsic value" (pp. 123, 127, 132, 152). Finally, Karl Polanyi (1971) suggests the neutrality of money symbolism by comparing it to the symbols of weights and measures. Of course, economists recognize that the money system affects and sometimes distorts the production and distribution of commodities,[5] but this does not affect the phenomenology of money, which is treated almost without exception as directly dependent on what money can buy.

But, in fact, money is symbolized in such a way as to be phenomenologically anything but neutral; it is invested with a variety of fears, obsessions, and inhibitions that distort its serviceability for market calculations. This elaboration of meanings is further complicated by the fact that the symbolization of money is often matched by a symbolization of particular commodities ("the fetishism of commodities"), and, it seems, from dream content, especially of automobiles

(Hall and van de Castle, 1966, appendix A). Tversky and Kahneman's study of the framing of decisions shows that there is often a mental framework for partic- ular commodities and a separate framework for money in general with the result that "this paradoxical variation in the value of money is incompatible with the standard analysis of consumer behavior" (Tversky and Kahneman, 1974, p. 457).

One measure of the difference in the hedonic value of money symbols and the commodities they purchase is suggested by their different contributions to mea- sures of subjective well-being. Thus, in one such account, a score on a "money index" contributes about 15 percent of the variance on an overall measure of life satisfaction, while a score on a "consumer index" contributes about 7 percent. If one were to follow economic practice and identify the sign value (as contrasted to the symbolic value) of the money to what money buys (the consumer index), the remaining symbolic value of money would contribute about 8 percentage points of the total 15 percent that the "money index" contributes to a sense of well-being. By this calculation, the symbolic value of money contributes more to well-being than does the sign, descriptive value (Andrews and Withey, 1976, p. 124).[6] Of course, these calculations are merely suggestive, but whatever measure of well-being is used ("satisfaction," "happiness," etc.), the overall result is the same.

A broad and tolerant concept of economic rationality can accommodate many of these symbolizations; the criterion for this accommodation is whether or not money symbols permit a person to maximize his or her utilities in the market. Following the above set of criteria, such symbolization interferes with individual "rationality" most generally when emotions dominate thought, and more specif- ically when the symbolization inhibits the formation of (i) consistent but flexible, (ii) comparatively assessed, (iii) ego-syntonic, or (iv) feasible preferences. It does this by distorting thinking about (v) how to achieve the goals implied by these preferences, and by (vi) ignoring or exaggerating the intrinsic value of the means employed. That is, those money symbols that bias perceptions, bend prefer- ences, inhibit transactions for desired goods, or invite transactions for undesired goods, or, like anxiety and obsessions, distort market calculations—these symbolic uses of money may be said to damage market rationality as we have defined it.

We may conceive of some of these money symbolisms as transaction costs, that is, the impediments to utility maximization imposed by money symbols increase the "price" of the commodities purchased. But it would be more accu- rate to think of them as price distortions, changing the values of the commodities in the market. In a clinical analogy they may be said to represent neurotic gain, short-term advantages purchased at the cost of long-term satisfaction. In the language of metaphor, inviting a person with some of the money symbolism we shall examine to enter the market is like inviting a person with agoraphobia to enjoy the view of a Kansas prairie. Sometimes, too, under the influence of symbolization, market calculations become like the decision to fly to an appointment in Paris made by a person who fears (or craves) flying. There is a lot more going on than calculat- ing the relative satisfactions to be derived simply from the objects purchased.

Money Symbolism

Condensation symbols of money, with their dense configurations of meaning "allowing for the ready release of emotional tension in conscious or unconscious form" (Sapir, 1934, p. 493) may be tapped in discursive accounts and word association tests. A simpler, though quite compatible, approach to money meanings is through conventional attitude research. In the discussions below we combine these approaches and attempt to synthesize the findings of the following studies.

1. In 1981 Carin Rubenstein reported four main clusters of attitudes (scales) derived from a nonrepresentative mail return sample of 20,000 respondents self-selected from the readers of *Psychology Today*. The sample was younger, more affluent, and included more professionals and business people than would a representative national sample.

2. In 1982, seeking to systematize psychoanalytic and other theories of money attitudes, Yamauchi and Templer found four main independent factors in a study using sixty-two questions given to a heterogeneous American sample of 300. These factors accounted for 33 percent of the variance.

3. In 1984 Adrian Furnham, using sixty-four questions (many of them borrowed from Rubenstein's and Yamauchi and Templer's items) in a study of a heterogeneous British sample of 226, found seven independent factors accounting for 17 percent of the variance.

4. Earlier, in 1972, Wernimont and Fitzpatrick employed a different method, the "semantic differential"; that is, they asked their 533 heterogeneous subjects to respond to forty statements of the following kind: "To me money is something that is ... 'good/bad,' 'embarrassing/not embarrassing,' 'successful/unsuccessful,' " etc. In many ways this method is better designed to discover the more subtle meanings of money. Again, the authors analyzed the results by factor analysis, finding six independent factors accounting for 55 percent of the variance.

5. Finally, we employ the reports of a psychoanalyst, Edmund Bergler (1951), on two of the many cases he treated that revolved around money problems.[7]

Obsession with Money and Money Consciousness

Agreeing with such propositions as the following obviously indicates an unusual concern about money: "I put money ahead of pleasure"; "I feel that money is the only thing that I can really count on" (Furnham, 1984); "Next to health, money is the most important thing in the the world."[8] In a more discursive vein, those who believe they think "much more" about money than others, or who say they fantasize about money "all or much of the time," may be said to be "money conscious" (Rubenstein, 1981). As might be expected, the poor more than the rich, the less well educated more than the better educated, fall into this classification. Microeconomics is silent about such obsessions. It may be that these are stable and transitive preferences fulfilling the usual criteria of market rationality. And they may even permit pursuit of feasible goals, pursued efficiently. But obsessions are not flexible; they block learning. Almost by definition, an obsession is not ego-syntonic in the sense that it does not correspond to those desires that, with more self-knowledge, a person would continue to desire; given help, people are happy to be free of obsessions. Evidence that such obsessive concern about money fails, for such reasons as these, to permit utility maximization comes from the studies themselves, for there is a reported tendency for people with such money obsessions to be dissatisfied with their work, their love lives, and their social relations. They are unhappy (Rubenstein, 1981, p. 42). Of course, we do not know whether their money obsessions contribute to their unhappiness or merely reflect a more general malaise, but it seems unlikely that such obsessions permit choices leading to happiness.

The word association study (Wernimont and Fitzpatrick, 1972) found one factor (out of six), called a "pooh-pooh attitude," revealing a tendency to deprecate the importance of money. Some of the adjectives associated with money in this factor were "weak," "unprofessional," "dissatisfying," "unimportant." This attitude seems, on the face of it, to represent the opposite of obsession with money.

Again, there is no reason to believe that such an attitude interferes with consistent, flexible, ego-syntonic, feasible preferences, although it may rule out one source of pleasure: for many people part of the fun of life lies in meeting economic challenges by making money. This form of utility maximization is apparently barred by the "pooh-pooh" attitude. On the other hand, this depreciation of the value of money may facilitate choices contributing to overall life satisfaction: for most people, satisfaction with leisure and with family life makes more of a contribution to life satisfaction than does satisfaction with standard of living. And, most strangely, satisfaction with the standard of living may itself be enhanced by considering money unimportant (Campbell, Converse, and Rodgers, 1976, p. 76). Unlike obsessions with money, there is nothing qualifying the "pooh-pooh" attitude as a violation of the criteria for economic rationality. Indeed, by limiting the scope of a person's aspirations, the "pooh-pooh attitude" may facilitate a more congenial ratio of aspirations to achievements. The irony flowing from the greater economic rationality of those who place a lower value on money will not be lost on a public taught to be believe that economic rationality depends on maximizing income.

Anxiety

In two studies "anxiety" emerged as a major factor differentiating responses to money; it is indicated by such sentiments as: "I show signs of nervousness when I don't have enough money"; "I spend money to make myself feel better" (Furnham,

1984; Yamauchi and Templer, 1982). For these people, it seems, money symbolism either stands for previous disturbing experiences or otherwise prompts chronic states of anxiety. These attitudes were independent of people's incomes, but they were closely associated with a general measure of mental disturbances.

Perhaps the attitude is compatible with consistent, comparative, and feasible preferences, but few clinicians would say that people choose ego-syntonically during anxiety. From social psychological studies we know that mild anxiety improves performance but more severe anxiety reduces the quality of performance because the individual is thinking more of himself than of the task at hand. Anxiety foreshortens perspectives and reduces realistic assessment (Spielberger, 1972, pp. 39–42).

Control over One's Money

Folk expressions and popular verse often reflect the sense that money is out of control: "That's the way the money goes, / Pop goes the weasel"; "Money burns a hole in my pocket." The sentiment is reflected in a group labeled "the money-troubled," characterized by their sense that they were poorer than their friends (even though they were not), aspirations beyond their means, inability to save, and the tendency to charge things they could not currently afford—and hence by their encumbrance by debt (Rubenstein, 1981; see also Furnham, 1984). In contrast, another group, called "the money-contented," have a sense of control over their finances and say that if they cannot afford something, they either save for it or forget it; they keep their aspirations within their means and (borrowing from a similar constellation in another study) such people report that "I always know how much I have in my savings account" (Furnham, 1984). Again, these attitudes towards money are not related to level of income.

There is nothing in the concept of consistent preferences that prevents overspending, or that implies a sense of control over one's finances, yet these attitudes and behaviors interfere with rational allocation of budgets over time. Specifically, this use of money violates the criterion for individual rationality represented by aspirations within one's means and rational ends-means calculations. Further, we know that a sense of control over one's fate is a central and indispensable ingredient of life satisfaction (Campbell, 1981, pp. 217–18), i.e., utility maximization. For those who have lost control over their money, money cannot represent a set of neutral symbols, like the weights and measures that Polanyi says are comparable to money symbols; rather, money is fraught with trouble entailing a sense of inadequacy in dealing with it.

Money Retention and Saving

A tendency to value saving over spending is not just the opposite of the lost sense of control (the corrective factor that would set things right), but rather a factor in its own right, and not a happy one. In two studies it is characterized by a tendency to agree with the statements: "I often say 'I can't afford it' whether I can or not"; and "Even when I have sufficient money I often feel guilty about spending money on necessities like clothes, etc." (Furnham, 1984; Yamauchi and Templer, 1982). There are no income differences that mark off this group. In another study, the author developed a "Midas scale"; those who scored high on this scale reported themselves to be "penny pinchers" and stated that they do not "really enjoy spending money" (Rubenstein, 1981).

For these groups the consistent preference is to deny oneself the commodities for which it is necessary to spend money; that is, there is a high transaction cost for every transaction. Since transaction costs (like information costs) represent charges against utility maximization, those who dislike spending money gain less from their purchases than others because the "price" has been increased. In assessing how this syndrome fits into the concept of economic rationality one could think of Midas himself as maximizing his utilities by hoarding, but, unlike Midas, the persons who rank high on "the Midas scale" derive little life satisfaction with their savings. For example, the attitudinal cluster includes agreement with the statement, "I often feel inferior to others who have more than myself, even when I know that they have done nothing of worth to get it." Rather, it seems, the retentiveness syndrome is (again) equivalent to a neurosis where the "neurotic gain" interferes with long-term, ego-syntonic satisfaction. For example, the "Midases" in this study had low self-esteem, were unhappy about their jobs, friends, sex lives, and had frequent headaches (Rubenstein, 1981, p. 43), evidence witnessing the implausibility of utility maximization along this route. But then, the Protestants who devised the Protestant ethic of thrift (and work) never placed a high value on happiness.

Impression Management

There is no reason to consider "conspicuous consumption," or impression management irrational in market terms; after all, Adam Smith held that the main reason people sought money was "to be observed, to be attended to, to be taken notice of with sympathy, complacency, and appreciation."[9] Thus, finding a cluster of attitudes towards money that indicates that the meaning of money for some people is the power they think it gives them over other people's attitudes towards themselves is not surprising or in itself economically irrational. Fashion is built on just such a set of attitudes. We see this cluster in the favorable responses to such statements as: "I sometimes buy things I don't need or want to impress people because they are the right things to have at the time"; "I sometimes 'buy' friendship by being very generous with those I want to like me"; and "I often give large tips to waiters/waitresses that I like" (Furnham, 1984).

The preference expressed, so far as we can tell, is consistent with other preferences, but it may lead to a kind of intransitivity in actual purchases. Seeking to buy friendship or approval from Group A today, the individual ranks commodity *X* over *Y*, but seeking to buy the friendship of Group B tomorrow, he ranks commodity *Y* over *X*. His preference for approval retains its priority, but, as others have observed, a person's intransitive commodity preferences risk his becoming a "money pump," trading a discounted *Y* for *X* today and then a discounted *X* for *Y* tomorrow. Going beyond the logic of the transactions, we might observe the risks of failure in the underlying "approval motive"; when it is severe, it is self-defeating, for people do not want to be courted insistently and they therefore spurn the suitor (Crowne and Marlowe, 1964). And recalling Marx's (1964) comment on the use of money to buy love, one might conclude that what is rational in market terms becomes irrational in terms of a larger life plan that reserves friendship for a separate domain.

Distrust and Suspicion

"When I make a purchase, I have a suspicion that I have been taken advantage of"; "I argue or complain about the cost of things I buy" (Yamauchi and Templer, 1982). Through such questions a cluster of attitudes marked off a group of distrustful purchasers, a group measurably (on a separate measure) more paranoid than most.

Like the group who purchases approval, this group risks having an intermediate purpose, in this case avoiding being taken advantage of, distort consumer preferences. There is nothing irrational about emphasizing reputations for integrity, choosing commodities according to the warranties offered, or going only to places where one is known, but the priority given to risk-aversive tactics at the cost of other properties of transactions and of things to be purchased seems likely to be costly in other ways. In any event, true paranoia cannot be reassured, for there are always grounds for suspicion. Therefore, the preference fails the feasibility criterion. It is comparable to Durkheim's insatiable appetites and any insatiability violates one of the canons of rational preferences: aspirations within reach of achievements. It also violates ends-means rationality, for no means can achieve these ends.

"Shameful Failure"

In the semantic differential study, a factor called "shameful failure" was the most discriminating of the factors found. The factor emerged as people responded to the question, "To me money is something that is. . ." with the adjectives "unsuccessful," "retreating," "embarrassing," "discouraging," "degrading." Those most likely to score high on this factor were hospital nurses, a group of unemployed in training, and freshmen and sophomores in college; the low scorers were managers and salesmen. That is, those for whom money was not (at least at the time of the questioning) important in their daily occupations viewed money as "embarrassing" or "discouraging," while those successfully engaged in making money did not. The same division occurs on another dimension, money as "socially acceptable or unacceptable" (Wernimont and Fitzpatrick, 1972).

Two forces affecting the stability of preferences seem to be at work in these responses: (1) this particular study was conducted in 1970 or 1971 when the counterculture was still active. For the students, at least, there was available a ready-made, negative response to money symbols that would disappear as the more conventional attitudes of the later 1970s reassumed their original force. Preferences cannot be expected to remain stable when the zeitgeists blow them hither and yon. (2) What is rational in one role is not rational in another. When the freshmen and sophomores become managers and salesmen, or when the unemployed in training have jobs, money symbolism will almost certainly not carry this freight of possible failure, embarrassment, and degradation. For only the mature hospital nurses is this likely to be a stable and transitive "preference," but for the others, something like Mannheim's (1948) "self-transformation" (with the aid of the changing zeitgeist and new responsibilities) seems at work—a different form of life rationality. In the meantime, to the extent that these attitudes imply behavior consonant with the attitudes reported (which is not always true), there remains an aversion to earning money that will frustrate certain forms of economic rationality.

"Money Masochism"

A taciturn and bitter criminal lawyer came into the office of the psychiatrist, Edmund Bergler, answered questions in resistant monosyllables, and when told that he must give more information, he broke down and wept. He then told a story of how he defended, by brilliant maneuvers, a group of chiseling clients in the plastics business. These "chiselers," however, persuaded the lawyer to accept, in lieu of payment, a partnership scheme in their business. In order to rescue his investment, the lawyer spent more and more time trying to save himself from losses, and as a consequence, neglected his legal work and lost more money.

A public accountant told Bergler a similar story. Deciding that he could not get rich by his accountancy practice, he was lured by his clients into investing in the cinderblock business. It turned out that the business was in a shambles and that in order to save his investment, he poured more money into the scheme with few prospects for success. Bergler asked him, "How could you, a specialist at figures and account sheets, fall for these crooks you allowed to become your partners?" "You know the human weakness for getting rich," he answered (Bergler, 1951, p. 234).

But, of course, the answer concealed the special forces at work in the accountant's own case. In both cases, given the special competences of lawyers and accountants, Bergler interpreted their failures as reflecting desires to punish themselves, a form of "money masochism," based on unconscious wishes to prove their own incompetence, or to assuage their guilt, or for some other reason.

Economic rationality makes no room for either the fear of success, now said to characterize some women in the professions and business (Tresemer, 1977), or masochistic tendencies. It would do no good to find that their preferences were consistent and feasible, and it would violate the canons of mental health to label masochism as ego-syntonic. The obvious problem for economic rationality, however, is how to interpret utility maximization through self-punishment, pleasure through pain.

Moral Evil

In the word association test, one group associated money with the adjectives: "dishonest," "dishonorable," "unfair." The syndrome was called "moral evil" and, strangely, was almost as frequently found among salesmen and managers as among students and hospital nurses (Wernimont and Fitzpatrick, 1972). For the salesmen, some inconsistency among "preferences" is apparent in the fact that they also found money "socially acceptable," and associated it with the adjectives "relaxed," "happy," and "dependable." One source of inconsistency is the ambivalence characteristic of symbols, that is, both positive and negative feelings about the same object, a frequent enough set of attitudes and yet qualifying as irrational by the economist's standards, especially since ambivalence might easily lead to intransitivity. For utility maximization, two unhappy outcomes might stem from ambivalence: (1) making and spending money might not lead to pleasure because the dark side of the ambivalence would detract from that pleasure; and (2) prior to consummation of an ambivalent desire, the individual might hold back as the negative side of his feelings made itself felt. Furthermore, with respect to money as "moral evil," the stage is set for a classic moral dilemma: achieving a desired good through means thought disreputable. It is hard to achieve utility maximization when each component pleasure is balanced by an associated, sometimes greater sometimes lesser, pain.

Money-Contented, Security, Acceptable

Some of the attitudes towards money and money symbolization reflect a sense of control over one's funds, a sense that money is desirable primarily as a source of security, and that it is a socially acceptable medium of exchange. In contrast to the "money-troubled," the "money-contented" say that if they can't afford something they save for it or forget it (Rubenstein, 1981). Those who find money a source of security report that "I always know how much I have in my savings account" (Furnham, 1984). The social acceptability of money is reflected in the word association study by such adjectives as "trusting," "loyal," "healthy," "friendly," "controllable" (Wernimont and Fitzpatrick, 1972). The studies indicate that these groups are reasonably populous but do not form a majority of the respondents studied. We do not know whether these attitudes are associated with rational economic behavior but they seem quite compatible with the criteria and conditions we have used.

Market Ideology

A somewhat different kind of attitude set, and a powerful one, is represented by acceptance or rejection of the market ideology itself. Labeled respectively "American Dream" and "American Nightmare," these two attitude sets both reflected and caused various aspects of money symbolism. The "American Dream" syndrome holds that (i) hard work always pays off; (ii) wealth is a measure of intelligence, mental health, and happiness; (iii) the Dreamers' own futures are considered bright; the Dreamers also tend to be (iv) more religious than others and (v) more money conscious. In contrast, the "American Nightmare" cluster holds that (i) success is a matter of luck or connections (or greed); and (ii) people have little control over their financial prospects. In addition, the Nightmare people are (iii) less happy and less optimistic than others, and (iv) they tend to be agnostic and skeptical about life (Rubenstein, 1981). This rich pair of syndromes tells us little about consistent, flexible, ego-syntonic, feasible preferences, but it tells us something about utility maximization. To increase one's happiness in a market economy, one's preferences should include support for market methods; one should believe in market fairness and one's own efficacy in the market. As it turns out, for some people these beliefs and preferences are indeed so stable that they survive every kind of misfortune in the market (including structural unemployment); that is, market system symbols are so strong that they foreclose some relevant learning from market misfortune. Even those who lose their jobs because of business failure or recession often continue to believe in that portion of the market ideology that holds that one is responsible for one's own fate, a belief that only increases their misery (Schlozman and Verba, 1979). In this sense, ends-means rationality is certainly not a feature of market ideology.

Symbolic Thinking and Rationality

If money were only a sign, or a neutral quantity, like measures of weights, it would be merely a tool for the normal processes of rational inference. But, as we have seen, this is not the case. The symbolization of money has implications for rational inference going beyond our confined definition of economic rationality.

Interpreting Meanings and Market Choices

At the beginning of this discussion we said that rationality in general implies emotions under cognitive control. The relationship between cognition and affectivity is not that of a single dimension, with rationality at one end and emotion at the other; rather, these two aspects of human responses are said either to lie along two different dimensions (McGuire, 1969, p. 202), or to be governed by two different systems. The psychologist, R. B. Zajonc, reports his findings this way:

> Affective responses to stimuli are often the very first reactions of the organism. ... Affective reactions can occur without extensive perceptual and cognitive encoding, are made with greater confidence than cognitive judgments, and can be made sooner. ... [A]ffect and cognition are under the control of separate and partially independent systems that can influence each other in a variety of ways, and ... both constitute independent sources of effects in information processing. [Zajonc, 1980, p. 151]

Responses to symbols tend to give priority to affect, the "like-dislike" dimension, and only secondarily to lead to a search for cognitive content or appropriate disposition. One of the purposes in the use of symbols is to arouse or pacify the emotions, playing on this primacy of affective responses. Certain things follow from this:

(i) It is hard to hold the affect-laden attitudes we have been examining in suspension while considering various alternative choices. Of course, people often try to do this in making their purchases or choosing jobs, but the symbolization of money makes this more difficult and is an impediment to the economist's idea of "value-weighing" rationality.

(ii) The relatively weak cognitive content of symbols means that the dispositions they arouse may be inconsistent and incoherent. "Affective reactions," says Zajonc "need not depend on cognition," and "may be separated from content" (1980, pp. 158, 159).

(iii) The multivalence of the symbolic meaning of money implies multiple possible referents from which the individual must choose (see, e.g., Eliade, 1969). For example, when money means "distrust and suspicion," or "shameful failure," the rich associations behind such interpretations are likely to suggest a multitude of responses that may be quite inconsistent and incoherent. In the cases of the lawyer and the accountant described by Bergler, the inconsistency of manifest and latent goals led to the self-defeating behavior that Bergler said was intended but which might also be interpreted as the result of cognitive confusion due to multivalent stimuli.

Inference and Truth Values

(i) The vague and underspecified cognitive content of the symbols makes logical inference difficult, for logic requires clear conceptual boundaries for its processes of inclusion and exclusion. If money were a neutral sign pointing to desired commodities or desired savings instead of a symbol of anxiety, suspicion, pride, and ideology, logical inference would be more nearly possible.

(ii) The truth or validity of a symbol cannot be verified or falsified, depriving rationality of one of the means of disposing of the untrue or invalid. Langer (1948, p. 58) suggests that a symbol is an affectively and imaginatively endowed concept; as Hempel (1952) said many years ago, concepts are neither true nor false, they are simply fruitful or unfruitful. But the test of fruitfulness in the case of money symbols is only partly that of utility maximization in the market; perhaps a larger part is subjective satisfaction from the symbolic process itself.[10] Using money symbols has its process benefits—and costs.

(iii) The noncausal nature of symbolic thinking limits rational assessment of the consequences of one's own acts or purchases in the market. And yet such questions as the following cannot be answered without careful attention to causes: What effects will buying a house have on my budget? How will an education affect my chances of getting a job? Does saving now for a vacation make sense in an inflationary economy?

(iv) One of the processes of inference is to infer from a little information some larger construct of meaning: What does a price/earnings ratio tell a person about a stock? What does price tell a person about the quality of a product? Money symbols tend to be overloaded with meaning. In this respect symbols are like stereotypes: they seem to offer more information (default values) than it is possible for them to convey. Thus, a money symbol is likely to be invested with inferences about a person who is poor that are quite unwarranted by the facts (Luft, 1957). Or an apparent desire to make money may give to the phrase, "promising investment," more meanings than the mere phrase can convey—as in the cases of Bergler's lawyer and accountant.

(v) The vivid, emotionally cathected, often personally relevant loadings of a symbol tend to dominate the background, sometimes statistical, situationally relevant information about the phenomena to which the symbol refers. In this sense, symbols invite what is called the availability heuristic, that is, the tendency to focus on what is readily available to the senses and memory rather than what is determinative for more scientific information processing (Tversky and Kahneman, 1974).[11] Thus, money symbols (standing for status, power, "moral evil," as well as price) may dominate information on the quality or usefulness of a commodity, again frustrating utility maximization.

(vi) Symbols are said to "represent" something but they may not be representative of the events or people for which they stand. Because they are so much "things-in-themselves," they do not lend themselves to concepts of sampling; they invite that common defect of thinking called the representativeness heuristic that says people tend to pick as representative of a set the exemplar that has the most immediately salient characteristics of the set being typified (Tversky and Kahneman, 1974). Asked to describe the characteristics of mammals, people describe the characteristics of dogs and cats—but forget about whales.

(vii) Thinking about condensation symbols is often metaphorical, using analogy to yield significance or meaning. Metaphors are fruitful sources of creativity and invention, but they may not be serviceable in providing consistent and coherent preferences or in leading to the ends-means rationality required to maximize utilities in the market. Like all analogies, metaphors select the similarities in some comparison but ignore the dissimilarities. Thus, government debt is compared to household debt, with bankruptcy as its perilous outcome. In the hidden interstices of language, economic metaphors convey subtle meanings: it has been pointed out that the phrase "labor is a resource" compares human labor to the "resource" of raw materials, concealing the dignity of labor (Lakoff and Johnson, 1980, p. 236). Psychoanalytic interpretations of money rely heavily on metaphor: the power of money triggers analogies to sexual potency, but thinking of money as sexual potency is not a preferred route to maximization of utilities in the market.

(viii) The interpretation of condensation symbols sometimes relies on insight, which may be defined as perception of a hidden pattern in some complex ground. The search for patterns is ubiquitous; from a few instances (and some indoctrination), one "finds" that "hard work pays off"; "people can't be trusted"; "people get what they deserve." Like analogies, these discerned patterns may lead to discoveries, but they are only ambiguously related to consistent, flexible, ego-syntonic, feasible preferences and appropriate ends-means rationality. Once the pattern has been discerned, it may trigger a response appropriate to that pattern—but, as in the case of the distrustful person who "finds" himself always being cheated, these discerned patterns may be inappropriate to the real-life situation. That is, given our bounded rationality, people use few (rational) reality checks on their "insights."

(ix) Symbols help to define situations and thus to guide responses considered appropriate to that situation. The British anthropologist Geoffrey Gorer (1948) said that Americans were exceptionally generous until the situation was defined as a business situation, at which point they became shrewd and calculating.[12] But defining situations by using money symbols, such as those suggested by the labels "money retentiveness," "uncontrollability," or "distrust and suspicion," is likely to lead to responses frustrating utility maximization in any long-term, ego-syntonic sense.

(x) Finally, when a proposition is symbolized, the task of interpreting its meaning is complicated by the fact that a respondent must disentangle the meaning of the symbol from that of the context or situation. Borrowing from the literature of symbolic politics, we turn to a study by Lance Bennett in which similar population samples were offered two statements, one straightforward and the other symbolized: "This country should take some of the money it spends on defense and the space program and use it to solve problems here at home." And "Above all, the flag should fly with pride above America. We should take some of the money we spend on defense. . . ." The consequence of adding the symbolic rhetoric was, first, to stabilize opinion, and second, to cause ideas on the use of defense money to cluster these now stabilized opinions in ways reflecting the symbol rather than the proposition to which it was attached. For the less sophisticated the symbol simplified their thought on the matter, for the symbol dominated policy considerations, but for the more sophisticated it complicated things, for they recognized that they had to sort out the separate meanings of symbol and statement, rather than confabulate them (Bennett, 1975, pp. 98–101). In some such fashion the symbolization of money complicates the meaning of a purchase, for there are two messages to be sorted out: the money message and the commodity message.

Ranking Preferences

(i) Ranking implies that a good, A, is ranked higher than another good, B, because A has more of the desiderata for that class of goods than B (Baier, 1969). But if it is money, rather than the goods themselves, that has the desiderata, it may be because one is interested in warding off being cheated, or avoiding moral evil, or fearful of failure. If that is the case, then these fears and desires are what is ranked and the utility maximization lies in successfully coping with these symbolic concerns. This form of utility maximization is just as "real" and just as rational as the ranking of pleasures to be derived from each item in an array of candidates for purchase. But it is certainly a different market from the one envisaged by market economists. This picture represents an "economy of love and fear," although in quite a different sense from that used by Boulding (1973).

(ii) There are several properties inherent in symbolism that help to explain the problem of ranking goods or values in symbolic thinking:

Symbolic thinking is nonlogical, nonlinear, and, as we said, uses loosely bounded concepts whose wide and vague boundaries defy ranking.

Whereas money as a sign creates a unidimensional scale along which to rank and compare the value of goods, money as a symbol treats such references as "moral evil," "impression management," "ideology of the market," and "shameful failure" as different and often incomparable dimensions. Thus, when we symbolize money we deprive it of one of its main functions: to serve as a standard of value permitting all goods to be ranked on a single dimension.

And two of the properties of symbols already mentioned impose barriers to sensible ranking: the ambivalence arising from the simultaneous positive and negative feelings that symbols arouse in the same person at the same time; and their situational specificity.

Ego-Syntonic Preferences

Just as "affective judgments implicate the self" in a way uncharacteristic of more cognitive judgments (Zajonc, 1980, p. 157), so symbols are incorporated in the personality in a way not characteristic of signs. There is some irony in this, for, according to Simmel (1950), one of the values of a money economy is the way money frees its owners from entanglements of personality and permits a certain detachment or blasé attitude toward life. The incorporation into the self of money symbols and the definition of the self in terms of money shatters this detachment and with it some portion of a person's capacity to assess each situation without believing that one's self-concept is at stake. Rubinstein's study shows that those who are "money-troubled" and those who are niggardly and savings-conscious tend to have lower self-esteem than others.

Information costs

Both the market and individuals perform better when information costs are minimal, but it is characteristic of condensation symbols to conceal as well as to distort information for the purpose of arousing or influencing an audience. This goes beyond the selective use of metaphor mentioned earlier, or the more obvious case of advertising, for it points to such problems as those revealed in the discussion of obsession with money. As mentioned, obsessions shut out other information, hence a person with a money obsession who answers "I put money ahead of pleasure" (i.e., utilities) is shielded from information about other kinds of pleasures—and forfeits utility maximization. In this respect, obsession with money is like any other obsession, except that in economic matters its scope is probably wider than that of other obsessions. Quite frequently the symbolization of money impedes information searches and shuts out relevant available information, thus violating the comparison condition in the formation of preferences.

As Marx observed, money conceals and remedies such personal deficiencies as unloveability and lack of taste. Research shows that this concealment works: without meaning to, we attribute to the wealthy favorable attributes denied to the poor (Luft, 1957).

Risk Assessment

We already know that people are poor judges of probability: the heuristics they use often "lead to large and persistent biases with serious implications for decision making in areas as diverse as financial analysis and the management of natural hazards" (Slovic, Fischhoff, and Lichtenstein, 1982, pp. 464–65). Behind these general attitudes lie certain individual differences associated, in the case of money, with such attitudes as distrust, as were mentioned earlier. More generally, the goodness and badness of money symbols seem sufficient in themselves to accept or reject them, distorting calculations of risk even beyond the "large and persistent biases" that frequently prevail. This is the function of patriotic symbols in war and, in lesser degree, is evident in money calculations as well. But without some consideration of risk of failure, enterprises will be more vulnerable to bankruptcy, and without some grasp on probability, investment in education, career choices, and the purchase of consumer durables will certainly not maximize satisfaction.

Borrowed Meanings

Finally, money symbols borrow meanings from other life domains, meanings used by the market, but not generated by it. For example, the meanings of money influence and are influenced by family life: people who grew up in families where money was a central feature of conversation are more likely to be "money-troubled" (Rubenstein, 1981). As cause or symptom, family quarrels often center on the handling of money (Neisser, 1960). Thus, in assessing market rationality we must allow for the fact that in using their money, people are fighting old quarrels (which they never win) or reflecting childish illusions of omnipotence that Bergler reports linger in adult life. This is a rather different and less satisfying way of "maximizing satisfaction" than that described by market rationality.

Conclusion

A more realistic approach to market behavior includes the treatment of money as a symbol as well as a sign pointing to price or exchange value. Money symbols stand for, suggest, imply such things as personal inadequacy, the fruits of effort or luck, shameful failure, moral evil, social unacceptability, suspicious behavior, comfortable security, and much more. In the many ways we have suggested, money symbols distort economic rationality, the formation of consistent, flexible, comparative, ego-syntonic, feasible preferences; they inhibit rational ends-means calculations while they reveal and often exaggerate the intrinsic value of money. Symbolization of money increases transaction costs, distorts "prices," and impairs judgments for many people; for others it makes the transaction itself the primary object of attention. As a consequence money symbols undermine utility maximization in the market.

And yet, if the political literature is any guide, the rational pursuit of monetary self-interest is more or less inert (see Kinder and Kiewiet, 1979; and Sears et al., 1980). Without symbolizing money, few (beyond the subsistence level) would exert themselves to earn much more of it, few would value it once they had it, seldom would men rouse themselves for great enterprises, and we would "silently unbend the springs of action" that make the system go.

Notes

1. "At a minimum, rationality comprises two ideas: consistency and the choice of appropriate means to one's ends" (Barry and Hardin, 1982, p. 371). See also Robbins (1935), p. 78.

2. With certain exceptions, economists are usually satisfied to take preferences as given. (See Becker and Stigler, 1977.) One can imagine an economist responding to the suggestion that economic formulae include the elements of symbolic thinking by observing that these may be absorbed by simple notations. The symbolist might respond with gratification—but only if the notations referred to empirical findings and not merely hypothetical difficulties, and if the theories of economic behavior that the notation represented were accordingly modified. Economists might argue further that commodity bundles are as "multivalent" as are money symbols and do not pose difficulties for traditional economic analysis, but, the symbolist would point out, that is because the multivalence of the bundles are in fact reduced to the single dimension of money value. I am indebted to James Bennett for suggesting elements of this imaginary discourse.

3. From the point of view of the social system, altruism is not irrational, but from the point of view of the economy, the matter is less certain, an uncertainty we do not need to enter upon here. Most economists assume self interest, but it has been said that "to run an organization entirely on incentives of personal gain is pretty much a hopeless task" (Sen, 1977, p. 335). Further, some arguments claim that self-interested rationality leads to societal irrationality. (Cf. Barry and Hardin, 1982.) Moreover, there are sufficient treatments of how the market may accommodate altruism to accept the view that the kind of individual rationality required of the market is not necessarily dependent on self-interest. See Margolis (1982); Collard (1978); and Frank (1988).

4. Neale goes on further to desymbolize money meanings: "What matters is that there is a record which can be used to enforce rights and duties of members of the society. [Demand deposits] are analogous to the records of land deeds in a county court house."

5. See, for example, Pigou, (1949).

6. The money index was composed of the following questions: "How do you feel about. . . "; "How secure you are financially?"; "The income you (and your family) have?" "How comfortable and well-off you are?" The consumer index was composed of answers to the following questions: "How do you feel about . . . "; "The way you can get around to work, schools, shopping, etc."; "The doctors, clinics, and hospitals you would use in this area?"; "The goods and services you can get when you buy in this area—things like food, appliances, clothes?" Admittedly, they diverge from ideal questions for the point at hand.

7. Regarding these five sources, we must enter certain caveats on the general applicability of the data: surveys and clinics are not markets—people behave differently in these differing situations; attitudes often do not predict behavior (see Ajzen and Fishbein, 1980); the representativeness of the samples used is uncertain. Our claim is only that some of the people, some of the time, are guided by such symbolism as is reported in these works.

8. This item has been added to an "Anomia" scale originally devised by Leo Srole. See Robinson and Shaver (1969, p. 175).

9. The social psychologist, Albert Bandura (1977, pp. 97–98), makes the same point: reinforcements, such as money, influence behavior more because they promise sympathetic attention than because they promise other forms of benefits.

10. "The symbol itself is enjoyed. . . . Here aesthetic factors in a wide sense become relevant" (Lasswell and Kaplan, 1950, p. 113).

11. One should not, however, exaggerate the power of price information to determine consumer decisions. See Stigler (1961). Examining research evidence on consumer behavior, Lea et al., comment: "It seems that the economy of information is not a major influence on real consumer behavior" (Lea, Tarpy, and Webley, 1987, p. 530).

12. Defining situations is like employing the "frameworks" discussed by Tversky and Kahneman (1974).

References

Ajzen, Icek, and Martin Fishbein. 1980. *Understanding Attitudes and Predicting Social Behavior.* Englewood Cliffs, NJ: Prentice-Hall.

Andrews, Frank M., and Stephen B. Withey. 1976. *Social Indicators of Well-Being: Americans' Perceptions of Life Quality.* New York: Plenum.

Baier, Kurt. 1969. "What Is Value? An Analysis of the Concept." In Kurt Baier and Nicholas Rescher, eds., *Values and the Future.* New York: Free Press.

Bandura, Albert. 1977. *Social Learning Theory.* Englewood Cliffs, NJ: Prentice-Hall.

Barry, Brian, and Russel Hardin, eds. 1982. "Epilogue." In *Rational Man and Irrational Society?* Beverly Hills, CA: Sage.

Becker, Gary, and George Stigler. 1977. "De Gustibus Non Est Disputandum." *American Economic Review* 67:76–90.

Bennet, Lance. 1975. *The Political Mind and the Political Environment.* Lexington, MA: Heath/Lexington.

Bergler, Edmund. 1951. *Money and Emotional Conflicts.* Garden City, NY: Doubleday.

Boulding, Kenneth E. 1973. *The Economy of Love and Fear.* Belmont, CA: Wadsworth.

Campbell, Angus. 1981. *The Sense of Well-Being in America.* New York: McGraw-Hill.

Campbell, Angus, Philip E. Converse, and Willard L. Rodgers. 1976. *The Quality of American Life.* New York: Russell Sage.

Collard, David. 1978. *Altruism and Economy: A Study of Non-Selfish Economics.* New York: Oxford Press.

Crowne, Douglas P., and David Marlowe. 1964. *The Approval Motive.* New York: Wiley.

Eliade, Mircea. 1969. *Images and Symbols: Studies in Religious Symbolism,* trans. by P. Mariet. New York: Sheed & Ward. (Originally published in 1952).

Elster, Jon. 1983. *Sour Grapes: Studies in the Subversion of Rationality.* Cambridge: Cambridge University Press.

Frank, Robert H. 1988. "If Homo Economicus Could Choose His Utility Function, Would He Want One with a Conscience?" In *Passions within Reason: The Strategic Role of the Emotions.* New York: Norton. (Originally published in *American Economic Review.*)

Fried, Charles. 1970. *The Anatomy of Values: Problems of Personal and Social Choice.* Cambridge, MA: Harvard University Press.

Furnham, Adrian. 1984. "Many Sides of the Coin: The Psychology of Money Usage." *Personality and Individual Differences* 5:95–103.

Gauthier, David. 1975. "Reason and Maximization." *Canadian Journal of Philosophy* 4:418–33. Reprinted in Brian Barry and Russell Hardin, ed., *Rational Man and Irrational Society?* Beverly Hills, CA: Sage, 1982.

Gorer, Geoffrey. 1948. *The American People.* New York: Norton.

Hall, Calvin S., and Robert L. van de Castle. 1966. *The Content Analysis of Dreams.* New York: Appleton-Century-Crofts.

Hempel, Carl G. 1952. "Fundamentals of Concept Formation in Empirical Science." In *International Encyclopedia of Unified Science,* vol. I-I, *Foundations of the Unity of Science.* Chicago: University of Chicago Press.

Juster, F. Thomas. 1985. "Preferences for Work and Leisure." In F. Thomas Juster and Frank P. Stafford, eds., *Time, Goods, and Well-Being.* Ann Arbor, MI: Institute for Social Research.

Kinder, Donald R., and D. Roderick Kiewiet. 1979. "Economic Discontents and Political Behavior: The Role of Personal Grievances and Collective Economic Judgments in

Congressional Voting." *American Journal of Political Science* 23:495–527.

Koopmans, Tjalling C. 1957. *Three Essays on the State of Economic Science.* New York: McGraw-Hill.

Lakoff, George, and Mark Johnson. 1980. *Metaphors We Live By.* Chicago: University of Chicago Press.

Langer, Suzanne K. 1948. *Philosophy in a New Key.* New York: Mentor. (Originally published in 1942.)

Lasswell, Harold D., and Abraham Kaplan. 1950. *Power and Society: A Framework for Political Inquiry.* New Haven, CT: Yale University Press.

Lea, Stephen E.G., Roger M. Tarpy, and Paul Webley. 1987. *The Individual in the Economy.* Cambridge: Cambridge University Press.

Luft, Joseph. 1957. "Monetary Value and the Perception of Persons." *Journal of Social Psychology* 46:245–51.

Mannheim, Karl. 1948. *Man and Society in an Age of Reconstruction,* trans. by E. Shils. New York: Harcourt Brace.

Margolis, Howard. 1982. *Selfishness, Altruism, and Rationality.* Cambridge: Cambridge University Press.

Marx, Karl. 1964. "The Power of Money in Bourgeois Society." In *Economic and Philosophical Manuscripts of 1844,* trans. by M. Milligan, ed. by D. Struik. New York: International Publishers.

McGuire, William. 1969. "The Nature of Attitudes and Attitude Change." *Handbook of Social Psychology,* vol. 3, 2nd ed. Reading, MA: Addison-Wesley.

Neale, Walter C. 1976. *Monies in Societies.* San Francisco: Chandler & Sharp.

Neisser, Edith. 1960. "Emotional and Social Values Attached to Money." *Marriage and Family Living* 22:132–38.

Pigou, Arthur C. 1949. *The Veil of Money.* London: Macmillan.

Polanyi, Karl. 1971. "The Semantics of Money." In *Primitive, Archaic, and Modern Economies.* Boston: Beacon Press.

Robbins, Lionel. 1935. *An Essay on the Nature and Significance of Economic Science.* London: Macmillan.

Robinson, John P., and Philip R. Shaver. 1969. *Measures of Social Psychological Attitudes.* Ann Arbor, MI: Institute for Social Research. Appendix B.

Rubenstein, Carin. 1981. "Money, Self-Esteem, Relationship, Secrecy, Envy, Satisfaction." *Psychology Today* 15(May):29–44.

Sapir, Edward. 1934. "Symbolism." In *Encyclopedia of the Social Sciences,* vol. 14. New York: Macmillan.

Schlozman, Kay L., and Sidney Verba. 1979. *Injury to Insult: Unemployment, Class, and Political Response.* Cambridge, MA: Harvard University Press.

Sears, David O., Richard R. Lau, Tom R. Tyler, and Harris M. Allen, Jr. 1980. "Self-Interest vs. Symbolic Politics in Policy Attitudes and Presidential Voting." *American Political Science Review* 74:670–84.

Sen, Amartya K. 1977. "Rational Fools: A Critique of the Behavioral Foundations of Economic Theory." *Philosophy and Public Affairs* 6:315–344.

Simmel, Georg. 1950. "The Metropolis and Mental Life." In *The Sociology of Georg Simmel,* ed. and trans. by Kurt H. Wolff. Glencoe, Il: Free Press.

———. 1978. *The Philosophy of Money,* trans. and ed. by T. Bottomore and D. Frisby. London: Routledge & Kegan Paul. (Originally published in 1907.)

Slovic, Paul, Baruch Fischhoff, and Sarah Lichtenstein. 1982. "Facts versus Fears: Understanding Perceived Risk." In Daniel Kehneman, Paul Slovic, and Amos Tversy, eds., *Judgment under Uncertainty: Heuristics and Biases.* New York: Cambridge University Press.

Spielberger, Charles D., ed. 1972. *Anxiety: Current Trends in Theory and Research,* vol. 1. New York: Academic Press.

Stigler, George J. 1961. "The Economics of Information." *Journal of Political Economy* 69:213–225.

Tresemer, David W. 1977. *Fear of Success.* New York: Plenum.

Tversky, Amos, and Daniel Kahneman. 1974. "Judgment under Uncertainty: Heuristics and Biases." *Science* 185:1124–31.

Wernimont, Paul F., and Susan Fitzpatrick. 1972. "The Meaning of Money." *Journal of Applied Psychology* 50:218–26.

Yamauchi, Kent T., and Donald I. Templer. 1982. "The Development of a Money Attitude Scale." *Journal of Personality Assessment* 46:522–28.

Zajonc, Robert B. 1980. "Feeling and Thinking: Preferences Need No Inferences." *American Psychologist* 35:151–175.

Markets, Competition, and Efficiency

6

PETER B. DOERINGER

The Socio-Economics
of Labor Productivity

Institutional economists have frequently observed systematic differences among firms in their wage strategies (Dunlop, 1957; Doeringer and Piore, 1985; Hildebrand, 1963). Some firms deliberately adopt policies of paying high wages, others pay the "going or average" rate, and still others offer below-average compensation (Reynolds, 1951). More recent quantitative studies of inter-establishment wage structures confirm this finding and there is evidence that these pay differences persist over long periods of time (Groshen, 1988a, 1988b).

One interpretation of this finding is that apparent differences in pay by firm or by industry simply relfect differences in worker productivity or in the nonpecuniary aspects of jobs; a second is that pay is not uniquely a function of labor force quality so that earnings can also depend on the firm or industry in which a worker is employed (Katz, 1986). The latter interpretation has led to a body of "efficiency wage" theory postulating a causal relationship between above-market pay premiums and higher profits (Groshen, 1988a, 1988b).

Most of the economics literature explaining how pay is related to labor efficiency sees high wages as a means of overcoming market failures that result in principal-agent problems and other sources of allocative inefficiency. There are several different versions of efficiency wage theories—selection and matching, turnover, and monitoring/motivation—each positing a different set of stylized facts about the workplace (Katz, 1986; Weiss, 1990).

Selection and matching theories postulate the existence of certain hard-to-measure abilities that are particularly productive under some technologies and work settings. Where such abilities are required, employers seek efficient ways of recruiting such workers. Under the assumption that the reservation wages of workers with these "superproductive" qualities are higher than those of other workers, high wage employment offers can lower recruitment costs by expanding the pool of qualified applicants and improving the efficiency of worker-job matching (Weiss, 1980, 1990; Katz, 1986; Weitzman, 1989).

Turnover theories assume that there are technologies or work settings that require enterprise-specific recruitment and training investments. Because these investment costs are partly borne by the firm, employers try to minimize these costs by controlling labor turnover. High wages are simply a vehicle for discouraging quits so that the recruitment and training investments can be amortized over longer periods of time, and so that increased productivity streams from enterprise-specific training are not prematurely terminated (Salop, 1979; Stiglitz, 1974).

Monitoring and motivation theories postulate a relationship between pay and worker performance that is also rooted in the technology of production. These theories argue that where individual effort or responsibility are difficult and costly to monitor, there is a principal-agent conflict between managers and employers. The agency model views the payment of high wages, coupled with the threat of discharge, as a means of motivating effort and of discouraging workers from shirking (Katz, 1986; Leonard, 1987). A variant on the agency model treats high pay as a "gift" from employers to workers that creates a sense of obligation in employees that motivates them to set higher effort norms (Akerlof, 1982, 1984).

While efficiency wage theories propose quite specific mechanisms linking profits to high wages, it is sometimes argued that these mechanisms are a metaphor for a larger class of organizational and behavioral incentives for improved labor productivity (Katz, 1986). However, these alternative incentives are usually illustrated by other economic regimes, such as employee bonding (Lazear, 1981) or "tournament" rewards (Lazear and Rosen, 1981). Social or psychological features of work force behavior—loyalty to the firm, morale, and commitment to the goals of the firm—are sometimes alluded to (Katz, 1986), but are usually incorporated in formal models in ways that are similar to effort or skill as sources of productivity (Akerlof, 1982, 1984; Akerlof and Yellen, 1990).

All the efficiency wage theories conform to the basic conventions of microeconomics. They are conceived within a choice-theoretic framework that leads to the usual equilibrium conditions for profit and utility maximization; they emphasize how firms can achieve static efficiency through economic incentives that compensate for various kinds of market failure; and the standard assumptions are made about the exogeneity of technology and worker preferences.

In the basic monitoring/motivation model of efficiency wages, for example, firms have production functions in which effort enters with a positive derivative and workers have utility functions in which wages have a positive derivative and effort a negative one. The employer maximizes profits subject to worker maximization of utility. A wage and employment equilibrium for the firm is reached when the elasticity of effort with respect to wages is unity and the wage is equal to the marginal product of labor. The only unusual feature of this model is that labor markets may not clear in the aggregate because there may be involuntarily unemployed workers who would be willing to work at "efficiency" wage levels (Katz, 1986; Bulow and Summers, 1986).

Collectively, efficiency wage theories have considerable appeal in that they provide a microeconomic basis for explaining a number of seeming paradoxes in the labor market. These include persistent interindustry wage effects, wage rigidity, long-term employment contracts, the failure of aggregate labor markets to clear, and the presence of dual labor markets (Bulow and Summers, 1986).

In contrast, the literature on social and organizational behavior at the workplace suggests that labor efficiency, at least in the kinds of large enterprises that are thought to pay efficiency wages, is more often addressed through various organizational regimes than through economic incentives. These regimes include human relations approaches, industrial relations and collective bargaining, and "superefficient" human resources development (Doeringer, 1989). In smaller firms, paternalism and kinship play a similar role.

There have been a number of recent attempts to unite these economic and managerial literatures, often under the general rubric of the "new personnel management" (Journal of Labor Economics, 1987; Kleiner et al., 1987; Winship and Rosen, 1988). However, they largely represent a recasting of personnel management issues into a neoclassical economic framework. Rarely is an integrated theory that draws upon social, economic, and organizational concepts attempted.

These various neoclassical approaches can lead to misleading conclusions about why some firms pay high wages and about how labor efficiency is managed in firms that seek to promote superefficient labor practices. This point will be developed by showing how principal-agent conflicts at the workplace are resolved by harmonizing the conflicting objectives of labor and management, rather than by altering economic incentives.

Evaluating the Economic Theories

Testing of efficiency wage theories has largely involved analyzing interindustry and interfirm wage differentials in a human capital framework (Krueger and Summers, 1988). Efficiency wage differentials tend to be found in industries and firms that are relatively capital intensive, have above-average levels of business concentration, employ workers with above-average education and experience, and have low rates of voluntary turnover. Efficiency wage firms tend to be large and unionized, or subject to the threat of unionization (Dickens and Katz, 1986; Ehrenberg and Milkovich, 1987; Leonard, 1987). Controls for measurable indicators of labor quality, and for characteristics of jobs, reduce, but do not eliminate, these efficiency wage differentials (Dickens and Katz, 1986; Dickens, Katz, and Lang, 1986; Groshen, 1988b; Krueger and Summers, 1988).

While these econometric findings are consistent with efficiency wage theory, data limitations have prevented conclusive tests that distinguish among the different theoretical formulations (Raff and Summers, 1987). Recent surveys of the literature on efficiency wages stress the complementarity among various versions of the theory, and the need for further elaboration of theory, but do not definitively narrow the scope of competing theories (Carmichael, 1990; Lang and Kahn, 1990).

The kinds of firms that are thought to pay efficiency wages, however, have also been the focus of managerial studies of labor efficiency. In contrast to the economic studies, most of the managerial literature is directed at improving dynamic efficiency by avoiding principal-agent problems and other types of conflict between managers and those of workers.

This correspondence between efficiency wage firms and those firms that are the subject of managerial studies of labor efficiency permits an alternative to econometric analysis as a way of both testing existing efficiency wage theories and developing additional theories based upon actual management practices. In a recently completed study (Doeringer, 1989), the social and organizational dimensions of efficiency wages were examined using a diverse set of research materials on workplace wage determination and effort motivation—theories of organizational development, case studies, and other empirical materials about organizational performance, textbook descriptions of "best" management practice, historical studies of management, and interviews and in-depth discussions with business executives and union officials about recent developments in corporate human resources strategies in large enterprises.

While no one piece of evidence was compelling, the combination of different sources of information cast considerable doubt on the accuracy of efficiency wage theories as literal descriptions of how labor productivity is controlled in large enterprises. With the possible exception of the efficiency wage experiment by Henry Ford in 1914 (Raff and Summers, 1987), efficiency wages do not seem to be the principal mechanism behind either effort-management or compensation strategies in the large enterprise sector.

Selection and Matching

While most high-wage firms do generate large pools of applicants, and do take advantage of this queue of applicants to select the best matches of jobs and workers, there is little evidence either in the management literature or from interviews with employers in the large-enterprise sector that high wages are a central feature of recruiting strategies. Instead, money is just one feature of a recruitment package in which employment security, job satisfaction, and corporate culture seem to be more prominent. Moreover, in the firms that place the greatest weight on the selection of workers with hard-to-measure qualities and on securing good "matches" with new hires, pay is the least important element of the recruitment strategy and recruitment and selection strategies are the least important source of labor efficiency.

Turnover Control

High-wage companies do report significant labor recruitment costs and provide considerable on-the-job training so that it is reasonable to conclude that turnover control is important to such firms (Gaudet, 1960; Merchants and Manufacturers Association, 1959; Stromsdorfer, 1981). Widespread managerial concern with high turnover in large firms and evidence of human resources policies targeted on the control of turnover, however, are much more characteristic of the early twentieth century (Slichter, 1919; Bloomfield, 1923) than of the contemporary labor market.

Even during this earlier period, however, high pay was less central to turnover control in best-practice firms than was a set of paternalistic programs designed to bond *experienced* workers to the firm. These included welfare and pension benefit packages that were tied to longevity of service, employee representation plans to give workers some measure of participation at the workplace, and the provision of a range of community and social services for workers and their families. The "best practice" management literature of the time attributes the subsequent reductions in turnover to these welfare practices, rather than to pay (Slichter, 1919; Jacoby, 1985).

More recent studies show that satisfaction with pay is important to keeping turnover low (Lawler, 1981). While this finding might be interpreted as supportive of turnover theories of high pay, the bulk of the empirical evidence points to the noneconomic aspects of the work relationship. Good human relations, participative decision making, job enrichment, work rotation, and *"fair"* pay are seen as more important than high pay in building job satisfaction and controlling turnover (Mowday, Porter, and Steers, 1982).

Monitoring and Motivation

While neither the matching nor the turnover versions of efficiency wage theory seem to describe the work force management strategies of high-wage firms, there is one group of such firms whose strategies superficially resemble monitoring and motivation theories of efficiency wages. These firms are "superefficient" in that they secure high levels of labor efficiency by creating a work force that is self-supervised and self-disciplined—the same work force characteristics that are postulated by monitoring and motivation theories of efficiency wages. Contrary to efficiency wage theory, however, these superefficient firms do not attribute their interest in fostering self-supervision and self-discipline to high monitoring costs, nor do they rely on pay incentives and the threat of discharge to motivate labor. Effort management in such firms is based on *altering the utility functions of workers, rather than altering the economic choices that they face.*

Social Efficiency or Wage Efficiency?

As the following brief review of workplace practices will show, labor efficiency in these "superefficient" firms is rooted far more in social, organizational, and psychological considerations than in technology or compensation incentives. The management of labor efficiency is directed at dynamic, rather than static, efficiency and it emphasizes the importance of social and organizational change as sources of labor productivity (Leibenstein, 1976; Nelson, 1981; Nelson and Winter, 1982; Weber, 1964; Crozier, 1964). Such efficiency management also takes into account the need to address issues of economic power and differing objectives for income distribution (Dalton, 1959; Edwards, 1979; Burawoy, 1979, 1985; Jacoby, 1985). For these reasons, effort management in superefficient firms is most in keeping with sociological theories of efficiency wages (Akerlof, 1982, 1984; Akerlof and Yellen, 1990), but even these sociological theories do not fully capture the motivational principles involved.

Technology

Work is not necessarily costly to monitor or supervise in superefficient firms and yet all employees, regardless of the technology and job duties, are encouraged to be self-motivated and self-supervised. This calls into question the technological necessity for efficiency wages and, therefore, diminishes the importance of the information imperfections and monitoring difficulties as problems that efficiency wages are supposed to address.

High Pay

High wages and the threat of discharge in superefficient firms do not appear to carry the motivational burden that they are assigned in efficiency wage theory. The prevailing assessment of pay practices in American industry is that management has largely abandoned the use of pay as a motivator in favor of noneconomic sources of motivation. This is particularly true in superefficient firms where pay is only a part of a larger package within which social and psychological motivators are far more important (Schein, 1965; Adams, 1965; Lawler, 1971).

Managers in superefficient firms explain the payment of high wages in terms of their concern with horizontal and vertical *pay equity* (Foulkes, 1980, Dunlop, 1957; Slichter, Livernash, and Healy, 1960; McGregor, 1960; Freeman and Medoff, 1984). High wages are thought to be the least costly way of demonstrating that pay policy is equitable. Since equity matters across all job levels, this explanation is consistent with the finding that high-wage firms and industries tend to pay high wages across all occupations, not just those for which various theories of efficiency wages are thought to apply.

This explanation somewhat resembles that offered by some efficiency wage theories that emphasize the reciprocal exchange of effort from workers for the voluntary sharing of economic rents by employers (Akerlof, 1982, 1984; Akerlof and Yellen, 1990). Managers in large enterprises, however, do not view high pay as a gift, but as a tangible signal of a commitment to fair treatment of employees. The importance placed on fairness is related less to the possibility that pay inequities will result in lower effort among disgruntled employees than to a larger concern with creating a set of corporate values that will be perceived as legitimate and moral by the work force (Habermas, 1970, 1975; Abercrombie, Hill and Turner, 1980).

Threat of Discharge

Although wages are typically near the top of the market in superefficient firms, the threat of discharge is deliberately eliminated as a motivational strategy. These firms guarantee employment for their workers. They also reject discipline and discharge as an instrument of labor control out of a concern that discharges will be perceived as arbitrary and will undermine labor efficiency. Social and psychological motivators are emphasized in place of pay incentives and threats of discharge, and rehabilitation is used in place of discipline as a means of correcting shortcomings in workplace behavior.

These employment guarantees are also consistent with a longstanding theme in the human relations and compensation literature that the main reason why work groups limit effort is the belief that greater effort will lead to a reduction in employment. Managers in superefficient firms act as if they take this concern seriously and they identify employment guarantees as prerequisite for greater worker effort.

Supervision and Monitoring

Just as high wages and the threat of discharge do not play the roles assigned to them by efficiency wage theory, neither do supervision and monitoring. The agency version of efficiency wage theory assumes that work is a source of disutility and economic payments are seen as the principal motivator of labor supply. Under these assumptions, unmonitored workers will "shirk" and supervision will ordinarily be needed to sustain effort. Where monitoring is costly, high wages and the threat of discharge are economic substitutes for supervisory costs.

Management studies have shown, however, that supervision of effort can actually have adverse effects on labor efficiency. While effort monitoring can produce improvement in productivity, as efficiency wage theory would suggest, it has been shown to have this effect only in the short term. Over longer periods, close supervision appears to reduce productivity in the longer term as workers respond negatively to being supervised (Likert, 1958). The negative consequences of monitoring on productivity are even common in routine work of the kind that efficiency wage theory predicts would be most easily monitored (Strauss, 1977).

Studies of how supervisory styles affect productivity further confirm this finding. They show that productivity is more strongly correlated with management that is supportive and that seeks to build effective work teams through social and psychological processes, than with close supervision and monitoring of workers (Likert, 1958; Gouldner, 1954). Good interpersonal relations are also thought to enrich jobs and enhance the legitimacy of management's objectives, even in situations where work is repetitious, routine, and easy to monitor (Strauss, 1977).

More generally, the assumption that employees prefer shirking to working seems largely to be discredited in the modern management strategies of large enterprises, particularly among superefficient firms. Instead, these firms follow work force management practices that are intended to enhance the intrinsic value of work and to ensure that shirking is not an inevitable result of unmonitored work (McGregor, 1960; Kochan, Katz, and McKersie, 1986).

Studies of what supervisors actually do (Walker, Guest, and Turner, 1956; Montgomery, 1987) and textbook recommendations of what supervisors should do (Davis and Newstrom, 1985; Baron, 1986), routinely show that coercive monitoring of the work force, backed by discipline and the threat of discharge, is no longer characteristic of large firms. In the modern factory, few supervisory resources are spent in monitoring worker effort. Instead, supervisors are concerned with production scheduling, quality control, inventories, and equipment maintenance, and with the social and psychological control of worker performance. "Time budget" studies also show that the supervisor's job typically has a large social component (Davis, 1987; Strauss, 1977)—talking with workers, training and assisting them in their job duties, and, in superefficient firms, helping to negotiate psychological "effort contracts" with workers.

Worker Motivation

The most significant inconsistency between efficiency wage theory and management practices lies in the assumptions about worker motivation. Agency versions of efficiency wages postulate differences between the effort objectives of managers/principals and workers/agents. Pay differentials and the threat of discharge are the instruments of effort control. Because these instruments have costs as well as benefits, profit-maximizing efficiency wage firms equate the marginal cost of higher wages with the marginal benefits of increased productivity.

Superefficient firms, however, seek to avoid the effort control problem by eliminating the conflict between the effort objectives of managers/principals and those of workers/agents. Using psychological "learning theory" and techniques of operant conditioning (Skinner, 1953; Vroom, 1964), these firms create an identity between the objectives of managers and workers. Workers are conditioned to identify with the goals of their managers and to commit themselves to psychological effort contracts that call for ever-increasing levels of output.

Social Learning versus Human Capital in the Superefficient Firm

The theoretical foundations of effort management in the superefficient firm come from sociology and psychology, rather than from economics. Superefficient firms adopt psychological techniques for motivating productivity drawn from behavioral theories of learning (Skinner, 1953; Vroom, 1964; Luthens and Kreitner, 1984). These behavioral theories rest on the concept of "operant conditioning" in which desired behavior is elicited through a process of stimulus and reinforcement in an environment where employment is guaranteed (Foulkes, 1980; Ouchi and Price, 1983; Lee, 1987).

Implementing operant conditioning at the workplace (or behavior modification, as it is often referred to in the management literature) involves identifying, and building upon, sequences of events that lead to the desired worker behaviors. It begins by identifying the behavioral events to be reinforced, such as "high effort" or cooperative "problem solving." The antecedents and the consequences of the behavior must then be determined and a strategy for reinforcing the behavior must be developed (Luthens and Lyman, 1976, pp. 333–52).

Second, operant conditioning relies heavily upon a kind of "social learning" that is distinct from traditional human capital investment (Bandura, 1977; Luthens and Kreitner, 1984). This social learning draws systematically upon the kinds of social reinforcements that are costless and that can be ever-present in the workplace environment. Such social learning is embedded in the workplace culture and is constantly reinforced through the daily routines of workers.

For example, a major responsibility of supervision is to reinforce continually the acculturation of employees to the values of the superefficient firm, to provide frequent feedback to employees about their performance, and to indicate how it might be improved. A combination of social, psychological, and economic incentives, rather than negative penalties such as discipline and discharge, is favored for motivating behavior in order to avoid the adverse reactions sometimes associated with negative reinforcement (Hammner and Hammner, 1983).

Social learning is also maintained through day-to-day interactions among workers who serve as role models for one another and who provide peer reinforcement of social "lessons." Because workers train and reinforce one another, social learning involves "public good" externalities.

The outcome of this conditioning process is a psychological "effort contract" reached between the superefficient firms and individual workers (Lee, 1987). These contracts embody understandings about the nature of individual effort and reward. They also involve the internalization by workers of the values of the firm and the responsibility for their own supervision.

Under these psychological effort contracts, the setting of effort norms occurs primarily through participatory goal setting by individual employees, rather than upon norms set by management, social groups, or collective bargaining. These goals are set as thresholds—the contracts call for individuals to achieve and then strive to exceed the goals. Supervision and monitoring of effort is provided by the worker, rather than by management; shortfalls in performance are self-disciplined rather than disciplined by supervisors; and the rewards for performance come from self-reinforcement, as well as from management and work groups.

Psychological effort contracting is facilitated by the corporate cultures of superefficient firms. Corporate culture in such firms is a means of continually directing workers towards higher levels of effort and it continually reinforces their behavior. Because the corporate culture is so embedded in the fabric of social relations at the workplace, it is particularly important as a control device in just those situations where efficiency wages have been argued to be most useful—where procedures are not standardized, where there is a need for discretion, and where measurement and monitoring of effort are most difficult (Pascale, 1986).

The principal criterion for an effective corporate culture is that it be perceived by employees to be just and legitimate. Legitimacy is particularly important in firms where high labor efficiency generates economic quasi-rents that can be shared with workers at the discretion of the employer. Where such discretion exists, there is the potential for internal conflict over distributional decisions regarding the allocation of income, employment, and economic security. Minimizing such conflict requires the development of legitimacy to validate such distributional decisions (Habermas, 1970, 1975; Abercrombie, Hill, and Turner, 1980). Without legitimacy, psychological effort contracts may be undermined (Habermas, 1975) and may lead to reduced labor efficiency and free rider problems.

It might be argued that psychological effort contracting and social conditioning could readily be encompassed within one or more theories of efficiency wages. For example, effort contracts and social conditioning might be analogous to investing in enterprise-specific human capital because they raise productivity only in the firm that provides it and because they also control turnover. Alternatively, the costs of effort contracting and social conditioning could be equated with wage payments that result in lower unit labor costs. Under both these interpretations, firms would balance the costs and benefits of effort management as they do in efficiency wage theories.

While there are costs to establishing the social and psychological environment necessary for such operant conditioning, these are largely one-time fixed costs. Once established, the social systems of superefficient firms are largely self-perpetuating through the corporate culture so that the social and psychological instruments of motivation are often costless at the margin.

Even where there are marginal costs to the motivational process, the marginal benefits may not be a limiting factor. The type of self-discipline and self-motivation that is developed in the work force leads to effort levels that are potentially open ended and there is evidence from learning theory that there may even be decreasing costs to social conditioning (Hilgard and Marquis, 1961). These considerations suggest that there can be increasing returns to social and psychological motivation. For these reasons, marginal cost and benefit calculations relating to effort and pay to profits are unlikely to be the appropriate metaphor for analyzing the motivational processes that are used in full employment firms.

How Widespread Is Superefficiency?

The effort-management practices of superefficient firms demonstrate that the stylized facts of efficiency wage theory—persistent high wages across all occupations within firms that have high-effort and self-disciplined labor—are better explained by social and psychological factors than by traditional economic incentives. While these factors can account for effort management in large enterprises, they are also important to labor efficiency in smaller enterprises that exhibit quite different characteristics from those of large superefficient firms. Paternalistic firms and kinship enterprises are examples of other ways in which social and psychological practices can harmonize principal and agent conflicts in the employment relationship.

Paternalistic Firms

The paternalistic model of labor efficiency establishes a form of psychological contract between employers and workers based upon reciprocal responsibilities and loyalties. Reciprocity involves incentives of benevolence, such as welfare programs and discretionary economic incentives, that are exchanged for worker loyalty and attachment to the firm (Brandes, 1970; Jacoby, 1985; Brody, 1980; Newby, 1977, 1979).

In contrast to superefficient firms, paternalistic firms often offer relatively low levels of pay, but pay is augmented by the granting of discretionary benefits to workers based upon individual need, rather than individual performance (Doeringer, 1984). There are also no employment guarantees, no emphasis on uniform and fair compensation practices, and no elaborate operant conditioning process. Nevertheless, paternalistic firms and benevolent incentives result in many of the same labor efficiency effects achieved by the practices of superefficient firms. They increase work satisfaction, encourage cooperative relationships between workers and their companies, and raise productivity.

Kinship Firms

Kinship firms rely on the obligations and incentives of familial relationships to promote labor efficiency (Doeringer, Moss, and Terkla, 1986). The connection between reward and effort resembles neither the effort contracts, operant conditioning, and legitimacy objectives of the superefficient firm, nor the benevolent incentives and reciprocal loyalties of the paternalistic firm. Instead, kinship firms establish individual performance norms within the kinship teams and individual pay is based on various types of income-sharing arrangements. In many respects, the pay and performance relationship resembles "share economy" models of the firm (Weitzman, 1984), but the shares may not be equally distributed among employees in the kinship unit.

Harmonizing the Objectives of Labor and Management

Effort control and labor efficiency in a wide variety of workplace settings seem to hinge far more on the choice of organizational technologies than on technological imperatives and economic incentives. The history of innovation and diffusion of social technologies at the workplace suggests a progression away from traditional economic conceptions of labor efficiency, such as those embodied in scientific management, towards increasingly sophisticated human resources management procedures of the kind adopted by superefficient firms. Until recently, it would have been tempting to extrapolate this trend to predict the spread of superefficient practices throughout the economy. In the aggregate, this would point towards an economy with rising labor productivity, improved job security, and higher wages.

However, pressures from increased competition and falling profits in recent years have made it difficult for many superefficient firms to maintain career employment guarantees. Some of these firms, such as Eastman Kodak and Hewlett-Packard, have even had to abandon their no-layoff practices (Business Week, 1990). The concern among these firms is that the psychological "effort" contracts upon which their high performance depends will not be sustained if employment guarantees are eliminated. Without such contracts, these firms will be burdened with high wage costs that are not offset by high labor efficiency.

The uncertain economic climate and the need to reduce production costs is leading to a rethinking of superefficient workplace practices. Many superefficient firms are beginning to look at lesser forms of employment security such as "employability" guarantees, severance pay, and outplacement training that might replace employment guarantees in their psychological effort contracts with workers. There is also a growing use of contingent workers and some firms are considering the possibility of switching to employment-at-will practices to secure highly flexible labor at low human resources development costs. If the latter course were to prevail, this would mean the growth of employment relationships based upon economic, rather than social and psychological, incentives and the possibility of a more insecure labor market with slow growth in productivity and real income (Doeringer, et al. forthcoming).

References

Abercrombie, N., S. Hill, and B.S. Turner. 1980. *The Dominant Ideology Thesis.* London: Allen & Unwin.

Adams, J.S. 1965. "Inequity in Social Exchange." In L. Berkowitz, ed., *Advances in Experimental Social Psychology.* New York: Academic Press.

Akerlof, G. 1982. "Labor Contracts as a Partial Gift Exchange." *Quarterly Journal of Economics* 97, 4, (November): 543–70.

———. 1984. "Gift Exchange and Efficiency Wages: Four Views." *American Economic Review* 74 (May): 79–83.

Akerlof, G., and J.L. Yellen. 1990. "The Fair Wage-Effort Hypothesis and Unemployment." *Quarterly Journal of Economics* 105 (2): 255–83.

Bandura, A. 1977. *Social Learning Theory*. Englewood Cliffs, NJ: Prentice Hall.

Baron, R.A. 1986. *Behavior in Organizations*. Boston: Allyn and Bacon.

Bloomfield, D. 1923. *Problems in Personnel Management*. New York: H.W. Wilson Co.

Brandes, S.D. 1970. *American Welfare Capitalism, 1880–1940*. Chicago: University of Chicago Press.

Brody, D. 1980. *Workers in Industrial America*. Oxford: Oxford University Press.

Bulow, J.J., and L.H. Summers. 1986. "A Theory of Dual Labor Markets with Application to Industrial Policy, Discrimination, and Keynesian Unemployment." *Journal of Labor Economics* 4, 3, part 1:376–414.

Burawoy, M. 1979. *Manufacturing Consent*. Chicago: University of Chicago Press.

———. 1985. *The Politics of Production*. London: Verso.

Business Week. 1990. "A Japanese Import That's Not Selling." *Business Week,* February 26, pp. 86–7.

Carmichael, H.H. 1990. "Efficiency Wage Models of Unemployment: One View." *Economic Inquiry* 28 (April): 269–95.

Crozier, M. 1964. *The Bureaucratic Phenomenon*. Chicago: University of Chicago Press.

Dalton, M. 1959. *Men Who Manage*. New York: John Wiley & Sons.

Davis, K., and J.W. Newstrom. 1985. *Human Behavior at Work: Organizational Behavior,* 7th ed. New York: McGraw-Hill.

Davis, P. 1987. "Managerial Compensation in Theory and Practice." Unpublished doctoral dissertation, Boston University.

Dickens, W.T., and L.F. Katz. 1986. "Industry Wage Patterns and Theories of Wage Determination." University of California, Berkeley. Mimeo.

Dickens, W.T., L. Katz, and K. Lang. 1986. "Are Efficiency Wages Efficient." NBER Working Paper no. 1935, June.

Doeringer, P.B. 1984. "Internal Labor Markets and Paternalism in Rural Areas." In P. Osterman, ed., *Internal Labor Markets*. Cambridge, MA: MIT Press.

———. 1989. "Social, Organizational, and Wage Efficiency." Report to the National Science Foundation, November 30.

Doeringer, P.B., and M.J. Piore. 1985. *Internal Labor Markets and Manpower Analysis,* 2nd ed. Armonk, NY: M.E. Sharpe.

Doeringer, P.B., P.I. Moss, and D.G. Terkla. 1986. "Capitalism and Kinship: Do Institutions Matter in the Labor Market?" *Industrial and Labor Relations Review* 40, 1 (October): 48–60.

Doeringer, P.B. et al. 1991. *Turbulence in the American Workplace*. New York: Oxford University Press.

Dunlop, J.T. 1957. *Industrial Relations Systems*. New York: Henry Holt.

Edwards, Richard C. 1979. *Contested Terrain: The Transformation of the Workplace in the Twentieth Century*. New York: Basic Books.

Ehrenberg, R.G., and G.T. Milkovich. 1987. "Compensation and Firm Performance." In M.M. Kleiner, R.N. Block, M. Roomkin, and S.W. Salsburg, eds., *Human Resources and the Performance of the Firm*. Madison, WI: Industrial Relations Research Association.

Foulkes, F.K. 1980. *Personnel Policies in Large Nonunion Companies*. Englewood Cliffs, NJ: Prentice Hall.

Freeman, R.B., and J.L. Medoff. 1984. *What Do Unions Do?* New York: Basic Books.

Gaudet, F.J. 1960. *Labor Turnover: Calculation and Cost*. New York: American Management Association.

Gouldner, A.W. 1954. *Patterns of Industrial Bureaucracy*. Glencoe, IL: Free Press.

Groshen, E.L. 1988a. "Why Do Wages Vary among Employers?" Federal Reserve Bank of Cleveland. Mimeo.

———. 1988b. "Do Wage Differences Last among Employers?" Federal Reserve Bank of Cleveland. Mimeo.

Habermas, J. 1970. *Toward a Rational Society.* Boston: Beacon Press.

———. 1975. *Legitimation Crisis.* Boston: Beacon Press.

Hammner, W.C., and E. Hammner. 1983. "Behavior Modification on the Bottom Line." In J.R. Hackman, E.E. Lawler, III, and L.W. Porter, *Perspectives on Organizational Behavior.* New York: McGraw-Hill.

Hildebrand, G.H. 1963. "External Influences and the Determination of the Internal Wage Structure." In J.L. Meij, ed., *Internal Wage Structure.* Amsterdam: North Holland.

Hilgard, E.R., and D.G. Marquis. 1961. *Conditioning and Learning.* Rev. by G.A. Kimble. New York: Appleton-Century-Crofts.

Jacoby, S.M. 1985. *Employing Bureaucracy: Managers, Unions, and the Transformation of Work In American Industry.* New York: Columbia University Press.

Journal of Labor Economics. 1987. "The New Economics of Personnel." *Journal of Labor Economics* 5, 4, part 2.

Katz, L.L. 1986. "Efficiency Wage Theories: A Partial Evaluation." In S. Fisher, ed., *National Bureau of Economic Research Macroeconomic Annual.* Cambridge, MA: MIT Press.

Kleiner, M.M., R.N. Block, M. Roomkin, and S.W. Salsburg. 1987. *Human Resources and the Performance of the Firm.* Madison, WI: Industrial Relations Research Association.

Kochan, T., H. Katz, and R.B. McKersie. 1986. *The Transformation of American Industrial Relations.* New York: Basic Books.

Krueger, A., and L.H. Summers. 1988. "Efficiency Wages and the Interindustry Wage Structure." *Econometrica* 6 (2): 259–93.

Lang, K., and S. Kahn. 1990. "Efficiency Wage Models of Unemployment: A Second View." *Economic Inquiry* 28 (April): 296–306.

Lawler, E.E., III. 1971. *Pay and Organizational Effectiveness: A Psychological View.* New York: McGraw-Hill.

———. 1981. *Pay and Organization Development.* Reading, MA: Addison-Wesley.

Lazear, E.P. 1981. "Agency, Earnings Profiles, Productivity, and Hours Restrictions." *American Economic Review* 71, 14 (September): 606–20.

Lazear, E.P., and S. Rosen. 1981. "Rank Order Tournaments as Optimum Labor Contracts." *Journal of Political Economy* 89 (October): 841–68.

Lee, C. 1987. "The New Employment Contract." *Training* (December 4): 45–56.

Leibenstein, H. 1976. *Beyond Economic Man.* Cambridge, MA: Harvard University Press.

Leonard, J.S. 1987. "Carrots and Sticks: Pay, Supervision, and Turnover." *Journal of Labor Economics* 5, 4, part 2: S136–52.

Likert, R. 1958. "Measuring Organizational Performance." In B.L. Hinton and H.J. Reitz, *Groups and Organizations.* Belmont, CA: Wadsworth, 1971; originally published in the *Harvard Business Review,* March–April, 1958.

Luthens, F., and D. Lyman. 1976. "Training Supervisors to Use Organizational Behavior Modification." In R.A. Sutermeister, ed., *People and Productivity,* 3rd ed. New York: McGraw-Hill.

Luthens, F., and R. Kreitner. 1984. *Organizational Behavior Modification and Beyond: An Operant and Social Learning Approach.* Glenview, IL: Scott Foresman.

McGregor, D.M. 1960. *The Human Side of Enterprise.* New York: McGraw-Hill.

Merchants and Manufacturers Association. 1959. *Labor Turnover, Costs and Methods of Control.* Los Angeles: Merchants and Manufacturers Association.

Montgomery, D. 1987. *The Fall of the House of Labor*. Cambridge: Cambridge University Press.

Mowday, R.T., L.W. Porter, and R.M. Steers. 1982. *Employee-Organizational Linkages: The Psychology of Commitment, Absenteeism, and Turnover*. New York: Academic Press.

Nelson, R.R. 1981. "Research on Productivity Growth and Differences: Dead-ends and New Departures." *Journal of Economic Literature* 19, 3 (September): 1029–64.

Nelson, R.R., and S.G. Winter. 1982. *An Evolutionary Theory of Economic Change*. Cambridge, MA: Harvard University Press.

Newby, Howard. 1977. "Paternalism and Capitalism." In Richard Scase, ed., *Industrial Society: Class, Cleavage and Control*. New York: St. Martin's Press.

———. 1979. *The Deferential Workers*. Madison: The University of Wisconsin Press.

Ouchi, W.G., and R.L. Price. 1983. "Hierarchies, Clans, and Theory Z: A New Perspective on Organizational Development." In J.R. Hackman, E.E. Lawler, III, and L.W. Porter, eds., *Perspectives On Organizational Behavior*. New York: McGraw-Hill.

Pascale, R. 1986. "Fitting New Employees into the Company Culture." In W.B. Werther, Jr., W.A. Ruch, and L. McClure, eds., *Productivity through People*. St. Paul, MN: West Publishing Co. (Originally published in *Fortune*, May 28, 1984.)

Raff, D.M., and L.H. Summers. 1987. "Did Henry Ford Pay Efficiency Wages?" *Journal of Labor Economics* 5, 4, part 2 (October): 557–86.

Reynolds, L. 1951. *Labor Markets in Theory and Practice*. New York: Harper and Brothers.

Salop, S. 1979. "A Model of the Natural Rate of Unemployment." *American Economic Review* 69 (March): 117–25.

Schein, E.H. 1965. *Organizational Psychology*. Englewood Cliffs, NJ: Prentice Hall.

Skinner, B.F. 1953. *Science and Human Behavior*. New York: Macmillan.

Slichter, S.H. 1919. *The Turnover of Factory Labor*. New York: D. Appleton and Company.

Slichter, S.H., E.R. Livernash, and J.J. Healy. 1960. *The Impact of Collective Bargaining on Management*. Washington, DC: Brookings.

Stiglitz, J.E. 1974. "Wage Determination and Unemployment in L.D.C.'s: The Labor Turnover Model." *Quarterly Journal of Economics* 88 (May): 194–227.

Strauss, G. 1977. "Managerial Practices." In J.R. Hackman and J.L. Suttle, eds., *Improving Life at Work*. Santa Monica, CA: Goodyear Publishing.

Stromsdorfer, E. 1981. "Training in Industry." In P.B. Doeringer, ed., *Workplace Perspectives on Education and Training*. Hingham, MA: Martinus-Nijhoff Publishing.

Vroom, V.H. 1964. *Work and Motivation*. New York: Wiley.

Walker, C.R., R.H. Guest, and N. Turner. 1956. *The Foreman on the Assembly Line*. Cambridge, MA: Harvard University Press.

Weber, M. 1964. *The Theory of Social and Economic Organization*. New York: Free Press.

Weiss, A. 1980. "Job Queues and Layoffs in Labor Markets with Flexible Wages." *Journal of Political Economy* 88 (June): 526–38.

———. 1990. *Efficiency Wages*. Princeton, NJ: Princeton University Press.

Weitzman, M. 1984. *The Share Economy, Conquering Stagflation*. Cambridge, MA: Harvard University Press.

———. 1989. "A Theory of Wage Dispersion and Job Market Segmentation." *Quarterly Journal of Economics* 104 (February): 121–38.

Winship, C., and S. Rosen. 1988. *Organizations and Institutions*. Supplement to the *American Journal of Sociology* 94.

7

Lester C. Thurow

Competing Games: Profit Maximization versus Strategic Conquest

The profit maximizing firm is derived from the rational utility maximizing individual for whom more consumption and more leisure are the sole elements of individual motivation. Higher productivity at work is desired since it gives individuals higher incomes to buy more consumption goods and the ability to reduce work effort to obtain more leisure without sacrificing consumption. But work is a disutility tolerated solely because it provides the economic resources needed for consumption.

An alternative theory of the firm, however, can be built on the historical, psychological, and sociological observations that individuals wish to be social builders who belong to an expanding empire.[1] Man is a tool-using animal. Work defines what he is. Put bluntly, work allows humans to express their desire to conquer.

Technically, while individuals may be drafted, all armies are essentially voluntary. No one can force anyone to fight and die when he or she does not want to do so, yet historically there has been no shortage of people willing to fight and die. Armies clearly fulfill some fundamental human need.

Few wars would have been started if all decisions were based upon discounted net present values. The up-front costs of war almost always exceed the downstream benefits—even for the winner. On a risk-adjusted monetary basis, wars are a negative-sum activity to be avoided at all costs.

Historically, individuals were forming tribes and building empires long before they were talking about maximizing consumption and leisure. For reasons that are not at all clear, we have built behavioral models where the motivation of those who build empires is very different from those who build companies. They are not. One joins a firm for many of the same reasons that one joins an army.

In the modern world it is only in the economic sphere where one can hope to build empires and exercise authority. The nation-state normally rules out making war on the neighboring clan, the days of colonial empires are over, expanding one's national borders by conquest is now rare, and nuclear weapons make conquering the world a goal not worth pursuing. As a result, business is almost the only area where power is available. Business is where one exercises the territorial imperatives of yesterday.

To have power over others requires an institution where exit is not easy and where there are strong incentives to participate. One cannot really lead, exercise control over others, or organize activities where some real degree of personal sacrifice is both demanded and given unless there are real rewards and punishments. The modern industrial leader is not a general who can shoot deserters, but he is a leader who can hand out real punishments and rewards. Individuals can be demoted or fired (banished from the group), deprived of security, belongingness, and the esteem of others. Individuals can be promoted. Soldiers can be made into officers; majors can be made into generals. Together individuals can build something bigger than they could ever dream of building on their own.

Together they can also share the booty of conquest. In takeovers within a short period of time, the top management at the firm being taken over is almost always replaced by managers from the firm doing the takeover. If jobs were simply given to the best people, one would expect a random ex-post distribution of post-merger job opportunities. In fact, conquering managers are put in charge of captured provinces much as they were in the days of the Roman or British empires.

One cannot explain the ferocity with which incumbent managements fight to resist takeovers by looking at consumption privileges. With golden parachutes, most will have a higher lifetime income with an unfriendly takeover than they would have had without it. High-income executives often have no time to enjoy the consumption goods that their incomes would allow them to buy. A takeover would give them the time to be consumers.

Most incumbent managers could strike an even better consumption deal for themselves if they were willing to surrender without a fight. Why don't they do so? To do so is to surrender leadership and decision-making authority. Control over others, over decision, over events, is their goal. Consumption goods are not a substitute for the power to make decisions.

Japanese versus American Firms

If one wants to understand Japanese market-share-maximizing companies, one can learn more from an analysis of empire builders than from an understanding of the economics of profit maximization (Tsurumi and Tsurumi, 1985). If one looks at the successes of those same Japanese companies, perhaps their secret is to be found in the fact that they have tapped a universal human desire to build, to belong to an empire, to conquer neighboring empires, and to become the world's leading economic power. Attempting to motivate individuals to work smarter or harder to produce higher incomes for themselves just isn't as successful as enlisting individuals into an army to build a successful empire.

Profits are important to every firm. An empire-building firm needs them to finance the expansion of its empire. Conversely, there are probably few firms that are pure profit maximizers where the desire to build and conquer plays no role. Evidence would suggest, however, that Japanese firms to a much greater extent than American firms are built on the empire power maximization model rather than the consumption profit maximizing model.

If one thinks of a continuum with profit maximizing firms at one end and empire-building forms at the other, the exact placement of Japanese and American firms on the spectrum might be controversial, but the order of the positions on the continuum would not. American firms would be closer to the profit maximizing end of the spectrum, Japanese firms closer to the empire-building end of the spectrum. European firms would probably be placed somewhere in between.

Evidence: Real Interest Rates

In Japan a social and corporate system has been organized to maximize growth and market share at the expense of individual consumption privileges. For the passbook Japanese saver, real interest rates, for example, have been negative for much of the post–World War II period (Statistical Bureau, 1986, p. 418). At the same time, a variety of other factors (very limited consumer credit, large housing downpayments, rudimentary public and private monthly pensions, and land policies that lead to very high prices for housing) have forced the average Japanese consumer to save a large fraction of his or her income despite a negative rate of return on his or her effort.

The intrinsic rate of time preference may be lower in Japan than it is in the United States but there is no doubt that the Japanese would save much less if they were in the American system. Some of their high savings rate is forced saving. But this system is not an accident. Historically, it was deliberately designed to shift resources directly from consumption to investment.

There never has been a political rebellion among the Japanese voter against this system. They grumble, but they know what they are doing and they are willing to put themselves voluntarily in a consumption prison where they consume less than they would in other social settings. This willingness can only exist if the average Japanese consumer-voter has goals other than simply to maximize his or her own consumption. Empire building is the best alternative hypothesis.

The low American savings rate and shorter American firm time horizons are rational if the goal is simply individual consumption. Because of advances in technology and productivity, those who live in the future will be richer than those that live in the present. As a result, the present should not sacrifice to raise the living standards of the future. Technically, the present should not save to insure that the poor (the present) are not subsidizing the rich (the future).

Americans would seem to be following these rational utility maximizing principles. Domestic saving is at an all-time low and the trade deficit is at an all-time high. By saving little and selling off existing American assets to finance a trade deficit, today's Americans are insuring that tomorrow's Americans will not be richer than they.

If other societies are saving more for the future, this implies a reduction in the future relative standard of living in the country with the lower savings rate, but this is not a subject of concern for those who maximize their own consumption. Envy does not exist in their theoretical world and the fact that foreigners have more money does not lead to the conclusion that foreigners will exert power over them.

The high domestic Japanese saving rate and the large Japanese trade surplus are irrational from the perspective of conventional economic analysis. They impoverish the present (the poor) and enrich the future (the rich). The Japanese are, however, very rational if their goal is to own the world and have the owner's power to make decisions.

Conversely, from a rational economic perspective Americans seem too worried about Japanese investments in the United States. Those purchases, after all, raise our consumption standards of living. But perhaps Americans are learning that Japanese decision making comes with Japanese ownership. Something the theory denies, but reality confirms.

Evidence: Language

One hears differences in motivation in the very language of conversation. The average Japanese employee loves to tell how he works for a company with the biggest market share in its industry. He or she will even take pride in having the third largest market share—in being the third most powerful warlord in the industry. No one, from the head of a company to the lowest worker, ever refers to a high rate of return on investment as an aspect of success in which one should take pride. Expanding (maximizing?) market share is the objective.

In *A Japan that Can Say NO,* Morita and Ishihara (1989) talk of the twentieth century as the century of superpower military warfare (the two world wars, the Cold War), and of the twenty-first century as the century of "economic" warfare. They boldly state that Japan will win the economic war of the twenty-first century.

In a similar vein, Europeans talk about "fortress Europe" and in February 1990, Chancellor Helmut Kohl said on German television "the decade of the 1990s will be the decade of the Europeans and not that of the Japanese" (*Boston Globe,* 1990, p. 2).

If one systematically listens to European firms describing their strategies for Eastern Europe, one does not hear the language of profit maximization, one hears the language of reclaiming one's former empires and patrimony. Statements are often made that their firms are willing to invest for ten to fifteen years before profits will be made (MIT Symposium, 1990). No income maximizer would contemplate such investments; to anyone with such a perspective, recapturing the glories of former empires is of no interest.

This difference in orientation led to the widespread observation at the 1990 World Economics Forum in Davos that American firms would not be major players in Eastern Europe. Their goals (immediate profits) were different and therefore they could not compete with firms that had different objectives.

In contrast, Americans would feel uncomfortable if they said that they wanted to be empire builders, were planning to win the next economic war, and would make the next decade their decade to the exclusion of someone else. They are very comfortable, however, talking about having the world's highest consumption standard of living.

One can argue that these are just accidental metaphors or one can believe, as I do, that the selection of metaphors tells us something very important about the different ways in which people view the world.

Evidence: Relative Rankings

On a list of the world's largest companies by sales and market share, there would be many more Japanese companies at the top than there would be on a list of the world's most profitable companies with the highest rate of return per unit of employed capital.[2] American firms would rank much higher on the latter. The two rankings are not accidental. They are exactly what one would expect given the theories underlying the two sets of companies.

Evidence: Willingness to Accept Below Market Rates of Return

Many very successful firms in Japan have made rates of return over the past two decades much lower than they could have made by simply investing in government bonds at home or abroad. Honda is a good example during the fifteen years from 1965 to 1980 when it was getting into the auto manufacturing business.[3] They knew then and know now that these alternative opportunities exist, but they did not then and do not now divert their investments into these higher rate of return riskless opportunities. Growth and market share are the goal of such firms. This is rational behavior in an empire-building model, but irrational in a consumption maximization model.

Empires overinvest because they plan to last forever and their aim is the dynamic one of expansion, not the static one of maximizing current consumption. No rational *homo economicus* would have built the cathedrals that play such an important role in the kingdom of God. No rational *homo economicus* would have built the buildings and roads of Rome or the monuments of ancient Egypt. They lasted too long and required too much capital up front.

By contrast, if one examines the American consumer electronics industry, one sees its history of a profitable strategic retreat into oblivion (MIT Commission, 1989). When the Japanese attack came in black and white television sets, the American manufacturers simply refused to let their rate of return fall to Japanese levels and left the market. But in their remaining activities, they continued to earn their demanded 15 percent rate of return. As the attack and willingness to accept lower rates of return came in market segment after market segment (radio, stereos, color television), American firms systematically retreated until they were out of the consumer electronics business. But at every point in time, they made their demanded rate of return. Being rational, they would go out of business before they would accept a lower rate of return.

Empires fight to expand. Fighting for greater market shares is irrational to the rational consumption maximizer who would rather surrender than fight. Fighting lowers one's consumption. Besides, their theories tell them that they can always go to work for the winner. Individuals are, after all, paid in accordance with their individual marginal productivities. Whom one works for is not important. Nothing is supposedly lost by surrender since the winners will not reserve the highest-paying jobs for their own troops. The consumption maximizer is a mercenary who would rather switch than fight.

Evidence: Stock Exchange Values

Given P/E multiples (60 to 80 in recent years) on the Tokyo stock exchange, profit maximizing firms should have issued and sold shares until the stock exchange price/earnings multiples were brought back into line with the price/earnings multiples available on government bonds (Statistical Bureau, 1986, p. 427). By selling shares and buying government bonds, they could have risklessly raised firm profits and the income of existing shareholders substantially. They did not do so.

To do so they would have to have diluted ownership and control and they would have made themselves vulnerable to takeovers. Very high multiples mean that Japanese firms can easily buy foreign firms but foreign firms cannot buy Japanese firms. High P/E multiples are the modern financial equivalent of the ancient moat and wall that holds potential invaders at bay.

Evidence: The Takeover Wars

In contrast, *Barbarians at the Gates*, by Burrough and Helyar (1990), is an interesting story of complete individual income maximization even at the cost of destroying the industrial empire (RJR Nabisco) to which one belongs. Destroying one's own company simply isn't important to the profit maximizer. The name of the game is raising one's own income. Institutions and corporate loyalties are irrelevant.

What we know of the story of the demise of Drexel would indicate that some of the same individuals who played a central role in the takeover of RJR Nabisco were also willing to destroy their own firms just to get their annual bonuses. Today's income was more important than tomorrow's income. Tomorrow one can always get another job—rational income maximization behavior; irrational empire-building behavior.

The Viking raiders are a mere footnote in history since they were not interested in the hard work of empire building and did not last long. But they had the highest incomes of their age, and when it comes to psychic income, they probably had a lot more fun than those who raised the vegetable gardens they raided.

Evidence: Whom Firms Serve

If the executives of profit maximizing American firms were asked to state the order in which they serve various constituencies, the order would be shareholders first, with customers and employees a distant second and third. Many managers would argue that the sole purpose of the company is to maximize shareholder wealth. Customers and employees are only important to the extent that they contribute to shareholder wealth. If Japanese firms were asked the same question, the order of duty would be reversed—employees first, with customers second, and shareholders a distant third (Yamazaki, 1986). Conquering armies want the best men and equipment in their armies. The taxes and reductions in civilian standards of living that these taxes will require of the "citizen-owners" are not of prime interest to conquering generals.

When managers talk about shareholder wealth as their sole goal, they immediately create a problem for they explicitly deny the importance of the group. Only individual capitalists count. All others are simply rented factors of production. Employees are not on the team.

Can anyone imagine a general going into battle making similar announcements to his troops? They, the soldiers and officers, are merely mercenaries, not members of the team. Long ago we learned that soldiers who believe in what they are fighting for almost always beat soldiers who are simply paid to fight. Why should it be different in the business world?

What general would announce that he reserves the right to surrender if some group that is not on the field of battle (the shareholders) would enjoy more consumption privileges as the result of his surrender? Any such general would not be successful. We would say that he does not understand the nature of military combat. But why should the motivations of economic combat be any different? People obey and sacrifice because they wish to join. If there is nothing to join, they will neither obey nor sacrifice.

Evidence: Treatment of Labor

In a profit maximizing firm, labor is simply a factor of production to be rented at the lowest possible cost. Wages are to be beaten down whenever and wherever possible. An empire-building firm, in contrast, sees labor as a strategic asset to be maximized. One wants the highest-quality and best-fed soldiers. In the good old days, the troops got a share of the booty achieved in conquest. Today in Japan they get a bonus not normally keyed to profitability but to growth, productivity, and market share.

The differences in how that labor is regarded in Japan and the United States can be seen in wages, employment, and training. In the United States real hourly wages fell 11 percent and real weekly wages fell 16 percent from 1973 to 1989 for nonsupervisory workers, and in recent years have been falling at the rate of 1 percent per year despite the fact that the real per capita GNP rose 29 percent over the same period of time (U.S. Office of the President, 1990, p. 334). In the last two decades American firms have demanded and received wage reductions to raise profits. When the opportunity to beat down wages arises, American firms beat them down. Many industries such as retailing have also been able to reduce fringe benefits by moving workers from full-time to part-time, thus making them ineligible for fringe benefits. Similarly, American firms have rapidly moved production to lower-wage offshore production bases. American firms treat labor in accordance with the dictates of classical microeconomic profit maximization. Lower wages equal higher profits.

Neither Japanese nor European firms lowered wages during the same period. Nor did they go abroad or move to part-time employment to the same extent. One might argue that foreign unions are more powerful and foreign firms cannot do what they might like to do, but there is no evidence that foreign firms were interested over this period in a wage-reduction strategy. Perhaps they have learned from history that successful armies don't reduce wages and benefits on the eve of battle.

Lifetime employment is offered to core workers in Japanese firms and economic firings and layoffs are much less prevalent in Europe than in the United States. The United States is in a statistical class by itself when it comes to labor force turnover (U.S. Department of Labor, 1983, p. 180). A turnover rate of 4 percent per month is about equally divided between quits and firings. From an income maximization perspective, this is a sign of efficiency. Workers are dismissed when they aren't needed and workers accept new job offers whenever wages are higher. But if high turnover is a source of efficiency, why is productivity growing more rapidly in both Japan and Europe?

Successful armies know the value of a central cadre of experienced troops. Empires are built on mutual loyalty and resistance to seduction by the enemy. Armies continually need new blood and new recruits but they also need a core of committed, trained troops. The Japanese and European commitment to a core group of workers with employment guarantees that go far beyond those given to the temporary workers on the fringe of the firm is in accordance with military practice. Turnover is limited to maximize training and experience, to promote bonding, and to increase the willingness to sacrifice oneself for the good of the group.

The American army has decided that excessive individual turnover was one of its major mistakes in Vietnam. Rather than rotating groups (platoons and companies) in and out as their enlistments were up, individual soldiers were rotated in and out, and the bonding necessary to make soldiers willing to sacrifice for each other never developed. Without this bonding no one would sacrifice for anyone else and the American army failed on the field of battle.

Economic armies worry about similar problems. Consumption maximizers do not. In armies teamwork is always stressed as more important than individual brilliance. Medals may be given for individual heroism after the battle is over, but prior to battle it is teamwork that is stressed.

The takeover and buyout wave in the United States leads to the same conclusion about differences in how companies are viewed. Company divisions, including the employees, are bought and sold or restructured in manners that are reminiscent of kings buying and selling provinces in medieval Europe. As in medieval Europe, the employees are chattel serfs who are not consulted about whether or not they want to have different masters. Not much corporate loyalty can be expected if one has to expect to be treated as a slave and sold to the highest bidder.

The buying and selling of provinces ended in Europe with the rise of nation-states that could command nationalistic loyalties. People were bonded to the state and states where this bond was constructed were simply able to defeat armies and conquer territories where no such bond existed. Why would anyone expect the history of economic firms to be any different from the history of nations?

In Japan the ceremony that new employees participate in when joining their lifetime company is in fact very similar to that of baptism (joining the empire of God) or giving allegiance to medieval lords. One becomes part of a group whose purpose is bigger than simply to raise individual incomes. In the first year of employment in Japan, the company indoctrination process occupies a substantial amount of time. Armies do likewise. They believe that firms that succeed in bonding their employees to them simply have more reserves of good will and a work force more willing to make short-term sacrifices than those that do not. In contrast, U.S. firms make very little effort to indoctrinate their employees.

In *Made in America*, the MIT Commission on Productivity documents a very different pattern of training expenditures in Japanese and German firms than in American firms (1990, p. 81). Americans invest less per worker and concentrate their investments more heavily in management education.

If one looks at training investments for average workers, one finds that Americans invest less in general background skills and more narrowly focus their investments on the narrow job skills required for the next job. In doing so, they more closely follow the dictates of Becker's (1964) distinction between general and specific skills. Firms should only pay for skill investments when those skills can be used in one and only one firm, and since there are few such skills, firms should invest little. Army generals, on the other hand, want an overtrained labor force. The American armed forces, for example, do much more training than most American firms.

Narrow profit centers are a much more widely used form of corporate organization in the United States than are in either Japan or Europe. They fit with a model of the world whereby individuals are motivated solely by their own income and where group efforts are not important. They don't, however, fit into a model where the group's output and not the individual's output is the dominant factor in total production. Narrow profit centers often lead to noncooperation between different parts of the same firm. No one wants to sacrifice his output (and hence income) to help some other part of the firm raise its output (and hence income) even if that sacrifice would lead to higher output by the firm as a whole. In testimony to the *Made in America* commission at MIT, the former head of research at a major American steel company stated that he could not do the projects that he thought he needed to do. Plant managers did not want him to use their facilities to do research since that research would lower their annual throughput and their annual bonuses.

Evidence: R&D Spending Patterns

Procyclical patterns of research and development spending in the United States are an indicator of the same differences in motivation. In the United States, private R&D spending falls in recessions and rises in booms (U.S. National Science Foundation, 1989). In Europe and Japan it does not. To an American firm, cutting R&D is a technique for maintaining profits during a period of declining sales. In Europe and Japan, R&D is not cut since it is seen as the source of long-run competitive strength. The same differences in spending can be seen in training expenditures: American firms cut during recessions; Japanese and European firms do not.

Evidence: Legal Systems

The American, European, and Japanese legal systems express the differences we have already examined. A society of individual income maximizers needs a detailed system of legal rules and regulations, checks and balances. It is not possible to assume any degree of self-restraint that will prevent individuals from taking actions that maximize their own income at the expense of the income of others. Private law enforcement where everyone sues each other is in fact held up by those who believe in profit maximization as optimal. The role of the state (the community, the collective, the group) should be minimized even when it comes to rule enforcement. The implicit assumption is that the state isn't a profit maximizer and will therefore make the wrong decisions.

In empires, group norms limit individual behavior. The individual who is more dependent upon the success of the group and better indoctrinated can be assumed to be more aware of what it takes to facilitate the group's success and more apt to act in the appropriate manner. Fewer legal rules and regulations have to be written. More can be done with informal "administrative guidance," as the Japanese call it. Personal lawsuits are uncommon.

One can prevent theft by buying locks or one can prevent theft by inculcating the values that theft is wrong. In the end, both may stop thievery, but if inculcating values actually works, as a communitarian approach, it has the advantage of being much cheaper. Honest societies without locks can produce goods more cheaply than dishonest societies that must invest in locks.

More explicitly, the Japanese and German legal systems both directly encourage conquest and discourage foreign invasions. Under the Japanese legal system it is possible to establish formal alliances with cross-ownership between firms (the *keiretsu* groups such as Mitsui) to insure that firms work together to expand. Because a majority of the shares of each member of the group are owned by other members of the group, no member of the group can be bought by outsiders.

Under the German merchant banking system, banks such as the Deutsche Bank can buy controlling interests in different industrial firms to insure that firms work together to expand. Because one bank owns a controlling interest in each firm, no firm in the group can be bought by outsiders.

These legal systems are irrational if the aim is to maximize share prices (potential buyers are discouraged from buying), but very rational if the aim is economic power. German or Japanese groups can buy firms in other countries such as the United States but cannot themselves be bought.

American antitrust laws, in contrast, prohibit the formation of interlocking business groups, and American banking laws prohibit banks from owning shares in industrial firms. Our securities laws also prohibit pension funds and mutual funds (the majority owners of most publicly traded firms) from acting as owners. They are not allowed to own a dominant position in any one individual firm and are forced by law to be solely share buyers and sellers (speculators).

Who Wins?

In the abstract, firms based upon the motivation of strategic conquest and those based upon the motivation of profit maximization would each seem to have advantages. The strategic conquest firm is willing to work for a lower rate of return and can use this willingness to force profit maximizing firms out of business. And in theory, profit maximizing firms should be better cost minimizers. They are more concerned about lowering costs and more willing to do so (e.g., by firing workers) and this advantage could be large enough to allow them to meet their rate of return on investment targets and still sell products at prices equal to, or lower than, that of empire-building firms.

Empire-building firms may not have a high demanded rate of return on investment, but they do have a profit constraint. They cannot grow unless their profits are positive. If profit maximizing firms costs are low enough, they can defeat an empire-building firm by forcing losses upon it.

Recent empirical evidence would seem to favor the long-run success of empire building firms. The firms that seem to be based on these principles are clearly on the offensive in international markets. Those based upon profit maximizing are on the defensive.

Who wins in the long run depends upon the extent to which one believes that economic dynamics are fundamentally different from comparative statics. The cost-cutting advantages of profit maximizing firms would probably dominate if we really lived in a world of comparative statics. This is, after all, the world where the theorems were derived showing the superiority of profit maximization.

In the comparative statics, firms prove their efficiency by moving from inside the production possibilities curve to a place on the production possibilities curve. In getting onto the production possibility curve, the Japanese seniority wage system, for example, should be a handicap. Labor is not being paid in accordance with its individual marginal productivity.

In economic dynamics the central problem is getting the production possibility curve to move to the right as rapidly as possible—i.e., to make productivity grow as rapidly as possible. In this effort many of the cost-cutting advantages of comparative statics become liabilities. Reducing wages and firing people may allow costs to be cut but such practices lower the willingness of the work force to accept new technologies, lead to a less well trained labor force, and eliminate loyalty—the willingness to make short-run self-sacrifices for the good of the firm. The willingness to reduce R&D spending in recessions similarly may be a short-run static advantage that turns out to be a long-run dynamic handicap. In any case an empirical experiment is now under way. The profit maximizing firms of the United States are in competition with the empire-building firms of Japan and Europe. Twenty years from now we will know who won.

Our own history, however, probably gives us the answer. In the period (1865–1929) when America caught up with and then surpassed Great Britain, it was full of conquering economic generals (Carnegie, Rockefeller, Mellon, etc.) whose goals clearly went beyond maximizing their own consumption. They unabashedly wanted to build empires. Hill even called his Great Northern train across America the Empire Builder.

Notes

1. For this argument, see Thurow (1989, p. 9).
2. See the *Fortune* Magazine rankings, May and June, various years.
3. Honda's rate of return fell from 9 percent before entering the auto business, and fell

to 3 percent in the fifteen years thereafter. Given known profits in motorcycles, the auto division was operating with very low returns for this fifteen-year startup period (Hatsopoulos, Krugman, and Summers, 1988).

References

Becker, Gary S. 1964. *Human Capital*. New York: Columbia University Press.

Boston Globe. 1990. "Kohl to Reassure Soviets on Unification." February 9.

Burrough, Bryan, and John Helyar. 1990. *Barbarians at the Gates*. New York: Harper & Row.

Hatsopoulos, George N., Paul R. Krugman, and Lawrence H. Summers. 1988. "US Competitiveness: Beyond the Trade Deficit." *Science* (July).

MIT Commission on Industrial Productivity. 1989. "The Decline of U.S. Consumer Electronics." *The Working Papers of the MIT Commission on Industrial Productivity*, vol. 1. Cambridge, MA: MIT Press.

MIT Commission on Productivity. 1989. *Made in America*. Cambridge, MA: MIT Press.

MIT Symposium on Europe in the 1990s. 1990. Cambridge, MA: MIT Press.

Morita, Akio, and Shintaro Ishihara. 1989. *The Japan That Can Say NO: The New U.S.-Japan Relations Card*. Unofficial English language translation (unpublished).

Statistics Bureau. 1986. *Japan Statistical Yearbook 1986*. Tokyo: Prime Minister's Office.

Thurow, Lester C. 1989. "Producer Economics." *Industrial Relations Research Association (IRRA) 41st Annual Proceedings*. New York: IRRA.

Tsurumi, Yoshi, and Hitoki Tsurumi. 1985. "Value-added Maximizing Behavior of Japanese Firms and Roles of Corporate Investment and Finance." *Columbia Journal of World Business* 20 (Spring): 29–35.

U.S. Department of Labor. 1983. *Handbook of Labor Statistics*. Bulletin 2175. Washington, DC: Government Printing Office.

U.S. National Science Foundation. 1989. *R&D Expenditures*. Washington, DC: Government Printing Office..

U.S. Office of the President. 1990. *Economic Report of the President, January, 1990*. Washington, DC: Government Printing Office.

Yamazaki, Masakazu. 1986. "The Impact of Japanese Culture on Management." In Lester C. Thurow, ed., *The Management Challenge: Japanese Views*. Cambridge, MA: MIT Press.

8

JOHN D. DONAHUE

The Ideological Romance of Privatization

Two political legacies of the 1980s seem certain to color and constrain the economics of the 1990s. The first is a renewed cultural enthusiasm for private enterprise. The second is a deficit-induced imperative to limit government spending. In the confluence of these trends have been born great hopes for "privatization," the delegation of public duties to private businesses. These hopes are almost surely doomed to frustration. For while a good case *can* be made for turning many parts of the public's business over to private contractors, the arguments that stoke conservative ardor for privatization are chiefly ideological rather than pragmatic. Privatization's political appeal, moreover, tends to be greatest in precisely those cases where it makes the least sense.

Background, Definitions, and Distinctions

Popular distaste for government, never wholly absent from American politics, reached a level in the 1970s and 1980s that had not been seen for over half a century. Ronald Reagan won immense popularity in large part by tapping the electorate's hostility to politicians and its contempt for bureaucracy. The anti-government themes of both Jimmy Carter and George Bush were subtler and less strident than Reagan's but were nearly as central to their electoral successes. While government plumbed new depths of disfavor, however, citizens' appetite for roads and bridges, schools and hospitals, and protection from crime, foreign menaces, and nature's ravages failed to slacken. As spending outpaced revenues—at federal, state, and local levels—virtually any stratagem for paring budgets while cutting services as little as possible gained political allure. And those who had always believed in the inherent superiority of profit-seekers over bureaucrats judged that their moment had arrived.

The privatization movement is not simply a response to the day's fiscal panic, of course. Business has long been involved in public undertakings. Freelance revenue agents collected taxes on commission in ancient Greece and Rome and in *ancien régime* France. Armies-for-hire, organized by martial entrepreneurs, have figured prominently in medieval as well as modern conflicts. Thomas Cook's travel service transported British troops to Africa when the empire needed some quick maintenance. American government has routinely spent roughly as much on contractors as on employees, and the federal government first codified its preference for private suppliers during the Eisenhower administration.

But privatization as today's fiscally ambitious and ideologically charged phenomenon dates from the 1980s. Early in Reagan's presidency the Privatization Task Force of the Private Sector Survey on Cost Control (better known as the Grace Commission) called for cutting the federal payroll by one-sixth through contracting out governmental functions. Private firms were hired to check the backgrounds of job applicants, to collect on bad debts owed the federal government, and to audit the books of the General Services Administration. For-profit urban transit operations enjoyed an explicit preference in the allocation of federal subsidies, and the White House hired freelancers to write major speeches. All but a small fraction of the Superfund environmental cleanup program has gone to pay contractors. A new bureau within the Office of Management and Budget (OMB) was formed to promote privatization, and a blue-ribbon presidential commission celebrated the theme and issued a volume full of candidates for sale or contracting. By the second Reagan term, budget officials took to joking that virtually any proposal could become administration policy if it carried the label of privatization.

The Bush administration continues the campaign, albeit with somewhat less hoopla. The Coast Guard continues to slough off responsibilities to private firms, for example, and the OMB is pushing to privatize security services at the Bureau of Engraving, where America's currency is printed. And by law, most of the duties associated with the massive rescue of the savings and loan industry, from surveying the financial wreckage to managing the assets of failed thrifts, must be carried out by contractors, not federal bureaucrats. Fiscally straitened cities and states, meanwhile, have been placing a vast range of public services into private hands, from garbage collection and street paving to job training, tax assessment, and the management of jails and prisons.

"Privatization" is not just an inelegant term, but is a lamentably imprecise one as well. The word can signify something as broad as shrinking the welfare state (the primary meaning in Thatcher's Britain) or something as narrow as substituting a team of corporate employees for an all-but-identical team of civil servants. There is an almost infinite variety of possible organizational forms, moreover, with varying mixes of "publicness" and "privateness." Government workers may be elected, appointed, drafted, hired (under civil service rules or not), bound by contracts or not. Private organizations include profit-seeking firms, nonprofit corporations, voluntary service organizations, and so on.

Indeed, to speak of "government" producing something is to employ a convenient but misleading figure of speech. To examine any instance of government production is invariably to discover *people* doing the producing. Government produces by arranging relationships whereby individuals devote resources to common goals. Some of these arrangements we call "government jobs"; others we call "government contracts." The central question is how these two types of arrangements tend to *differ*—in efficiency, in accountability, in fidelity to the public purpose. And on this question it is soberingly easy to err.

Privatization's Proper Role

A richly elaborated theoretical tradition argues that private, profit-seeking organizations should perform with greater technical efficiency than do public organizations. This, it turns out, is broadly true. Empirical studies comparing public and private performance in comparable activities do identify a private advantage in simple efficiency—albeit with some significant exceptions and conditions. Consider first one of the humbler public missions, garbage collection. Natural experiments in comparative efficiency are strewn across the continent as municipal sanitation departments and hauling contractors operate simultaneously in adjacent towns or neighborhoods. Trash collection seems somehow fascinating to economic researchers, and the literature is strangely rich in careful empirical studies. The answer on efficiency is as clear as statistical conclusions ever get: public trash collectors are less efficient than competitive private contractors, by something like 10 to 40 percent (Young, 1972; Kemper and Quigley, 1976; Savas, 1977; Stevens, 1977; Bennett and Johnson, 1979; McDavid, 1985; Cubbin, Domberger, and Meadowcroft, 1987).

Similar studies find that privately owned and operated transit systems are run more efficiently than their private counterparts; that private airlines carry more freight and passengers and earn more revenue per worker than national carriers; that commercial office-cleaning services do the same job more cheaply than janitors on the public payroll; and even that for-profit fire fighters operate more efficiently than their colleagues in the public sector (Donahue, 1989).

Lower quality is *not* the key to contractors' lower costs, despite what natural skepticism might suggest (and some privatization opponents assert). While some private suppliers do provide shoddy services, most of the studies that establish superior private efficiency scrupulously control for quality. The major sources of contractors' productive advantages are precisely as theory advertises. Private firms operate closer to optimal scale. Their work rules are more flexible. Hiring and procurement are less rule-bound. Innovation is more rapid, machines are more up-to-date. Less money is spent on hiring employees, more on equipping them. Employee incentives and sanctions are subtler and more effective.

Recognizing that private organizations have distinct advantages in low-cost production is no slur on public servants. Productive efficiency is not what public organizations are *for*. Government agencies are structured to ensure procedural fairness, openness, and accountability. Just as science cannot breed a single strain of tomato for both top-drawer taste and the indestructibility that cross-continental shipping requires, no organization can be structured for both maximum fairness and maximum efficiency.

At the same time, it is essential to recognize that both theory and evidence identify only a *potential* private advantage in efficiency. That potential is only realized under certain conditions. The mere presence of the profit motive no more ensures efficiency than a bureaucrat's good intentions guarantee justice. At the core of the privatization issue lie two central truths, both distilled by Adam Smith out of older, deeper traditions, and both habitually ignored by many privatization enthusiasts. One truth: it is *competition*, and only competition, that transforms the profit motive from a base appetite into an engine of the common good. The other: the first and fondest desire of any sensible profit-seeker is to avoid competition. The same tradition of empirical studies that confirms private organization's potential for efficiency demonstrates that where competition is weak or absent—as with water or electricity utilities, to cite two well-studied examples—there is no private advantage at all.

What does all this tell us about privatization's proper role? It makes sense to delegate public functions that can be precisely defined (so that a meaningful contract can be written and meaningful bids solicited); whose performance can be evaluated accurately; and where contractors must constantly match the standard set by eager rivals, or else face replacement. There is less to be gained, and more to be lost, by privatizing tasks where criteria are vague or shifting, and where performance is hard to assess. If competition is lacking for any reason—and the potential reasons are legion, including technical barriers to entry, corruption, or the simple disinclination of public officials to keep contractors appropriately insecure—little can be expected from privatization. And of course, *some* public tasks are so dependent on procedural fairness or so intimately tied up with collective decision making that simple productive efficiency is a relatively minor concern (if it can even be defined). For functions like these—drafting budgets, presiding over courts, judging appeals for benefits—to delegate authority is often to pervert it.

Yet there are plenty of public tasks with the right mix of clarity, visibility, and openness to rivalry. One example, noted earlier, is garbage collection. For similar reasons, street sweeping, road repair, and park maintenance have proven good candidates for privatization (Stevens et al., 1984). The federal government has discovered significant savings by contracting for janitorial services in the buildings it owns or leases (U.S. General Accounting Office, 1981). The armed services have collected measurable gains by privatizing support services—laundry, test administration, motor-pool management, and so on—at U.S. military bases (U.S. General Accounting Office, 1985a). There are hundreds or thousands of other functions that could be delegated without great risk. Governments in the

United States spend roughly a half-trillion dollars a year paying public workers to deliver goods and services directly. Suppose we somehow managed to achieve just the right pattern of privatization. If one-quarter of these services could be delegated, at an average cost savings of 20 percent—and neither figure exceeds what is theoretically achievable—the savings would reach $25 billion per year.

Two common yet unconvincing objections to privatization must be aired before we turn to more telling flaws. The first concerns symbolism. Some people find it repugnant to admit the profit motive into the public realm. But even if we care intrinsically about the way the public's servants are organized, such concerns must be balanced against more mundane ones. If private delivery turned out to be sufficiently cheaper, better, or more accountable, most of us (though assuredly not all) would set aside our misgivings. What is more important, Americans simply differ on which way the symbolism issue cuts. Some no doubt feel that providing public services through civil service organizations reinforces their communal character, while the profit motive would pollute it. Others might feel that to accomplish our common goals through private institutions affirms our individualistic culture and that—precisely *because* symbolism matters—American government should shun bureaucracy even when it would be superior to the private alternative.

The second objection concerns the fate of public workers. Much of the cost savings from privatization—typically one-quarter or more, and sometimes over one-half—comes at labor's expense. Opponents make much of this, promoters try to obscure it, but the facts are fairly clear. Private contractors often pay less than the public agencies they replace. Even more frequently they offer leaner benefits, call for less restrictive work rules, and demand more flexibility of workers. What are we to make of this? On the one hand, public jobs have been the gateway to the middle class for millions of disadvantaged Americans. Government work offers job security and employee benefits that are uncommon in the private sector. To insist that nothing matters in public service delivery but the raw dollar cost is to adopt a needlessly narrow view of government. On the other hand, it is hard to discern any democratic mandate for redistribution through the public payroll. There is also a certain arbitrariness to making employees' stakes a trump argument in the privatization debate. If street sweeping should be public so that street sweepers will be well paid, why not automobile assembly? Equally troubling is the fact that government workers are frequently better off than a majority of the citizens whose taxes cover public payrolls.

On balance, it seems that those who value collective action cannot reject using private means to serve public ends simply out of distaste for the symbolism, or because government workers stand to lose. But admitting privatization as a serious option summons the question of whether it delivers as promised. To illuminate this question I turn—not to one of the triumphs trumpeted by proponents or the horror stories beloved by skeptics—but to an initiative in privatization that is widely thought to be at least modestly successful.

Subsidized Private Training and Covert Inefficiency

As he signed the Job Training Partnership Act into law in 1982, Ronald Reagan hailed it as "eliminating the bureaucratic and administrative waste" that had plagued its predecessor, the Comprehensive Employment and Training Act (better known and widely scorned under its acronym, CETA). The new jobs program, drafted during the giddy early days of the Reagan Revolution, reflected the prevailing contempt for the public sector and apotheosis of the private. Government would be relegated to its proper role, in Reagan's words, of "working with the private sector." (Reagan, 1982). The money would come from federal coffers. But most of the decisions about how to spend it, and most of the actual training, would be private.

In an era where job training is prescribed as the remedy for ills as fundamental and as diverse as widening class differences and ebbing international competitiveness, JTPA is a symbolically significant reform. It made American manpower development policy more "businesslike" in three broad ways. First, it stipulated that business representatives would control the local boards that actually run the program. Second, it encouraged much more reliance on for-profit providers of training, both in the classroom and (especially) on the job. And third, it mandated a "results-oriented," contractual approach to subsidized training.

Local JTPA programs must meet specified standards for placing trainees in jobs following training. Other standards set a floor under the average hourly wage trainees must earn, set a ceiling over the maximum average expense for preparing a trainee for the labor force, and require that a stipulated fraction of JTPA graduates *stay* placed for at least several weeks. The contracts that local programs write with training providers embody these criteria. Most JTPA contracts require results—generally defined as job placement—as a condition of payment, or set fees that vary with the number or quality of jobs graduates land.

At first blush, JTPA looks like a solid success. Most local programs exceed the standards, often by large margins. Business organizations, moreover, are much happier with JTPA than they were with previous training programs. Companies that had spurned any involvement with CETA hire JTPA graduates, and do training themselves under contract with local JTPA programs. Virtually every local program can list hundreds of cases of disadvantaged citizens who underwent subsidized training and graduated to gainful employment. There has been a certain amount of criticism that JTPA tends to neglect the hard-core unemployed (Orfield et al., 1986), but the program is broadly seen as worthwhile as far as it goes (even if it should go farther.) This good reputation is undeserved. But to understand why this is so—to see why JTPA illustrates the perils of delegating public tasks to profit-seekers—requires a look at the logic of creating public value.

Looming behind subsidized job training programs are the American economy's massive investments in human capital development. Adding up federal, state, and local budgets for formal schooling and vocational and military training, plus individual tuition payments and wages foregone during training, plus the sums businesses spend to run their own training programs, to pay employee tuitions, and to cover the costs of on-the-job training, and the total annual investment in human skills comes to something like $300 billion or more—comparable to national spending on medical care or defense.

Public budgets for job training for the disadvantaged account for only a minuscule fraction of this total. (Indeed, the budget for JTPA's core program is not much bigger than IBM's training budget.) The question of targeting is thus crucial. The JTPA legislation specifies that program funds "shall only be used for activities which are in addition to those which would otherwise be available." This is an indisputably sensible proviso, but rather harder to put into effect than it seems at first blush. When private-sector spending on training dwarfs JTPA, how can "otherwise available" training activities be identified? Should the baseline for each firm be defined as its training budget in the year JTPA passed (perhaps adjusted for inflation)? Or some average of the previous several years? What about firms that are growing, and would have increased spending anyway? Or shrinking, and planning to cut spending? How much of the cost of on-the-job training (where learning is a byproduct of marketable production) should be attributed to skill development? Unless it can somehow distinguish *incremental* investments from training that would take place in any event, the government may simply be shouldering more of the burden without increasing overall spending.

Restricting subsidized training to the disadvantaged is one means of targeting public funds. But while the poor *do* get less private training, they still get *some* (Lillard and Tan, 1986; U.S. Department of Labor, 1985). Moreover, "the disadvantaged" is a generic term for a large and diverse group of people with different goals, different kinds of problems, and different capacities and inclinations to benefit from training. Most people who are counted among the poor at some point in their lives escape from poverty (Bane and Elwood, 1985). It happens sometimes that the starving young artist becomes rich and famous. It happens frequently that the children of penniless immigrants become doctors and lawyers. And it happens routinely that people who slip for a time into poverty return, if not to affluence, at least to solvency. Large numbers of the poor leave the unemployment rolls or get better jobs every year by virtue of talent, hard work, maturation, or simple good luck. This does not soften the hard truth that many other people stay jobless or underemployed. But it does complicate efforts to assess the effects of manpower policies.

A training program for the disadvantaged creates value when a participant's productivity and earnings exceed what they *would have been* in the absence of any intervention. Now, in any random sample of poor Americans at any given time, a few are fated for prosperity, some for a modest but stable niche in the work force, some for several years more of dependency, and some for deepening misery. We can easily observe a trainee's status *before* and *after* participation. But such comparisons conflate the whole gamut of forces determining a worker's prospects. The real effect of training programs is the difference between each person's fate *with* and *without* the program. This we can never know for certain, and only through considerable care and effort can we know approximately. When a trainee earns dramatically more (or just the same, or less) after the program, it may be because the training was highly valuable (or ineffective, or harmful) or because she or he was for wholly unrelated reasons on an upward (or stagnant, or downward) earnings path. The *average* measured effect of a training program depends in part on the value the program creates. But it also depends on the mix of participants: With a large proportion of high-potential trainees, the program looks better, *no matter what* real but unobserved changes take place—or fail to take place—in participants' real prospects (Borus, 1979). The true impact of subsidized training, in other words, can be either more or less than meets the eye.

About 29 million Americans meet the age and income requirements for JTPA training. In addition, up to 10 percent of participants with special "barriers to employment"—including the handicapped, older workers, veterans, alcoholics and drug addicts, ex-offenders, and "displaced homemakers"—may be exempted from any means test. From among these potential participants, JTPA's budget suffices for roughly one million per year. In other words, something less than one out of thirty eligibles gets training. Aside from a stipulation that 40 percent of the funds must go for training young people, and repeated but toothless exhortations to serve welfare recipients and other subgroups "equitably," the Job Training Partnership Act leaves the selection of participants up to local officials and contractors.

Recall, now, that training providers are judged on the basis of post-program placement rates. The results are entirely predictable. High school graduates are chosen to participate much more frequently than their less educated neighbors. Women, Hispanics, and welfare recipients are relatively scarce in JTPA programs. Subgroups that are easy to plug into job slots—with or without subsidized training—rose as a fraction of all trainees with the transition from CETA to JTPA. Participation rates for groups that are harder to place—and especially welfare recipients and high school dropouts—fell sharply (Donahue, 1989; Walker et al., 1986; U.S. General Accounting Office 1985b). A study by the General Accounting Office (1988), covering 5,500 trainees in sixty-three local JTPA programs, found that less "job-ready" participants received relatively little training, and that most of the training they got was in low-skill occupations like custodial work, housekeeping, or laundering.

The point to observe, in seeking to assess JTPA's *efficiency*, is that the pool of eligibles is big enough and diverse enough that selection *alone* can explain most of the program's impressive performance on placement and wage goals. Ivy League graduates indisputably tend to earn more than the national average. If Ivy League schools selected their students randomly, this would be clear evidence that sitting through four years of lectures boosted productive capacity. But students are not selected randomly. The screening process is sufficiently intense that the people selected for admission would *still* tend to earn more than average even if they spent their four years in the Peace Corps, or learning to play the harp, instead of attending classes in ivied halls. It is extremely difficult to distinguish between the value *added* by the professors and the value *identified* by the admissions office. A similar ambiguity undercuts JTPA's contractual approach to training.

Consider the types of jobs, and the types of companies, that typify JTPA's on-the-job training programs. Fully 40 percent of training slots are in low-skill occupations like food service and dishwashing (U.S. General Accounting Office, 1988). Among the most important on-the-job training contractors are fast-food restaurants and convenience stores. Both types of enterprises hire large numbers of people—generally at the lower end of the income distribution—and train them in a limited range of fairly narrow skills applicable to low-wage, high-turnover jobs. It seems prudent to wonder how much these firms change their hiring or training— indeed, how much *room* there is for them to change their hiring or training—in response to subsidies.

Consider, too, the demonstrated lack of awareness among many JTPA decision makers of the contractual complexity of subsidized training. In the words of one Pittsburgh entrepreneur: "Just because a businessman has an on-the-job training contract and his two sons are his only employees, where's the conflict of interest? Is it wrong to upgrade the skills of your children?" (Bovard, 1986). Few officials or contractors, to be sure, are quite so unclear on the concept. But the basic problem is seldom conflict of interest in this blatant sense. Rather, it is that JTPA's celebration of the private sector's efficiency edge is accompanied by a nearly perfect obliviousness to the delicate task of harnessing that efficiency to clearly *public* goals. It is quite probable that the gentleman from Pittsburgh would have trained his sons without a JTPA contract. It is less obvious, but equally true, that most business people in the United States find it in their interest to train people, including large numbers of JTPA-eligible people, without subsidies.

One local program's staff director offers a fairly typical perspective: "Our placement rates and costs beat the federal standards. That proves we're efficient" (Walker et al., 1986). It proves nothing of the sort. There can be no doubt that JTPA does some good; it would be astonishing if the public and private partners, equipped with noble aspirations and $2 billion a year, did *not* do some good. But there can also be little doubt that JTPA does much less good than the statistics suggest and its proponents assert.

The problem, at base, is a preposterously underspecified contractual relationship. Most disadvantaged people work, most of the time; JTPA deals with about 2 or 3 percent of America's poor each year. But over 10 percent of the poor escape from poverty each year, most for reasons that have absolutely nothing to do with the program. The typical JTPA trainee ends up in a job paying little more than one-half the average wage. Most of the working poor move in and out of such jobs with dismal regularity. There is little within the contractual structure of JTPA to constrain training organizations to concentrate on people who would otherwise remain unemployed and impoverished. There are powerful incentives to select trainees from among the minority of the eligible population who—for wholly separate reasons—have the best prospects. It is rather as if Medicaid physicians were presented with a population of patients suffering complaints ranging from bursitis to brain tumors, were asked to choose 2 or 3 percent for treatment, and then were paid on the basis of how many were still breathing when they left the hospital.

Many officials in the JTPA system are fully aware of the tension between broad-gauge performance requirements and the unenforced imperative to create public value. Both critics and troubled proponents recognize that JTPA generally concentrates on the most job-ready fraction of the eligible population. But charges of "cream-skimming" miss an important part of the problem. The tendency to avoid the hard cases is seen as lamentable on ethical grounds, and it is. But it also means that the real impact of the program is far less than advertised. There is no convincing evidence that the Job Training Partnership Act system, on balance, makes much difference for the employment, earnings, or productive capacity of American workers.

Concluding Observations

Some of America's less happy experiences with private suppliers so dominate the political foreground that their value as evidence in the privatization debate is difficult to appreciate. Our reliance on for-profit weapons suppliers has ensured strong incentives for technological ambition, but it has also cost the nation billions of dollars in waste and incited corruption on a stunning scale. Our health care system, based largely on public financing and for-profit suppliers, is often considered at once the costliest and the worst in the industrialized West. But it is particularly sobering to find that even in the case of job training—where there is little blunt corruption, and where the *a priori* case for superior private efficiency is fairly compelling—the private-sector edge turns out to be largely illusory.

The quiet inefficiency of the Job Training Partnership Act illustrates the perils of America's curiously symbolic approach to privatization. Paeans to the profit motive substitute for clear thinking about how to harness it. Proponents reprise over and over the sound case for *potential* efficiency gains without considering, in the laborious detail required, how to realize this potential. Those who enjoy enumerating government's myriad ineptitudes forget that *writing contracts* is one of the hardest things to do well, and requires the kind of flexibility, foresight, discretion, and imagination that most public agencies—rule-bound for the very best of reasons—conspicuously lack. Vague calls for careful legal draftsmanship and monitoring simply beg the question.

There is an enormous element of nonsense in the privatization debate. Proponents invoke the efficiency that characterizes well-run companies in competitive markets and then trumpet their conviction that private firms must inevitably excel in *public* undertakings as well. To go from the observation that private companies tend to do what they do better than public agencies, to the assertion that companies should take over the agencies' duties, is much the same as observing that the clients of exercise centers are healthier, on average, than the clients of hospitals and concluding that workout coaches should take over from doctors. Public tasks are different, and mostly harder.

At the same time, to be sure, it would be perverse to reject privatization simply because some enthusiasts front hollow arguments in its favor. Even for those who believe in government—perhaps *especially* for those who believe in government—any opportunity to serve the public interest more expeditiously warrants respectful appraisal. And delegating tasks to profit-seekers *can* make collective action more efficient when contracts are clearly written and fairly enforced, and when suppliers' efforts to affect the public agenda can be bridled.

The privatization debate would more fruitfully center on hammer-and-tongs technical and economic studies to identify public tasks that can be delegated to business, followed by repeated rounds of contractual architecture to bind suppliers firmly to the public purpose. But ideological romance, not dull analysis, is the current fashion. George Bush is less smitten than his predecessor with the ideal of privateness *per se*, but is at least as inclined by temperament, and rather more sorely tempted by the urgency of his predicament, to lunge for quick fixes whose costs come later, or covertly, or confusingly. Privatization is thus apt to become one more bottle in a medicine cabinet full of fiscal patent remedies that promise cures but end up useless, addictive, and subtly destructive.

The problem with romantics, of course, is that they are easy prey for cynics. This is perhaps most poignantly clear at the Department of Housing and Urban Development, the federal government's privatization pacesetter in the Reagan years, where insouciant supervision let the dark side of the profit motive surge to the fore. The Department of Energy, similarly, turned America's nuclear weapons production over almost entirely to private contractors who escaped accountability so completely that they were able to bill one part of government to pay civil fines and criminal penalties levied by other parts. At the state and local level, there are opportunistic (and effective) pressures to privatize precisely the wrong functions—those that are hardest to define and evaluate, least amenable to ongoing competition, or most tied up with collective functions that cannnot be delegated. Jails and prisons are the most egregious examples. Local power and water utilities are not far behind.

Like fire in an earlier era of human history, the profit motive is a prodigious source of potential good that can be devastating when applied heedlessly. Much of the East is painfully thawing out from an epoch of tragically smothering this force. Patches of the West, meanwhile—the savings and loan industry, the victims of the drug trade—are smoldering consequences of profit-seeking that slipped free of its social constraints. It would be a shame to shun all opportunities for applying private energies to public tasks. With so many urgent, unmet common needs, America can use all the efficiency it can get. But the politics of the dawning decade ill equip us to identify the private sector's rightful public roles.

References

Bane, M.J., and D. Ellwood. 1985. "Slipping in and out of Poverty." Unpublished discussion draft, Cambridge, MA, August.

Bennett, J.T., and M.H. Johnson. 1979. "Public versus Private Provision of Collective Goods and Services: Garbage Collection Revisited." *Public Choice* 34 (page numbers unavailable).

Borus, M.E. 1979. *Measuring the Impact of Employment-Related Social Programs.* Kalamazoo, MI: W.E. Upjohn Institute.

Bovard, J. 1986. "The Failure of Federal Job Training." Cato Institute Policy Analysis Paper, Washington, DC, August.

Cubbin, J., S. Domberger, and S. Meadowcroft. 1987. "Competitive Tendering and Refuse Collection: Identifying the Sources of Efficiency Gains." *Fiscal Studies* (August) Page numbers unavailable.

Donahue, J.D. 1989. *The Privatization Decision: Public Ends, Private Means.* New York: Basic Books.

Kemper, P., and J.M. Quigley. 1976. *The Economics of Refuse Collection.* Cambridge, MA: Ballinger.

Lillard, L.A., and H.W. Tan. 1986. *Private Sector Training.* Santa Monica, CA: Rand Corporation.

McDavid, J.C. 1985. "The Canadian Experience with Privatizing Residential Solid Waste Collection Services." *Public Administration Review* 45: (page numbers unavailable).

Orfield, G. et al. 1986. *Job Training under the New Federalism.* Chicago: Illinois Unemployment and Job Training Research Project, University of Chicago.

Reagan, R.W. 1982. *Public Papers of Ronald Reagan,* vol. 2. Washington, DC: U.S. Government Printing Office.

Savas, E.S. 1977. "Policy Analysis for Local Government: Public vs. Private Refuse Collection." *Policy Analysis* 3 (Winter).

Stevens, B.J. 1977. "Scale, Market Structure, and the Cost of Refuse Collection." *Review of Economics and Statistics* 60 (March).

Stevens, B.J. et al. 1984. *Delivering Municipal Services Efficiently.* Washington, DC: HUD Office of Policy Development and Research, June.

U.S. Department of Labor, Bureau of Labor Statistics. 1985. *How Workers Get Their Training.* Washington, DC: U.S. Government Printing Office, February.

U.S. General Accounting Office. 1981. "GSA's Cleaning Costs Are Needlessly Higher than in the Private Sector." Washington, DC: U.S. Government Printing Office, August.

———. 1985a. "DOD Functions Contracted out under OMB Circular A–76: Contract Cost Increases and the Effects on Federal Employees." Wasihngton, DC: GAO, April.

———. 1985b. "The Job Training Partnership Act: An Analysis of Support Cost Limits and Participant Characteristics." Washington, DC: GAO, November.

———. 1988. "Job Training Partnership Act: Participants, Services, and Outcomes." Washington, DC: GAO, September.

Walker, G. et al. 1986. *JTPA: Impelmentation and Performance,* New York: Grinker-Walker and Associates.

Young, D. 1972. *How Shall We Collect the Garbage?* Washington, DC: Urban Institute Press.

9

Klaus Nielsen and Ove K. Pedersen

From the Mixed Economy to the Negotiated Economy: The Scandinavian Countries

The Scandinavian countries have not only developed from a market economy to a mixed economy, but have experienced important trends that might be interpreted as a development from a mixed to a negotiated economy. The concept of the negotiated economy is no doubt rather unknown outside of Scandinavia, although others have expressed similar concepts (Devine, 1988; Moore and Booth, 1989). The expression was coined about ten years ago in connection with a lengthy and ambitious Norwegian public investigation that sought to uncover the power relations in modern Norwegian society (Hernes, 1979; NOU, 1982). Since then, theoretical discussions have taken place and efforts have been made to apply this concept in empirical studies of the different Scandinavian countries (Nielsen and Pedersen, 1988, 1989a; Berrefjord and Nore, 1988; Midttun, 1988; Pestoff, 1988a, 1988b).

In our view, the "negotiated economy" approach is a promising new field of inquiry even if it is still in need of a coherent body of concepts and theories. In this paper we present some general theoretical considerations related to all the Scandinavian countries.

The Approach and the Model

Negotiation: An Instrument for Decision Making

In the Scandinavian countries negotiations are widely used as instruments for decision making in relation to both allocation as well as (re)distribution. The classical example is the labor market. Wages, working hours, and other conditions of work are generally determined neither by individual market agents nor by legislation, but rather through institutionalized negotiations between the collective organizations of the agents. Furthermore, large investment projects are normally accompanied by negotiations between private firms and public authorities about infrastructure, sharing of risk, etc. Either institutionalized or informal negotiations precede decision making in many different parts of the economy.

Negotiation appears as an appropriate instrument in many different situations. It can be a preferable instrument in cases of conflicts of interest, especially when none of the involved parties has full control of the implementation and/or any possibility of exit. Compromise and agreement achieved by means of negotiation is an established method to handle such situations.

But negotiation is not only an instrument to resolve conflicts between opposing interests. It is also an instrument for achieving mutual understanding. Thus, it is not only an instrumental technique for decision making; it also involves communication, compromising, and achieving a consensus.

Certainly, negotiation is just one of many instruments for collective decision making. The classical instruments are the price mechanism, voting, and (bureaucratic) rules—connected to the ideal-type conceptions of the market, the democracy, and the bureaucracy. Neither the economy nor the political institutions, however, function in accordance with the ideal-type prescriptions. A mixture of many different types of instruments characterizes both the economic and the political sphere in all modern societies. This mixture is often rearranged. The instruments might interact in a supplementary way but they might also compete, disturb, and eventually supersede one another. No stable equilibrium mixture can be expected.

This instability is perhaps especially pertinent as far as the role of negotiations is concerned—also in the Scandinavian countries. In spite of a long tradition for negotiation-based decision making, history in general, and recent changes in particular, have shown that how, what, and when to negotiate, and even if one should negotiate at all, is always controversial.

Despite such controversy the importance of negotiations should not be ignored. No doubt this instrument is more prevalent in the small, open economies of Europe than elsewhere (Katzenstein, 1985), and this is probably even more true in the Scandinavian countries, which are characterized by homogeneous populations, relative symmetry of power in the capital-labor relationship, and a long history of compromise, integration, and mediation.

It is our assertion that the Scandinavian countries are increasingly assuming the character of a negotiated economy. An essential and even a growing part of the allocation of the productive resources as well as the (re)distribution of the output is determined neither on the market, by individual agents adapting to market changes, nor through autonomous decision making by public authorities. Instead, the decision-making process is conducted via institutionalized negotiations between the relevant interested agents, who reach binding decisions typically based on discursive, political, or moral imperatives rather than on threats and economic incentives, even if such threats and rewards as well as persuasive measures might be essential elements of the framework that surrounds the negotiations.

The Negotiated Economy: A Model

The negotiated economy is the result of a long process characterized by the development of a multitude of institutions and interinstitutional networks—formal and informal. It is neither a coherent system nor the effect of some grand design. The negotiated economy has been constituted in an organic way by the contributions of many different actors with diverse and often short-term motivations. No streamlined or ideal-type structure can be identified. On the contrary, if we look at the economic structure as a whole, we see a muddy mixture of features from the market economy, the mixed economy, and the negotiated economy. But, we also see a general long-term trend in the direction of a negotiated economy, and rather advanced states of such a structure have developed in important sectors of the economy. The following model identifies the characteristics of the *pure* negotiated economy.

The negotiated economy is much more than an instrument for decision making and the actual negotiations that take place around a negotiating table. These elements are parts of the overall structure of the negotiated economy encompassing the normative and institutional framework as well.

The overall structure and the comprehensive process are sketched in Figure 9.1. On the left is not only the instrument but also the institutional arrangements developed above, around, or in connection with the actual application of negotiation as an instrument for decision making. On the right is an illustration of the comprehensive societal process where the events around the negotiation table constitute just one instance—heavily influenced by the other processual links. It is impossible to understand the function of the negotiated economy unless one analyzes the overall structure and the total process. The application of the instrument in actual decision making should not be seen as an isolated event.

The five institutions listed on the left in Figure 9.1 cover different functions within the negotiated economy. They support the application of negotiation as an instrument, and they complement each other. They might be considered cogwheels in the machinery of the negotiated economy.

Some of the institutions attempt to mobilize mutual understanding of the socioeconomic situation, which functions as an ideological (normative) framework for the negotiations. We call this the socioeconomic ideology. Within this normative framework the involved parties engage in institutionalized negotiation games developing compromises on themes and procedures for the negotiations. Then in some other institutions *the roundtable negotiations* take place on the basis of the agreed-upon themes and procedures.

The activities taking place around the negotiation table—which may or may not physically exist—are integrated into the overall structure of the negotiated

Figure 9.1. **A Model of a Pure Negotiated Economy**

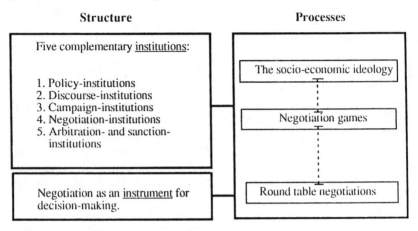

economy. The roundtable negotiations are just one link in a comprehensive process.

This sketch is, of course, a model rather than an actual description. In some parts of the economy, a negotiated economy with all the above characteristics has developed through a long historical process. In other areas only a part of the structure exists while some others even appear relatively unaffected by this development.

The Negotiated Economy: A Power Struggle

The negotiated economy is characterized by constant struggle and conflict at all levels, while simultaneously, mutual understanding is mobilized and compromises are established between the conflicting parties.

The parties communicate, but they also struggle about the formulation and transformation of socioeconomic experience into perceived problems, ends, and alternative means. In this way the political agenda is formed around an agreed-upon conception of the society at a given point of time. The preferences and expectations of the societal agents cannot be assumed to be given; they are constantly being formed through such an institutionalized struggle—and institutionalized communication.

In a similar way the procedures and criteria for decision making cannot be assumed to be given. There is constant struggle about the formation and change of institutions. On the other hand, both the discursive and the institutional results of the ongoing process constitute a framework for behavior with more or less balanced power relations between the parties. In other words, the agents struggle not only about the results of the actual negotiations, they are also engaged in conflict—and communication—about the interpretation and the selection of problems, means, and ends. Furthermore, they struggle about where and how to negotiate about what. A power struggle is going on about discursive and institutional objectives as well as about the outcome of actual negotiations. Although the overall structure of the negotiated economy appears rather stable, it is for obvious reasons surrounded by controversy and challenged by alternative arrangements.

The neoliberal critique of the negotiated economy maintains that negotiations should be replaced by market transactions because of a supposed rigidity and inefficiency of the negotiated economy brought about by the influence of the interest organizations. Another critique, coming from an ideal-type democratic position, asserts that negotiations should be replaced by voting in parliament, which is considered the only legitimate representational form of popular rule.

Others defend the negotiated economy as a smooth and efficient procedure that guarantees the legitimacy of the decisions and the loyalty and consent of the involved parties in the process of implementation that is often decisive. According to this position, many conflicts will remain unresolved if the parties behave in an uncoordinated way. Negotiations prior to decision making are expected to prevent this from happening.

However, neither the critics nor those who sympathize with the reality of the negotiated economy seem to judge its functions from a fully satisfying conception of it. They often restrict themselves to an evaluation of the events around or closely connected to the negotiation table. They do not couple these with the processes that produce the discursive and institutional framework for negotiations. Were this done, the question of the efficiency of the negotiated economy would appear much more complex as quite different forms of rationality were combined. We shall return to this below.

From the Mixed Economy to the Negotiated Economy

The Ideal of the Mixed Economy

The concept of the mixed economy is well known and widely used, although there is still no well-established definition. It has mainly been used to distinguish the Western industrialized countries in the period after World War II from societies with all-embracing market mechanisms and from societies dominated by central planning and state ownership of the means of production. In the mixed economies, neither the market nor the state is completely dominant. On the contrary, a balanced relationship is assumed to exist (Shonfield, 1984). Prices and supplies of goods and services are supposed to be largely determined by market processes. At the same time, the state and its agencies are supposed to have large capacities for intervention to secure objectives that the market would not achieve automatically.

The mixed economy might be defined as a society composed of various systems of allocation (market, state, organizations, collectives, etc.). While this is not wrong *per se,* in our view it is a rather inappropriate description, for according to this definition, one should be able to identify no other alternatives to mixed economies than pure ideal-type market economies or command economies. Accordingly, all presently existing societies might be characterized as mixed economies—and all possible future forms might be covered by this label too.

We consider it more appropriate to define the concept of the mixed economy in a stricter and narrower way, for three reasons: first, we wish to identify the concept with the specific historical background for its propagation; second, we want the definition to correspond to the dominant conceptions of the ideal function of the mixed economy; and third, we wish to specify the concept in such a way as to make it possible to identify recent divergent trends. Accordingly, we wish to stress an important feature of the mixed economy that is omitted from the above definition: this is the clear-cut division of labor between market and state—decisions are made *either* by autonomous market agents *or* by equally autonomous state bodies. There is not only a balanced mix of state and market but also a clear distinction between the areas covered by the authority of the sovereign state and areas where market agents are supposed to have full autonomy. All the important social and institutional innovations of the mixed economy, such as demand management and the welfare state, are characterized by such a clear-cut division of labor.

The ideal of the mixed economy has been formulated in Keynesian macroeconomics and, first of all, in economic welfare theory (Tinbergen, 1963), according to which optimality is secured if the resources are allocated through the market mechanism provided the nonexistence of market failure. In case of market failure, however, intervention of the state is required: that is, *either* allocation of resources by voluntary interaction of market agents, or corrective measures taken by a sovereign state. No direct cooperation is needed. A carefully designed division of labor is considered sufficient.

No society corresponds fully to this ideal of the mixed economy. Nevertheless, it seems obvious that following the 1930s and especially in the first decades after World War II a development in the direction of a mixed economy took place in all the Western industrialized economies. It is also obvious, however, that more recent developments diverge from this trend. It has become still more difficult to designate the line of demarcation between market and state. Economic decisions are no longer either private or public. Now, a growing part of the allocation of resources is determined neither on the market by individual agents adapting to market changes, nor through decision making by sovereign public authorities. Instead, the decision making is conducted via institutionalized negotiations between various autonomous private, semipublic, and public agents. The state delegates powers and participates in decision-making processes without full authority. Also, the discretion of private agents is restrained by the results of the negotiations. Different rationalities are combined, and private and collective interests are mixed as agents engage in direct cooperation.

The Negotiated Economy: A Definition

There are different ways to characterize these recent features and different ways to evaluate their implications. In our view, they represent a transition from a mixed economy in the direction of a negotiated economy. We take the term "negotiated economy" to mean a structuring of society where an essential part of the allocation of resources is conducted through institutionalized negotiations between independent decision-making centers in state, organizations, and/or corporations. Unlike decisions made by public authorities, negotiation-based economic decisions are reached on the basis of interaction between *independent* agents, and the relevant public authority is just one of several participants. Unlike authoritative decisions, negotiation-based economic decisions are usually not subject to the possible use of sanctions. They are typically based on discursive, political, or morally binding—rather than legally sanctioned—agreements. And unlike market decisions, which are made by individual agents each acting separately and on the basis of given preferences and resources, negotiation-based economic decisions are made through a process characterized by the deliberate shaping of preferences.

We do not assert that all economic resources in the Scandinavian countries are allocated and distributed in accordance with this ideal-type version of the negotiated economy. We do maintain, however, that we are experiencing a development away from a mixed economy in the direction of the negotiated economy as defined above. For instance, we get a mixed picture if we look at the determination of (various) prices. In some branches prices are determined by the market mechanism, with no interference by the state. Other branches are characterized by autonomous price determination by market agents coexisting with state regulation, taxation, or subsidizing, while still other prices (including free services) are set by public producers—all in accordance with the ideal of the mixed economy. Simultaneously, however, an essential—and growing—part of wages, prices, interest rates, and profit ratios is determined through the process of the negotiated economy.

Studying the Negotiated Economy

Institutional Analysis

In the negotiated economy decisions are made through institutionalized negotiations between the appointed agents who reach binding decisions based on discursive, political, and moral imperatives rather than formal contracts and legal sanctions. The behavior of the agents is regulated not by authoritative means but rather through normative forms of regulation, through incentives broader and more indirect than economic gains, and through measures intended to influence the preferences of the counterpart, his perception of the room for maneuver, and so on.

As a result of this process, two fundamental—and coherent—assumptions in economic theory appear problematic: (1) the assumption of given preferences; and (2) the assumption of given institutions.

In the negotiated economy the formation and manipulation of preferences must be perceived as a rationale for behavior. Attempting to influence the counterparts preferences is part of the behavior function of each agent. Systematic accumulation of experience, shaping of opinions, and influencing of attitudes is even to a considerable extent institutionalized in the policy, campaign, and discourse institutions.

Some economists have attempted to endogenize preferences (see Weizsäcker, 1984; Hirschman, 1982). These, however, deal with vastly less complex feedback processes than those referred to earlier. The conscious and systematic measures adopted to mold preferences and map *the negotiation space* through institutional action is omitted.

Traditional economic theory also ignores the problems and the effects of institutional change. This is not acceptable when studying the negotiated economy. The institutional setting is constantly changed and constitutes a dominant item on the political agenda. For this reason it is essential to study how the institutions of the negotiated economy have been established historically. Only through such endeavors can one recognize the dynamics and the functioning of this economic structure.

Institutional History

Most of the institutional innovations identified above with a negotiated economy did not begin in the Scandinavian countries until the end of the 1950s, but the institutional foundation for these innovations was established long before then. In all the Scandinavian countries the tradition of institutionalized class cooperation is very strong. In Denmark this tradition dates back to the turn of the century. A "general agreement" was made between organized labor and capital as early as 1899. About thirty-five to forty years later the same development occurred in Sweden (1938) and Norway (1935). As a result we experienced a profound civilizing of the class confrontation. This civilization is in our view a decisive premise for the development of a negotiated economy in the Scandinavian countries. We distinguish four phases:

1. In the first phase, the *juridification* of class relations, the peak organizations on the labor market entered into general agreements specifying the rights and duties of each party but also including acceptance of one another's legitimate existence. Furthermore, the organizations were given autonomous rights and obligations vis-à-vis their members. The organizations were thus turned into autonomous legal subjects.

2. Juridification was followed by a phase of *institutionalization*. A highly complex pattern emerged. Private and semipublic as well as public institutions were established in order to regulate the relations between the two main classes.

3. The next phase was one of *integration* of the organizations into the public administration. This actually implied a transfer of public authority to the organizations, enabling these to formulate policies and make authoritative decisions in connection with the labor market.

4. As a result of the lengthy and in-depth civilizing of class conflict, public authority has been delegated to many different types of institutions where organizations are represented and thus generally dispersed. Public authority became multicentered, thereby creating coordination problems. From the end of the 1950s until today various problems have been formulated as coordination problems. This started a fourth phase of innovative institutionalization: *the coordination of decision making through discursive and institutional means.*

The Socioeconomic Frame of Meaning

The existence and the autonomy of the above-mentioned institutions were accepted as a basic premise making coordination by legal administrative means impossible. Instead, a strategy for ideological or discursive coordination was formulated and new institutions were erected to facilitate such coordination.

The main objective in this process was the formulation and propagation of a socioeconomic ideology: *the socioeconomic frame of meaning.* This is a general conception of the relationships between public administration, organizations, corporations, and households as part of an economic *organism.* The health of this organism is not automatically established. It is only created if the different agents observe a normative injunction to act in the interests of the society as perceived through the socioeconomic frame of meaning. This incentive is being mobilized through many new institutions designed for this purpose. These institutions formulate problems and designate ends, means, and strategies in various policy fields within the overall, normative socioeconomic frame of meaning.

In particular, wages—or incomes—policy and public expenditure policy have been formulated and propagated within the socioeconomic frame of meaning. Not all policy areas have been subjected to this socioeconomic ideological conception, and the process of the negotiated economy has certainly not reached the same stage of development in all areas of potential application. Nonetheless, we may justify our reference to a general trend by asserting that macroeconomic policy is increasingly assuming these contours, and that similar although embryonic tendencies can be shown to exist in a number of areas of policy.

Institutional Arrangements

Since the end of the 1950s, five new types of institutions have developed:

1. *Policy institutions* are public commissions and committees—usually composed along corporative lines—to formulate problems and to recommend steps to be taken.

2. *Campaign institutions* are set up by interest organizations, corporations, public authorities, or even along corporative lines in an attempt to formulate and propagate specific interpretations of problems and specific solutions in order to influence the political agenda.

3. *Discourse institutions* are scientific or other institutions that test the consistency of the dominant conceptions and try to reformulate these into analytically coherent codes of languages.

4. *Negotiation institutions* are either *ad hoc* or permanent bodies—usually consisting of two or three parties—to outline frameworks and timetables and to reach concrete agreements by means of negotiations.

5. *Arbitration and sanction institutions* are private or semipublic institutions that are supposed to deal with disputes and to impose sanctions in case of violation of agreements.

These institutions are complementary; they fulfill mutually dependent functions within a coherent process. Actually existing institutions might cover more than one function. This is the case, for instance, with the economic secretariats of the budget departments, which function simultaneously as campaign and as discourse institutions.

The five institutions probably exist to some extent in all the Western European countries. They seem to follow from institutionalized class cooperation everywhere. It is not their mere existence that distinguishes the Scandinavian countries in this context. It is rather their elaboration and their complementariness that have made possible a specific institutional process: the negotiated economy:

• The formation of new institutions has made it possible to formulate and propagate a specific ideological conception (the socioeconomic frame of meaning) as a normative frame of reference.

• Other new institutions systematize and develop this ideological conception to constitute a rationale for individual and collective behavior.

• Institutions mobilize and produce an elite (and to a certain extent, also a popular) consensus about how to connect individual interests and socioeconomic objectives.

• Within the normative framework dictated by the socioeconomic ideology and the institutional restrictions imposed by general procedures and rules, a complex form of negotiation game is set into motion.

• The specific procedures and rules established via negotiation games ensure compromises and agreements in concrete negotiations between independent agents with opposite interests.

A Process of Institutional Learning

The negotiated economy is also a learning process; in an ongoing process, objectives are reformulated, experience with old means is evaluated, and alternative means are formulated. This has been made possible precisely through the formation of the numerous policy, campaign, and discourse institutions. The continuous campaigning and reformulation of discourses and problems is conducted not merely by proposing a particular interpretation of the current economic situation on the political agenda; it also creates the semantic frame of reference and the discursive environment for connecting individual agency and socioeconomic objectives.

The very act of recording the experience gained necessarily involves constant reinterpretation and reformulation. Forecasts are tested and maybe falsified. Project calculations are modified. The correlation between phenomena is confirmed or denied. Earlier approaches to problems or solutions already tried are labeled invalid or obsolete. Alternative forecasts and calculations are produced. As a result, new problems are formulated, alternative solutions are discovered, and new terms and conceptual contexts are created. The socioeconomic frame of meaning is constantly being reformulated as a rationale for the understanding of society's relationships, problems, and patterns of development.

This process is constantly evolving in the Scandinavian countries. By no means a natural necessity, such a learning process follows from the systematic and continuous verbalization of the various conflicts of interests. It follows from the fact that the various institutions are not only capable but also are forced to engage in the process. This is so not only because the socioeconomic development constantly produces evidence to confirm or invalidate earlier forecasts and assumed relationships, but also because of the impossibility of avoiding a constant verbal confrontation with institutions representing opposing interests. If they want to influence the political agenda, the various participants in this confrontation are forced to analyze, comment, and criticize the data, the models, the formulated problems, and the proposed solutions put forward by the other participants.

The Negotiated Economy and Social Science Dogmas

A Challenge to Ideal-type Conceptions

The emergent reality of the negotiated economy implies challenges to the dominant ideas within economic as well as political theory. Within economic theory, the debate is still dominated by the ideal types of either the market economy or the mixed economy. Within political theory, the constitutional interpretation of the distinction between the authority of the sovereign state and civil society still seems to dominate. In addition, theories of corporatism have also gained prominence. However, none of these dominant theoretical perspectives seems appropriate in relation to the negotiated economy.

Economic Theory

In most economic theory, allocation of resources is evaluated either in relation to the market ideal of perfect competition or in relation to the ideal of a perfect and sharp demarcation between autonomous action by market agents and supplementary or corrective measures taken by a sovereign state. The dominance of these ideals of either the market economy or the mixed economy results in blindness in relation to the coherence and the specific rationality of the negotiated economy.

The development of economic theory in the last decade does not even seem to move in that direction. Instead we have seen a lot of criticism of the established theories of the mixed economy (Keynesianism, welfare theory) based on the ideal of the market economy. For instance, the inherent assumptions concerning the capacity and the necessity for stabilization policy has been criticized by proponents of monetarism and new classical macroeconomics. Also, advocates of public choice theory, which focuses on various government failures, have criticized the implicit assumption in welfare theory concerning the capacity of the state for correction of market failures. Even the necessity for correcting perceived market failures has been denied by property rights theory, which suggests massive extension and careful specification of private property rights as a more effective alternative.

One might argue that a whole new branch of theory has been developed to analyze these phenomena within the paradigm of traditional economic theory. The implications of negotiations or bargaining in economic life are analyzed by means of formalized bargaining theory. Negotiations are seen as strategic games and analyzed with a game-theory framework. Even if these contributions are no doubt helpful, their helpfulness is limited. In game theory, the participants, the preferences, the bundle of choices (the strategies), and the outcome (dependent on the chosen strategy) are all assumed to be *given,* rather than products of the game itself. This corresponds to the institutional reality of what we have called *roundtable negotiations.* It is not possible, however, to comprehend the processes of *the negotiation games,* let alone the total institutional process of the negotiated economy, by these analytical means.

As suggested above, two basic assumptions are challenged. Neither the institutional setting (including the definition of the participants and the strategies of the game) nor the preferences of the agents can be considered "given" in a profound theory of the negotiated economy. Part of the institutional setting is actually an outcome of *the negotiation game* rather than a given framework for action. Furthermore, the formation of meaning and the molding of preferences as a result of the formulation and propagation of the socioeconomic frame of meaning has critical implications concerning the assumption of given preferences. Of course, this assumption has been challenged by many sources, perhaps most prominently by the Carnegie School (Herbert Simon), most basically by cognitive psychology, and most articulately by Geoffrey Hodgson (1988). The inadequacy of the assumption of given preferences is certainly not restricted to the negotiated economy, but the necessity for an alternative is especially urgent, in this context.

It is not at all illegitimate or inconsistent to exclude the formation of preferences from the theoretical horizon, as is the case in traditional economic theory.

We maintain, however, that such an exclusion seems at least rather inappropriate in the reality of the negotiated economy, where choices and formation of preferences are integrated in one continuous process.

Neocorporatist Theory

Political science has produced many different theories about the relationship between state and organizations. The theoretical development has been dominated by two general traditions: pluralism and neocorporatism. During the last fifteen years there has been a trend—at least in Western Europe—away from pluralism to neocorporatism. Formerly, the political agents seeking to influence the political process were most often perceived as formally independent groups. In recent decades this tradition has been challenged by a perception of organizations as integrated in the political process in a stable, long-term manner, by institutional or other means.

The pluralist tradition originates from the so-called *group theory* (Greenstone, 1975), according to which political groups are seen as autonomous in relation to the political institutions. A clear distinction is supposed to exist between the political institutions (regulated through constitutional norms and principles) and the private organizations (regulated through statutory rules about membership and decision making).

This is challenged by the neocorporatist theories. At least three types of neocorporatist theories can be identified (Kastendiek, 1981):

• *Ideal-type theories:* corporatism is seen as an actual or potential mechanism at the systemic (the economy, the political system, or the social system) level.

• *Functional theories:* corporatism is seen as functional in relation to class domination and hegemony in the bourgeois state.

• *Institutional theories:* corporatism is seen as historical specific, concrete, and partial institutional arrangements.

Other theories stress the coordination of such specific, concrete, and partial arrangements. In the Scandinavian context, a lot of evidence concerning the creation of integrated policy fields within public administration has been produced by the Norwegian Power Study (Egeberg, Olsen, and Sætren, 1978). Other theories stress the importance of more loose and informal forms of coordination: institutional networks or just *networks* (Benson, 1981; Pedersen, 1988). Still other theories perceive the elements of the neocorporative structure as a comprehensive network of cooperation and conflict functioning as a generalized political exchange among the organized agents (Marin, 1985).

All those theories share certain features: they stress the stable and institutionalized character of the relationship between state and organizations. Furthermore, they assume that the political institutions and the private organizations are no longer separated by a clear-cut borderline; as a result new political processes and structures have developed that integrate the formerly separated parts.

The neocorporatist theories—especially the theory on generalized political exchange—resemble our approach. Such theories recognize the ensemble of institutional and discursive prerequisites for the emergence of political exchange and the institutional processes put in motion. They differ from our approach, however, in various ways. While neocorporatist theories focus on relations between organizations representing objective societal functions or interests, we stress that interests are created or formed by institutions. Generally, in addition to the existing institutional structures, we also stress the discursive aspects and the emerging institutional processes. This leads us to recognize the fluidity and instability of the specific neocorporative arrangements.

For these reasons we do not use the concept of neocorporatism. We distinguish between the concept of *institutional integration* to designate the concrete and partial structures developed through integration of organizations and the political system, and the concept of *the negotiated economy* to cover those forms of allocation and (re)distribution that have been developed through the coordination of decision making in autonomous centers in states, organizations, and corporations by institutional and discursive means. This analytical separation of the institutional structure and the coordination is meant to underscore the decisive argument that the negotiated economy is founded on a specific institutional history and on the emergence of specific measures for discursive coordination.

Formal Rationality and the Rule of Law

The institutional integration of public administration and private organizations contradicts the institutional conditions presupposed in the ideal legal conception of the rule of law. According to the rule of law, the state is the autonomous, hierarchically organized, internally power-balanced, but externally undifferentiated administrator of legalized compulsion. Limits are imposed on state intervention in civil society. These limits can be exceeded only on defined, specific, and *a priori* conditions. A space for individual and collective freedom of behavior is thus created. Modern law separates state and market and establishes the framework for instrumental behavior by free market agents.

Furthermore, according to the ideal, the public administration constitutes an entity. The administration's status as an entity is based on the minister's dual status as political leader and administrative head. The status as an entity is ensured through the hierarchical (superior/subordinate) structure—i.e., successive levels of competence and responsibility. In formal terms, the administration is at the same time subject to the requirement that the decisions it makes are sanctioned by legislation adopted by parliament.

Involvement or cooptation of the organizations and the creation of integrated policy fields within the public administration contradict the ideal conceptions. In this context the following features of the observed trend are significant:

- The number of institutions outside the ministers'—and thus parliament's—direct sphere of influence is increasing, as is the importance of such institutions. Authority has been dispersed. Various corporative institutions have been delegated legal authority.

• In such corporative institutions less emphasis is being placed on direct legal authorization for decisions made. The chain of legality has been lengthened and the so-called principle of legality has been diluted.

The integration of public administration and private organizations has resulted in the formation of a large number of administrative bodies that are more or less independent of the relevant minister(s). The political order has thus become multicentered, and the administrative structure less hierarchical. The boundaries between public authority and civil society are no longer distinct; encroachments on liberty are no longer based on defined, specific, and *a priori* rules.

At the same time, institutional networks are formed, destroying the entity of the administration and the principle of legality. Since networks are not subject to any jurisdiction, they do not have to play any subordinate role. A network, being a combination of public, semipublic, and private institutions, makes it impossible to distinguish the boundaries separating the public from the private sector. Here the legal limits are laid down in extremely complex combinations of public and private law. The boundaries between the state hierarchy and civil society do not exist. The rule of law has been shattered.

The integration of public administration and private organizations has produced features clearly different from those qualities of modern law that were, according to Max Weber, an expression of formal rationality. The ideal-type modern law is independent of morality and tradition. It is formal, value-free, and impersonal. It is abstract and general—i.e., not discriminating, not directed to special persons or groups. It is a coherent and systematic structure of established norms. It is formed by a legislative assembly following constitutional rules while the executive branch and the courts are obliged to follow formal and material rules in the administration and interpretation of the law. The ideal-type formal law enfranchises a civil society. It produces the necessary preconditions of an arena where individual agents are free to pursue individual ends through instrumental choices among alternative means, i.e., pure instrumental behavior by market agents.

The recent development is in sharp conflict with this ideal pattern. Actual law has no rationality independent of morality; it is not value-free. The formulation and propagation of the socioeconomic ideology has introduced a moral foundation in actual law:

• The ideological conception of the socioeconomic frame of meaning has forced all the major political as well as market agents to make moral or political choices. The socioeconomic frame of meaning has become a normative premise. All the various agents are obliged to relate to this conception. On the labor market, for instance, the peak organizations cannot avoid weighing socioeconomic considerations against the self-interests of their members when they engage in negotiations about collective agreements.

• Furthermore, this necessity of weighing different considerations is a built-in characteristic of the welfare state itself. Typically, welfare state law specifies ends and purposes and authorizes the executive power to make discretionary decisions while weighing different interests and considerations.

• Finally, the decision-making authority has been obliged to legitimize the actual decisions with normative arguments. It is no longer sufficient that a decision is formally correct; it must also be normatively reasonable.

Actual law has become more complex and indeed very different from the ideal-type image presented by Weber. As a result of the integration of public administration and private organization and the propagation of the socioeconomic ideology, actual law no longer produces the necessary preconditions for instrumentally rational behavior by market agents. On the contrary, it defines the conditions for more complex forms of rationality.

Rationality and Efficiency

The Negotiated Economy—A Combination of
Different Forms of Rationality

The emergence of the negotiated economy has produced a new context for rational behavior. We argue that the specific process of the negotiated economy produces a combination of different forms of rationality in conflict with the conceptions of the formal rationality of law and the instrumental rationality assumed in traditional economic theory.

In traditional economic theory, agents are assumed to be rational in a certain sense. They are supposed to choose the best possible means in relation to the predetermined goals. This assumed rationality is clearly dependent on the assumptions of given institutions and given preferences. When preferences (or ends) and the institutional surroundings can be considered given, it is possible to deduce the economic behavior of the agent as a logical effect of the assumed means-end rationality. This is not so, however, if molding of preferences cannot be segregated from choices. It seems appropriate to abandon the traditional assumption of instrumental rationality in recognition of the fact that in the negotiated economy, this specific form of rationality is interwoven with other forms of rationality connected to discursive processes and formation of meaning.

In one unbroken process the agents are confronted with different demands. They have to act *rational* in different ways. In roundtable negotiations they have to choose those means of action that are the most rational in relation to their ends within a given institutional framework. In negotiation games they also have to choose the most rational means in relation to their ends with the institutional framework as the product, rather than the precondition. Simultaneously, they have to act rationally in the process of formulation and propagation of the socioeconomic frame of meaning.

However, the different stages of the process of the negotiated economy are only partly separated in time and space. Accordingly, the agents are confronted with rather complex criteria for action in almost every instance of (negotiation) interaction. They are integrated parts of a process characterized by systematic and institutional interpretation of the situation, formation of meaning, and molding of preferences. Often this takes place by means of direct verbal communication between the agents. Accordingly, unambiguous behavioral conditions, stable institutional frames, and given preferences cannot be assumed to exist.

The behavior of the agents appears irrational when judged from an ordinary instrumental point of view. However, according to Etzioni "means selected to realize goals are often chosen partially or solely on normative-affected grounds and not on the bases of logical/empirical considerations" (Etzioni, 1988, p. 14). This is no doubt generally true. In the negotiated economy, however, this may be even more evident because of the institutionalization of the normative-affective aspects of the decision-making process.

The different forms of rationality present in the negotiated economy also resemble the forms identified by Hargreaves-Heap (1989) in *Rationality in Economics*. Hargreaves-Heap distinguishes three forms: in addition to "instrumental" rationality, he mentions "procedural" rationality and "expressive" rationality. Procedural rationality is not directly related to any ends. On the contrary, the rationality of behavior is defined by the procedure or the means chosen. On the other hand, expressive rationality has nothing to do with any means. The rationality is connected to the process of formulating or finding ends. The formulation and propagation of the socioeconomic frame of meaning introduces elements of procedural as well as expressive rationality in the negotiated economy.

The specific combination of rationality forms can also be conceived through the concepts of Habermas (1982), who also identifies three forms: "instrumental," "strategic," and "communicative" rationality. While instrumental and strategic rationality are concerned with results and efficiency, communicative rationality is concerned with mutual understanding and truth. The distinction between instrumental and strategic rationality is due to the difference between the decision-making environment in the two situations. If the environment is *objective*—i.e., independent of the behavior of the agent—then Habermas talks of instrumental rationality. If it is social—i.e., consists of social agents who are dependent on the behavior of other agents—then he talks of strategic rationality.

While roundtable negotiations constitute situations of instrumental (and strategic) rationality, and negotiation games seem to embody strategic rationality, the socioeconomic ideology is then a result of a process characterized by communicative rationality.

The concept of communicative rationality is perhaps the most interesting in this context. Habermas uses the concept in a prescriptive way. He imagines an idealized situation of communication without power-related differences as far as admittance and influence are concerned. The interaction (the communication) is considered rational if the participants are free and equal, if they openly and publicly discuss common interests in order to achieve mutual understanding about disputed normative matters.

The formulation and propagation of the socioeconomic frame of meaning through policy, campaign, and discourse institutions resemble such discursive processes as sketched above. However, they are also different from the imagined idealized communicative situation.

The interaction between the involved parties in the above-mentioned institutions is not free from power-related constraints. Nor is it free from instrumental and strategic considerations. The campaign institutions, for instance, are meant to influence the political agenda and the preferences of the other participants in the discursive process. They engage in a conflict between different conceptions based on different interests.

Fundamentally, however, several features of the process bear resemblance to the ideal-type communicative rationality. Also, here the participants attempt, by means of verbal interaction in a continuous process of critique and self-critique, to coordinate different conceptions into a mutual understanding of the current situation with its alternatives and constraints. Furthermore, the agents have to live up to certain legitimacy requirements in order to be accepted as legitimate participants in the discursive process. These requirements are not fundamentally different from the universal requirements to participants in ideal-type communication as formulated by Habermas. In the discursive process concerning the socioeconomic frame of meaning, the involved parties are obliged to fulfill the following requirements:

• The arguments must be normatively correct, viewed in relation to existing value perceptions of future developments of society.

• They must be technically credible, in relation to the prevailing professional standards and norms.

• They must be cognitively true, in relation to the cognitive conception of the reality the frame of meaning theoretically seeks to reflect.

Irrational Man and Rational Society?

In our discussion above the concept of rationality was attached to individual behavior. The transformed context for rational individual behavior was explained as an effect of the emergence of the negotiated economy. In this last section we shall briefly approach the concept of rationality at the systemic level instead.

Is the negotiated economy an efficient way of allocating and (re)distributing the resources of society? From the point of view of a traditional economist, the answer is in the negative. Johansen concludes the following about what he called "the bargaining society":

> Bargaining will often be an inefficient decision procedure in the sense that it tends to distort the information basis for decisions, it tends to use or waste

resources in the process, particularly delay decisions for reasons which are not technically necessary, it will more or less frequently lead to breakdown and failure to realize the potential gains, and threats will sometimes be carried out. [Johansen, 1979, p. 23]

If one assumes instrumentally (or strategically) rational agents and uses the criterion of Pareto optimality, Johansen's conclusions appear well founded. No doubt, bargaining processes will rarely lead to Pareto-optimal allocation if one systematically omits the specific rationality of the communicative process.

The rationality of a *system* must also be related to the discursive processes needed to achieve mutual understanding of a normative frame of meaning. Certain arrangements might be considered irrational or wasteful when judged from the traditional criterion of efficiency. They might, however, appear rational as a means to achieve mutual understanding.

Unfortunately, we are only able to reformulate the problem of efficiency and to reject the answers given by such authors as Johansen and by formalized bargaining and game theory. We are, of course, not able to present any new composite concept of efficiency.

Other observations, however, confirm the hypothesis that inefficiency need not be an inescapable effect of a negotiated economy. According to Katzenstein (1985) the process of the negotiated economy (although Katzenstein does not use that term) seems to be at least part of the reason for the smooth and relatively successful process of adapting to world market changes that characterizes small states in Western Europe including the Scandinavian countries. These qualities of the Scandinavian countries still seem to be intact (Nielsen and Pedersen, 1989b), although the present formation of a new technoeconomic paradigm poses new and more difficult challenges to the small Scandinavian countries (Mjøset, 1989).

In general, flexible adjustment in Scandinavia seems to depend on its coexistence with political stability (Nielsen, 1989). In case of relative political instability the capacity for flexible adjustment of resources is hampered. The structure of the negotiated economy has produced a process that has shown capacity for learning and adjustment—although not always as fast as some might wish.

It seems at least justified, however, to reformulate the problem posed by Barry and Hardin (1982), who identified the paradox of "the rational man and the irrational society"—because of the prevalence of such situations as described by the "prisoners' dilemma" and "the impossibility theorem." Perhaps individual behavior that appears irrational by traditional standards might produce a rational society within the structure of the negotiated economy.

References

Barry, B. and R. Hardin. 1982. *Rational Man and Irrational Society.* Beverly Hills: Sage.
Benson, J.K. 1981. *Networks and Policy Sectors: A Framework for Extending Interorganizational Analysis.* Columbia: University of Michigan.

Berrefjord, O. 1990. "Economically Motivated Decisions and the Behaviour of Firms in a Negotiated Economy." Paper presented at the second Annual International Conference on Socioeconomics, Washington, DC, March 16–18.

Berrefjord, O. and P. Nore. 1988. "Political and Economic Policy Planning on a National Level—Exorcism and Laws of Gravity." *Scandinavian Political Studies* 2:103–14.

Devine, P. 1988. *Democracy and Economic Planning.* London: Polity Press.

Egeberg, M., J.P. Olsen, and H. Sætren. 1978. Organisasjonssamfunnet og den segmenterte stat. In J.P. Olsen, ed., *Politisk Organisering.* Oslo: Universitetsforlaget.

Etzioni, A. 1988. *The Moral Dimension: Towards a New Economics.* New York: Free Press.

Greenstone, J.D. 1975. "Group Theories." In F.C. Greenstein, and W.P. Nelson, eds., *Handbook of Political Science,* vol 2. Reading, MA: Addison-Wesley.

Habermas, J. 1982. *Theorie des Kommunikativen Handelns,* vol. 1 and 2. Frankfurt am Main: Suhrkamp.

Hargreaves-Heap, S. 1989. *Rationality in Economics.* London: Basil Blackwell.

Hernes, G., ed. 1979. *Forhandlingsøkonomi og blandingsadministrasjon.* Oslo: Universitetsforlaget.

Hirschman, A. 1982. *Shifting Involvements. Private Interests and Public Action.* Oxford: Martin Robertson.

Hodgson, G. 1988. *Economics and Institutions.* London: Polity Press.

Johansen, L. 1979. "The Bargaining Society and the Inefficiency of Bargaining." *Kyklos* 3:497–522.

Kastendiek, H. 1981. "Die Selbstblokierung der Korporatismusdiskussion." In U.V. Alemann and R.G. Heinze, eds., *Korporativer Staat und Korporatismus: Dimensionen der Neokorporatismus-diskussion.* Frankfurt am Main: Suhrkamp.

Katzenstein, P. 1985. *Small States in World Markets. Industrial Policy in Europe.* Ithaca, NY: Cornell University Press.

Marin, B. 1985. *Generalized Political Exchange.* EUI, no. 85/190. Florence: European University Institute.

Midttun, A. 1988. "The Negotiated Political Economy of a Heavy Industrial Sector: The Norwegian Hydropower Complex in the 1970s and 1980s." *Scandinavian Political Studies* 2:115–43.

Mjøset, L. 1989. "Norway's Full-Employment Oil-Economy—Flexible Adjustment or Paralysing Rigidities?" *Scandinavian Political Studies* 4:313–41.

Moore, C., and S. Booth, 1989. *Managing Competition: Meso-Corporatism, Pluralism and the Negotiated Order in Scotland.* Oxford: Clarendon Press.

Nielsen, K. 1989. "Flexible Adjustment and Political Stability." *Scandinavian Political Studies* 4:297–312.

Nielsen, K., and O.K. Pedersen. 1988. "The Negotiated Economy. Ideal and History." *Scandinavian Political Studies* 2:79–101.

———, eds. 1989a. *Forhandlingsøkonomi i Norden.* Copenhagen: Jurist- og Økonomforbundets Forlag.

———. 1989b. "Is Small Still Flexible?—An Evaluation of Recent Trends in Danish Politics." *Scandinavian Political Studies* 4:343–71.

NOU [Norwegian Official Report]. 1982. *Maktutredningen. Slutrapport.* Oslo: 1982:3.

Pedersen, O.K. 1988. "Den sønderdelte stat. Om interesseorganisationernes integration i den offentlige forvaltning og effekterne heraf." *Statsvetenskaplig Tidskrift* 3:259–78.

———. 1990. "Learning Processes and the Game of Negotiation. Wage Formation and Negotiated Economy in Denmark." Paper presented at the Second Annual International Conference on Socio-Economics, Washington, DC, March 16–18, and at the Seventh International Conference of Europeanists, Washington, DC, March 23–25.

Pestoff, V. 1988a. "Joint Regulation, Meso-Games and Political Exchange in Swedish Industrial Relations." In B. Marin and A. Pizzorno, eds., *Generalized Political Exchange*. New York: Walter de Gruyter.

———. 1988b. "Exit, Voice and Collective Action in Swedish Consumer Policy." *Journal of Consumer Policy* 1:1–27.

———. 1990. "Organizational Participation and Negotiations in Swedish Consumer Policy." Paper presented at the Second Annual International Conference on Socio-Economics, Washington, DC, March 16–18, and at the Seventh International Conference of Europeanists, Washington, DC, March 23–25.

Shonfield, A. 1984. *In Defence of the Mixed Economy*. Oxford: Oxford University Press.

Tinbergen, J. 1963. "The Organization of the Economy in the Service of Man—A General Review." *Annals of Public and Cooperative Economy* 34, 96–109.

Weizsäcker, C.V. 1984. "The Influence on Property Rights of Tastes." *Journal of Institutional and Theoretical Economics* 1:90–95.

4

The Moral Dimension
of the Firm

10

Norman E. Bowie

The Firm as a Moral Community

Amitai Etzioni (1988) advocates a new paradigm for understanding the economic actor. Etzioni's paradigm is based on deontological moral theory, according to which people not only seek pleasure but they also do their duty; they are not only concerned about themselves, they are concerned about their impact on others. Sometimes they will act unselfishly; that is, they will sacrifice their own pleasure in order to do their duty with respect to others. Hence, in human activity there is an "I" and a "We" dimension. Etzioni refers to his new paradigm as the I/We paradigm.

In this paper I extend Etzioni's analysis to the business firm, which has traditionally been viewed almost entirely as an economic institution. I ask you to join me in a thought experiment. If we were to conceptualize the firm as a moral community, what would it look like? By what principles would it be managed? In the first part of this paper, I will develop this notion of the firm as a moral community by calling on the political and ethical theory of Aristotle, Kant, Rousseau, and Rawls. In the latter part I will speculate about whether such a firm could be a viable economic entity.

Despite appearances to the contrary, it is widely accepted that business has a moral purpose. The making of profits is an instrumental goal not an intrinsic one. Profits are merely a means to an end and business gains legitimacy only if that end is a moral end. Thus, many who take an economic perspective on capitalism argue that a competitive business system provides the greatest good for the greatest number. A competitive profit-oriented business system is maximally efficient and hence serves a utilitarian end. Others, however, argue that business can serve deontological ends. Milton Friedman in *Capitalism and Freedom* (1962) argues that a competitive profit-seeking business community is necessary to maximize human freedom; a competitive economic system is a necessary condition for democracy.

I wish to acknowledge the helpful comments of Dennis Quinn of Georgetown University, Phil Bromiley of the University of Minnesota, Donald L. McCabe of Rutgers University, and Gregory A. Danke of the University of British Columbia.

The view that economic institutions must serve moral ends is ancient. Both Plato and Aristotle recognized that a sufficient number of material goods was necessary for happiness. As Aristotle said in *Politics,* "no man can live well or indeed live at all unless he be provided with necessaries" (McKeon, 1966, p. 1131). Although Aristotle left the production of material goods to the household, this role is generally fulfilled by business. In the *Republic*, Plato argued that businesspersons such as craftsmen and artisans had developed specialties so that the totality of businesspersons provided for the material needs of the citizens (Hamilton and Cairns, 1961). Indeed, for Plato, providing for the material needs of people was the proper function of business. However, since Plato believed our physical appetites were the lowest and most inferior part of the soul, businesspeople had the least status in the well-ordered state.

One might reject Plato's denigration of our physical appetites and still argue that the moral function of business is limited to the production of goods and services to satisfy our physical needs. In contemporary language the moral function of business might be to produce quality goods and services and to stay close to the customer.

Such an approach, however, would be sufficient only if businesses were limited to single proprietorships—to individual craftsmen and artisans. Once a business consists of multiple persons, a nexus of moral relations is created that is internal to the business itself. If Sally and Tom establish a partnership and operate a business—a Chinese restaurant, for example—their moral responsibilities are not limited to the patrons of the restaurant. Their moral responsibilities extend to the employees they hire and to each other. In a large corporation the number of moral relationships internal to the firm is even greater.

To understand the firm as a moral community, suppose we begin with the narrow view of a stakeholder. On the narrow view, a stakeholder is a member of a group whose existence is necessary to the firm. Traditionally, stakeholders include managers, employees, stockholders, suppliers, customers, and the local community. For any firm *X*, the moral community for *X* is constituted by its stakeholders.

In his classic work on justice, the contemporary philosopher John Rawls never discussed how individual business firms should be organized. He did say that every organization should be a social union. To develop his notion of a social union, Rawls (1971) contrasts two views regarding how human society is held together: *In the private view human beings form social institutions after calculating that it would be advantageous to do so. In the social view human beings form social institutions because they share final ends and value common institutions and activities as good in themselves.* Rawls, in the tradition of Aristotle, believes that the social view of human nature is the more accurate. Those who take the social view can form a social union that is defined as a group in which there is an "agreed scheme of conduct in which the excellence and enjoyments of each are complementary to the good of all. Each one of them can take pleasure in the actions of the others as they jointly execute a plan acceptable to everyone" (1971, p. 526).

Part of the task of this paper is to explain how a business firm could be conceptualized as a social union and hence be viewed as a moral community in Kant's and Rawls's sense.

The difficulty with most analyses of the moral obligations of the firm is that they focus only on one of the relationships—the obligations of managers to stockholders or the obligations of managers and employees to customers. A complete account of the firm as a moral community would need to consider the total set of stakeholder relationships.

Moreover, a comprehensive account would need to prioritize and harmonize the set of relationships so that there are no contradictory obligations or conflicts. For example, it is of no help to a manager to decide where her duty lies if she is told that doing X will fulfill her duty to employees but violate her duty to stockholders and that there is no way of settling the conflict and determining what her real duty is. One of the great weaknesses of stakeholder theory today is that it provides little if any help in settling such conflicts and establishing priorities. An account of the firm as a moral community may provide a beginning to the solution of some important problems in contemporary stakeholder theory.

Let us begin with the moral philosophy of Kant. In 1785, Immanuel Kant tried to put ethics on a rational foundation because rationality is the characteristic universally common to all human beings (Kant [1785] 1969). All human beings recognize the requirement of consistency. Thus, if one person were permitted to lie when it was to his or her advantage, then everyone else would have the same privilege. However, if everyone were permitted to lie whenever it was to their advantage, language would become unstable. Liars free-ride off truth tellers and obviously a world cannot exist when everyone is a free-rider. Such a world is conceptually impossible; such a world is irrational.

Kant then took this insight about consistency and applied it to the person itself. Kant argued that each person considered him or herself to be the locus of unconditioned value. A person had this value because of the kind of thing a person is, specifically a rational, autonomous, responsible agent. Such agents are objects worthy of respect. Each individual recognizes himself or herself as an agent in the sense described and hence has a right to respect. But consistency requires that all agents have similar rights to respect. Therefore, it is a fundamental principle of morality that every person ought to be treated with respect.

All of this is familiar even to those with the most cursory knowledge of Kant. Kant, however, combined the two insights discussed above to describe what a moral community would look like: a moral community would be a community of moral equals. Each member of the community is intrinsically valuable and is equally worthy of respect. This egalitarian view of moral agents is accepted by Rousseau and Rawls as well.

In a moral community, the interests of every member of the community are equal to the interests of every other member. If a business firm were viewed as a moral community, the interest of one stakeholder would never automatically predominate over any other. Hence, if the interest of one stakeholder is given priority over another, then there should be a moral justification that establishes the priority. For example, if the issue at hand is reward for risk and stakeholder X took more of the risk then stakeholder Y, stakeholder X deserves more of the reward then stakeholder Y. This seems relatively uncontroversial. The real difficulty occurs in matching and balancing different categories of contribution. How do you reward the contribution of the risk taker who put up the capital as compared with the employees who actually produce the product or service?

One might respond that this is the kind of question a manager should decide. That's what managers are hired to do. But in a moral community, that cannot be the right solution. If the manager decides, the autonomy of the other stakeholder has not been respected.

To show proper respect for the various stakeholders would require that the stakeholder participate in the decision-making process and give consent to the way a decision is to be reached. Managers might object to giving stakeholders autonomy in this sense on the grounds that it would make business decisions slow and chaotic.

This type of problem is similar to a problem in traditional political philosophy. In a state, some would argue, any decision procedure chosen is either tyrannical or anarchical. Even in a democracy where the decision is made on the basis of majority voting, it might be argued that the autonomy of the minority has not been respected. Their wishes are thwarted. But achieving unanimity is impractical and if you let each person make a decision on his or her own, the stability of the group is undermined and anarchic disintegration starts to set in. How can human beings reap the necessary advantages of working through groups without surrendering their rights to autonomy? This is one of the problems addressed by traditional political theory.

Kant, Rousseau, and Rawls all develop a contract model to attempt to resolve the problem. Kant's solution to the problem was to see what the categorical imperative required in a social setting. Since, by the principle of consistency, moral rules must apply to everyone and be accepted by everyone, anyone could propose a rule and if it were truly rational, everyone else would freely adopt it. As Kant put it, everyone in a moral community is both subject and sovereign:

> For all rational beings stand under the law that each of them should treat himself and all others never merely as a means but in every case also as an end in himself. Thus, there arises a systematic union of rational beings through common objective laws. This is a realm which may be called a realm of ends . . . because what these laws have in view is just the relation of these being to each other as ends and means. ([1785] 1969, p. 59)

Kant argues that in a kingdom of ends, any proposed rule would have to be universal and that such rules could not appeal to self-interest:

> Reason, therefore, relates every maxim of the will as giving universal laws to every other will and also every action toward itself; it does so not for the sake of any other practical motive or future advantage but, rather from the idea of the dignity of a rational being who obeys no law except that which he himself also gives. ([1785] 1969, p. 60)

Two modern philosophers have expanded on Kant's point. In *The Moral Rules*, Bernard Gert (1966) proposes ten moral rules that he claims every rational person would adopt. Such adoption is only possible for rules that can be publicly advocated and that are without bias in favor of the person who advocates them. Under such a scheme everyone is the equal of everyone else. No one can operate as a moral elite and set the rules of the game. Since the proposed rules are rational, they would be accepted unanimously. No one's autonomy would be violated and anarchy would not prevail.

A similar Kantian insight can be found in the work of John Rawls (1971). Rawls wants to know what principles of justice would be unanimously adopted by rational agents. To get such unanimity Rawls knew that personal bias must be eliminated. He proposed that persons proposing principles of justice would have to reason behind a veil of ignorance where all knowledge of individual characteristics would be eliminated. If such bias were eliminated, Rawls believed people would unanimously agree on two principles that could be used in the construction of a just society.

The problem with Kant's solution is that often no universal rule can be found to settle the problem. A manager considering whether to institute a program of random drug testing can ignore self-interest and still not know whether to give priority to the right of the customer not to be harmed or the right of the employee to privacy. At best Kant's categorical imperative offers a negative test. It rules out certain proposed actions as immoral. But that is not sufficient for dealing with the problem at hand.

Jean-Jacques Rousseau raised the problem in its classic form in 1762, arguing that the social contract could provide the ideal solution:

> Find a form of association that defends and protects the person and goods of each associate with all the common force, and by means of which each one, uniting with all, nevertheless obeys only himself and remains as free as before. This is the fundamental problem which is shared by the social contract. (Rousseau [1762] 1978, p. 53)

Rousseau argued that in civil society persons must aim for the good of all. The genuine good of each individual can only be found in the good of all and decisions should be made from that perspective. A decision made from that perspective represents the general will.

The plausibility of Rousseau's theory depends on whether he is correct in asserting that the genuine good for any individual in society rests with the good of all. In giving the general will priority over his perceived current interest, the citizen certainly does lose something:

> What man loses by the social contract is his natural freedom and an unlimited right to everything that tempts him and that he can get; what he gains is civil freedom and the proprietorship of everything he possesses. (Rousseau [1762] 1978, p. 56)

One can make the following argument on behalf of Rousseau's position: in the absence of a state, we could not satisfy our interests since the satisfaction of these interests is dependent on others. Since a human being is a social creature, social institutions are in his best interest. But social institutions are only possible when individuals are willing to subordinate their immediate interest to the interests of all.

In the economic sphere, our interests are often best achieved in cooperation with others. To get others to cooperate, however, we need to forego the achievement of the totality of our immediate interests. Otherwise, the requisite cooperation will not be forthcoming. So long as the general will represents the good for all, our best interest rests with decision rules in accordance with the general will—or so Rousseau argues:

> As each gives himself to all, he gives himself to no one; and since there is no associate over whom one does not acquire the same right one grants him over oneself, one gives the equivalent of everything one loses, and more force to preserve what one has. (Rousseau [1762] 1978, p. 53)

Rousseau, however, leaves a number of problems untouched. First, different stakeholders bring different assets to the table. Suppose the good for all as captured by the benefits of cooperation is far more dependent on some stakeholders than on others. Shouldn't the more powerful stakeholders set the terms for cooperation? Should the more productive stakeholders demand that more of their interests be satisfied as a condition for their cooperation? If a group of people want to take a drive, the person who owns the car has the greatest bargaining power. Does the common good require that the car owner's first choice of destination predominate?

Second, Rousseau seems to come down on the side of the sovereign whenever there is a disagreement by an individual as to whether a decision of the general will really is in the long-run best interest of the individual:

> It follows that the general will is always right and always tends toward the public utility. But, it does not follow that the people's deliberations always have the same rectitude. One always knows what is good for oneself, but one does not always see it. (Rousseau [1762] 1978, p. 61)

In the traditional hierarchical context of business decision making, the boss is sovereign. If the employee's idea of the good of the organization conflicts with that of the boss, the boss would be right. Rousseau allows much more democracy. He would endorse something like quality circles. But suppose one member of the quality circle disagrees with the others on whether a particular action really was in the firm's best interest. In Rousseau's view, the individual would be mistaken.

John Rawls drew on Rousseau's contract notion as well as on Kantian moral philosophy to develop his notion of justice as fairness. There is much in Rawls's analysis that will be of assistance to us in escaping the difficulties in Rousseau's view. Rawls did not think it was sufficient to reach the good for all by having each person try to vote for policies in the public interest. Rawls thought more explicit instructions were needed for our thought experiment in order to eliminate bias. That is why he proposed his notion of the veil of ignorance. To operate behind the veil, one needed to think away all the particular characteristics (e.g. sex, intelligence, wealth) one might have. Notice that if such a psychological thought experiment could succeed, the contractees would be in the condition of equality Rousseau desired. No one would have a bargaining advantage since behind the veil the contractees would not know if they had any characteristic that would give them an advantage. In that way Rousseau's first problem was supposedly put to rest.

For the second problem, Rawls made a distinction between imperfect and perfect procedural justice. He observed that the ideal state of affairs occurred when a just procedure yielded just outcomes, such as when a person cutting a cake agreed to take the last piece. In such circumstances, society has a case of perfect procedural justice. However, perfect procedural justice is often a practical impossibility. With respect to criminal justice, a perfect procedure would punish all the guilty and only the guilty. In the absence of a system that would yield such a result, a system of innocent-until-proven-guilty is the closest practical approximation. However, under such a system a few nonguilty are punished and quite a few guilty are not. Such a system is imperfect and is an example of imperfect procedural justice.

What legitimizes a system of imperfect procedural justice? For Rawls, it would be its conformity to the principles of justice. In this case, a Rawlsian would argue that a system that gives priority to protecting the innocent would be justified if it were chosen from the social contract perspective, that is, by the contractees designing a legal system behind the veil of ignorance.

With respect to our political dilemma between autonomy and anarchy, Rawls argued that a constitutional democracy with a place for civil disobedience was in accord with justice. A place for civil disobedience was necessary to recognize that democratic decision making was an example of imperfect procedural justice.

In the economic arena Rawls thought that fairly traditional market institutions passed his justice test so long as the government was given the power to keep the price system reasonably competitive, to work to achieve full employment, the power to provide for a social minimum, and the power to preserve approximate justice in distributive shares. "A further and more significant advantage of a market system," says Rawls, "is that, given the requisite background institutions, it is consistent with equal liberties and fair equality of opportunity" (1971, p. 272). Notice that Rawls corrected for the distributive imperfections of the market by providing government as a regulator, stabilizer, and safety value for an adequate standing of living.

Kant, Rawls, and Rousseau make a number of points that aid our understanding of what constitutes a moral community. First, everyone's interest should count. Second, everyone should have a voice in the decision. Third, if there are benefits in a cooperative scheme, the interests of one stakeholder should not be given priority; otherwise there would be no incentive for the other stakeholders to cooperate. Why should they if some of the gains of cooperation don't go to them? We shall adapt these insights for the business context as conditions for a firm that wishes to represent itself as a moral community.

1. The firm should consider the interests of all stakeholders in any decision it makes.

2. That consideration should involve getting input from all the affected stakeholders.

3. It should not be the case that for all decisions, the interests of one stakeholder take priority.

4. Each business firm must establish procedures designed to insure that relations among the stakeholders are governed by principles of justice. There principles of justice are to be developed in accordance with conditions 1 through 3 and must receive the endorsement of representatives of all stakeholders.

These moral conditions are not without some bite if they are used to judge current business practice.

A firm whose decision-making procedure is hierarchical often violates condition 2 and hence is not a moral community. Neither is a firm where every decision gives priority to the needs of the stockholders. A firm that applies the "employment at will" doctrine or refuses to develop policy statements indicating what employee actions constitute grounds for dismissal violates condition 4.

Some might criticize the requirement in condition 4 that the procedures designed to provide justice must receive the endorsement of representatives of all stakeholders. They might argue that the level of trust and good will required does not exist. However, achieving unanimous approval from the stakeholder representatives is not a utopian dream. Labor and management have bargained successfully over issues far more specific and controversial than those involved here. The chief interests of each stakeholder group are readily identifiable. What is needed is an agreement among the various stakeholders for institutionally balancing out the conflicts and insuring that the goals of each stakeholder are at least partially met by the firm. As difficult as this task is, it is hardly impossible.

Finally, it should be noted that viewing a firm as a moral community requires that we change our perspective that stakeholder relationships in a firm are solely economic. Under the traditional perspective, if an individual stakeholder and a firm enter into a business relationship, then each believes there is an economic benefit to be gained. From that perspective, stakeholder relations are simply sets of economic relationships.

I believe the traditional view is impoverished. Rather than merely providing economic benefits, a moral firm should contribute to the development of the individual's autonomy and self-respect. Before turning to the real world of business and to management theory, let us add one last element to the firm conceptualized as a moral community. What would the stakeholders' relationships look like in such a firm?

Let us begin by discussing the relationship such a firm would have with its employees. If the firm is simply a set of economic relationships, then the employer will pay the worker as little as he or she can in order to get the job done. On the other side, employees will try to maximize pay and minimize the amount they will have to do. But if we assume that people have a need to work, the moral firm provides more than a paycheck; it provides a job. But not just any job. To support autonomy and self-respect the firm should provide meaningful work. In this context, meaningful work is defined as work that is useful, challenging, and respectful of autonomy. Obviously, how far a business firm can go in eliminating monotony can be limited by technological factors. Some jobs by their very nature don't require much in the way of complex skills. Philosophers know that *ought* implies *can* and that if you can't do something, it makes no sense to tell you that you ought to. Still, taking the moral point of view will go a long way toward making each kind of work as meaningful as it can be.

If the firm provides employees an element of self-realization by providing work and, furthermore, provides opportunities for work that enable people to use their creative talents, then that firm is treating its employees with respect. The moral responsibilities, however, do not fall exclusively on the employer. By providing an employee with meaningful work, the employer contributes greatly to the employee's self-actualization. The employee owes his or her allegiance to the employer and should not suddenly change jobs for a higher wage. In a firm organized as a moral community, there would be far less turnover.

It is even more important that the employees should provide high-quality products and services to customers. The customer and the employee are in a moral relationship where the employee is doing something she or he considers valuable and the customer is gaining something he or she considers valuable. As the Delta Airlines ad says, "We love to fly and it shows." That ad captures the spirit of the firm as a moral community that I am trying to convey.

In this view the manager is engaged in a service profession with the task of facilitating these various moral relations. If management is viewed this way, then it is obvious why the hierarchical view of management is so out of place. Also, from within the moral perspective, to call someone a boss is to commit a category mistake. Perhaps Bill Gore, founder of W.T. Gore, was on to something when everyone in the Gore company was called an associate. In an economic paradigm such terms are just eccentric devices for trying to motivate employees to produce more. From a moral perspective, where a firm is a genuine social union, such terms reflect a psychological and moral truth about the relations within the firm.

What about the stockholders? Is their relation to the firm anything more than economic? The answer to this question depends on one's perspective. Are stockholders merely a provider of capital or are they partners in providing something useful to the collective enterprise? From the perspective of the firm as a social union, they are partners who provide a commodity that makes the moral relations within the firm possible. So long as they are genuine partners, then the four conditions govern stockholder-firm relations in the same way that they govern other firm-stakeholder relations. The stockholders in such circumstances should be concerned with the overall health of the firm. They should be active and involved, rather than passive. And, most importantly, they should not be holding stock in the firm merely to make money. That would reduce a moral relationship to a merely economic one. Rather, the stockholders should purchase stock in firms because they share the firm's goals and ideals. They own stock because they think the firm can both do good and do well.

If, however, the stockholders do not see themselves as partners, then from the moral point of view their relation to the firm is more at an arm's length and it is the relations among the managers, customers, and the employees that are morally central. As Berle and Means pointed out a half-century ago (1932), stockholders are not actively involved in the managing of the firm. Most stockholders are in it merely for the money. This is true for both individual and institutional investors. The separation of owners from managers reduces moral obligations to the stockholders.

Some might object that the stockholders of necessity must play a large role in the moral firm. After all, they are the owners of the firm. Although ownership is a significant economic fact, ownership is less significant as a moral fact. It is the significance of the relations that carries moral weight.

Many employees and managers have an attitude toward the firm that resembles that of the homeowners. That is why the interests of these stakeholders have greater moral weight than the interests of absentee stockholders. Investment property is different from other personal property. Most stockholders in a corporation are not property owners in the way that most single-family homeowners are. Most homeowners do not own homes simply to maximize a real estate investment. A homeowner lives in a home, manages it, and provides for its upkeep. Often improvements are made in the home that any competent real estate agent would agree would not return the investment if the house were sold. Indeed, this type of homeowner usually develops an attachment to the home. A house takes on a special meaning (a house is not a home). It is simply more than an investment. Frequently, this homeowner will not sell the home even when it is financially advantageous to do so. I know of people who have not sold their home for an astronomical profit despite the fact that it is literally surrounded by fast-food outlets. They wish to die in the home that has been such a part of their lives for many years.

I am well aware that this analysis is not consistent with the legal analysis. Under the law, managers are in a fiduciary relation with stockholders and as a result have strict moral duties to them. But my analysis here is moral, not legal. Moreover, the business judgment rule as developed by the Delaware courts has weakened the strictness of the obligation. Several states have passed legislation that permits corporate managers to consider the needs of stakeholders other than the stockholder, and a few states require that the interests of the other stakeholders be considered. It seems to this observer that both the courts and statutes are moving closer to the philosophy espoused here.

This completes my analysis of the firm as a moral community. A manager in such a firm is constrained by four conditions. So long as a manager recognizes the needs of the various stakeholders as described above and manages in accord with the four conditions, the management of the firm will be done from the moral perspective. The other stakeholder groups would in a similar fashion honor their moral obligations. Such a firm would be a social union in Rawls's sense and it would contribute to the individual self-realization of the various stakeholders. In such a firm all the stakeholders would be treated with the respect required by morality.

Until this point, I have done my conceptual analysis oblivious to the real world and without any reference to the vast literature and insights of management theory. Instead, I have looked to moral and political philosophy to see if I could develop some principles that would govern a firm organized as a moral community. It is now time to enter the world of business and ask a couple of hard questions: (1) Is there anything in management theory that would lend either theoretical support or help to implement the four conditions? (2) Could a firm organized as a moral community make money? The remainder of this paper considers these questions and examines how we can answer both affirmatively, albeit with caution.

Despite the strangeness of the language and the idealistic tone, there are many points where the management literature and the arguments of this paper coincide. Both the popular business literature and the more scholarly literature of management journals urge managers to take the interests of the various stakeholders, especially customers and employees, into account in order to improve the bottom line. My philosophical description of some of the ethical ways to treat employees parallels what labor relations experts describe as enlightened labor management relations. Quality circles, employee stock option plans (ESOP), and participatory work involvement are all ways of implementing the Kantian categorical imperative that we should treat people as ends and not merely as means. Agency theory has had a great impact on a number of business disciplines. Agency theory seeks solutions to so-called agency problems that arise when agents who are obligated to act on behalf of others (principals), behave opportunistically and act on behalf of themselves at the expense of their principals. The more effective nonopportunistic moral norms are in a business, the less serious are the agency problems. Monitoring costs decrease. In a firm organized as a moral community, opportunistic behavior would be rare and monitoring cost would be minimal.

Another concern of management theorists is transaction costs. High levels of trust lower many types of transaction costs. Legal costs can be reduced if every contingency does not have to be written into the contract. As the United States faces the challenges of international competition, improved technology and more innovation are considered essential. A better record in these respects may require joint ventures—between a supplier and a manufacturer, for example. However, the success of these joint ventures is dependent on both nonopportunistic behavior and high levels of trust. A manufacturer will not work with a supplier unless she or he can be assured that the supplier will not sell the improved product that resulted from their collaboration to the manufacturer's competitor. A firm where stakeholder relations are moral rather than merely economic would have less cause to worry.

Can a firm conceived as a moral community make money? Other things being equal, I think it can. Of course, managerial competency and luck are necessary. But if these two elements are present, would a firm organized as a moral community have a competitive edge?

This issue cannot be settled empirically. Empirical attempts to establish a relationship between corporate social responsibility and profitability have given contradictory results. To this author's knowledge no studies have been published to overturn the judgment of Aupperle, Carroll, and Hartfield (1985). Their own study of CEO orientation supported neither those who claim a positive nor those who claim a negative relation between corporate social responsibility and profitability. In addition, their analyses of ten earlier studies showed that the results of the studies were mixed (some studies supported a correlation and some did not) and all the studies were conceptually flawed. Given the multiplicity of factors that contribute to profitability, the attending difficulty in determining the significance of the factors, and the conceptual ambiguity surrounding the notion of corporate responsibility, definitive empirical results may be a long time in coming.

Theoretical considerations, however, lend support to the notion that, other things being equal, especially managerial competence and luck, a moral firm will have a competitive advantage. Two arguments deserve our attention.

One argument is based on Robert Frank's commitment model (1988). Frank argues that most of what passes for altruism can really be reduced to enlightened self-interest. All acts of reciprocal altruism (when people act benevolently to-

ward others in the expectation of being recognized and rewarded by some reciprocal acts of kindness in the future) can be so reduced. So can cooperative
strategies to avoid prisoner's dilemma problems and the various tit-for-tat strategies described by Axelrod (1984).

Frank argues that evidence shows that in addition to acts of reciprocal altruism, people commit acts of genuine altruism—acts of "hard-core altruism" as
Frank calls them. Cases of hard-core altruism occur when people sacrifice their
interests when there is no hope of reward for doing so, for example, returning a
wallet with $100 in it found on a deserted street.

Persons who have personality traits that result in acts of hard-core altruism
have an advantage. Since they will be more trustworthy in situations where the
purely self-interested person would not, these persons will be much sought after
in positions that require trust. Note, however, that these persons must be genuine
altruists. One would not really trust reciprocal altruists because they would (or
might) defect in situations where there is no possibility of a reward. Such people
must be emotionally disposed to altruism rather than adopt altruism as a strategy.
To get the benefits of altruism, one has to be a genuine altruist. As Frank says:

> For the model to work, satisfaction from doing the right thing must not be prem-
> ised on the fact that material gains may later follow; rather it must be *intrinsic* to
> the act itself. Otherwise a person will lack the necessary motivation to make
> self-sacrificing choices, and once others sense that, material gains will not, in
> fact, follow. Under the commitment model, moral sentiments do not lead to
> material advantage unless they are heartfelt. [1988, p. 253]

The other argument is based on what I have referred to elsewhere as the
paradox of profit (Bowie, 1988). The paradox of profit is analogous to what
philosophers call the hedonic paradox, which contends that the more one seeks
happiness, the less likely one is to find it. I maintain that a similar paradox can
operate in business. Although many businesspersons believe one should always
keep an eye on the bottom line, I argue that the more a business becomes
obsessed with profits, the less likely it is to achieve them. I can illustrate this
point by looking at the various responses of employees to quality circles and
other programs designed to show concern for employees.

If management were to indicate publicly that a program of management-
worker teams was to be introduced in order to increase shareholder profits, the
program would probably fail. Why? Suppose that the management-worker teams
objectively improved the conditions of the workers. Isn't that sufficient? No.
Empirical research shows that individuals refuse a bargain they perceive to be
unfair even if the bargain would make them better off (Goth, Schmittberger, and
Schwarze, 1982). If the workers believe that the stockholders already keep too
much of the profits, then a program that increases stockholder wealth even more
may be resisted even if the workers are better off as a result. The workers would

see the increased wealth to shareholders as unfair.

Perhaps management should focus on employee self-realization while keeping profits in the back of its mind. In that way management can keep its eye on the quarterly reports. Leaving aside the moral issue of deception, such an approach can be dangerous. If profits aren't sufficiently in the back of management's mind, the employees will develop the same kind of cynicism described above when profit is the conscious goal of "moral" behavior.

Before we leap to the conclusion that the profits-in-the-back-of-the-mind strategy is the only practical one, let us conduct another thought experiment. Suppose a firm is having difficulty with employee morale and management believes that taking steps to increase employee morale will lead to greater profits. What steps do they take? Unless management adopts a strategy that is convincingly altruistic, the employees are likely to treat management overtures cynically and to behave in accordance with such cynicism. Any gains in productivity are likely to be suboptimal. Management needs a strategy that represents what Frank calls altruistic commitment. A no-lay-off policy during an economic downturn is an example of such a policy. It communicates to the employees that management is concerned about them even when that concern does not yield greater profits. Such a policy would be adopted because it is right, rather than because it leads to greater profits. It is the kind of policy one would expect in a firm managed as a moral community.

Recent philosophers and game theorists have elaborated on Plato's theme that morality is in the interest of society. Morality is in the interest of everyone. That is certainly true in a moral firm. A moral firm in which the interests of all stakeholders are taken into account may have a competitive advantage. Being moral will not protect the firm from bad business decisions or from external calamities. But all else being equal, it should both do good and do well.

References

Aupperle, Kenneth E., Archie B. Carroll, and John D. Hartfield. 1985. "An Empirical Examination of the Relationship between Corporate Social Responsibility and Profitability." *Academy of Management Journal* 28:446–63.

Axelrod, Robert. 1984. *The Evolution of Cooperation.* New York: Basic Books.

Berle, A.A., Jr., and Gardiner Means. 1932. *The Modern Corporation and Private Property.* New York: Commerce Clearing House.

Bowie, Norman. 1988. "The Paradox of Profit." In N. Dale Wright, ed., *Papers on the Ethics of Administration.* Provo, UT: Brigham Young University Press.

Etzioni, Amitai. 1988. *The Moral Dimension: Toward a New Economics.* New York: Free Press.

Frank, Robert. 1988. *Passions within Reason.* New York: W.W. Norton.

Friedman, Milton. 1962. *Capitalism and Freedom.* Chicago: University of Chicago Press.

Gert, Bernard. 1966. *The Moral Rules.* New York: Harper & Row.

Goth, Werner, Rolf Schmittberger, and Bernd Schwarze. 1982. "An Experimental Analysis of Ultimatum Bargaining." *Journal of Economic Behavior and Organization* 3:367–88.

Hamilton, Edith, and Huntington Cairns, ed. 1961. *Collected Dialogues of Plato.* New York: Pantheon Books. Reprint. Princeton: Princeton University Press, 1984.

Kant, Immanuel [1787] 1969. *Foundation of the Metaphysics of Morals,* trans. by Lewis White Beck. Indianapolis: Bobbs-Merrill.

McKeon, Richard, ed. and trans. 1966. *The Basic Works of Aristotle.* New York: Random House.

Rawls, John. 1971. *A Theory of Justice.* Cambridge, MA: Harvard University Press.

Rousseau, Jean-Jacques [1762] 1978. *On the Social Contract,* ed. Roger D. Masters; trans. Judith R. Masters. New York: St. Martin's Press.

11

Max B.E. Clarkson

The Moral Dimension of Corporate Social Responsibility

Neoclassical economists have denied the necessity or even the validity of the concept of Corporate Social Responsibility (CSR). Milton Friedman called it a "fundamentally subversive doctrine" and stated that businessmen who believe that "business has a 'social conscience' and take seriously its responsibilities for providing employment, eliminating discrimination [and] avoiding pollution . . . are preaching pure and unadulterated socialism" (Friedman, 1970). By 1971 the Committee for Economic Development had effectively rebutted Friedman's position. Nevertheless he would continue his anathemas against deluded "do-gooder" businessmen and intellectuals for another twenty years, defiantly denying what was happening in the real world and presenting no empirical evidence in support of his own position.

Friedman notwithstanding, the concept of CSR has stayed alive and well, as its meaning has broadened and become more inclusive. Twenty years ago the term was interpreted, within the neoclassical paradigm, to mean that the firm had two sets of responsibilities in two separate arenas, one economic and the other social. The "I" of the profit-maximizing corporation was viewed as standing detached from the "We" of the community and its values. The underlying assumption, despite the evidence, was one of separation and compartmentalization.

Carroll (1979) was the first to develop a model of Corporate Social Responsibility that recognized and incorporated economic performance, or profit, as the most important principle of social responsibility, but without excluding the other and necessary legal, ethical, and discretionary responsibilities. Thus, for the first time, the "I" of profit maximization was integrated with the "We" of the community and society.

Wartick and Cochran (1985) developed a model based on Carroll's construct, and Clarkson (1988) tested the validity of this model and its conceptual foundations, as part of a major research project to evaluate the corporate social performance of forty-two large Canadian corporations. A key conclusion of this study was:

The Wartick and Cochran model, based on the Carroll construct, provides a usable and relevant framework for analyzing and evaluating CSP. As a result of this approach, economic responsibility and public policy responsibility are integrated into the definition of social responsibility. No longer is it possible to view economic responsibility as being inconsistent with, or in opposition to, social responsibility. Economic responsibility is . . . the first and most important social responsibility, but it is not the only one. Business does not carry on its affairs in a compartment labelled "economic," separate from the society of which it is a part. Average or above-average economic performance in an industry group over several years is related to the integration of social, ethical and discretionary responsibilities and goals with the strategic planning of the company, which is, in turn, linked with management performance and decision-making at the operating level. To be socially responsible is to be ethically responsible and profitable. [p. 263]

In the words of socioeconomic theory: "Instead of the neo-classical assumption that people seek to maximize one utility, whether it is pleasure, happiness or consumption, the I/We paradigm assumes that people pursue two irreducible utilities and have two sources of valuation, pleasure and morality" (Etzioni, 1988, p. 4). If "economic performance and profits" are substituted for "pleasure and happiness," the conclusions of the empirical research reported on above clearly can be stated in terms of socioeconomic theory.

If a business cannot fulfill its economic responsibilities by being profitable, clearly it cannot fulfill any other social responsibilities, no matter how they are defined. "The basic proposition is that managerial organizations cannot operate successfully over the long run in conflict with their environments" (Preston, 1986, p. 6). A business organization fulfills its social responsibilities by being profitable over an extended period of time and by responding to the changing values, needs, and expectations in the society of which it is a part.

Business conducts its affairs in a democratic society and is not separate therefrom. Talking and writing about "Business and Society" has led to the belief that they are in separate compartments. It is this compartmentalization that has led to the false antitheses between business and society. This in turn has led to the fruitless and sterile debates that have been the result of the neoclassical separation of economic from social responsibilities. As soon as this can be seen for what it is—theoretically convenient but realistically false—we can revise Friedman's well-known dictum by stating that "the business of business is business in society," and move on.

This argument leads to the conclusion that Corporate Social Responsibility can be defined only in normative terms that include both the profit-making or economic utility and the public policy or moral utility. To be socially responsible, a corporation must be both profitable and responsive to the changing values, needs, and expectations of the community and society in which it operates.

The three areas, or domains, in society of values, needs, and expectations are interrelated. There have been significant changes in recent years in the relative importance of some key values. The needs of different groups and segments of society to exert influence on the processes of corporate decision making have resulted in significant changes in the management of corporate stakeholders. The expectations of society and of corporate stakeholders have resulted in significant changes in perceptions of the role of the manager. In each of these three domains, the changes have been congruent with the development of socioeconomic theory and the I/We paradigm.

Values

The values of technology and of profit have taken priority over human values throughout most of the twentieth century. The technological imperative has had us in its grip: if it could be built, it should be built, whether it was a ten-lane superhighway on land or its equivalent in space. The imperative of profit maximization has led us into environmental and social dilemmas that can be ignored no longer.

The imperatives of technology and of profit require that managers ignore any ethics but utilitarianism or consequential ethics. Utilitarianism—achieving the greatest good for the greatest number—is basically indifferent to the welfare of the individual. When the "greatest number" consists of the shareholders and managers of a corporation, the harm or benefit to individual members of society is irrelevant to the corporate manager's decision-making processes. Utilitarianism has been constrained and has become the ethic of cost-benefit analysis, risk assessment, and market analysis whereby the ends of greater technological efficiency or greater profits justify whatever are the necessary means. And those means, as we now know full well, can result in pollution, unsafe products, unhealthy working conditions—"ends" or results that, judged by other moral standards, are unethical.

These results, or ends, are judged unethical when we weigh them against human values such as justice, equity, security, self-respect, and respect for individual human rights. Utilitarianism does not confront these human values or try to deal with them very effectively. Thus, what we are experiencing today in this context is the struggle to give human values some kind of parity with the values of technology and profit in corporate and governmental decision making processes. And, of course, as soon as we allow the consideration of human values, of rights, justice, equity, and self-respect, into the calculus of decision making we have entered the domain of moral responsibility. The "I" must act within the social context of the "We."

The increased level of concern with ethics in business and in government shows that we are beginning to understand that unless we can bring human values—the "We"—back into our decision-making processes, we shall be condemning ourselves to a contaminated world, an environmentally wounded world, a world unfit for human life, unable to maintain the five billion who are here now, let alone the ten billion who may be inhabiting the earth in less than fifty years. Human values, the values of survival and security, of justice, equity and self-respect, are also changing our views about stakeholders in the decision-making processes of corporations.

Stakeholders

It has become clear in recent years that the shareholder is no longer the sole or even necessarily the primary stakeholder in a corporation. The concept of the shareholder and profit maximization is being replaced by the concept of stakeholders, of whom the shareholder or investor is only one class. This represents a profound change in the ideology of business in North America. The shareholder is no longer the preeminent stakeholder. The "I" no longer has unquestioned priority over the "We."

There are still some unreconstructed Friedmanites, some neoclassical economic isolationists, who maintain that the nature, purpose, and responsibility of a corporation is solely economic; that capitalist society is constructed in such a way that everything to do with free enterprise and profit-seeking takes place in a separate compartment, insulated in some mysterious way from the rest of society and labeled "economic," a compartment in which corporate managers can pursue their own and their shareholders' assumed self-interest by maximizing profits, regardless of the results, as long as their actions are within the letter of the law. But these neoclassicists are a minority, as society, government, and corporations themselves recognize the claims of other stakeholders for just and equitable treatment.

Today the customer comes first in many corporate statements of mission or purpose. These same statements promise the shareholders a "fair return," in effect admitting that maximizing shareholder returns is incompatible with the effective management of the claims of competing stakeholders. Employees, suppliers, the communities in which corporations have their operations, and even competitors are all recognized now as stakeholders. And of course environmental groups and special interest groups have a place at the corporate table, whether or not they have been invited.

The moment that we recognize the existence and legitimacy of several or multiple stakeholder groups, we have entered the domain of moral principles and ethical performance. So long as managers could maintain that shareholders and their profits were supreme, the claims of other stakeholders could be subordinated or ignored. There was no need for the manager to be concerned with fairness, with justice, or even with truth. The single-minded pursuit of profit justified any necessary means, so long as they were not illegal.

We have seen the results and there is no need to dwell on them now, except to point out that the whole subject of inquiry called "Corporate Social Responsibility" is a direct outcome of what was perceived, by an increasing number of people, as Corporate Social Irresponsibility.

As soon, therefore, as we talk and act in terms of stakeholder management, we have entered the territory of moral principles and ethics. We have been slow to recognize this, since we have been brought up to deny the moral responsibility of corporations and their managers for the results of their activities. We forget that Adam Smith was Professor of Moral Philosophy. In order to manage the interests of different stakeholders, ethical analysis of business decisions, a concern for the results of decisions on different stakeholders and on human beings must become as integral a part of our decision-making processes as cost-benefit analysis, risk assessment, internal rate of return, and all the other analytical tools available to the modern manager.

The time has come therefore to redefine "Corporate Social Responsibility" in terms of its two principal components: profits and ethics. Corporate Social Responsibility is both economic and moral, a definition represented by the formula: $CSR = ER + MR$. This definition leads us to confront the fundamental strategic question, which is how to reconcile these two different kinds of responsibility and how to keep them in balance. How do we resolve the inherent conflict between cost-benefit analysis or end-point ethics and the ethics of moral rules, of distributive justice, and of social contracts? The neoclassical assumption that the corporation seeks to maximize only one utility, profit, is replaced by the assumption that the corporation pursues two "irreducible utilities" and has two sources of valuation—profit and morality. But the core of the problem remains, which is the resolution of the "creative tension and perpetual search for balance between the two primary forces" of profit and morality (Etzioni, 1988, p. 8).

Just as corporations have learned to be explicit about their marketing and financial objectives and responsibilities, so they must now learn to be explicit about their stakeholder objectives and their responsibilities towards stakeholder groups. The time has come when corporations must define their objectives, and consequently their responsibilities, towards their customers, employees, suppliers, and competitors, towards government and the communities in which they operate, just as they have defined their economic objectives and responsibilities toward their shareholders.

What about our customers? Do we consider them as "means" or as "ends"? Do we believe in *caveat emptor,* so that customers are regarded primarily as the means by which we increase our profits, at the expense of safety, health, quality, or truthfulness? Or do we value the customer as an end, to be satisfied and maintained, to be served honestly and fairly as well as profitably?

What about our employees? Do we treat them as "means" or "ends"? Do we regard them as means, as extensions of machines, as instruments to be used solely in order to maximize profits, to be terminated or laid off when they are no longer immediately useful? Or do we manage people as ends in themselves, as individuals with potential who are entitled to respect and fair treatment? Are we prepared to state what we mean by "respect" and "fair treatment"?

Similar questions must be asked and answered about the corporation's relationship with suppliers and competitors, with the community, the environment, and government. Are these relationships governed primarily by a utilitarian, cost-benefit calculus, in which the "other" is simply a means towards the end of greater profit? Or do we also determine and define our relationships with these other stakeholders on the basis of our moral responsibilities towards them? This then requires that we define the ground rules of justice, equity, and rights that will govern our behavior in these relationships. These are questions of fundamental strategic importance. The answers will determine our behavior and have a profound influence on the processes of decision making.

In many statements of corporate purpose or mission today we find such words and phrases as "ethical," "integrity," "fairness," "quality," "respect for the individual," "service to the customer." These words of moral responsibility and ethics are common currency even though we are still learning to speak the new language of business ethics: "Fairness, rights, discrimination, affirmative action"; "duties, obligations, loyalties"; "environmental pollution." We need to understand more clearly the implications and meaning of these words in terms of our behavior and our decision making.

For example, if Exxon and Aleyaska had been obliged to define clearly their objectives and responsibilities towards their stakeholders, including the communities of Valdez and Prince William Sound, Alaska, the local people and their governments would have known that these two companies were prepared to spend no more than $x on standby equipment and $y on emergency crews, because additional costs could not be justified by cost-benefit and risk assessment analysis. The communities would have known that the companies' objectives were to move a maximum number of barrels of oil through the pipeline, into the tankers, and down the coast at a defined cost per barrel. Such a cost would allow for certain clearly stated precautions, which, based on risk assessment assumptions, were deemed sufficient to prevent or contain disastrous situations.

But the companies were not obliged to be explicit about anything, not even to justify how little they were doing, except to have claimed, in 1981, that they were doing too much at too high a cost. From the viewpoint of human values and stakeholder management, the fundamental flaws and inadequacies in the processes of cost-benefit analysis and risk assessment are revealed clearly and tragically in this disaster, as has happened so many times before: Bhopal, Challenger, the Dalkon Shield, and asbestos merely top the current list. These tragedies are the direct result of the separation of the "I" of these profit-maximizing corporations from the "We" of the communities and societies in which they operated.

It does not seem unreasonable, therefore, to require that corporations not only define their economic or market responsibilities to society, but also define their responsibilities to the different stakeholder groups who are actively or passively involved in the corporation's activities, those groups, in effect, without whom the corporation could not operate or make a profit, and those groups who may be affected by the corporation's actions.

The Role of the Manager

What is the role of the manager? To whom is the manager responsible? Is the role of the manager solely that of the loyal and faithful agent of the corporation and its shareholders, as Milton Friedman and other neoclassical economists would have us believe, or does it involve responsibilities to stakeholders other than the shareholders? These are important and fundamental questions, the answers to which have profound impact on the decisions and behavior of managers.

The utilitarian, rationalist, and individualist view of the role of the manager is expressed clearly by Friedman:

> In a free-enterprise, private property system, a corporate executive is an employee of the owners of the business. He has direct responsibility to his employers. That responsibility is to conduct the business in accordance with their desires, which generally will be to make as much money as possible while conforming to the basic rules of the society, both those embodied in law and those embodied in ethical custom. . . .[T]he key point is that in his capacity as a corporate executive, the manager is the agent of the individuals who own the corporation . . ., and his primary responsibility is to them. [Friedman, 1970]

The "resource converter" model presents a different definition of the role of the manager, one that is consistent with socioeconomic theory and the I/We paradigm, and places the manager's role in a social context:

> The basic function of managers in society is to convert resources . . . into outputs. The managers are the middlemen who keep the conversion process going. . . . As a resource converter the manager is cast in a role that is clearly vital to society. He is not a protagonist for any one resource group. Instead, the social values that the manager seeks to satisfy when he makes decisions for his company are the values of all the various resource contributors.
>
> Of course, two crucial and complicating factors qualify this simplified source of values. First, all wishes of contributors cannot possibly be met. . . . Second, the desires of resource contributors change. . . . Thus, the manager is an active participant in shifting values. In this framework the manager is no reluctant Scrooge. Rather, his success depends to a large extent on how well he perceives value issues and how ingenious he is in meeting highest priorities. He is moral because he is responsive to human wants.
>
> Picturing the manager as a resource converter at least emphasizes one point—future managers will be inextricably concerned with change in social values. [Newman, 1978, pp. 126–27]

In business, which comes first when the manager must resolve conflicting needs and values: the profits of the corporation, the well-being of the employees, customer satisfaction, paying suppliers on time, respecting the environment? What happens when it is not possible to satisfy all these different stakeholders?

Is the manager's responsibility only to the corporation and its owners or shareholders (the "I")? Or is the manager responsible also to the corporation's employees, its customers and suppliers, and to society as a whole (the "I and the We") for the results or effects of his or her decisions, the implementation of policies and strategies?

There has been a significant change in the way these questions are being answered today from the answers of not so many years ago. This change was documented by Feldman, Kelsay, and Brown (1986), who analyzed articles in the *Harvard Business Review* from 1940 to 1980 and showed that there has been a shift in the concept of managerial responsibility from a narrowly focused "role" to a more widely oriented "moral" responsibility:

> Under the concept of Role Responsibility, the manager:
>
> a) is answerable only to the claims of the owners/stockholder for the corporation's profits, survival and growth,
>
> b) promotes the corporation's profitability and thereby its bottom-line, using cost-benefit calculations in order to maximize the productive and efficient use of its resources,
>
> c) is not directly answerable to the claims of society, of employees, or of consumers,
>
> d) and can justify breaches of ordinary moral norms, such as truthfulness, with reference to the claims of other interest groups of stakeholders, such as employees, consumers, society. Thus misleading advertising, bluffing, deception and even bribery can all be justified,
>
> e) finally the manager is answerable only to the stockholders and the corporation, and justifies all actions, regardless of their ethical significance, with reference to the claims of these overarching constituencies.
>
> Under the concept of Moral Responsibility, however, the manager:
>
> a) is answerable to the claims of members of society, consumers and labor,
>
> b) is obliged to answer the claims of persons affected by company policies and decisions, whether inside or outside the company,
>
> c) and is obliged to observe ordinary moral norms, and can justify breaches of one norm only when it is overridden by another. [Feldman, Kelsay, and Brown, 1986, pp. 93–117]

In the *Harvard Business Review* of the 1940s through the 1960s, the concept of "role" responsibility was preeminent. This meant that the manager's responsibility was to the market system, to the system of free enterprise, and not to the people who were assumed to be the beneficiaries of the working of the invisible hand. Actions and decisions were justified primarily on the basis of their beneficial consequences for the corporation and the market system. The implicit norm was the utilitarian cost-benefit calculus, whatever provided the greatest good for the shareholder and the corporation. "What's good for General Motors is good for the country" represented this viewpoint perfectly.

The manager's primary commitment was to "the rules of the game" (Carr, 1968), and thus he could justify deception and other practices that are normally viewed as violations of the ordinary obligations due to persons. Under "role responsibility" the manager experiences a totally different purpose and meaning of his business life than in his personal life. The values of the free enterprise system and of the corporation justify any actions that will contribute to success and profit (ends justify means). Consequently, the principle of respect for persons, for individuals, does not apply to the manager. Any lingering sense of moral responsibility on the part of the manager must be subordinated to the responsibility of his or her role as an agent of the employer. Managers have been trained to hang up their personal values and ethics with their coats as they enter the office.

Feldman et al. (1986) identified that there has been a shift, as reflected in the pages of the *Harvard Business Review,* and showed that stress is now being placed on a wider sense of responsibility, which may be called "moral." It is now being argued that, since corporate strategies and decisions are made by managers, who as individuals possess the capacity for moral reasoning, the corporation itself is responsible for taking "the moral point of view." This argument rests on the premise that managers can and do inject their own values into the culture and decision-making processes, a view strongly expressed by Andrews (1971). This view has also received significant support from *The Pursuit of Excellence* (Peters and Waterman, 1982) and the tidal wave of books that have followed. Values, culture, and ground rules come from the top, and so do ethics. Role responsibility and moral responsibility cannot be compartmentalized. Both are essential for the successful management of stakeholders with conflicting or competing claims on the corporation.

The Problem of Balance

Defining Corporate Social Responsibility in terms of its two principal components, economic responsibility and moral responsibility, makes it essential to confront the difficulties of reconciling these responsibilities when they are in conflict and of keeping them in balance.

When the value system of a corporation gives unquestioning priority to the values of profit and technology, then economic responsibilities will be emphasized at the expense of moral responsibilities, the purpose of the corporation will be to maximize profits for the shareholders, and the role responsibility of its managers will be solely to the corporation and its shareholders. Its economic orientation, its emphasis on the bottom line, will be at the expense of its social, or moral, orientation. Profits take priority over ethics. The utilitarian, rationalist, individualistic "I" of the corporation takes priority over the "We" of the community and society.

By contrast, when the value system of a corporation explicitly acknowledges the importance of human values by granting them parity with the values of profit and technology, then economic responsibilities will be balanced with moral responsibilities, the corporation will seek to balance the interests of the stakehold-ers without sacrificing its economic responsibilities, and the responsibilities of its managers will be not only to the corporation and its shareholders but also to other stakeholders. The corporation's economic orientation will not come at the expense of its social, or moral, orientation. Profits and ethics coexist. The "I" and the "We" are integrated into the strategic planning and decision making of the corporation.

In a recent research study that evaluated the social performance of forty-two large corporations (Clarkson, 1988), "emphasis on the bottom-line (economic orientation) at the expense of social orientation [was] shown to be related to economic performance which is below average within an industry groups" (p. 262). However, those corporations in the study that balanced their proactive economic orientation with a proactive social orientation were profitable at aver-age or above-average levels in their industries. In the corporations included in this research project, unbalanced concentration on the maximization of profits was counterproductive and resulted in lower ratios of profitability than their competitors during the preceding three to five years. There was, in these less profitable companies, no evidence of a conscious attempt "to weave social con-cerns into their long-term, strategic planning . . .[or] to ensure that social perfor-mance is built into the whole organization, its policies and day-to-day practices. There is a lower level of awareness and analysis of social and public policy issues, and consequently of policy development and implementation" (Clarkson, 1988, p. 262).

"Balance," clearly, is not an easy concept to define in the context of social responsibility. The measurement of economic performance is governed by a multitude of generally accepted accounting principles. The balance sheet of a corporation "balances" assets and liabilities, but no mechanisms exist whereby moral responsibilities and ethical performance can be quantified or measured in such a way as to satisfy accountants or academics, let alone the general public. The imperative of quantification must be resisted. Instead of attempting to quan-tify the unquantifiable, the principal elements of moral responsibility and ethical performance must be defined and analyzed, together with the corporate data necessary in order to evaluate levels of performance.

Defining Economic and Moral Responsibilities

Managers enter the domain of moral principles and ethics and of socioeconomic theory, whether they know it or not, as soon as they recognize the existence and legitimacy of several or multiple stakeholder groups. The sophisticated cost-benefit analytical tools of utilitarian ethics cannot by themselves provide satis-factory answers to dilemmas and problems involving moral rules, distributive justice, or social contracts and trust. Corporations that are morally aware under-stand this difficulty. They confront it by explicit statements about their mission, about codes of ethics or conduct, and in the basic principles by which the company is managed. For example, in 1986, a large industrial company, as an integral part of a major strategic restructuring, made explicit statements about its corporate purpose, principles, and policies, and initiated an ongoing program of communication and education for all employees. The CEO stated that the purpose was:

> to remind ourselves of what we, as a corporation, are trying to become, to clarify our corporate purpose and identify those basic, enduring values or principles that bind all units of the company together. These essential elements taken together form the very heart and corporate character of (the company) and are critical to our success. [Clarkson, 1987, p. 32ff]

The four "basic, enduring values or principles" of the company can be summarized as follows:

> 1) The company "is in business to serve the needs of its customers" by producing high quality products and services and by providing value to customers through continuing effort to increase productivity.
> 2) "Profit is essential and the ultimate measure of corporate performance." Shareholders are entitled to an "appropriate" return on investment, and profits are intended to contribute to the well-being of all stakeholders in the company.
> 3) "Employees make the crucial difference." This principle provides the basis for the company's policies covering human resources, health and safety.
> 4) "In all its dealings [the company] must act reasonably and with a sense of public accountability." [Clarkson, 1987, p. 33]

Thus, this company defines both its economic and its moral responsibilities, and aims to achieve a balance between them: customers are mentioned first, ahead of profits and the shareholders, who are entitled to a fair but not a maximum return, so that all stakeholders can benefit from their association with the company. Thus, responsibilities towards both the "I" and the "We" are stated explicitly.

From these four principles established by this company major policies were derived, covering the management of human resources, care of, and responsibility for, products and the environment, and the safety, security and maintenance of physical assets. Finally, their Code of Business Conduct serves as a special statement of policy, which provides guidance to individuals in their business dealings and is based on the fundamental ethical principles of honesty, integrity, and trust.

This company demonstrates how economic, moral, and social issues can be integrated with the formulation and implementation of strategic goals. The statements of principles are qualitative in nature, excluding numbers and quantification. They are not, however, motherhood statements or variations on the golden rule. As statements of purpose, of values and of principles they can be made operational only by means of policies and objectives derived from them, which in turn are linked with management style and performance at the operating level.

Role responsibility and moral responsibility are both essential for the successful management of stakeholders with conflicting or competing claims on the resources and capabilities of the corporation. In order to exercise moral responsibility, managers must have, from top management, the guidance and support of clear corporate statements, which explicitly affirm the importance in policy and decision making of human values, moral rules, distributive justice, and social contracts. The behavior and performance of senior managers must demonstrate their belief in, and understanding of, these principles and values. Otherwise cynicism and corporate social irresponsibility will prevail.

Corporations and "community are both completely essential, and hence have the same fundamental standing. The individual and the community make each other and require each other" (Etzioni, 1988, p. 8). The "I" of the corporation cannot survive and prosper apart from its communities and society. The business of business is not just business. The business of business is business *in* society. Effective and satisfactory social performance is both profitable *and* ethical. Corporate social responsibility is both economic *and* moral.

References

Andrews, K.R. 1971. *The Concept of Corporate Strategy.* Homewood, IL: Irwin.

Carr, Albert. 1968. "Is Business Bluffing Ethical?" *Harvard Business Review,* Jan./Feb., 93–98.

Carroll, Archie B. 1979. "A Three-Dimensional Conceptual Model of Corporate Performance," *Academy of Management Review* 14:497–505.

Clarkson, M.B.E. 1987. "The Strategic Management of Corporate Social Performance." Administrative Sciences Association of Canada, Conference Proceedings.

———. 1988. "Corporate Social Performance in Canada 1976–1986." *Research in Corporate Social Performance and Policy* 10:241–65.

Etzioni, Amitai. 1988. *The Moral Dimension: Toward a New Economics.* New York: Free Press.

Feldman, J.D., H. Kelsay, and H.E. Brown. 1986. "Responsibility and Moral Reasoning: A Study in Business Ethics." *Journal of Business Ethics* 5:93–117.

Friedman, Milton. 1970. "The Social Responsibility of Business is to Increase Its Profits." *New York Times Magazine* (page nos. unavailable).

Newman, W.H. 1978. *Managers for the Year 2000.* Englewood Cliffs, NJ: Prentice Hall.

Peters, T.J., and R.H. Waterman. 1982. *In Search of Excellence.* New York: Harper & Row.

Preston, L.E. 1986. "Social Issues and Public in Business and Management: Retrospect and Prospect." Center for Business and Public Policy, College Park, MD: University of Maryland.

Wartick, S.L., and P.L. Cochran. 1985. "The Evolution of the Corporate Social Performance Model." *Academy of Management Review* 14:4758–769.

12

John Oliver Wilson

The "Junk Bond King" of Wall Street: A Discourse on Business Ethics

In March 1989, Michael R. Milken was indicted on charges of racketeering, securities fraud, and mail fraud. Known on Wall Street as the "junk bond king," Milken had made a meteoric rise from relative obscurity and modest means to become one of the richest men in the world. During 1987 alone, he received compensation of $550 million from Drexel Burnham Lambert Inc., where he was head of the high-yield bond department. And during the four-year period from 1984 through 1987, he received a total compensation of $1 billion. His indictment, and the revelation of his massive income based on fees earned from engineering leveraged buyouts of some of the best-known and revered American corporations, has reverberated and occasioned soul searching far beyond the confines of Wall Street.

Reaction to the Milken affair has ranged from stunned amazement to support in principle to outright rage. Wall Street professionals and corporate moguls, hardly a group to be awed by numbers in the millions, were stunned by the size of his earnings. David Rockefeller stated that "such an extraordinary income inevitably raises questions as to whether there isn't something unbalanced in the structure of the way our financial system is working" (*New York Times,* 1989, p. C1).

The general public was outraged. Milken's actions were viewed as just the latest event in a long series of examples of graft, greed and unethical behavior on Wall Street. Ivan F. Boesky, T. Boone Pickens, Drexel Burnham Lambert, and RJR Nabiso Inc. had all become household names. On May 25, 1987 *Time* magazine captured the mood of the country with the following headline emblazoned across its cover: "What Ever Happened to Ethics?" Assaulted by "sleaze, scandals and hypocrisy, America searches for its moral bearings," the magazine went on to inform its readers.

Yet not all reaction was stunned amazement or blatant rage. Many in corporate and academic America felt that the increase in mergers and acquisitions was a good thing. Rational reasons were offered to explain why corporate takeovers had suddenly exploded upon the financial scene, and many of these reasons were advanced as being good for both corporate America and the economy in general.

Mergers and acquisitions are viewed by many experts as introducing a new dynamics of efficiency into a bloated and bureaucratic corporate America. Long protected from competition because of government regulations, a large domestic market that offers easy opportunities for growth, and until recently the lack of serious foreign competition, American management has become stagnant. If America is to compete against the onslaught from Japan and Western Europe, our management has to become more efficient. Mergers and acquisitions are one means of improving corporate efficiency.

The lack of a clear consensus on the activities of Milken and his peers is not surprising, for it represents an underlying conflict between two different sets of social values: those that relate to economic efficiency and those that relate to social justice.

While, for instance, David Rockefeller may castigate Milken for his presumed greed, he is unlikely to call for an end to the free enterprise system that allows merger and acquisition activity to occur. Nor is Rockefeller likely to advocate increased government regulation to curtail significantly the opportunity for one company to acquire another. Rockefeller would undoubtedly admit that when mergers and acquisitions occur as "friendly takeovers" and involve far less ostentatious fees paid to investment bankers, then such activity is a good thing, something that enhances economic efficiency.

On the other hand, the general public is reacting out of rage to a visceral sense of social injustice. While the average American family works full-time to earn an average income of $32,000 a year (generally requiring two workers), Milken earned $1,500,000 a day for every day of the year during 1987. And he did not earn this money through making what was perceived as a direct contribution to economic output; he earned it simply by manipulating financial markets and stock prices in a transfer of wealth from one group of investors to another. His actions were inappropriate when judged by what most Americans perceive to be "fair play" or "equitable" or "just." Such judgments are a matter of social justice.

Corporate and academic America appears to be mired somewhere between these two camps. It is well recognized that mergers and acquisitions can enhance economic efficiency, for if markets are presumed to be reasonably efficient, then they will value such activity at its true or efficient value. Thus, the commercial banks that are providing much of the leveraged buyout (LBO) financing will charge appropriate interest rates to reflect the increased risk of such activity, the bond market will establish appropriate bond ratings to reflect the underlying value of the merged assets, and the stock market will reflect the earnings of the new company. Yet this intermediate camp also clearly recognizes that there seems to be something "unfair" about the size of the fees earned by certain individuals involved in the takeover business, and these few individuals give the rest of the industry a "bad name." In this arena, the judgments are a matter of both economic efficiency and social justice.

How do we disentangle these competing sets of social values? How far should we go in improving the efficiency of the economy? What is fair play, equitable, or just? If Milken had earned only $250,000 during 1987 and had not engaged in any alleged illegal manipulation of the markets, would his activities in engineering mergers and acquisitions be viewed as a useful contribution to society? Where do we draw the line between those activities that enhance economic efficiency and those activities that increase social justice? In sum, the Milken case confronts us with an issue that is far deeper and more profound than simply that of personal greed and alleged wrongdoing on the part of one individual investment banker. It is an issue of business ethics in general.

It is my intention to shed some light on the complexity of the competing social values revealed by the reaction to the Milken case among different groups of Americans. I will first examine the meaning of ethics in terms of the economic environment in which the academic and business communities and the general American public are attempting to judge the merits of merger and acquisition activity. This environment is that of the conventional neoclassical model of economic behavior. I will then broaden the discussion of the neoclassical model to consider the issues of social justice. This entails the introduction of utilitarian and contractual models of economic behavior. Finally, I will offer some observations on what these models imply for the broader issue of ethics in business.

Ethics and the Neoclassical Model

Two major questions arise in discussions of ethical behavior and social justice: First, what is the essential nature of individual motivation in determining economic behavior? And second, how do we assess the social desirability of individual economic behavior as it affects the economic system?

The traditional business answer to these two questions is that individuals are inherently moral or ethical in nature and that when employed, they will work to advance the best interests of the firm and society. This view was well expressed in a speech given by A.W. Clausen, former Chairman of the Bank of America at the first forum on "Ethics and American Business in the 1990s": "Our ethics reside in that still small voice of conscience inside each of us that tells us right from wrong."[1] But that still small voice—while certainly intuitively correct—is not sufficient to explain our behavior when we confront difficult decisions of moral choice in business.

Nor is it at all clear that no matter how moral or ethical the employee may be, he or she will make the right decision when confronted with a difficult choice in which alternative courses of action both may be viewed as right. What is right is largely determined by the context in which the decision is made, and this is not generally intuitively clear. Therefore, we must turn to more sophisticated models of economic behavior to explain the behavior of Michael Milken and ourselves when confronted with difficult decisions of moral choice in business. The first of these models is the neoclassical model of economic behavior.

The neoclassical model answers that the individual is motivated by considerations of rational behavior and maximization of self-interest. The individual is assumed to confront a range of alternative socioeconomic choices, and in making a choice the individual will behave in a rational manner. Rationality extends from the choice among competing bundles of economic commodities to choice regarding work and occupation to choice between public and private goods. In making a choice the individual will attempt to maximize his or her own self-interests.

For example, the individual will attempt to maximize the level of consumer utility to be derived from consuming a bundle of private and public commodities, and to maximize the profitability of the firm where he or she works. In maximizing the profitability of the firm, the individual will receive compensation that reflects the market-determined value of his or her contribution to the firm's output, and it is this compensation that enables the individual to pay for the commodites that are consumed in the current time period and to save (accumulate wealth) for consumption in the future.

If each individual behaves in this manner, and we assume the existence of perfectly competitive economic markets and the ability of government to adjust appropriately for social externalities, then the economy will be operating efficiently. All scarce resource inputs such as land, labor, capital, and technology will be allocated among all potential uses to achieve the highest possible level of total output for the economy.

This is generally assumed to be a positive model of economic behavior; that is, it only considers how individuals actually behave, and not how they ought to behave in any normative sense. This dichotomization between positive and normative behavior was most eloquently stated some years ago by Lionel Robbins (1962) in his influential essay on the nature and significance of economic science: "Economics deals with ascertainable facts; ethics with valuations and obligations. The two fields of enquiry are not on the same plane of discourse" (p. 148).

The second matter of concern is assessing the relative social desirability of one economic system compared with another. On this issue the neoclassical model is quite explicit: the "best" economic system is the one that is most efficient in its use of scarce resources. It is the system that will generate the greatest output for a given quantity of resources. Any alternative economic system that is less efficient will achieve a lower level of total output and is judged inferior. It is well recognized that such an economic system can produce great inequality in the distribution of income—a few rich indulging their most extreme desires while the masses live in abject poverty—as much as it can produce greater equality—all individuals able to enjoy a satisfactory standard of living.

Ethics and Utilitarianism

The neoclassical model of economic behavior is not totally devoid of ethical considerations, as has thus far been implied. The ethical version of the neoclassical model is utilitarianism. In general, utilitarianism assumes that an economic system is most socially desirable when its rules and regulations, positions of power and influence, institutions, and so on are arranged to achieve the greatest satisfaction for the largest number of people. Such an economic system is viewed as being "rightly ordered, and therefore just, when its major institutions are arranged so as to achieve the greatest net balance of satisfaction summed over all individuals belonging to it" (Rawls, 1971, p. 22).[2]

The utilitarian model of moral behavior is strongly teleological, that is, the "good" (achieving maximum social utility as an aggregate of all individuals in society) is defined independently from the "right" (achieving justice between all individuals in society), and then the right is defined as that which maximizes the good.

When we apply the utilitarian model to the behavior of Michael Milken and other investment bankers involved in LBO financial transactions, we can explain a good deal of the public reaction to such activities.

First, to the extent that any financial dealings are found to be unlawful by the courts, they would be judged unethical. A basic condition of the utilitarian model is that all financial transactions must be lawful for the model assumes that all economic exchanges occur in free and competitive markets. Illegal transactions are not allowable in such markets.

Second, to the extent that Milken enjoyed a monopoly position within the financial industry that enabled him to earn extraordinary profits for Drexel Burnham Lambert and bonuses for himself, then his activities would be judged as unethical. Again, monopoly is not allowed in free and competitive markets, for it does not lead to maximum social utility.

Third, if the activities of Milken contributed to the inefficient use of financial resources in our economic system, then his actions could be judged as inappropriate for they created a less efficient economic state than existed prior to his activities. Since justice is defined as that which maximizes the good, then inefficient actions would be judged as unjust behavior.

In summary, the utilitarian model assesses ethical or just behavior on the part of Milkin according to two criteria: (1) were his activities legal? and (2) did his activities reduce economic efficiency and hence total social utility? The answer to the first question is for the courts to determine. The answer to the second question is not at all clear.

We know that the firm for which Milken worked—Drexel Burnham Lambert—is now out of business and thousands of its employees have lost their jobs. But it may well be that the overall economy is more efficient with the demise of this particular investment firm, and that its former employees will serve the economic system better by becoming engaged in other activities. And we know that American corporations are more highly leveraged than they were before the rise of the junk bond kings, but whether such leverage is "better" or "worse" from the point of view of economic efficiency is not at all certain. Only time will provide that answer, if at all.

These answers, however, hardly empower us to analyze the full extent of public reaction to the Milken case. They cannot explain the general public's perception that what Milken received was "unjustly acquisitive" or that his actions represented "unethical business behavior." They cannot tell us whether the activities of Wall Street in general are to be judged as "unjust" from a social point of view. To address these concerns we must turn to a far broader moral model than utilitarianism.

Ethics and Contractualism

The contractual model has a long and distinguished intellectual history; it is associated with such names as Locke, Rousseau, Kant, and Rawls. But rather than review this literature, it is my intention to present a generic version of the contractual model that can serve as a basis for discussing the actions of Milken and the issue of business ethics.

The basic elements of the contractual model for an economic system are: (1) a set of initial conditions; (2) a model of exchange of economic commodities; and (3) a set of socially acceptable outputs (see Figure 12.1).

Stage I of the contractual model establishes the basic set of initial conditions that are to be "guaranteed" by the economic system. The guarantee is assumed to take the form of rights or primary goods that are to be honored and preserved in the rules of acceptable behavior governing economic production and exchange within the economic system.

While there is a broad range of initial conditions that can be adopted, I have chosen a limited number: (1) rights against injury from others; (2) rights to freedom of choice and action; (3) rights to own and exchange property (economic commodities including labor services); and (4) rights to a minimal level of basic economic needs (food, shelter, education, health care).[3]

In Stage II of the contractual model the distribution of initial conditions is altered through the process of production and exchange of economic commodities. At this stage there can exist a number of different models of exchange, including free market economy, welfare-state economy, and command economy. I have assumed a free market economy in this discussion as most appropriate for judging the behavior of Milken and the public reaction to that behavior.

In Stage III the outputs of the economic system are defined as consisting of a matrix of outputs that satisfy the following human needs: (1) material needs (food, clothing, shelter, medical care, safety, security); (2) social needs (self-esteem, esteem of others, a sense of belongingness and participation); and (3)

Figure 12.1. **Basic Structure of the Contractual Model**

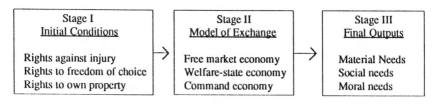

moral needs (the right to meaningful work, the right to actualize our maximum human potential, the right to social justice).

Given this generic contractual model, we return to the basic issue of our role as individuals within the economic system. It is assumed that each of us has the inherent capacity to act as a moral being with a sense of right and wrong (that is, some concept of social justice), that we desire to cooperate with other persons for the mutual benefit of all, and that we act within the economic system to advance our own specific ends.

The first condition, that we are capable of moral behavior, does not mean that we will necessarily always make the right moral or ethical choice; this will depend on the circumstances in which our socioeconomic choices are made and whether we choose to act upon our moral preference function. But this condition does require that we understand what is right and wrong and that we are capable of making moral choices if we so desire.

The second condition, that we desire to cooperate with others for the mutual benefit of all, accounts for the socialization aspect of our nature. We recognize that we belong to a broader community in which our actions will be shaped by the socioeconomic environment in which we act out our individual choices.

Our relationship to the community occurs on many different levels. The most simple is the existence of social externalities, that is, our individual actions will generate social benefits (our consumption of certain goods such as education will benefit others) and social costs (our production of pollution will harm others). At a somewhat higher level we possess "extended sympathy" with other persons. The effect of extended sympathy on our behavior can range from the inclusion of others' feelings in our own moral preference function (an effect that will most commonly occur within a close-knit community such as the family) to a sense of moral commitment to others arising from religion or a metaphysical source (a Kantian form of categorical imperative rationality).[4] And at a still higher level, we might hold an organic or totality view of the true essence of society. Such a view sees the universe as one living organism of identical and interdependent parts.[5]

The third condition is that we act within the economic system to advance our own specific ends. There is no single all-dominant goal or output in the economic system, such as consumer utility. Rather, there is a matrix of socioeconomic outputs provided by a given economic system to all persons in that system. That matrix of outputs consists of material, social, and moral needs.

Each of us has the opportunity, within the constraints imposed by the availability of initial conditions and the institutions of the economic system that determine the process of exchange, to realize whatever subset of that matrix we desire. Some may choose to maximize consumption of material outputs. Others may place more emphasis on realizing certain social outputs, such as participating in the community, while still others may pursue social justice as a primary goal.

As we participate in the economic system, we will form our assessments of the social justice with which that system operates. Social justice is not simply a matter of the distribution of initial conditions and certain rules imposed at the first stage of the contractual model (see Rawls, 1971). Nor is social justice an externally imposed condition at the final stage, such as a socially determined social welfare function as expressed in traditional neoclassical theory. Social justice involves three different conditions that permeate all stages of the economic system: commutative justice, productive justice, and distributive justice.

Commutative Justice

The concept of commutative justice was first asserted by Aristotle. The philosophical basis for commutative justice is rooted in the fundamental moral prohibition against harm, and in economic exchange harm is avoided when there is equivalence of exchange. Therefore, within the condition of commutative justice one has to determine the meaning of equivalence of exchange. It was this problem that Aristotle attempted to answer in discussing the relationship of a "just price" and "value in exchange" for a commodity exchanged in an economic market.

Aristotle defines commutative justice as involving private voluntary transactions, consisting of such transactions "as selling, buying, lending at interest, giving security, lending without interest, depositing money, hiring" (Welldon, 1892, p. 142). In such transactions, "that which is unjust is unfair, that which is just is fair." Recognizing that in economic exchange the two parties to that exchange are not equal, Aristotle argued that there should be neither "excessive profit" nor "undue loss" resulting from a just or fair voluntary exchange (Welldon, 1892, p. 149).

Adam Smith expressed these principles most completely when he laid out the principles of a competitive market of exchange. He began by distinguishing between natural price and market price: the natural price is that price sufficient to pay rents, wages, and earn normal profits; the market price is the actual price at which the commodity is sold in the market, and this price "may either be above, or below, or exactly the same with its natural price" (Smith, 1937, p. 55).

There may be a gap between the natural and market price for a number of reasons: monopoly; great distance between the buyer and the seller; secrets in manufacturing such as technological advantages that reduce costs; or natural conditions such as particularly fertile land. While admitting that some of these conditions may last for centuries (e.g., uniquely fertile land), or for the life of the individual producer (e.g., technological advantage), Smith argues that such cases are unique. The laws of supply and demand in a competitive market will eliminate any unusual profits enjoyed by a particular producer, and thus a competitive market will equate the actual market price with the natural price. And for Smith, following the same reasoning as that of Aristotle, the natural price is a just price.

However, implicit in the discussion of Adam Smith is an assumption that exchange takes place between a buyer and a seller who are roughly equally competent to judge the commodities, their quality, and their value. Smith discusses competitive conditions existing in what he calls "a society or neighborhood." There is "in every society or neighborhood an ordinary or average rate both of wages and profit in very different employment of labor and stock. This rate is naturally regulated. . .partly by the general circumstances of the society [and] partly by the particular nature of each employment" (Smith, 1937, p. 55).

Smith appears to have in mind individuals who exchange commodities in "a world of shared meanings and mutual knowledgeability" (Gunnemann, 1986, p. 104). It is a world that involves trust and credibility, or as Kenneth Boulding states the matter—suppose that we cure all of the ills of the market, what then?

> No matter how well we take care of all neighborhood effects and external economies and diseconomies, no matter how exactly the seven marginal conditions of welfare economics are fulfilled, there remains a residue of elements in social relations that are not accounted for by exchange. It is these residues that constitute what I call the integrative system, involving such things as status, respect, love, honor, community, identity, legitimacy, and so on. I would argue indeed that without an integrative framework, exchange itself cannot develop, because exchange, even in its most primitive forms, involves trust and credibility. [Boulding, 1967, p. 68]

It is clear that commutative justice involves far more than the occurrence of voluntary exchange in a competitive market. While these conditions are basic to achieving a just or fair price, other factors are involved. Aristotle suggested that justice would occur in a market where there is neither excessive profit nor undue loss. Adam Smith postulated the conditions of a competitive market that would eliminate excessive profit, but the basis of this market is grounded in a society of shared meanings and mutual knowledgeability. Kenneth Boulding characterized this society in terms of an integrative framework of values based on trust and credibility.

Productive Justice

Like commutative justice, the roots for the concept of productive justice can also be traced back to Arisotle, who along with Thomas Aquinas some centuries later, gave definition to what has been variously known as legal justice and social justice. According to Aristotle, justice is not absolute but exists "in relation to our neighbor" (Ferree, 1942, p. 11). While this relative nature of justice is traditionally interpreted as compliance with a particular code of law or positive legalistic justice, Aristotle offered an alternative meaning to legal justice from which productive justice emanates: that state of a society by which it is called good through the proper ordering of its parts.

It was Thomas Aquinas, however, carefully building upon the philosophical base of Aristotle, who is credited with formulating the basis for our modern understanding of productive justice. Rooted in the acceptance of the essentially social nature of human beings, justice "can be neither specified nor understood apart from the web of social interdependence which entails mutual obligation and duty" (Hollenbach, 1977, p. 210).

It is social interdependence that sets this form of justice apart from commutative and distributive justice, both of which are inherently much more individualistic. The communal nature of justice was further developed by Roman Catholic theologians during the past century into its modernday form. In 1891 the Roman Church proclaimed that "one cannot specify the meaning of justice without examining the social relationships, patterns of mutuality and structures of interdependence which bind human beings together in communities."[6] This was followed by an encyclical published in 1931 that proclaimed that the justness of any society is to be judged in terms of the way in which the institutions of that society "promote human dignity by enhancing mutuality and genuine participation in community."[7] The latest statement on social justice, published by the National Conference of Catholic Bishops in the United States in 1986, requires "that persons have an obligation to be active and productive participants in the life of society and that society has a duty to enable them to participate in this way" (National Conference of Catholic Bishops, 1986, p. 36).

In summary, productive justice relates to the fairness of participation by individuals in the economic system. It considers the impact of the methods of production on the fulfillment of basic needs, employment levels, patterns of discrimination, environmental quality, and sense of community. Furthermore, it requires that society operate so that all individuals can contribute in ways that respect their freedom and the dignity of their labor.

Distributive Justice

In the most general terms, distributive justice concerns the allocation of the benefits of an economic system among all the members of that system. But how those benefits are defined and how a just criterion for the allocation is determined are highly debatable issues. Aristotle proposed one of the earliest suggestions: justice requires that a society treat equals equally and unequals unequally but in proportion to their relevant differences. John Rawls, the best known of the current writers on the issue, proposes that all social primary goods—liberty and opportunity, income and wealth, and the bases of self-respect—are to be distributed equally unless an unequal distribution of any, or all, of these goods is to the advantage of the least favored (Rawls, 1971).

Both Artistotle and Rawls, along with a host of thinkers on the issue of justice in the ages between these two, raise as many complex questions as they answer. What do we mean by equality? What are the relevant economic differences between individuals that would justify inequality in the allocation of economic benefits within an economic system? When would an unequal distribution of benefits be to the overall advantage of the entire economic system?

While it is impossible in this short discussion to address these complex questions, a few comments about the nature of distributive justice are relevant to our discussion of Michael Milken. The most narrow interpretation of distributive justice is that it must satisfy the conditions of merit. If the original distribution of certain fundamental rights is fair, and all subsequent exchanges are fair, then the final distribution is just.[8]

While our society apparently has judged that distributive justice should adhere essentially to the merit principle of allowing the individual to realize his or her rewards from the operation of a just economic system, the outcome must satisfy some generally perceived conditions of fairness. These conditions relate to fairness in earning that income, fairness in functioning in an economic system in which all individuals have an opportunity to participate, and fairness in that the individual contributes to the overall good of the economic system.

Moral Choice and Business Ethics

Given the contractual model of economic behavior, can we now explain the range of public reaction to the Milken case and derive knowledge that is applicable to all individuals in business?

The basic assumption that the individual is motivated by a set of values that include ethical considerations as well as by a set of considerations that relate only to self-interests raises the issue of the moral nature of the activities of Milken or any other individual engaged in business. All of us must make moral choices in our jobs, whether those choices are only routine matters or are unique decisions that affect hundreds of individuals or involve millions of dollars. Moral choice is an inherent part of our daily business life.

Therefore, while we do not know exactly what motivated Milken, the results of his actions suggest that he was acting upon a quite narrow set of self-interest values. He clearly was not acting on a broader set of values that involved a consideration of the impact of his actions upon other individuals or upon society in general. But did his narrow set of self-interest values lead to unethical behavior? To answer this we must turn to the issue of his impact upon the economic system. That impact can be explained most readily through our broader concept of social justice.

Much of the attitude of the public towards Milken is explained by the concept of commutative justice. The public's sense is that Milken manipulated the markets to his personal advantage. He was able to create a unique demand for his product of junk bonds, to control the information provided to the public regarding the nature of the transactions, and to structure a personal agreement with Drexel Burnham Lambert that ensured him extraordinary fees for his services.[9] In other words, Milken was not paid for any market valuation of his productive efforts, but rather for his ability to generate new business through use of "the vast resources at his disposal to exert unprecedented control over the junk bond market and corporate America" (*New York Times*, 1989, p. C2).

Such activities clearly do not meet the test of Aristotle that there should be neither excessive profit nor undue loss in a free voluntary exchange in the market. They do not meet the conditions of Adam Smith that market prices must represent a normal return for services rendered. Nor do they satisfy the conditions of trust and credibility in all market transactions expounded by Kenneth Boulding. It is not surprising, then, that David Rockefeller could question whether there is something wrong with the way our financial system is working.

When we turn to the concept of productive justice, the ethical indictment is even more pronounced. Applied to the Milken case, productive justice raises questions regarding the mutual obligations and duties that all those involved in business have with society. It suggests that the basis of the naturally regulated society of Adam Smith or the integrative community of Kenneth Boulding (both expounded as essential in commutative justice) is found in the web of social interdependence that is characteristic of productive justice. Just behavior requires that we consider the duties and obligations to society that go along with our rights to engage in activities that maximize our economic self-interests.

Finally, can we explain the visceral sense of social injustice that characterizes the general public reaction to the fact that Milken earned $1,500,000 a day during 1987 while the average American family earned only $32,000 during the entire year? This is a matter of distributive justice. But it is a complex matter, for the public reaction involves a commingling of all three concepts of justice. For instance, the sense of social injustice arises from a view that what was earned was not the result of meritorious activity but of manipulation of the financial markets (commutative justice) emanating from greedy and self-centered behavior on the part of Milken (productive justice). Distributive justice enters the picture through the concept of declining utility of income, the fact that the utility of the last dollar earned by a millionaire is viewed by society in some general sense as of less value than the last dollar earned by the average American.

In conclusion, when we broaden the meaning of social justice to include commutative and productive justice as well as distributive justice, and postulate that each individual behaves with a set of ethical as well as self-interest values (regardless of whether we choose to act upon our ethical values), the activities of Milken and his junk bond peers involve ethical issues of moral choice. And the

Milken case is not unique. All business decisions involve moral choice. Business cannot treat ethical issues as a separate consideration from mainstream business decisions, segregating such issues into a "social policy committee" or looking to government to solve what is viewed as "a social problem" rather than "a business problem." The Milken case, and the public reaction to it, point out once again the importance of dealing with the issue of moral choice and business ethics.

Notes

1. Walter A. Haas School of Business, University of California at Berkeley, November 27, 1989.

2. While Rawls (1971) is no friend of the utilitarian school of thought, he does have a good summary and criticism of both the classical version of utilitarianism and the more current versions such as rule utilitarianism.

3. The nature and extent of these conditions gives shape to the economic system far more than any other aspect of the contractural model. For instance, Nozick (1974) specifies in his model a minimal set of initial conditions: rights against injury by others, rights to freedom of choice and action, rights to own property. Out of this set of minimal rights, Nozick fashions a model in which exchange occurs in a market economy and the resulting distribution of output is defined as just. Rawls (1971), on the other hand, has a far more extensive list of what he terms primary goods: (1) basic liberties including political liberties, freedom of thought and association, freedom of the integrity of the person; (2) freedom of movement and choice of occupation; (3) powers and prerogatives of offices and positions of responsibility; (4) income and wealth; (5) social bases of self-respect. Given this set of primary goods, Rawls builds a social system in which all primary goods are to be distributed equally unless an unequal distribution would benefit the least advantaged of society. These two models probably represent the extreme positions of the contractual model: that of Nozick producing such extremes in the distribution of final output that no rational individual would voluntarily adopt this economic system and that of Rawls so constraining the economic system at the initial stage with his essentially distributive justice limitations that it is unlikely that the economic system would produce the necessary output to satisfy the conditions of distribution that are imposed upon it by Rawls.

4. Smith (1937) is the best-known economist who expounded the extended sympathy view. This view has, however, been updated by Harsanyi (1982) in his version of rule utilitarianism.

5. Alfred North Whitehead is well known for propounding this philosophy. Yet the most sophisticated statement of a philosophy of totality is that of Hua-yen Buddhism. See Cook (1977) and Cleary (1983).

6. This view of social justice was contained in the encyclical, "On the Rights and Duties of Capital and Labor" (Refum Novarum) by Pope Leo XIII. See Hollenbach (1977, p. 210).

7. The second major statement by the Roman Catholic Church on social justice was the encyclical, "On Reconstructing the Social Order" (Quadragesimo Anno) by Pope Pius XI. See Hollenbach (1977, p. 213).

8. This is the conclusion of Nozick (1974) from his contractual model. A more complete statement would be: If the original distribution of certain fundamental rights is fair (equal distribution of rights against injury by others, rights to freedom of choice and action, rights to own property), and all subsequent exchanges are fair (defined as being

achievable in a free competitive market economy), then the final distribution of income and wealth is by definition just.

9. Milken apparently was guaranteed up to 35 percent of the commission on each leveraged buyout transaction he engineered as a reward for helping his firm move from being "a third-tier investment house" to "a Wall Street powerhouse."

References

Boulding, Kenneth E. 1967. "The Basis of Value Judgments in Economics." In Sidney Hook, ed., *Human Values and Economic Policy*. New York: New York University Press.

Cleary, Thomas. 1983. *Entry into the Inconceivable, An Introduction to Hua-yen Buddhism*. Honolulu: University of Hawaii Press.

Cook, Francis H. 1977. *Hua-yen Buddhism, The Jewel Net of Indra*. University Park: Pennsylvania State University Press.

Ferree, William. 1942. *The Act of Social Justice*. Washington, DC: Catholic University of America Press.

Gunnemann, John P. 1986. "Capitalism and Commutative Justice." In *The Annual of the Society of Christian Ethics, 1985*. Washington, DC: Georgetown University Press.

Harsanyi, John C. 1982. "Morality and the theory of rational behaviour." In Amartya Sen and Bernard Williams, eds., *Utilitarianism and Beyond*. Cambridge: Cambridge University Press.

Hollenbach, David. 1977. "Modern Catholic Teachings Concerning Justice." In John C. Haughey, ed., *The Faith That Does Justice*. New York: Paulist Press.

National Conference of Catholic Bishops. 1986. *Economic Justice for All*. Washington, DC: NCCB.

New York Times. 1989. "Wages Even Wall St. Can't Stomach." April 3.

Nozick, Robert. 1974. *Anarchy, State, and Utopia*. New York: Basic Books.

Rawls, John. 1971. *A Theory of Justice*. Cambridge, MA: Harvard University Press.

Robbins, Lionel. 1962. *An Essay on the Nature and Significance of Economic Science*. London: Macmillan.

Smith, Adam. 1937. *The Wealth of Nations*. New York: Modern Library.

Welldon, J.E.C. 1892. *The Nichmachean Ethics of Aristotle*. London: Macmillan.

13

KAREN N. GAERTNER

The Effect of Ethical Climate
on Managers' Decisions

The purpose of the research described in this paper was to examine the effect of a firm's ethical climate on the criteria used in decision making and on the decisions ultimately made within the firm. This has become an extremely important topic among managers and teachers of managers, as we see examples of unethical decision making causing harm to individuals, organizations, markets, and potentially to the economy. Understanding how and why ethical criteria are used in the decision-making process can help us educate managers and eventually change their propensity to use ethical criteria in the decision process.

Theory

Individual decision making has been a topic of research in the behavioral and social sciences for many years. Models have been developed that describe decision making as an individual-level activity, bounded by people's ability and will to process information (March and Simon, 1958). These so-called "bounded rationality" models of decision making focus attention on the limits of human cognition and information-processing capacity. Recently, Etzioni (1988) extended this line of reasoning in his discussion of moral considerations in decision making. He argues that logical/empirical decision making is constrained both by cognitive factors and by noncognitive factors, and he suggests that normative commitments and affective involvements are important criteria in choice processes because they shape the limits within which the cognitive aspects of decision making operate. Normative/affective considerations delimit the range of

This research was supported by a grant from the Center for Creative Leadership. Mary Beth Lyons helped with Looking Glass from beginning to end in every way imaginable. Lynn Paine insisted that decision criteria would be important and offered other conceptual help throughout. Stan Nollen provided methodological clarity at exactly the right moment.

acceptable alternatives from which one may be chosen. Normative affective criteria may also compete directly with logical/empirical criteria in the choice process. Thus, the choice process is heavily laden with normative preferences of individuals.

While Etzioni does not address characteristics of the situation that may shape the use of normative criteria in much detail, Simon's (1979) discussion of aspirations suggests that people select goals according to what they believe can be accomplished. Thus, in friendly, supportive environments, aspirations will be high; in more difficult environments, aspirations will be lower.

Other models of decision making take specific aspects of the situation into account, emphasizing the quality of information available or the uncertainty under which decisions are made (Bass, 1983). Seldom is explicit attention paid to an organization's culture or climate as a source of variation in individual decision making. Yet culture and climate ought to affect decision making by prohibiting consideration of a range of alternatives considered to be inconsistent with the firm's culture or by giving greater weight to alternatives considered consistent with the firm's culture (analogous to Etzioni's discussion of normative criteria at the individual level).

By organizational culture we mean the norms and values shared by organizational members that guide behavior (Smircich, 1983). Culture is manifested in customs, rituals, myths, and other behaviors, and is reinforced by reward systems and criteria. The ethical climate, therefore, is one aspect of an organization's culture, defined as the implicit norms and values about ethical behavior in the firm, derived from perceptions of practices and policies (Victor and Cullen, 1988).

Just as decision making has been examined at both the individual and the situational level, causes of ethical (or unethical) behavior are attributed to both individuals and situations. Trevino and Youngblood (1990) found moral development and locus of control directly related to the ethical quality of decisions. Hegarty and Sims (1978) similarly found locus of control and value orientation related to the ethical quality of decisions, while subjects in both of these studies were more likely to make unethical decisions if their "company" supported such decisions through rewards or modeled behavior. In other words, individual and organizational normative criteria appear to have an effect on the choice process.

Although Victor and Cullen (1988) were not testing actual decision-making behavior, they found that organizations vary in their ethical climates. They identified five ethical dimensions along which their firms varied: the extent of *caring* about others ("What is best for everyone in the company is the major consideration here"); reliance on *law and code* ("People are expected to comply with the law and professional standards over and above other considerations"); reliance on company *rules* ("People in this company strictly obey the company policies"); prevalence of *instrumental* behavior ("People are expected to do anything to further the company's interests, regardless of the consequences"); and reliance on one's own *independent* values ("In this company, people are guided by their own personal ethics"). They found considerable variability across companies and locations in ethical climate, as well as differences by employees' level, age, and tenure within company. They conclude that ethical climates may influence the criteria brought to bear in decision making, and thus influence the ethical quality of decisions.

We have extended this line of research to examine both individual and organizational factors that might result in more or less ethical decisions. Specifically, three research questions are addressed:

1. Does an organization's ethical climate affect the criteria that are brought to bear in decision making?

2. Does an organization's ethical climate affect the ethical quality of decisions made by employees?

3. Do individual characteristics affect the ethical quality of their decisions independent of the ethical climate within which they work?

This study combines the contributions of others as we examine ethical climate and individual characteristics. It extends their work as we assess the effect of decision criteria explicitly.

Methods

Looking Glass, Inc.

Data for this study were gathered via a complex management simulation, *Looking Glass, Inc.*, a hypothetical firm in the glass manufacturing business. The simulation is a $3^1/_2$-hour "day in the life of" in-basket involving the top nineteen or twenty managers in the company. We ran four separate companies among full-time MBA students.[1] For the students it was the culminating exercise in an organizational behavior course. Most students were assigned to write their final paper for the course on their Looking Glass experience.

Looking Glass is an ethically neutral company. There are problems to be solved in the simulation that have ethical dimensions, but there is no information in the simulation indicating the company's historic approach to such problems. To increase the likelihood of differences in ethical climate owing to something other than individual differences, we added eight memos to the in-baskets (a typical in-basket has about fifty memos). In two companies these memos indicated that the firm had policies and practices that reinforced a *caring* and *law and code* climate in Victor and Cullen's terms, and indicated that dishonest or ethically suspect behavior would not be tolerated (similar to Trevino and Youngblood). Examples include a statement of values and a memo to managers announcing that an employee had been fired for stealing from one of the plants.[2]

In the other two companies memos on the same topics were added, but their content emphasized *instrumental* values and either rewarded or explicitly tolerated ethically suspect behavior (for example, inappropriate use of the company airplane by sales people for certain clients and a personal relationship between a purchasing employee and a buyer in another firm).

Students were not told about the differences in the companies prior to the simulation. They were told about the differences afterwards, as part of the debriefing process.

Measures

Systematic data were collected in two ways. First, participants completed the Defining Issues Test (Rest, 1979) separate from Looking Glass. The DIT measures the type of ethical reasoning used in moral dilemmas, following Kohlberg's (1969) and Rest's work on moral reasoning. For this analysis we use the "P" score from the test, which is the percentage of time the respondent used *principled reasoning* in working through the problems. This is clearly a limited measure of individual normative criteria, but it has been used by many researchers in work on moral judgment and has well-known psychometric properties (Rest, 1979).

Second, a questionnaire was completed by all participants directly following Looking Glass in which we asked about ethical climate, decision criteria, and a number of other aspects of their experience.

Ethical Climate

We asked about the ethical climate that evolved in the organization, adapting the instrument developed by Victor and Cullen (1988).[3] The five ethical climate dimensions measured are the same as those described above: caring, law and code, rules, instrumental, and independent. For this analysis we emphasize the caring and instrumental climates, consistent with the changes induced in the companies through new memos.

Criteria Used in Decision Making

We asked about decisions made during the simulation and the criteria used for those decisions. The criteria included such things as one's own ethical values, costs, company policies, the needs of employees, and efficiency. We sorted these criteria into five groups, supported by factor analysis and corresponding roughly to the five ethical climate dimensions.[4]

Decision Made

We measured an actual decision with responses to a hypothetical situation given in the questionnaire. This decision was whether to purchase machinery that would improve air quality inside and outside the plant but that was not required by law, was not commonly installed in the industry, and would not result in any increase in productivity. The participants were asked how likely they would be to buy the machinery, assuming they were still working for their Looking Glass

Table 13.1

Means, Standard Deviations, and Reliabilities

Variable	Mean	Standard Deviation	Alpha
1. Ethical Climate			
Instrumental	3.31	1.13	0.714
Independent	4.13	0.97	0.673
Law and Code	4.58	1.23	0.815
Rules	3.82	1.22	0.753
Caring	4.29	1.15	0.821
2. Decision Criteria			
Caring	4.99	1.47	0.521
Law and Code	3.66	1.44	0.673
Rules	4.59	1.32	0.738
Independent	5.23	1.47	0.615
Instrumental	4.76	1.18	0.614
3. Moral Development			
P—Percent Principled Reasoning	48.60	13.80	
4. Decision			
Buy new machinery	5.34	1.48	

company. Responses were on a seven-point Likert scale that ranged from (1) very unlikely to buy, to (7) very likely to buy.

This decision is most relevant for the *caring* ethical dimension and the *instrumental* dimension. The independence, law, and rules ethical dimensions do not have an obvious role in this decision.

A total of 76 students participated in the study. There were 72 usable questionnaires and 65 completed Defining Issues Tests. The analyses are based on the 72 completed questionnaires unless otherwise noted. The means, standard deviations, and reliability coefficients (where appropriate) for all variables are shown in Table 13.1.

Results

1. Does an Organization's Ethical Climate Affect the Criteria That are Brought to Bear in Decision Making?

The zero-order correlations among the five climate scales and the five decision criteria are shown in Table 13.2. For three ethical climates there are strong relationships with corresponding criteria used in making decisions. In the other two ethical climates there are no strong relationships between climate and decision criteria.

Those who perceived an instrumental ethical climate also report instrumental criteria being used in decisions ($r = 0.353$). Those who report an independent ethical climate (behavior based on one's own personal beliefs about right and wrong) say their own ethical values were used as criteria for decisions ($r = 0.389$). In addition, those who report an independent ethical climate say employee needs and company policy and values were used as criteria ($r = 0.318$ and 0.247, respectively). Finally, those who report a caring ethical climate (valuing the needs of others) say employee needs ($r = 0.341$) and company policy and values ($r = 0.473$) were criteria for decisions.

Perceptions of ethical climates emphasizing laws and company rules were not clearly associated with the use of any particular decision criteria. This makes sense in light of the memos we added to the in-baskets. It is also consistent with Victor and Cullen's (1988) results as they report no strong association between these two ethical climate perceptions and satisfaction with criteria used in decision making.

These results show clear connections between perceived ethical climate and the criteria participants report using in decisions. Note that these decision criteria are largely independent of the type of decision being made. We averaged criteria across three decisions for this analysis. Only one decision, the hypothetical decision, is constant. The other two could have been on anything from purchasing raw materials to job transfers. Yet even with this heterogeneous collection of decisions implicated in decision criteria, we find expected relationships between climate and criteria. Had we been able to control for the type of decision made we would probably have seen even stronger relationships.

2. Does an Organization's Ethical Climate Affect the Ethical Quality of Decisions Made by Employees?

To answer this question the relationships among ethical climate, decision criteria, and the hypothetical decision made by all participants after the completion of Looking Glass (presented in the questionnaire) were examined.[5]

This decision is most relevant for the *caring* ethical dimension and the *instrumental* dimension (and the corresponding criteria). We expect, therefore, that participants who perceive a more instrumental ethical climate will invoke instrumental criteria for the decision and not buy the machinery. Similarly, those who perceive a more caring ethical climate will invoke caring criteria and buy the machinery. In other words, ethical climate should affect the purchase decision indirectly through the criteria that are invoked for the decision.

To address this question, the purchase decision was regressed on the two relevant decision criteria, instrumental and caring. The two relevant ethical cli-

Table 13.2

Zero-Order Correlations between Ethical Climate and Decision Criteria

		Decision Criteria				
		Caring	Rules	Law	Indep.	Instru.
	Instru.	−0.276*	−0.207*	−0.044	−0.175	0.353**
	Indep.	0.318**	0.247*	0.241*	0.389***	0.130
Ethical	Law	0.051	0.241*	−0.004	−0.049	−0.032
Climate	Rules	−0.105	0.109	−0.057	−0.187	−0.032
	Caring	0.341**	0.473***	0.121	0.143	−0.030

*$p < 0.05$, one–tailed test
**$p < 0.01$, one–tailed test
***$p < 0.001$, one–tailed test

mate dimensions were then added to the equation to determine whether either of these dimensions had a direct effect on the purchase decision. Finally, each decision criterion was regressed on the two climate variables to ascertain the direct links between the decision criteria and ethical climate dimensions (and therefore the indirect links between ethical climate and the purchase decision). The results of this analysis are shown in Table 13.3.

As expected, use of the two relevant criteria was a strong predictor of the purchase decision. Those who took into account the needs of others were more likely to purchase the machinery. Similarly, those who invoked efficiency and cost criteria (the instrumental criterion) were less likely to purchase the machinery. These results are shown in the left column of Table 13.3.

We also see that perceptions of ethical climate *per se* did not have any direct effect on the purchase decision. Neither of the coefficients for climate perceptions is statistically significant. These results are shown in the second column of Table 13.3.

Finally, the indirect effects of climate on the purchase decision can be discerned through the results shown in the third and fourth columns of Table 13.3. Here we show the direct relationships between the relevant climate dimensions and the decision criteria. Clearly, the perception of an instrumental climate is the most powerful for this decision. There is a positive relationship between instrumental climate and instrumental criteria and a slightly stronger negative relationship between instrumental climate and the use of caring criteria (betas of 0.225 and −0.275, respectively). In other words, for this decision, the perception of an instrumental climate corresponds to use of instrumental criteria and a no-purchase decision. Similarly, perception of an instrumental climate also affects the decision by making it *unlikely* that caring criteria will be used. Thus, an instrumental climate affects the purchase decision in two ways, via commission and omission, if you will.

Table 13.3

Regression of Purchase Decision on Climate and Decision Criteria

	Purchase Decision Dependent		Decision Criteria Dependent	
	I. Decision Criteria	II. Ethical Climate	III. Instru. Criteria	IV. Caring Criteria
Variable	Beta[a]	Beta[a]	Beta[a]	Beta[a]
Caring Crit.	0.337***	0.367***		
Instru. Crit.	−0.396***	−0.415***		
Caring Climate		0.028	−0.061	0.200*
Instru. Climate		0.121	0.225*	−0.275*
Adj. R^2	0.311	0.302	0.039	0.139
F =	17.233	8.793	2.472	6.793
	$p < 0.001$	$p < 0.001$	$p < 0.1$	$p = 0.002$

[a]Standardized regression coefficients
*$p < 0.05$; **$p < 0.01$; ***$p < 0.001$.

Perceptions about a caring climate have a weaker but still predicted effect on use of criteria. Those who perceive a caring climate are more likely to use caring criteria that result in the decision to purchase. However, perception of a caring climate is unrelated to use of instrumental criteria. Thus, a caring climate does not *prevent* the use of such criteria. It just seems to *add* a criterion to the process.

In sum, we have strong evidence that the criteria used do affect the decision and that perceptions of ethical climate correspond to the criteria used. Moreover, we see some evidence that instrumental climates may actively discourage breadth in the criteria used in decision making, while caring climates encourage caring criteria and neither support nor inhibit the use of instrumental criteria.

3. Do Individual Characteristics Affect the Ethical Quality of Their Decisions Independent of the Ethical Climate within Which They Work?

The last step in the analysis is to examine the relationship between individual moral reasoning and decision making. To do this we added individual moral reasoning (the "P" score from the DIT) to the regression equations discussed above. This analysis, too, was done in several steps. First, moral reasoning was added to the regression of the purchase decision on criteria and climate (the left panel in Table 13.4). Then it was added to the equations with the decision criteria dependent (the next two panels in Table 13.4). Finally, it was used as a predictor of climate perceptions, although, because neither of these was significant, the equations are not shown in this table. A note of caution is appropriate

Table 13.4

Regression of Purchase Decision on Climate, Decision Criteria, and Moral Reasoning

Dependent Variables

I. Purchasing Decision		II. Decision Criteria	
		Instrumental	Caring
Variable	Beta[a]	Beta[a]	Beta[a]
Caring Crit.	0.387***		
Instru. Crit.	-0.413***		
Caring Climate	0.018	-0.062	0.247*
Instru. Climate	0.120	0.223*	-0.228*
Moral Reasoning	-0.047	-0.012	0.348***
Adj. R²	0.294	0.026	0.250
F =	6.989	1.628	9.008
	$p < 0.001$	$p = 0.19$	$p < 0.001$

[a]Standardized regression coefficients.
*$p < 0.05$; **$p < 0.01$; $p < 0.001$.

before examining the results shown in Table 13.4. Because of missing data from the DIT, we used mean substitution for missing DIT scores rather than lose the cases. This is a fairly conservative procedure and tends to diminish relationships.

We see that moral reasoning has no direct relationship with the purchase decision. Nor has it any direct relationship with the perception of ethical climate, as noted above. This is good news, since it suggests that ethical climate is not merely a function of one's individual ethical values but exists independent of one's values. Moral reasoning does, however, show a strong relationship with the use of the caring criteria for decision making. Those who use more principled reasoning are also more likely to invoke concern for others as a decision criterion. At the same time, there is no relationship between moral reasoning and use of instrumental criteria. Those who use more principled reasoning are no more or less likely to use instrumental criteria than others. The results of the analyses shown in Tables 13.3 and 13.4 are summarized in Figure 13.1.

Discussion and Conclusions

At the outset we asked how and why managers make the decisions they make, and to what extent they invoke ethical criteria in making decisions. This research demonstrates that the criteria people invoke affect the ethical quality of decisions

Figure 13.1. **Summary of Results**

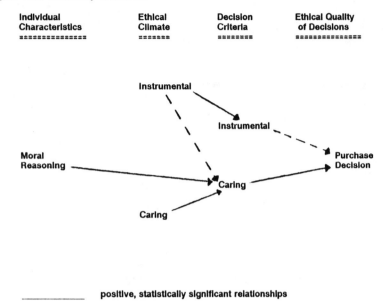

made and that the criteria invoked are a function of both the perceived ethical climate of the organization and the individual's values. We did not find any direct effect of moral reasoning on decision making. It operated only through the criteria invoked. Those who use principled reasoning do not make "knee jerk" ethical decisions (the absence of a direct relationship between principled reasoning and the decision). Rather, they are likely to invoke criteria that are consistent with their judgment process (the strong relationship between moral reasoning and use of caring criteria). It is interesting that moral reasoning does not have a corresponding dampening effect on instrumental criteria. Those who use principled moral reasoning are as likely to use instrumental criteria as others. The difference is that they are able to add caring criteria to their decision process.

There was also no direct effect of ethical climate on the purchase decision. Again, the effect of ethical climate is manifested in its effect on the criteria used in the decision process. Our results are similar to those of Trevino and Young-blood, as we found both individual and situational determinants of decision behavior. At the same time, our results extend their work by identifying the strong mediating effect of decision criteria on the final decision. Our results also extend the work of Victor and Cullen by identifying the decision criteria through which ethical climate works to affect decision making.

Perhaps the most interesting results are those that have to do with the determinants of the use of decision criteria rather than the decision itself. The pattern of relationships we found suggests that instrumental criteria are invoked in a very different way from caring criteria. Caring criteria are invoked when the climate is supportive, when there is no countervailing pressure from instrumental criteria, *and when people use principled reasoning.* By contrast, instrumental criteria are invoked when the climate supports them. Use of instrumental criteria is not influenced by individual characteristics (though we tested only a small number of individual characteristics—not reported here). Nor is it dampened by the use of caring criteria. The same study done with a more heterogeneous population may be more revealing regarding the determinants of instrumental criteria.

These results suggest that instrumental climates affect decisions as much through the criteria they prohibit as through the criteria they encourage. Classroom discussions with students support this interpretation. Students in MBA programs refer to ethical criteria as "soft" and "not business-like" and "emotional." They have a hard time seeing decisions from a stakeholder perspective, including the legitimate needs of others. They believe that in business there is no room for "soft," "emotional" criteria in decision making.

Moreover, much of the coursework in an MBA program rests, at least implicitly, on an economic model that assumes rational behavior is motivated by individual self-interest. Business students know this model, are comfortable with it, and believe it, notwithstanding evidence concerning its weaknesses (Etzioni, 1988). Ethical reasoning, on the other hand, asks for consideration of the needs of others. It is not based on the assumption that self-interest is optimal. It is therefore not surprising to find that business students are uncomfortable with ethical reasoning and do not readily see its place in business decisions.[6]

Methodologically, we lent some support to Victor and Cullen's work. Factor analysis supports the same factors in our data as theirs, even though the populations are quite different and some of the individual items were different. We also found a similar pattern of interscale correlations as Victor and Cullen (not shown).

Substantively, we add to their results in two ways. First, we support their supposition that different criteria are invoked in different ethical climates. Second, we see that the caring ethical climate is not quite as strong an indirect predictor of ethical decision making as is moral reasoning. The path from caring climate to the purchase decision is a little weaker than the path from moral reasoning to the purchase decision. The difference is small, but may be indicative of the difficulty in creating and maintaining an ethical climate in which it is acceptable to invoke *both* caring and instrumental criteria.

Finally, instrumental climate has a stronger indirect effect on the purchase decision than either the caring climate or individual moral reasoning. Victor and Cullen found a strong negative relationship between instrumental climate and *satisfaction* with criteria used. This suggests that managers may feel they have to use instrumental criteria too much in decision making. Anecdotal evidence from practicing managers supports this supposition. Future research might explore the reasons for dominance of this climate dimension, particularly in other organizational settings (nonprofits, for example) and in other cultures.

These results are clearly tentative. The sample is small, Looking Glass, Inc. is a simulation, the decision used for the analysis was hypothetical, outside the simulation (although participants were asked to respond as they would as an employee of their Looking Glass company), and our measurement of decision criteria is imperfect. However, these limitations notwithstanding, we are encouraged by the results because they indicate that decision criteria can be managed and therefore that the ethical quality of decisions can be improved.

Notes

1. These were full time students in a daytime MBA program. As a group they have nearly three years of full time work experience. About 75% are from the USA. The others are from a dozen different countries around the world.

2. Complete information about the added memos and the simulation is available from the author. *Looking Glass, Inc.* is a product of the Center for Creative Leadership.

3. In a pretest with another group of students we used all 26 items in the Victor and Cullen scale, plus 10 new items they were testing. Based on analysis of the pretest data and examination of Victor and Cullen's results we administered a 26-item scale that includes some items from the original scale and some from the ten new items for this study. For exact items used, contact the author.

4. There were two questions in the questionnaire about decisions made during the exercise and one hypothetical question to which all participants responded. For each decision respondents were asked to indicate how important different criteria were in their decision. Factor analysis was run separately for each of the three decisions. The three factor analyses yielded similar but not identical results. The groupings finally used represent the similarities among the three factor analyses together with correspondence to Victor and Cullen's (1988) climate dimensions. More detail is available from the author.

5. For this analysis we used decision criteria only for the hypothetical decision rather than the three-decision scales used in the previous analysis.

6. I am indebted to my colleague, Dennis Quinn, for making this point so clearly.

References

Bass, Bernard M. 1983. *Organizational Decision Making.* Homewood, IL: Irwin.

Etzioni, Amitai. 1988. *The Moral Dimension: Towards a New Economics.* New York: Free Press.

Hegarty, W.H., and H.P. Sims, Jr. 1978. "Some Determinants of Unethical Decision Behavior; An Experiment." *Journal of Applied Psychology* 63:451–57.

Kohlberg, L. 1969. "Stage and Sequence: The Cognitive-Developmental Approach to Socialization." In D.A. Goslin, ed., *Handbook of Socialization Theory and Research.* Chicago: Rand McNally.

March, James G., and Herbert A. Simon. 1958. *Organizations.* New York: Wiley.

Rest, J.R. 1979. "Development in Judging Moral Issues." Minneapolis: University of Minnesota Press.

Simon, Herbert A. 1979. "Rational Decision Making in Business Organizations." *American Economic Review* 69, 4 (September): 493–513.

Smircich, L. 1983. "Concepts of Culture and Organizational Analysis." *Administrative Science Quarterly* 28:339–58.

Trevino, L.K., and S.A. Youngblood. 1990. "Bad Apples in Bad Barrels: A Causal Analysis of Ethical Decision Making Behavior." *Journal of Applied Psychology* 75:378–85.

Victor, B., and J.B. Cullen. 1988. "The Organizational Bases of Ethical Work Climates." *Administrative Science Quarterly* 33:101–25.

5

Sociopolitical Context
of Economic Activity

14

JOHN L. CAMPBELL AND LEON N. LINDBERG

The Evolution of
Governance Regimes

Social scientists have produced a massive literature about governance transformations—changes in the institutional arrangement of economic activity. In this paper we first identify five general theoretical traditions in this literature that try to specify the key determinants of governance transformations. We then derive from these traditions a new evolutionary model of the governance transformation process and assess this model in light of evidence from case studies of transformations in the U.S. steel, automobile, commercial nuclear energy, telecommunications, dairy, meatpacking, hospital, and railroad sectors.[1] We argue that these transformations begin with the development of pressures for change that cause actors to search within certain limits for alternative *governance regimes*, by which we mean combinations of specific organizational forms of economic activity. These organizational forms, or *governance mechanisms*, include markets, corporate hierarchies, associations, and several types of networks (such as long-term subcontracting, research consortia, joint ventures, interlocking corporate directorates, and so on).[2] Finally, we explore the implications of this analysis for debates about the long-term institutional development of advanced capitalism.

Five Models of Governance Transformation

Economic Efficiency

Economists typically attribute governance transformations to shifting economic conditions, including variations in the supply and price of production factors,

Revised and reprinted with permission from John L. Campbell, J. Rogers Hollingsworth, and Leon N. Lindberg, eds., *Governance of the American Economy* (New York: Cambridge University Press, 1991).

fluctuations in demand, and other things that inhibit firms from operating efficiently; that is, maximizing output with a given set of inputs. Within this tradition it is assumed generally that governance through markets is the norm (e.g., Alchian and Demsetz, 1972), but that alternative governance mechanisms will develop when markets fail to operate efficiently. For example, actors may build corporate hierarchies when they perceive that market pricing has become an inefficient way of coordinating transactions (Coase, 1937), or when they believe that economies of scale may be achieved (Scherer, 1970, p. 81)—a goal that may also lead to the creation of joint ventures and other networks (e.g., Pfeffer and Salancik, 1978, p. 153).[3] Oliver Williamson (1975, 1985) developed one of the most sophisticated explanations of governance transformations within this tradition. He argued that when the costs of conducting and monitoring transactions through the market become excessive, because they involve the recurrent exchange of products whose manufacture requires substantial investments in idiosyncratic factor inputs (high asset specificity) and, therefore, small numbers bargaining, actors will turn to alternative governance mechanisms that reduce these transaction costs. When the frequency of exchange and level of idiosyncratic investments is high, Williamson argued, actors will replace markets with hierarchies. When the level of such investments is moderate, they will turn to less stable subcontracting relations among a few firms (Williamson, 1985). In either case, the alternative to market contracting is an allegedly more efficient form of governance. Thus, unless noted otherwise, efficiency refers throughout this paper to the capacity of transacting organizations within the production system to obtain the resources and information they need and manufacture their products at lowest possible cost.

In addition to arguing that economic inefficiencies create pressures for changing existing governance regimes, this tradition assumes that the most efficient form of governance will eventually emerge. Not only have others criticized this perspective for ignoring the fact that market-based governance may be transcended for reasons unrelated to efficiency (e.g., Perrow, 1986), but also for relying on a functionalist logic to explain which specific governance mechanisms finally emerge in different situations—a logic that is flawed insofar as it maintains that the most efficient mechanisms will eventually develop simply because they are the most efficient (e.g., Robbins, 1987). This difficulty reflects, and perhaps stems from, the fact that adherents to this tradition, such as Williamson, fail to incorporate into their analysis a regorous account of the process whereby actors decide how to solve their economic and organizational problems.

Technology Development

At least since Marx argued that changes in the forces of production created the possibility for shifts from capitalism to socialism, observers of economic history have recognized that technological developments often contribute to governance transformations. Alfred Chandler (1977), for example, argued that the revolutions in transportation and communication technologies that occurred in the United States during the nineteenth century fostered rapid growth in markets, mass production technologies, and, thus, the creation of modern industrial hierarchies with which capitalists could more efficiently stabilize and exploit these markets and technologies, respectively.[4] Following Chandler, others argued that mass production technology tends to produce long hierarchies and bureaucracy, while craft production technology often yields more subcontracting and short hierarchies (e.g., Caves, 1980; Piore and Sabel, 1984; Stinchcombe, 1983, pp. 111–15).

Whereas the development of new technologies is generally viewed as a pressure for change that triggers a search for new governance regimes, efficiency criteria are often offered to explain why one form of governance emerges from the search rather than another. This is an important parallel with economic arguments and is perhaps most obvious in Chandler's (1977) work where he argued that hierarchies are most likely to develop in mass production industries because they are the most efficient way to organize the scheduling and flow-through requirements of such production technologies. Similarly, he maintained that associations frequently preceded the emergence of corporate hierarchies, but were short-lived largely because they were unable to manage efficiently the problems associated with mass production and distribution (Chandler, 1977, chap. 4). Similarly, although recognizing the importance of political and other struggles around the creation of governance regimes and, therefore, offering a more multidimensional account than Chandler's, Michael Piore and Charles Sabel (1984) suggested that with the advent of computers and numerically controlled machines we have the opportunity to create more decentralized, flexible economic institutions that can adapt more effectively to the shorter product cycles and other instabilities of the late-twentieth-century-world economy.

We are not suggesting that this literature succumbs to crude technological determinism. In fact, deliberate attempts are often made to avoid such pitfalls while establishing the causal links between changing technologies and institutions. At least passing reference to the important role of the state, class struggle, and other factors in determining institutional outcomes is common (e.g., Torstendahl, 1984). Even Chandler (1977, chap. 4) recognized that the replacement of federations and pools by corporate hierarchies during the late nineteenth century was premised in part on the lack of support from the state for these more collective forms of governance. Piore and Sabel (1984) recognized that technological change simply created the *opportunity* for governance transformations, and that political and other struggles would ultimately determine which technology and accompanying set of governance mechanisms actors would select.

Yet it is the effect of technological change that these scholars *theorized,* not these other influences.[5] Hence, the emphasis on the technological determinants of social organization is unmistakable, but also because this literature tends to pay much less attention to the processes whereby actors, responding to new technological possibilities, or pressures for change, actively search for alternative governance regimes through which to realize these possibilities—a second parallel with the economic tradition. Ann Markusen (1985), for example, developed a fascinating argument about how technological and product innovations typically drive an industry's profit cycle and, thus, transform its governance arrangements. She argued that the initial, unprofitable stages of innovation foster lots of small-firm subcontracting that gives way first to intense market competition, as the innovation becomes very profitable, and then to corporate hierarchies, as weaker competitors exit the market and barriers to entry develop. Later, as new innovations cut into existing markets, profits sag and actors begin to deconstruct hierarchies and resort once again to subcontracting. Associations play a greater role in trying to prevent further industrial decline. However, Markusen paid very little attention to the processes by which actors who face these technologically driven profit cycles decide which governance mechanisms to adopt.[6] Indeed, one of the most common criticisms of Chandler's work is that he tended to neglect the struggles that occur over the selection of governance mechanisms in different industries (e.g., Perrow, 1981).

Power and Control

In contrast to arguments about economic efficiency or technological change, a third tradition maintains that governance transformations occur when actors try to increase their power and control over each other and whatever resources and information they deem to be important for their economic survival and prosperity. For example, some have argued that firms build corporate hierarchies through horizontal mergers in order to reduce and control market competition (Perrow, 1981, 1986, chap. 7; Scherer, 1970, chap. 4), and through vertical integration to minimize the degree to which one firm depends on another for key resources (Aldrich, 1979; Pfeffer, 1987). They have also maintained that firms create networks, such as corporate interlocks and joint ventures, and associations to better manage various types of resource interdependencies (e.g., Aldrich, 1979, chap. 12; Pfeffer, 1987; Pfeffer and Salancik, 1978, pp. 152–57).[7] In this literature, power generally refers to the capacity of an organization to extract for itself valued resources, including wages or profits, and information in a system where other organizations seek to do the same thing for themselves, or otherwise to control the behavior of other organizations within the system (e.g., Perrow, 1986, p. 259).

According to this tradition, because the desire to gain power and control, and to avoid becoming the object of another's power and control, is the critical impetus for change, it is easy to see that actors will struggle among themselves over the formation of new governance arrangements, particularly to the extent that governance transformations will institutionalize new power relationships. The frequent zero-sum nature of these relationships means that one actor's gain in power will often come at the expense of another.[8] Hence, in addition to offering additional insights about what may constitute pressure for changing existing governance arrangements, this tradition creates a broader analytical space for understanding the search process itself than either the economic or technology traditions which tend to lapse into arguments that confuse efficiency with causality. This is not to say that the power and control position does not have problems of its own. Williamson (1981, pp. 572–73), for example, charged that proponents of this tradition had not developed a precise, multidimensional definition of power that would permit researchers to determine when power did or, more important, did not influence organizational changes. Some of the more radical representatives of this tradition, who have suggested that power and control tend to accumulate in increasingly centralized organizational forms, have difficulty explaining why hierarchies are not found everywhere (Perrow, 1986, p. 241). Nevertheless, the merits of this perspective are clear: it shows how the balance of power among actors will help determine the institutional outcomes of the search for new governance regimes.

Culture

Karl Polanyi (1944, p. 46) argued that "man's economy, as a rule, is submerged in his social relationships." More recently, sociologists have reminded us of this by arguing that the determination of governance mechanisms is due as much to cultural and ideological factors, including norms, values, levels of trust, and so on, as it is to economic or technological imperatives, or struggles over power. Michel Crozier (1964, p. 312) claimed that values and cultural trends influence the form of hierarchy that emerges in different countries, and that as these cultural attributes change, so does the nature of hierarchy. Cultural explanations of institutional structure have proliferated in the literature on organizations (Smircich, 1983), and have proven useful in explaining the conditions under which actors will organize themselves in networks, rather than hierarchies, where Williamson would have predicted otherwise (e.g., Lazerson, 1988). Mark Granovetter (1985, p. 503), for example, suggested that when the economic conditions exist for the development of transaction-cost problems, hierarchies are not likely to develop if there is an already well-established network of personal relations that mitigates against opportunism and malfeasance among economic actors. Thus, he maintained that both Williamson and Chandler had adopted "undersocialized" views of economic activity that neglected the importance of trust in economic transactions, particularly insofar as the creation of networks is concerned.[9] Others have shown that common cultural background also contributes to the development of networks, such as class-based social clubs, through which economic and political activity may be coordinated tacitly (e.g., Domhoff, 1974, 1983).

The point is not that representatives of this tradition believe that cultural arguments should entirely replace economic and other explanations of governance transformation, but that they should complement them. Geoffrey Hodgson (1988, p. 156), an ardent critic of orthodox economic explanations of institutional change, including transaction-cost theories, suggested that "the basis of [exchange] agreements is not simply the rational calculation of abstract individuals with a view to their perceived costs and benefits; it is a combination of both formal legislation and legitimation, and inherited custom and tradition of a less formal kind." Yet the use of culturally focused arguments has been criticized for failing to define precisely what is meant by culture (Smircich, 1983), and for failing to specify clearly the mechanisms that link cultural conditions with the development of specific governance mechanisms. This later criticism has been especially pronounced in studies that seek to determine how different national economic structures emerged in countries with similar cultural traditions (e.g., Hamilton and Biggart, 1988).[10] Indeed, this suggests that cultural explanations also tend to overlook the search process through which culture may affect governance transformations.

State Policy

Hodgson's point that economic activity is embedded partially in a political context is important and has been reiterated by others who have noted that governance transformations are caused, at least occasionally, by shifts in legislation and other state policies. Some have gone so far as to argue that the primary source of governance transformations is the state itself, such as those who have claimed that changes in the definition and enforcement of property rights policies by the state are the fundamental sources of the transaction-cost and other inefficiencies that Williamson and others believed to be so important in explaining the development of economic institutions (e.g., North, 1981).[11] In contrast to these arguments that are sympathetic to economic efficiency models, some cross-national studies of economic development have suggested that politicians and state bureaucrats successfully promoted different governance regimes in different countries in order to legitimize their political authority (Hamilton and Biggart, 1988), and to compete more effectively with other nation-states in economic and geopolitical affairs (Weiss, 1988). Of course, Polanyi (1944, pp. 139–41) was among the first to suggest that the state was often directly responsible for governance transformations. He demonstrated that during the nineteenth century the British market system, allegedly the epitome of laissez faire capitalism, developed, ironically, out of deliberate state action, and had to be supported by the state thereafter, or face self-destruction. Finally, a vast literature has shown that the state is often directly responsible for the development of associative forms of governance, primarily as a means of avoiding state intervention (e.g., Streeck, 1983; Streeck and Schmitter, 1985; Useem, 1984, chap. 6).

Not all of this literature views state policy and politics as the primary independent variables in governance transformations, i.e., the factors that are responsible for generating the central pressures for change. Some authors see them in a more indirect role, orchestrating the search process when other factors have already created pressures for change. For example, in an argument that is sympathetic to the power and control tradition as well as Piore and Sabel's technological arguments, Scott Lash and John Urry (1987) noted that advanced capitalism experienced an institutional disorganization during the 1970s and 1980s, triggered not by the state, but largely by the globalization of economic activity and transformation of national class structures. However, they showed that this led to the breakdown of class-based politics, the fragmentation of political struggle, and, as a result, the decline of corporatism, associative governance, and even the partial deconstruction of corporate hierarchies.

Elsewhere we discuss the literature about how the state affects governance transformations (Campbell and Lindberg, 1990; Lindberg and Campbell, 1991). For now, it is sufficient to understand that political struggles within and around the state may play important roles in the governance transformation process, in terms of both creating pressures for change and constituting an important part of the search process.

An Evolutionary Model of Governance Transformation

Each of these five theoretical traditions has distinctive strengths and weaknesses, which suggests that a more comprehensive approach is required for understanding governance transformations. We cannot, however, develop such an approach simply through an eclectic addition of elements selected from each tradition because many of these are rooted in incompatible philosophical positions. Consequently, we must specify the institutionalist assumptions that we hold about rationality, and the relationship between human agency and institutional structure. This will help us fuse the useful elements of previous traditions into a more precise composite and evolutionary model of governance transformations.

The basic ontological premise that informs our evolutionary model is that although actors, including individuals, groups, and organizations, are subject to economic, technological, institutional, cultural, and other constraints, they are at the same time creative, active forces that can shape and reshape these constraints. In other words, these constraints generally limit the *range* of interests and opportunities available to actors, but they do not determine the *specific* interests and opportunities that actors select. Thus, rationality is contingent and there is some, though not unlimited, room for actors to select their goals and actions, a condition that creates the possibility that actors may occasionally interpret and react to their problems in new and unexpected ways. Conversely, although actors may process information, evaluate circumstances, and make purposeful decisions that reshape, intentionally or unintentionally, the constraints they face, these constraints cannot be reduced to the interests and acts of *individual* actors. This is because their choices are somewhat limited in the first place, but also because these constraints, interests, and acts arise from the *interactions* that occur among actors. Indeed, actors produce, cooperate, exercise power, and struggle with each other frequently in situations where resources and power are distributed unequally.[12]

Governance regimes constrain production and exchange relationships among diverse economic actors and the state according to various types of rules and means of compliance (Lindberg, Campbell, and Hollingsworth, 1991). These regimes change over time as actors, whose range of choices is constrained in ways that we have just discussed, adjust to exogenous and endogenous forces. This process of governance transformation, however, is rarely smooth. First, as noted above, economic signals and technology are not usually decisive in determining specifically the direction of change or the outcomes of governance transformations. Second, because governance transformations involve significant changes in a governance regime's structure of rights, rules, and compliance procedures, these matters are of intense, often strategic, interest to most actors. As a result, prolonged processes of trial and error learning, negotiation and cooperation, and coercion and struggle will occur over the structure of new governance regimes. We have referred to this as the search process.

The point is that the reciprocal effects between actors and social constraints, as well as the presence of contingent rationality and the search process, suggest the need for an evolutionary explanation of governance transformations, although one that is neither teleological nor functionalist. The elementary logic of such an explanation begins by recognizing that endogenous and exogenous forces episodically disrupt production and exchange. In response, actors search for solutions to these disruptions through a series of complex decisions in which economic, organizational, and political choices that were institutionalized in the most recent governance regime limit the options that are currently available to actors during the search. In turn, these actors institutionalize their choices in a new governance regime that constrains their future options. This process repeats itself, usually in a gradual manner, as new governance regimes evolve out of old ones, again and again, in the stepwise historical process illustrated in Figure 14.1.[13]

The centerpiece of such an evolutionary view of sectoral development is what we have thus far summarized heuristically as the search—a process whereby sectoral actors pursue their interests within a variety of constraints and eventually *select* a new governance regime by combining in intended and unintended ways their individual strategies for coping with the dilemmas of production and exchange. Indeed, the concept of *constrained selection* captures the essence of

Figure 14.1. **An Evolutionary View of Sectoral Development**

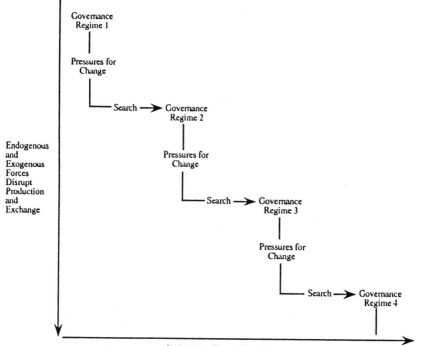

Institutional Change Over Time

the search process as it embodies the reciprocal relationship between actor and constraint, or strategy and structure, as outlined above.

Our model of governance transformation as the selection of new governance regimes is summarized schematically in Figure 14.2, which represents the intricacies of one step of the evolutionary process depicted in Figure 14.1. Three sets of actors are linked to each other through complex relationships of dependence and interdependence. These include *producer organizations*, such as firms, *other organizations* that typically respond reactively to producers, including suppliers, labor, financial institutions, public interest groups, and consumer groups, and the ensemble of *state organizations* which behave reactively, but also on the basis of their own interests. Governance transformations are usually initiated by producers, but occasionally by other organizations, who respond to new problems and opportunities created by changes in economic conditions and technology. We have referred to these problems and opportunities as pressures for change. Of course, shifts in state policy, the efforts of actors to increase their power and control over exchange, and other factors may alter economic conditions and technology in the first place, or create pressures for change in their own right to which producers and other organizations may respond. However, if the state

Figure 14.2. **The Selection of New Governance Regimes**

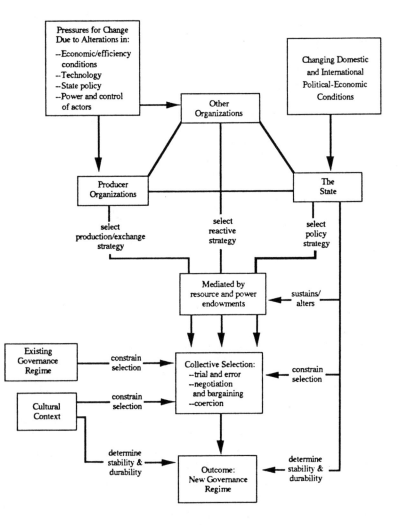

initiates a transformation, it does so in response to changes in domestic or international political-economic conditions.

Actors do not respond automatically to pressures for change in a knee jerk fashion, but rather select the ones, if any, to which they will react. The state does the same thing insofar as changing political-economic conditions are concerned. Of course, some pressures for change may be more difficult to ignore than others, so the existing set of pressures constrains the choices that are initially available to actors. Furthermore, pressures for change are not always exogenous to the model. The institutional character of the existing governance regime, or the specific actions of actors within the sector may contribute to the formation of these pressures. However, to avoid excessive complexity we have not included these feedback loops in Figure 14.2.

For ease of presentation we make two further simplifications. On the one hand, we tell the story, depicted in the model, from the producers' point of view. That is, the producers initiate change. On the other hand, we recognize that these three sets of actors should not be treated as mysterious black boxes. Producers, for example, have distinctive interests, organizational routines, time horizons, and performance standards through which they interpret the flow of information about economic and technological options (e.g., Nelson and Winter, 1982). These develop within the context of previous governance regimes and represent the cumulative momentum and/or drag of earlier decisions about economic conditions, technology, and relationships with other groups and the state. In this sense, they constitute the producer organization's institutional memory. Of course, other organizations, including the state, also have their own interests, routines, time frames, and standards. However, because this model focuses on interorganizational relations, we will not elaborate on this point further.

Three streams of action constitute the central dynamic of the selection process. First, producers initiate the search for a new governance regime, sometimes without realizing it, by selecting in an opportunistic manner new production and exchange strategies to optimize their interests on the basis of endogenously and exogenously produced problems and opportunities—strategies that they seek to implement by manipulating their own organizations and their relationships with other actors. Second, these efforts are constrained by the strategies of other economic organizations, reacting to producers. Finally, the state may pursue its own interests and strategies, such as maintaining its legitimacy in the face of public controversies, initiated by producer strategies, or dealing with international pressures from other states and economies, in ways that constrain the actions of producers and other organizations. The state may also become involved if producers or other actors mobilize politically to implement their strategies and achieve their interests.

The idea that one actor's strategy may constrain the implementation of another's strategy suggests an interactive process. Indeed, actors eventually select a new governance regime as these streams of action intermingle in complex ways. Trial and error learning as the result of spontaneous interaction may predominate in some instances, such as when actors learn how to coordinate their actions around emergent common conventions, incrementally discard unsuccessful strategies, or tacitly align themselves with other especially powerful actors. In this sense selection is very much a process of muddling through. In other cases, deliberate negotiations among organizations will take the place of, or supplement, trial and error. Contracts and legislative bargains that formally reflect the interests, institutional capacities, and relative bargaining power of different actors, including the state, can be important steps along the path to new governance regimes (e.g., Young, 1989). Finally, selection may involve elements of coercion through political and economic struggle. For example, producers may exercise economic and organizational power to force labor or suppliers to accept a new governance regime. Recognizing that selection involves the intermingling of streams of action helps to highlight how our model departs from conventional rational choice conceptions of transformation, and suggests that selection is in many ways a *collective* process.

Of course, these complex interaction processes are mediated initially by the resources and power with which actors are endowed insofar as the strategies selected by powerful actors are more likely to be implemented than those of weak ones. In addition, the institutional arrangements within the existing governance regime, such as systems of labor-management relations and finance, constrain the selection process to the extent that existing patterns of interaction usually embody a degree of institutional rigidity or inertia out of which it is difficult to break. For instance, when actors have already established extensive networks or associations in their sector and, thus, the capacity for selecting far-sighted, cooperative strategies, they can more easily devise new multilateral governance mechanisms than actors from a sector where short-sighted, bilateral mechanisms, such as markets, dominate the governance regime. (By multilateral, we mean mechanisms where exchange simultaneously involves many actors from a sector, such as in a research consortium, association, or price-leading system. Bilateral mechanisms involve only a few actors at a time in an exchange.) Furthermore, the state constrains the selection process. The state's actions, such as defending or modifying property rights, sustains or alters the relative endowments of resources and power. Likewise, the procedural and legal principles that state actors choose to promulgate and enforce may temper the *use* of these endowments, and may constrain the types of interactions that occur during the selection process. So does the state's institutional structure (e.g., Campbell and Lindberg, 1990). Similarly, cultural factors, including norms of fairness, justice, competition, and cooperation, either of a general or sector-specific nature, may constrain the use of power and resources.

The degree to which trial and error, negotiation and bargaining, or coercion prevail during the selection process will determine, and be reflected by, the new governance regime that emerges. However, the nature of the selection process will also help to determine the stability of the new governance regime. Presumably a regime that is imposed through coercion will be less stable, and perhaps less durable, than one that is crafted through cooperation. In this regard, stability and durability also depend critically on the ability and willingness of the state to ratify and help legitimate the regime. For example, if state actors provide political support, resources, and legal enforcement for a regime, its stability and durability are likely to be enhanced. The same will probably occur if the emergent regime is organized in ways that are consistent with the current cultural and normative context.

An Empirical Assessment

We have outlined how five theoretical traditions attempt to explain governance transformations, and we have offered an evolutionary model that we argue helps to integrate these theoretical traditions. Our strategy of integration has been to suggest through what mechanisms the central, purportedly causal relationships that are offered by each tradition actually operate. Our model does this through a theory of action that is based on assumptions about the reciprocal effects of strategy and structure. That is, we recognize how various actors respond to changing conditions by selecting strategies, first individually and then through complex collective processes, that eventually become institutionalized as new governance regimes, but in ways that are constrained by the already existing governance regime as well as other factors. Thus, the model implies that explanations of governance transformation cannot simply postulate dependent and independent variables, but must explain the mechanisms that link these variables—mechanisms through which causal factors actually enter into the evaluations and choices of actors. However, we also recognize that the variables in which we are interested, particularly economic and technological conditions, power, culture, and state policy, are loosely coupled in the sense that over time, the manner in which they affect actors and the transformation process will vary under different internal and external conditions (e.g., Sorge and Streeck, 1987). Let us now demonstrate *empirically* how our model helps to link the separate stories that these five theoretical traditions offer by considering in turn the central arguments of each theoretical school from the perspective of our model and case studies.

Economic Efficiency

Our case studies revealed several examples of governance transformations that resulted from actors selecting production and exchange strategies that they believed would help improve economic efficiency. For example, manufacturers in the automobile sector created huge corporate hierarchies by extending their operations through vertical integration, both forward and backward, in order to achieve economies of scale. Indeed, General Motors experienced much greater demand for its products than American Motors and, as a result, became more vertically integrated due to the promise of greater economies of scale. In the meat-packing industry during the late nineteenth and early twentieth centuries, vertical integration proceeded downstream from meat packers into wholesale distribution. Retailing, however, was not subject to as much integration, and beef production upstream rarely became integrated with the large packing houses—a finding that supports Williamson's transaction-cost theory insofar as asset specificity was relatively low in beef production and retailing, but rather high elsewhere where special capital-intensive railroad refrigeration systems had to be built to transport slaughtered meat to distant markets. Similarly, a reduction in capital-intensive specific assets after the Second World War, due to the development of readily available refrigerated trucking, lowered barriers to entry in meat packing and contributed to vertical *dis*integration. Vertical disintegration also occurred during the 1960s and 1970s as corporations tried to improve their efficiency by reducing labor and production costs through plant closings in both sectors, and in the automobile sector through the development of precisely coordinated subcontracting schemes between parts suppliers and manufacturers where parts were scheduled to arrive at the manufacturer just in time for assembly, thus minimizing inventory costs.

Nevertheless, it was often the case that even when interests in economic efficiency, through either promises of reduced transaction costs, or improved economies of scale, helped spark the search for new governance regimes, there were additional forces that helped set the selection process in motion. After all, it was breakthroughs in transportation technologies that created the conditions under which vertical integration and then disintegration could be economically efficient in meat packing. In automobiles the development of new computerized information and production systems created the possibility for just-in-time scheduling. The economies of scale that actors hoped to achieve by building large integrated steel companies were only possible because of the capital-intensive nature of the technologies involved. Thus, as suggested earlier with respect to Chandler's work, the interconnection between economic efficiency and technology explanations of governance transformations is often very tight.

Equally important, however, there were times when actors selected hierarchies and other governance mechanisms for reasons completely *unrelated* to efficiency considerations. For example, in the hospital sector after 1965 companies began to integrate vertically through hospital management corporations and later through diversification schemes, not because actors believed that this would reduce transaction costs or improve economies of scale, but because state policy rewarded them for doing so through larger Medicare payments. In fact, these hierarchies emerged in an environment where there were very few incentives to minimize costs at all because Medicare paid a patient's medical expenses on a cost basis—a situation, it turned out later, that actually led to a *decrease* in economic efficiency insofar as the creation of corporate hierarchies increased the organizational costs of providing health care. Furthermore, when vertical disintegration occurred in our cases, it was not always due to the perception of private actors that markets or subcontracting networks had become a relatively more efficient governance alternative, but because state policy forced the transformation for political reasons, as happened when the federal government invoked antitrust law to break up both AT&T in the telecommunications sector in 1982 and some of the vertically integrated hierarchies in the meat-packing sector during the first half of the twentieth century. Indeed, many of the transformations that occurred in our cases do not appear to have been caused primarily by private actors searching for greater economic efficiency. Rather, they stemmed from shifts in technological, political, and other conditions, elaborated below.

It is worth mentioning that economy of scale or transaction-cost models were only helpful for understanding those transformations that resulted in the selection of *bilateral* forms of governance. Often these were related directly to the creation or undoing of corporate hierarchies. In addition to the examples already discussed, formula pricing developed in the meat-packing sector where, in response to the vertical disintegration that occurred after 1960, beef producers established flexible long-term contracts with packing houses well in advance of product exchange through an agreement that allowed them to specify prices at a later date. They selected this form of governance to reduce the transaction costs associated with what would have been a constant series of price negotiations. Similarly, steel manufacturers sought long-term contracts with customers to stabilize demand, a necessary precaution taken to ensure that their expensive mills would run continuously and realize the economies of scale that they were designed to achieve. In contrast, when actors pursued *multilateral* forms of governance, they often did so to counteract what they believed was excessive price competition, a problem that is very different from those of efficiently obtaining production factors or manufacturing products that we have been discussing, and that are typically the focus of the economy of scale or transaction-cost literatures. Formally organized associations and pools emerged during the nineteenth and early twentieth centuries in steel, meat packing, and railroads to reduce price-based competition. Steel companies also orchestrated explicit price-fixing agreements through the infamous Gary dinners and actors in the meat-packing, steel, and automobile sectors pursued tacit price-leading strategies at various times. All of these were attempts to extract greater profits from consumers, and therefore illustrate governance transformations driven by the collective exercise of power, rather than the quest for greater efficiency.

Furthermore, although that conventional economic efficiency models appear to be helpful for identifying important pressures for change, at least in some cases, they are less useful for understanding how and why actors eventually selected one alternative governance mechanism, rather than another, to be dominant, particularly insofar as *multilateral* forms are concerned. We cannot, for example, understand why meat packers first selected pools, then a holding company, and then the least formally organized multilateral form of all, price leading, to control cut-throat price competition between 1880 and 1920, or why price leading, rather than these other forms, finally succeeded in solving the problem unless we introduce a political analysis that includes a discussion of the struggles that erupted around the antitrust issue. Transaction-cost or economies of scale models are of little value here.

Perhaps we should not be too critical. After all, the economic efficiency literature has been preoccupied with developing models to explain the conditions underlying the formation of bilateral, not multilateral, forms of governance

(Etzioni, 1988, p. 5; Schneiberg and Hollingsworth, 1989). This is ironic because orthodox economists have tried to apply their models to many social phenomena that others consider to be beyond the traditional domain of economics, such as politics (e.g., Downs, 1957) and the family (e.g., Becker, 1976)—an exercise that some have condemned as a dangerous form of economic imperialism (e.g., Granovetter, 1989; Swedberg, 1991). However, orthodox economists have not done so in this case.[14] We must turn to other explanations if we are to understand the forces that precipitate searches for the full range of governance transformations that have occurred in the United States.

Technology Development

Innovations in technology created possibilities for governance transformations in many of our case studies by providing actors with an opportunity to devise new strategies for production and exchange. In the extreme, these opportunities permitted actors, previously excluded from participating in the sector, a chance to carve out a niche for themselves. For example, we have seen that the increasing availability of relatively low-cost highway transportation reduced barriers to entry in the meat-packing industry and helped to foster market competition where an oligopoly had exercised control for decades, in part through its control over enormously expensive railroad distribution systems that were made possible in the first place by the development of railroads and refrigeration technology during the nineteenth century. The geographical expansion of milk distribution, due to improvements in railroads, refrigeration, and sanitation, established the possibility for transforming the dairy sector during the late 1800s from an economy of locally based milk markets into one where central distributors had a chance to develop, form oligopolies, and dominate the distribution system in urban areas. The development of microwave technologies during the 1950s and 1960s created the opportunity for independent firms to break into a telecommunications industry that had been monopolized by AT&T and its affiliates for nearly a century.

This is not to say that major technological breakthroughs automatically trigger governance transformations. As Piore and Sabel (1984) suggested, new technologies simply broaden the range of production and exchange strategies from which actors may select in organizing economic activity. In our cases it was always an open question which option actors would eventually choose, and, once they had decided, it often took a long time before the institutional effects of their decisions began to materialize. Although companies began trying to utilize microwave technologies, for instance, in the 1950s to penetrate AT&T's monopoly on telephone service, it was not until 1971, after years of litigation and regulatory haggling that culminated in an FCC decision to permit long-distance competitors to interconnect with the Bell System's local exchanges, that they began to establish competitive services for customers. Thus, new technology created the *possibility* for a governance transformation, but struggles over regulatory policy determined the final outcome. Similarly, in the nuclear sector, adoption of the light water reactor established the possibility for the kind of accident that occurred at Three Mile Island. In turn, the accident created the conditions that prompted actors to search for a new governance regime, one where they selected self-regulatory associations and networks to improve the sector's performance and public image. Yet the accident was also due in part to mismanagement of the technology—that is, laxity in safety research and regulation, problems that stemmed from the already existing governance regime. Thus, a variety of factors, including state policy and the structure of governance itself, modify the influence that technological developments have on the transformation process.

On the other hand, once the decision has been made to pursue and institutionalize one technology, rather than another, in a particular regime, the availability of alternative technologies and regimes tends to decrease as movement along the chosen path develops a momentum of its own out of which it is hard for actors to break (Dosi, 1984, p. 85; Piore and Sabel, 1984). Although most members of the nuclear sector recognized the benefits of standardizing reactor designs, this became virtually impossible to do after manufacturers and utility companies decided to commercialize two different versions of the light water reactor and to market them competitively. Elsewhere, massive capital investments by the big steel hierarchies in old brownfield sites during the 1950s and 1960s made it extremely difficult for them to abandon these traditional mill technologies in favor of new, more flexible minimills later, even though the minimills appeared to be a more appropriate technology for the shifting economic climate of the late twentieth-century steel sector. As a result, it was not the old steel oligopoly that innovated with the minimill technology, but a new group of competitors that selected a more market-oriented governance regime. The point is that although dramatic changes in technology periodically *expand* the range of choices for organizing governance, once these choices have been made, actors tend to become locked into the technology and the governance regime in which it is embedded in ways that *constrain* future choices in an evolutionary manner.

Many of the technological developments that occurred in our case studies, including minimills, truck transport, and microwave communications, encouraged the selection of new production and exchange strategies that eventually led to major governance transformations. However, in light of the arguments reviewed earlier which suggest that technological change is often the driving force behind governance transformations, we need to explain why in some cases new developments in technology did *not* induce change, such as the hundreds of innovations that occurred in the telecommunications sector as a result of AT&T's extensive research and development efforts. Following Giovanni Dosi (1984), we can divide these technological innovations into two categories. The development of these steel-making, transportation, and communication technologies are examples of *extraordinary* technological innovations because they were so revolutionary that they opened up a new range of production and exchange opportunities for actors, whereas the latter AT&T innovations are examples of *normal* innovations that merely refined *already existing* technologies and therefore did little to alter the range of strategic opportunities, unlike the development of microwave transmission technology.

Not only does extraordinary innovation tend to create pressure for change, it appears to do so in ways that often foster market competition. The advent of microwave technology enabled actors to create competitive markets in telecommunications, as did trucking in meat packing, and minimills in steel. This is consistent with Dosi's (1984) prediction that when extraordinary innovation occurs, it tends to induce competition as many actors try to pursue the new technological path and to take advantage of new commercial opportunities. However, Dosi also suggested that once the new technology becomes firmly established, normal innovation becomes the typical pattern, and oligopoly tends to emerge as some firms begin to internalize the process of technology development thereby constructing barriers to entry, a process that is similar to that which Markusen (1985) described. This was precisely the purpose of AT&T's research and development strategy, where the company spent tremendous sums of money to stay at the forefront of technological development in telecommunications, and patented its innovations to create barriers to entry that contributed to the development and reinforcement of its monopoly position. In fact, as this case suggests, actors may use normal innovation more generally as a strategy to stabilize the already existing governance regime. In the nuclear sector a variety of normal safety innovations, such as those developed during the 1970s in response to the public outcry over inadequate emergency systems, appear to have been devised, at least in part, to stabilize a politically volatile situation that threatened to disrupt the current regime. Thus, extraordinary innovation tends to generate pressures for new governance regimes and normal innovation tends to help actors adjust to changes in their sector's political economic environment in ways that help them stabilize or reinforce already established regimes.[15]

Of course it is difficult to determine *in advance* whether an innovation will be extraordinary or not. This was another reason why AT&T pursued its aggressive policy of developing and patenting as many innovations as it could. If the corporation discovered a potentially extraordinary innovation, AT&T's patent would prevent another firm from using the technology to challenge the existing monopoly. Thus, this is an example that also suggests that powerful actors, endowed with substantial resources, are often able to control the range of technologically determined strategies that are available to others.

In addition to these change-inducing and adjustment-inducing influences, technology also seems to provide certain background conditions that help us anticipate how different sectors are likely to be organized. Our cases indicate that actors in sectors that are based on expensive, mass production or process technologies tend to form governance regimes that are dominated largely by hierarchies, such as occurred in railroads, steel, automobiles, and nuclear energy, a finding consistent with much of the literature (e.g., Caves, 1980; Chandler, 1977; Stinchcombe, 1983). When the large capital requirements for adopting expensive technologies are not met easily by single firms, actors also appear to form bilateral networks. Examples include the joint ventures among utility companies who sought to build nuclear plants together after investment capital became more expensive in the early 1970s, and the joint venture between the Bell System and the Morgan banking interests during the early 1900s that provided the capital Bell needed to buy out independent telephone operators, obtain telegraph technology, and initiate its research and development program. The Morgan-Bell network dissolved after the Bell company turned to public stock offerings as an alternative source of finance capital. However, when the new technologies involved are less expensive relative to the old ones, as they were in microwave communications and minimills, or when they are craft-based, as they were in dairying which until recently was based on relatively small farms, corporate hierarchies appear less likely to emerge than either market competition (steel, telecommunications), or perhaps multilateral forms of governance (dairy cooperatives).

Finally, although an elaborate discussion is well beyond the scope of this paper, our case studies shed some light on one of the fundamental disagreements about economic change that continues to rage between orthodox and institutional economics. The orthodox school treats the development of technology, as well as the possibilities and constraints it poses for the economy, as a phenomenon that is exogenous to the economic system and, therefore, as something which economists do not have to explain in order to develop a theory of economic change. In contrast, institutionalists maintain that technological change is endogenous to the economy and requires explanation if we are to construct such a theory (Elliott, 1984; Hodgson, 1988, pp. 12–21; Stevenson, 1987). On the one hand, we have seen that some important technological innovations occurred outside of the sectors that were eventually affected. The development of truck transport, a technology that helped transform the meat-packing sector, had little to do with anyone connected directly with this sector. On the other hand, a vast proportion of the technology improvements that occurred in the telecommunications sector were the deliberate work of AT&T as part of its patent wall strategy. The selection and refinement of the light water reactor as the nuclear sector's technological cornerstone was largely due to the military and political interests of Congress, and the financial interests of a few large manufacturers who already had a stake in this technology. In both cases, technological innovation did not spring magically from the heads of independent entrepreneurs as Markusen implies. Nor was it developed because it was believed to be the most administratively or technologically efficient way to proceed. Instead, these innovations were primarily the result of a search for greater political and/or economic power by actors who *already* played substantial roles in economic governance, and who sought to reinforce them institutionally through further technological development. So in addition to lending some support to the institutionalist position on the origins of technological pressures for change, these examples also suggest the need for an analysis of struggles for power (see also Noble, 1977; Stone, 1981).

Power and Control

In addition to technological developments and problems of economic efficiency, the interests of actors to increase or maintain their power over each other, and their control over critical resources and information often constituted pressures for change in many of our case studies. Steel manufacturers, for example, integrated backwards into coal mining during the 1800s to discourage others from entering the steel manufacturing business, as well as to guard against the opportunism of mining companies. In the dairy sector, milk distributors, seeking to augment their already considerable power to force prices on dairy farmers, established urban milk exchanges and networks through which they banded together to set the purchase price of milk without input from farmers. In telecommunications, the Bell company granted certain local companies exclusive rights to use its technology in specific geographical areas in exchange for which the companies eventually relinquished all of their stock to Bell and agreed not to interconnect with other independent operators. This was a deliberate attempt by Bell to increase its control over these firms, and a strategy that contributed to the eventual development of a single corporate hierarchy in the sector.

In response to offensive drives for power, such as these, actors often took defensive steps, selecting *reactive strategies* that led to the further transformation of governance. Most obviously, workers in the railroad, steel, meat-packing, and automobile sectors tried to counteract the power of large corporate hierarchies by creating unions. When they succeeded, union-based wage bargaining and long-term labor contracts replaced competitive labor markets as the mechanism for setting wages. In turn, corporations themselves occasionally banded together to deal with organized labor, as was the case in the steel sector where they formed multiemployer bargaining groups to negotiate with the United Steel Workers. Similarly, dairy farmers formed cooperatives to deal from a position of collective strength with powerful milk distributors—a strategy to which distributors responded by creating their own associations. When AT&T tried to eliminate independent telephone companies by refusing to interconnect them with its long-distance lines during the late 1800s, the independents formed associations to counter these tactics. In the hospital sector physicians fostered and supported such collective organizations as the American Hospital Association and the American Medical Association in order to defeat the movement for national health insurance, and to reinforce their own autonomy and control over the health care system. Finally, shippers who objected to the rate fixing of railroad companies formed associations to stop these practices. Indeed, in our case studies when one group of actors sought to alter the balance of power, or increase its control over resources through multilateral forms of governance, others who were threatened often responded in kind—an *evolutionary* process, noted by some sociologists (e.g., Aldrich, 1979, p. 321; Offe and Wiesenthal, 1985, p. 189; Useem, 1984, chap. 6), where strategic selections build upon each other in a serial fashion. As will be discussed shortly, the evolution of governance regimes in this manner is very much the result of an interactive process among different actors.

Two points are worth noting here. First, although we have seen that concerns about economic efficiency generated pressures for change in some cases, more often it was a concern about power and control that created this pressure, at least in part. This supports the position of scholars, such as Charles Perrow (1981, 1986), who argued that although efficiency considerations may lead occasionally to transformations, it is the desire of firms—and we would add other groups as well—to control markets, labor, and production that is most often the critical stimulus. Second, although much of this debate has been cast in terms of the conditions under which markets and hierarchies emerge, our data indicate that it is also relevant to the formation of multilateral forms of governance. In our cases, concerns with power and control triggered searches that led to the selection of multilateral forms of governance far more often than did concerns with economic efficiency. We have already reviewed several key examples where defensive reactions to power led to the creation of multilateral governance mechanisms, such as unions and associations (see also Schneiberg and Hollingsworth, 1989). Hence, it appears that analyses based on power are more useful generally than those based on efficiency, although not exclusively so, in explaining the development of pressures for change, regardless of whether the governance regime that emerges is dominated by multilateral or bilateral governance mechanisms.

Those who have argued for an analysis of governance transformations based on power, including Perrow, have focused on struggles among actors *within* sectors of the economy as the key source of pressures for change. Yet these are not the only conflicts over power that precipitate transformations, especially those leading to the formation of multilateral governance mechanisms. The same may occur when actors perceive that *outsiders* threaten their common interests. For example, foreign competition in the automobile sector led members to search for ways to improve their competitive position, particularly against the Japanese. Eventually they selected networks, including industry conferences and collaborative research and information exchanges among suppliers, manufacturers, and dealers. Similarly, in steel the American Iron and Steel Institute organized industrywide research and development projects to help the sector compete more effectively against foreign imports. In meat packing, as consumption of red meat declined nationally during the late 1970s and 1980s due to consumers turning to other products, such as poultry, trade associations assumed an increasingly important role in promoting the sector's products. In all of these cases, threats of product substitution, either from foreign competition or other sectors, caused actors to realize and defend their common interests. This is consistent with those who have argued that multilateral forms of governance are more likely to appear when the primary interests of actors are homogeneous (e.g., Aldrich, 1979, pp. 319–21), and when actors are bound up in relationships with each other that are marked by what Jeffrey Pfeffer (1987) called commensalistic interdependence—a structural relationship among organizations that is derived from their mutual dependence on the same resources. Indeed, what better way to sensitize actors within a sector to their common interests than to threaten, through foreign competition or product substitution, the most critical resource that they share: the total pool of available customers for the finished product.

What most distinguishes the power and control tradition from the economic efficiency and technological development models is that in addition to helping us understand the origins of pressures for change, the power and control view also provides insights about the selection process. As noted earlier, the relative resource and power endowments of actors *mediate* the selection process by affording more richly endowed actors with greater capacities to implement the governance mechanisms of their choice. For example, although the Carter White House selected a corporatist strategy to rejuvenate the ailing steel industry in the late 1970s, a scheme that would have led to a multilateral governance regime, large steel manufacturers and organized steel workers opposed the plan, for different reasons, and were powerful enough politically to block the Carter initiative. Similarly, although independent telephone companies during the late 1800s organized associations in an attempt to counter the coercive tactics of AT&T, the associations were short-lived because AT&T had enough resources to undermine their effectiveness by buying out some of the members, and because the state invoked antitrust and other policies that further crippled their operation. Hence, the power and resources of other actors prevented the development of effective associative behavior among the independents. In railroads, the substantial political strength of farmers who were opposed to railroad pools and associations around the turn of the century contributed to the failure of these forms of governance, in part by helping to persuade federal officials that state, not private, railroad regulation was necessary. Finally, in telecommunications, the Bell company was able, through its possession of patents, to license technology to local companies for building and operating telephone exchanges during the late nineteenth century, thus establishing hundreds of long-term bilateral arrangements that enabled the Bell system to shift much of the risk and capital costs in establishing local telephone service on to these smaller and less powerful companies.

A second way in which the power and control tradition sheds light on the selection process is by focusing on the *interactive and collective dynamics* involved. We have already examined the evolutionary nature of the selection process insofar as one actor's strategic choice often induces another's strategic response. Through repeated interactions, such as these, actors collectively construct new governance regimes through power struggles and coercion. Sometimes, however, selection is more of a bargaining process, as was the case in the dairy sector when, during the early twentieth century, the Federal Food Administration orchestrated corporatist-style price bargaining between dairy cooperatives and distributors, a new multilateral form of governance. At other times, selection is at least partially a matter of trial and error, such as when meat packers first formed pools, then a holding company, and finally tacit price-fixing schemes to eliminate excessive price competition, although in this case state power was also operating to the extent that government officials challenged the legality of the pools and the holding company.

Richard Nelson and Sidney Winter (1982) and others who have advocated that economic efficiency models be supplemented, if not replaced, with evolutionary models of economic change have started to recognize that power and control models are useful for explaining not only pressures for change, but also the selection process that results. They have done so by arguing that the search for new economic arrangements often involves conflict *within* firms among people who are responsible for choosing organizational options.[16] Yet, as we have demonstrated, this is not enough. We must push beyond such micro-level organizational analysis and explore how conflicts *among* firms and other organizations within and beyond sectoral borders determine new governance regimes.

Culture

Although there are relatively few examples in our case studies that provide insights about the effects that culture and ideology (i.e., general systems of beliefs, norms, and values) have on governance transformations, we do find some that suggest that these factors constrain the selection process, facilitating or inhibiting the formation of different types of governance mechanisms, and helping to determine how effective and stable a new governance regime will be once it emerges. For example, steel executives formed a cooperative ethos or "corpsgeist" through the Gary dinners between 1907 and 1911, much as meat packers developed a cooperative ideology through earlier pools and holding companies. Later, actors in these sectors were able to establish monitoring arrangements, particularly price-leading schemes, that operated successfully for years because they had already developed, through these earlier networks, a familiarity with each other's practices and a sense of cooperation—a collective consciousness about what was best for their sectors. In dairying, immigrant farmers brought to the midwest European ideals of collectivism and cooperation that helped to shape an early dairy culture. This served as the ideological foundation upon which they later built dairy cooperatives. During the 1910s the development of a multilateral network of farmers, cooperatives, agricultural extension agencies, and land-grant universities throughout the region reinforced and contributed further to the articulation of the sector's long-term collective goals which, in turn, helped farmers to form associations of dairy cooperatives during the 1920s in response to a variety of economic problems. Furthermore, the Grange movement of the 1870s cultivated a collective militancy among midwestern farmers that also served dairy men who sought to found cooperatives and associations.

These cases stand in stark contrast to the railroad sector where actors formed pools and associations to control cut-throat price competition, scheduling, and other collective economic problems, but where such multilateral governance failed in part because members could not resist the temptations of short-term, individual gains that could be won by betraying their collective commitments. These temptations might have been tempered had there been a stronger cooperative ideology among railroad executives. Yet apparently there was not, even though the federal government passed legislation in 1866 that encouraged the formation of these multilateral forms of governance.

As noted earlier, Granovetter (1985) argued that actors are likely to create long-term subcontracting networks instead of hierarchies, if transacting parties have well-established, trusting relationships with each other, thus reducing the need for actors to control opportunism and malfeasance with administrative controls. Our data suggest that we can extend his argument to multilateral forms of governance insofar as they may also serve as an alternative to hierarchy, if cultural and other conditions are right. Ironically, support for this proposition comes from the meat-packing and railroad sectors, two cases where hierarchies *replaced* pools and associations, but for different reasons. In meat packing, where economic activity was embedded in a milieu of familiarity and cooperation, multilateral governance enabled actors effectively to control the difficulties associated with excessive market competition until the state forbade it, largely through antitrust policies. As a result, actors created hierarchies to resolve these sectoral problems. On the other hand, in railroads, although the state tried to promote these multilateral mechanisms, at least until the late nineteenth century, the project was undermined by rampant individualism, the antithesis of a cooperative ideology. Given the differences in cultural context, had the state not interfered, multilateral governance might have succeeded in meat packing; but without even stronger doses of political support, it was still probably doomed to failure in railroads. Thus, these cases substantiate the claim of Piore and Sabel (1984, pp. 255–65), and others, that multilateral forms of governance generally require a sense of community, common background, or other ideological or cultural adhesives to sustain them.[17]

Yet these examples also suggest that culture and ideologies are not free-floating, but rather are institutionally based systems of beliefs. The dairy culture, for instance, was nourished in the United States through an elaborate institutional network of private and public organizations. It seems, then, that William Domhoff (1974) was correct when he argued that the development of class consciousness—and we would add all consciousness that contributes to governance transformations—is facilitated by institutions that contribute to the production and reproduction of culture and ideology, an idea that has been echoed recently by other scholars from different theoretical traditions that are critical of orthodox economic models of transformation insofar as these models provide no room for cultural influences (e.g., Etzioni, 1988; Foster, 1987). The more important point, however, is that the effects of institutions and culture are reciprocal. That is, a current governance regime may facilitate the development of an ideological and cultural milieu that contributes to governance transformations later, as was the case when the dairy sector's multilateral network supported a dairy culture that, in turn, helped foster the collective consciousness that was central to the formation of associations of dairy cooperatives. Unfortunately, our case studies do not provide enough data to pursue this point further.

Nevertheless, all of this sheds light on arguments that have been critical of culturally based explanations of governance transformations, such as those posed by Gary Hamilton and Nicole Biggart (1988) who argued that cultural explanations of institutional change in East Asian economies were unconvincing because, although the entire region's culture was fairly homogeneous and static, substantial variations in governance regimes, both historically and cross-nationally, emerged within the region after the Second World War. Their analysis was insightful in many ways. Our data indicate, however, that one must move very cautiously when attributing a general set of cultural or ideological traits to regions or national economies, something that critics as well as proponents (e.g., Crozier, 1964) of cultural explanations have often failed to do. Our cases reveal tremendous cultural and ideological variation across sectors within the U.S. economy. Furthermore, we have seen that these features tended to change, often in an evolutionary manner, as they did in steel where a cooperative ideology developed gradually through repeated interactions among steel executives. In short, if one recognizes that culture is heterogeneous and dynamic at the sectoral level, then there may be a more significant role for cultural explanations in the analysis of governance transformations than critics have been willing to admit.[18]

We must also recognize, however, that in our examples, cultural and ideological factors did not serve as pressures for change that triggered the selection process, as other factors did. Nor did they determine in any immediate or direct sense the new governance regimes that actors selected. This was largely a matter of the interactive selection processes that we described earlier. Instead, where they could be clearly identified, cultural factors served a much more subtle and indirect role insofar as they provided a social context within which the selection process occurred. In other words, they helped to define the *range* of available governance mechanisms from which actors might choose, and influenced the *probabilities* that actors would institutionalize their choices on a relatively permanent basis and use these mechanisms successfully. This latter point is an important one to the extent that emergent governance regimes that were clearly inconsistent with surrounding cultural and ideological parameters were often ineffective in helping actors solve the problems for which they devised new regimes. As a result, these regimes were short-lived. This is what happened in railroads, where associations proved to be only transitional forms of governance that preceded other more permanent ones because they conflicted with the politically dominant laissez faire ideology of the time, expressed in antitrust policy. Of course, this raises again the issue of the state's role in the selection process.[19]

State Policy

We have referred repeatedly to the many ways in which the state influenced governance transformations in our cases. Although we have discussed these influences elsewhere (Campbell and Lindberg, 1990; Lindberg and Campbell, 1991), it is worth sketching, however briefly, the major aspects of the state's roles in order to highlight their complexity and to round out the preceding discussion.

Perhaps more than any of the other factors discussed here, the state is capable of influencing governance transformations throughout the entire transformation process. First, state actors may devise policy that creates *pressures for change* either intentionally or unintentionally. In the former category we have seen how policy makers deliberately manipulated antitrust laws in the dairy, steel, railroad, meat-packing, and telecommunications sectors either to facilitate or to break up corporate hierarchies, multilateral networks, and associations. In the latter category, the passage of Medicare legislation helped indirectly to spawn the development of capital markets in the hospital sector.

A second way in which the state influences governance transformations is by facilitating the *selection* of a new governance regime once pressures for change have materialized. Sometimes state actors select policies specifically designed to solve problems for a sector, such as when federal regulators passed beef-grading regulations during the 1920s that increased the amount of information about beef quality available to consumers, thus helping inadvertently to create competitive markets in the meat-packing sector. At other times the state sustains or alters the balance of power among actors, as was the case during the 1920s when the Federal Food Administration protected fledgling dairy cooperatives from antitrust prosecution, and orchestrated producer-distributor price bargaining throughout the sector. At other times, the state's influence is much more subtle, as its legal principles and institutionalized procedures constrain the selections of other actors. In the automobile sector, for instance, right-to-work laws in the South helped to keep labor costs low for Southern parts suppliers, a situation that encouraged automobile manufacturers, who were looking for ways to reduce costs during the 1970s and 1980s, to reduce the level of vertical integration in their operations by establishing just-in-time subcontracting arrangements with these suppliers. Finally, the state often helps to ratify and stabilize new governance regimes once they emerge. In telecommunications, for example, independent firms frequently challenged the Bell company's monopoly by asking the courts to determine whether Bell was entitled to control telephone technology through its patents. Judges generally sided with Bell thereby legitimizing and further stabilizing the company's hierarchical domination within the sector.

Our cases reveal that the state not only plays important roles throughout the transformation process, but that it does so with respect to the creation of all types of governance mechanisms. One of the most interesting of these involves the creation of markets. Much of the literature on governance transformations has focused on the conditions under which corporate hierarchies replace markets as the principal institution for coordinating transactions. A good deal of this literature implies that markets occur naturally or spontaneously, in the sense that actors do not deliberately plan or construct them in advance of actual transactions, and that the existence of markets precedes the development of hierarchies insofar as actors will begin to organize their activity through hierarchies only when extenuating circumstances arise that cause markets to break down.[20]

Yet our analysis of the state's role in governance transformations suggests that there is nothing natural or inevitable about the existence of markets, and that markets are not necessarily the precursors to all other forms of governance. Instead, we found that actors select and socially construct markets, just as they do other forms of governance. For example, although utility companies were reluctant to begin buying nuclear reactors for the commercial generation of electricity during the 1950s, Congress finally convinced them to do so by threatening to build government-owned nuclear plants that would compete with private utilities. In telecommunications a series of regulatory rulings from the Federal Communications Commission and the courts between 1968 and 1982 led directly to the creation of competitive markets for long-distance telephone service where once there had been only the AT&T monopoly. Of course, we have already seen how state policy contributed to the formation of markets in meat packing and hospitals. The trend toward deregulation may help precipitate a shift away from associative forms of governance in the dairy sector toward an economy organized more through markets. In these examples, the state played an active role in helping to construct markets where there had never been commercial exchange to begin with (nuclear), or where alternative governance mechanisms had come to coordinate exchange (hospitals, meat packing, telecommunications, dairy). Thus, we agree with Hodgson (1988, p. 210) who argued that "the onus is as much to explain the existence of the market as it is to explain the existence of the firm," and we would add other governance mechanisms as well. Indeed, as Polanyi (1944) suggested years ago, an analysis of the effects of state policy must be an integral part of these explanations, particularly insofar as they concern the social construction and maintenance of markets. Perhaps the reason why economists and others have granted such a privileged status to markets in the first place is that they have systematically ignored the empirical effects of political and other social processes by which actors have selected markets histor-ically—an omission that our case studies help to correct.[21]

To summarize briefly, we have demonstrated that the insights of all five theoretical views of governance transformation are valuable, although in differ-ent ways, for developing a more comprehensive, evolutionary model of the transformation process. We have done this by showing the extent to which each view is particularly relevant for explaining how the selection process proceeds at *different stages* of our evolutionary model. Most perspectives helped us to iden-tify the origins of pressures for change. Theories that emphasize the importance of power and control, as well as the state, were especially useful for understand-ing how actors collectively produce new governance regimes by blending their individually selected strategies in complex ways. Those that stress cultural and political factors provided important clues for understanding how emergent re-gimes are stabilized and become durable. In addition, we have shown that the new evolutionary model conforms in many ways to the empirical stories of our case studies.

As a result, it is clear that exclusively economic arguments about governance transformation, including the so-called new institutionalism, offered by William-son and his followers, are myopic to the point of reductionism. Without an analysis of politics, technology, culture, and other social factors, one cannot arrive at a solid theoretical understanding of the governance transformation pro-cess. Yet we are not trying to *replace* economic analyses of this phenomenon with other forms of social analysis. To do so would be to engage in the same sort of intellectual imperialism for which economists have recently been accused. Rather, we suggest that a far more eclectic approach is required, one that squares well in this regard with the socioeconomics that scholars have recently proposed, and one that refuses to reduce governance transformations to any narrowly fo-cused category of variables (e.g., Etzioni, 1988). It would be a mistake, however, simply to search for an assortment of economic, political, technological, and other variables that seem to trigger transformations. Although insights may be gained from such an exercise (e.g., Hollingsworth, 1991), we concur with Nelson and Winter (1982) who argued that the key to understanding economic transfor-mations is an analysis of the search process. Indeed, the evolutionary model we have developed gives pride of place to the processes through which actors select new governance regimes. Without such an analysis governance transformations will appear to be knee jerk reactions to various constellations of independent variables, and explanations will lack much appreciation or insight as to the causal mechanisms involved.

Trajectories of Capitalist Development

Our discussion of governance transformations bears directly on debates about the long-term institutional development of advanced capitalism. During the 1950s and 1960s both liberals and Marxists argued, for different reasons, that the imperatives of economic and technological rationality were propelling all capitalist societies toward a common institutional structure, characterized by large firms, concentrated industries, and mass production technology (e.g., Baran and Sweezy, 1966; Galbraith, 1967). Later, critics, who were concerned with explaining the presence of industries and parts of industries consisting more of craft-based production and small firms than of colossal corporate hierarchies, argued that these *convergence* theories had grossly overstated the case. They offered instead theories of *dualism* that suggested, for example, that more traditionally organized sectors persisted because large modern firms often sought to avoid a variety of labor problems and restrictive regulations that were commonly associated with modernization, and because volatile market demand occasionally required the flexibility in production offered by more traditional institutional arrangements (e.g., Berger and Piore, 1980; Goldthorpe, 1984).

The evidence reported above supports the dualism thesis to the extent that we have found some sectors, such as automobiles, telecommunications, steel, and meat packing, that are hierarchically organized and highly concentrated, while others retain a more decentralized, traditional structure, such as dairying where relatively small farms still conduct most production. We also find evidence for dualism insofar as parts of the production process *within* some sectors are organized increasingly in a relatively decentralized fashion. Subcontracting to small firms has been rejuvenated in automobile manufacturing, and minimills have developed in steel—two sectors where one would expect the highest levels of hierarchically organized mass production, particularly in light of Chandler's (1977) argument that mass-produced consumer and producer goods bring forth corporate hierarchies. Furthermore, we have seen that in steel and automobiles, managers eventually selected less hierarchical forms of governance to avoid, at least in part, the costs and problems associated with unionized labor, environmental regulations, and to respond more quickly to changing demand in the marketplace—factors routinely offered to explain dualism.

However, scholars who are interested in production systems based on flexible specialization and diversified quality production have recently identified several problems with the dualism thesis.[22] For example, Linda Weiss (1988, chap. 1) criticized adherents to the dualist perspective for adopting an overly society-centered view insofar as they generally attribute dualism to problems and imperatives that stem from civil society—a perspective that systematically neglects how the state, confronting geopolitical and international economic crises, often deliberately promotes different institutional configurations within the economy. She also maintained that dualism tends to slip into functionalist and, at worst, teleological explanations when theorists claim that the traditional sector persists because it serves the needs of large-scale capitalism, such as controlling the demands of organized workers or providing certain special machinery for other mass production firms, and that such needs and, therefore, traditional sectors develop as inevitably as does large-scale capitalism itself. Recognizing that the state plays an important and autonomous role in helping to determine the institutional forms that capitalism assumes, and rejecting functionalist explanations, Weiss concluded that the process of capitalist development is inherently neutral to the extent that there is no preordained form that will necessarily emerge. Although Weiss cast her argument primarily in terms of the development of flexible specialization in Northern Italy, others, examining a wider range of cases, made similar arguments. Charles Sabel (1989) and Wolfgang Streeck (1989), for instance, also suggested that the state plays an important role in fostering or inhibiting the development of different types of production; that firms develop flexible specialization and diversified quality production for a variety of reasons, not just to control or more efficiently exploit labor; and that because the interactions among labor, capital, and the state determine (we would say select) the course of capitalist development, certain structural conditions do not inevitably determine this course through teleological or functionalist processes.[23]

We find some support for this position. First, we have already discussed many cases where the state was responsible for the creation of all sorts of governance arrangements, although not always for reasons having to do with war, economic crises, or the preservation of national security. Society-centered views, as implied above, are often inadequate by themselves. Yet Weiss overstates her case to the extent that she would apparently *abandon* these explanations in favor of a completely state-centered approach. We advocate a more balanced position between these two extremes, as do Sabel and Streeck. After all, we have also seen cases where the state had very little to do with transformations. (Indeed, we see no reason *a priori* why either perspective must necessarily take precedence over the other with respect to explaining governance transformations.) In addition, as suggested above, the state plays a much more complex set of roles in the transformation process than Weiss recognized—roles that include not only creating pressures for change, the primary thrust of her analysis, but also facilitating in complex ways the selection process. Second, our cases support the claim that there does not appear to be an inherently teleological momentum to the development of capitalism where sectors evolve toward a common governance arrangement, dualist or otherwise. There is simply too much diversity in the examples that we have explored to support such a position. Furthermore, if one takes seriously the proposition that the selection process is largely a collective interaction among many actors, struggling and bargaining with each other, and that the outcomes of these struggles and bargains are never guaranteed in advance, then teleological arguments are even more difficult to sustain.

Weiss (1988, p. 6) argued that dualist theories tend to fall into the same trap as the convergence theories they attack; that is, to argue that traditional sectors survive because they are needed to support large-scale capitalism requires an assumption about the inevitability and general direction of economic development in the first place. The same could be said about recent studies that suggest that advanced capitalist societies are undergoing a prolonged period of disorganization. For example, in a fascinating and insightful study of five advanced capitalist nations, including the United States, Scott Lash and John Urry (1987) argued that during the late nineteenth and early twentieth centuries these societies moved through a period of increasing organization, characterized by high levels of union density, industrial concentration, trade association activity, state centralization, and the strengthening of class-based political parties, but that since the Second World War many of these patterns have started to be reversed. Thus, we are witnessing, they claimed, the end of organized capitalism. However, the disorganization that Lash and Urry saw transpiring across national political economies is much less uniform *within* these societies, at least within the United States. On the one hand, we have seen a degree of disorganization, or at least reorganization in a decentralized and less formally organized direction, with the development of minimills in steel, just-in-time subcontracting in automobiles, increasing competition in meat packing, and declining union strength in all three—evidence that tends to confirm the disorganization thesis. Yet, on the other hand, automobile manufacturers organized multilateral networks during the last twenty years to coordinate research and development aimed at solving engine emission and other industrywide problems, and trade associations became more, not less, active in meat packing as the market for red meat dwindled. In addition, we have seen increasing levels of vertical and horizontal integration in the hospital sector due to the 1965 Medicare legislation, and a dramatic increase in associative governance in the nuclear sector due to the accident at Three Mile Island. Furthermore, there was a shift from associative to hierarchical governance in the California dairy industry—certainly a reorganization, but not disorganization because the decline in associative activity was accompanied by an increase in hierarchy. What we have, then, is a set of examples, albeit an admittedly small set, that illustrates the *uneven* and *multidirectional* character of institutional development within and across sectors in the United States, rather than a consistent process of disorganization.

The point is that many of the pitfalls that have marked these debates about the trajectory of capitalist development, including functionalist and teleological reasoning, excessively state- or society-centered explanations, and sweeping historical generalizations, could have been avoided if scholars adopted a sectoral analysis and employed an evolutionary theory of governance transformation, as we have, that theorized the causal mechanisms involved in the selection process. Others have also suggested the need for such a theory, but have offered little in the way of empirical evidence to substantiate their theoretical contributions (e.g., Foster, 1987; Nelson and Winter, 1982). We have started here to fill these gaps by arguing that actors respond to pressures for change by trying to select new governance regimes within a variety of limits, but that they do so in ways that often lead to the eventual transformation of these limits themselves. Thus, we have argued for a theory of governance transformation that neither over-emphasizes the actor's free will, nor succumbs to excessive institutional deter-minism. In short, we have offered a theory that takes very seriously Marx and Engels's (1970, p. 59) famous methodological dictum that "circumstances make men just as much as men make circumstances."

Notes

1. These studies, all based on primary and secondary data, were written by Patricia Arnold (hospitals), Ken Bickers (telecommunications), John Campbell (nuclear energy), Rob Kennedy (railroads), John Portz (meat packing), Christoph Scherrer (steel and auto-mobiles), and Brigitte Young (dairy) and appear in Campbell, Hollingsworth, and Lindberg (1991).

2. See Lindberg, Campbell, and Hollingsworth (1991) for a discussion and typology of different types of governance mechanisms.

3. For criticisms of this view, see Nelson and Winter (1982) and Hodgson (1988).

4. Chandler's argument is not entirely removed from the economic tradition insofar as he argued that, with the advent of these technological breakthroughs, existing markets were unable to handle the scheduling and distribution problems associated with new mass produced goods. Hence, he also incorporated a market failure model into his analysis.

5. Although Chandler, for example, recognized the state's role in undermining col-lective governance mechanisms, his theoretical discussion does not address the state's role (e.g., Chandler, 1977, pp. 6–12, 484–90).

6. The presumption that technology is the primary, but certainly not the only, force behind governance transformations is clear insofar as a host of additional variables are discussed in this literature as modifying the effects of technology. For example, many who work within this tradition have recognized that the extent to which technological change leads to the replacement of markets by hierarchies is influenced by such things as product type, the existence of already well-developed distribution systems, the availability of finance capital and skilled managerial talent, wage levels, the centralization of urban markets, state policy, and historical tradition (Chandler and Daems, 1980; Kurth, 1979; Markusen, 1985, chap. 5).

7. For criticisms of the resource dependence school from within the power and control tradition, see Mintz and Schwartz (1985, chap. 2).

8. This assumes that economic exchange rarely occurs between actors with equal power—a fundamental departure from theories that are rooted in the economic efficiency tradition, and a point stressed by others (e.g., Etzioni, 1988, p. xii).

9. For further discussion of the important effects that trust and other relatively sub-jective factors play in the organization of economic activity, see Eccles (1981), Johanson and Mattsson (1987), Lorenz (1988), MacCaulay (1963), and Ouchi (1977, 1980).

10. Some do a better job of establishing these linkages than others. Compare, for example, Crozier's (1964, chap. 8) rather vague discussion of the culturally based differ-ences in French, U.S., and Soviet bureaucracy with Lazerson's (1988) excellent analysis of how cultural traditions contributed to the formation of extensive subcontracting net-works in Italy.

11. For a review of this property rights school, see Bowles (1984), and for a critique, see Hodgson (1988, chap. 7).

12. For elaborations of this ontological position, see Baumgartner, Burns, and DeVille (1984, 1985), Giddens (1984), and Hodgson (1988).

13. Ikenberry (1988) develops a stepwise, evolutionary analysis of U.S. energy policy

regimes that illustrates the kind of developmental logic we have in mind, although his analysis does not focus on institutional transformations *per se*. Evidence for this kind of logic supports our contention that in order to understand governance transformations, one must have a historical analysis of distinctive sectoral and national experiences that accounts for the contingent nature of structural change.

14. Of course, beginning with Olson's (1965) path-breaking study, many economic theories have been offered to explain the collective action of individuals. Yet we are not aware of any that explicitly try to understand the development of multilateral types of *interorganizational institutions*. Knoke and his colleagues, however, appear to be moving in this direction (e.g., Knoke and Wood, 1981; Knoke and Wright-Isak, 1982).

15. This argument is consistent with recent work in economics on long waves and macroeconomic development where it is argued that fundamental breakthroughs in technology, such as the invention of the steam engine, the automobile and low-cost petroleum products, and, most recently, microelectronics, have triggered long-term swings in economic performance (Freeman, 1984, 1986).

16. Insofar as Nelson and Winter recognize that conflict within organizations may help determine the course of organizational change, it is somewhat surprising that they express reservations about including an analysis of power in their models (e.g., Nelson and Winter, 1982, p. 44). See Foster (1987, chap. 7) for a macroeconomic argument in favor of evolutionary models that is sympathetic to Nelson and Winter, but that includes an explicit analysis of power.

17. We are not claiming that such cultural support is always *sufficient* to foster and sustain multilateral forms of governance, just that it often appears to be necessary. We have already noted that there is a substantial body of literature that suggests that political support from the state is also usually important (e.g., Streeck and Schmitter, 1985), as these cases illustrate. Similarly, Weiss (1988, p. 202) suggested that although culture may have some effect, the more important determinant in facilitating the development of networks is the state.

18. Biggart seems to have recognized this point more recently and has tried to build a normative element into her analysis of the formation of different types of markets (e.g., Abolafia and Biggart, 1991).

19. The state is very important in this regard because it both helps to define the politically dominant ideologies, and plays a very important role in ratifying, or refusing to ratify, new governance regimes.

20. For examples of those who create this impression, see Williamson (1975, 1985) and Chandler (1977). For recent criticisms, see Lazonick (1986) and Hodgson (1988, chaps. 8 and 9).

21. Others have recognized recently that markets are not necessarily naturally occurring phenomena. For example, Abolafia and Biggart (1991) suggest that such diverse forms of governance as the Chicago Board of Trade, Japanese business groups, and direct sales organizations, all of which they consider markets, were created deliberately through a complex variety of social forces, often including political struggle. Coase (1988, pp. 8–9), an early proponent of transaction-cost economics, a school that often leaves the impression that markets are naturally occurring precursors to other forms of governance, has also recognized recently how political forces often play important roles in the deliberate planning and social construction of markets.

22. By flexible specialization we mean production that utilizes flexible purpose machines and skilled workers to manufacture special or customized products, a form of production that is quite the opposite of mass production in this sense (e.g., Piore and Sabel, 1984). Scholars who prefer the term "diversified quality production" (e.g., Streeck, 1989) refer to the same form of production, but stress that its development may occur

gradually through either cooperation among artisanal firms or the decentralization of large hierarchical firms; that this is not a new phenomenon historically in some national econo-mies, such as West Germany; and, thus, that its discovery by scholars does not represent a radically new set of opportunities for organizing industry, as the flexible specialization literature often suggests.

23. Weiss's critique of dualism, although insightful in many respects, tends to go a bit overboard. First, some of the dualist theories that Weiss targets are not as society-centered as she claims. Suzanne Berger (Berger and Piore, 1980, p. 144), for example, recognizes the important role the state plays in perpetuating small-firm sectors. Second, although Weiss's concerns about functionalism are generally well founded, there are exceptions. Again, Berger (Berger and Piore, 1980, pp. 146–48) rejects functionalist logic.

References

Abolafia, Mitchel, and Nicole Woolsey Biggart. 1991. "Competition and Markets: An Institutional Theory." In Amitai Etzioni, ed., *Socio-Economics: Toward a New Synthesis*. Armonk, NY: M.E. Sharpe.

Alchian, Armen, and Harold Demsetz. 1972. "Production, Information Costs, and Economic Organization." *American Economic Review* 62 (December): 777–95.

Aldrich, Howard. 1979. *Organizations and Environments*. Englewood Cliffs, NJ: Prentice Hall.

Baran, Paul, and Paul Sweezy. 1966. *Monopoly Capital: An Essay on the American Economic and Social Order*. New York: Modern Reader.

Baumgartner, Thomas, Tom R. Burns, and Philippe DeVille. 1984. *The Shaping of Socioeconomic Systems*. New York: Gordon and Breach.

———. 1985. "Actor and System: Toward a Theory of Social Action and System Structuring." In Tom Burns, Thomas Baumgartner, and Philippe DeVille, *Man, Decisions, Society: The Theory of Actor-System Dynamics for Social Scientists*. New York: Gordon and Breach.

Becker, Gary. 1976. *The Economic Approach to Human Behavior*. Chicago: University of Chicago Press.

Berger, Suzanne, and Michael Piore. 1980. *Dualism and Discontinuity in Industrial Societies*. New York: Cambridge University Press.

Bowles, Roger. 1984. "Property and the Legal System." In David Whynes, ed., *What Is Political Economy?* New York: Basil Blackwell.

Campbell, John L., J. Rogers Hollingsworth, and Leon N. Lindberg, eds. 1991. *Governance of the American Economy*. New York: Cambridge University Press.

Campbell, John L., and Leon N. Lindberg. 1990. "Property Rights and the Organization of Economic Activity by the State." *American Sociological Review* 55, 5:634–47.

Caves, Richard. 1980. "Industrial Organization, Corporate Strategy, and Structure." *Journal of Economic Literature* 18, 1:64–92.

Chandler, Alfred. 1977. *The Visible Hand: The Managerial Revolution in American Business*. Cambridge, MA: Harvard University Press.

Chandler, Alfred, and Herman Daems. 1980. *Managerial Hierarchies: Comparative Perspectives on the Rise of the Modern Industrial Enterprise*. Cambridge, MA: Harvard University Press.

Coase, Ronald. 1937. "The Nature of the Firm." *Economica* 4:386–405.

———. 1988. *The Firm, the Market, and the Law*. Chicago: University of Chicago Press.

Crozier, Michel. 1964. *The Bureaucratic Phenomenon*. Chicago: University of Chicago Press.

Domhoff, G. William. 1974. *The Bohemian Grove and Other Retreats*. New York: Harper Colophon.

————. 1983. *Who Rules America Now?* Englewood Cliffs, NJ: Prentice Hall.

Dosi, Giovanni. 1984. "Technological Paradigms and Technological Trajectories: The Determinants and Directions of Technical Change and the Transformation of the Economy." In Christopher Freeman, ed., *Long Waves in the World Economy.* London: Frances Pinter.

Downs, Anthony. 1957. *An Economic Theory of Democracy.* New York: Harper & Row.

Eccles, Robert. 1981. "The Quasifirm in the Construction Industry." *Journal of Economic Behavior and Organization* 2(December): 335–57.

Elliott, John. 1984. "The Institutional School of Political Economy." In David Whynes, ed., *What is Political Economy?* New York: Basil Blackwell.

Etzioni, Amitai. 1988. *The Moral Dimension: Toward a New Economics.* New York: Free Press.

Foster, John. 1987. *Evolutionary Macroeconomics.* Boston: Allen & Unwin.

Freeman, John. 1984. *Long Waves in the World Economy.* London: Frances Pinter.

————. 1986. *Design, Innovation and Long Cycles in Economic Development.* New York: St. Martin's Press.

Galbraith, John Kenneth. 1967. *The New Industrial State.* New York: Mentor.

Giddens, Anthony. 1984. *The Constitution of Society: Outline of the Theory of Structuration.* Cambridge: Polity Press.

Goldthorpe, John. 1984. "The End of Convergence: Corporatist and Dualist Tendencies in Modern Western Societies." In John Goldthorpe, ed., *Order and Conflict in Contemporary Capitalism: Studies in the Political Economy of Western European Nations.* New York: Oxford University Press.

Granovetter, Mark. 1985. "Economic Action and Social Structure: The Problem of Embeddedness." *American Journal of Sociology* 91, 3:481–510.

————. 1989. "Summary and Background of Talk Prepared for the Conference on Socio-Economics." Paper prepared for the First Annual International Conference on Socio-Economics, Harvard Business School, Cambridge, MA.

Hamilton, Gary, and Nicole Woolsey Biggart. 1988. "Market, Culture, and Authority: A Comparative Analysis of Management and Organization in the Far East." *American Journal of Sociology* 94, suppl.:52–94.

Hodgson, Geoffrey. 1988. *Economics and Institutions: A Manifesto for a Modern Institutional Economics.* Philadelphia: University of Pennsylvania Press.

Hollingsworth, J. Rogers. 1991. "The Logic of Coordinating American Manufacturing Sectors." In John L. Campbell, J. Rogers Hollingsworth, and Leon N. Lindberg, eds., *Governance of the American Economy.* New York: Cambridge University Press.

Ikenberry, John. 1988. *Reasons of State: Oil Politics and the Capacities of American Government.* Ithaca, NY: Cornell University Press.

Johanson, Jan, and Lars-Gunnar Mattsson. 1987. "Interorganizational Relations in Industrial Systems: A Network Approach Compared with the Transaction Cost Approach." *International Journal of Management and Organization* 17(Spring): 34–48.

Knoke, David, and James Wood. 1981. *Organized for Action: Commitment in Voluntary Associations.* New Brunswick, NJ: Rutgers University Press.

Knoke, David, and Christine Wright-Isak. 1982. "Individual Motives and Organizational Incentives Systems." In Samuel Bacharach, ed., *Research in the Sociology of Organizations,* vol. 1. Greenwich, CT: JAI Press.

Kurth, James. 1979. "The Political Consequences of the Product Cycle: Industrial History and Political Outcomes." *International Organization* 33, 1:1–34.

Lash, Scott, and John Urry. 1987. *The End of Organized Capitalism.* Madison: University of Wisconsin Press.

Lazerson, Mark. 1988. "Organizational Growth of Small Firms: An Outcome of Markets and Hierarchies." *American Sociological Review* 53, 3:330–42.

Lazonick, William. 1986. "Organizations, Markets, and Productivity." Paper presented at the Economic History Association meetings, Hartford, Connecticut.

Lindberg, Leon N., and John L. Campbell. 1991. "The State and the Organization of Economic Activity." In John L. Campbell, J. Rogers Hollingsworth, and Leon N. Lindberg, eds., *Governance of the American Economy*. New York: Cambridge University Press.

Lindberg, Leon N., John L. Campbell, and J. Rogers Hollingsworth. 1991. "Economic Governance and the Analysis of Structural Change in the American Economy." In John L. Campbell, J. Rogers Hollingsworth, and Leon N. Lindberg, eds., *Governance of the American Economy*. New York: Cambridge University Press.

Lorenz, Edward. 1988. "Neither Friends nor Strangers: Informal Networks of Subcontracting in French Industry." In Diego Gambetta, ed., *Trust: Making and Breaking Cooperative Relations*. New York: Basil Blackwell.

MacCaulay, Stewart. 1963. "Non-contractual Relations in Business: A Preliminary Study." *American Sociological Review* 28, 1:55–67.

Markusen, Ann. 1985. *Profit Cycles, Oligopoly, and Regional Development*. Cambridge, MA: MIT Press.

Marx, Karl, and Frederick Engels. 1970. *The German Ideology*. New York: International Publishers.

Mintz, Beth, and Michael Schwartz. 1985. *The Power Structure of American Business*. Chicago: University of Chicago Press.

Nelson, Richard, and Sidney Winter. 1982. *An Evolutionary Theory of Economic Change*. Cambridge, MA: Harvard University Press.

Noble, David. 1977. *America by Design*. New York: Oxford University Press.

North, Douglass. 1981. *Structure and Change in Economic History*. New York: W.W. Norton.

Offe, Claus, and Helmut Wiesenthal. 1985. "Two Logics of Collective Action." In Claus Offe, *Disorganized Capitalism*. Cambridge, MA: MIT Press.

Olson, Mancur. 1965. *The Logic of Collective Action*. Cambridge, MA: Harvard University Press.

Ouchi, William. 1977. "Review of *Markets and Hierarchies: Analysis and Antitrust Implications* by Oliver E. Williamson." *Administrative Science Quarterly* 22, 3:540–44.

———. 1980. "Markets, Bureaucracies, and Clans." *Administrative Science Quarterly* 25, 1:129–41.

Perrow, Charles. 1981. "Markets, Hierarchies and Hegemony." In Andrew Van de Ven and William Joyce, eds., *Perspectives on Organization, Design, and Behavior*. New York: John Wiley & Sons.

———. 1986. *Complex Organizations: A Critical Essay,* 3rd ed. New York: Random House.

Pfeffer, Jeffrey. 1987. "A Resource Dependence Perspective on Intercorporate Relations." In Mark Mizruchi and Michael Schwartz, eds., *Intercorporate Relations: The Structural Analysis of Business*. New York: Cambridge University Press.

Pfeffer, Jeffrey, and Gerald Salancik. 1978. *The External Control of Organizations: A Resource Dependence Perspective*. New York: Harper & Row.

Piore, Michael, and Charles Sabel. 1984. *The Second Industrial Divide*. New York: Basic Books.

Polanyi, Karl. 1944. *The Great Transformation*. Boston: Beacon Press.

Robbins, James A. 1987. "Organizational Economics: Notes on the Use of Transaction-Cost Theory in the Study of Organizations." *Administrative Science Quarterly* 32, 1:68–86.

Sabel, Charles F. 1989. "Flexible Specialization and the Re-emergence of Regional Economies." In Paul Hirst and Jonathan Zeitlin, eds., *Reversing Industrial Decline? Industrial Structure and Policy in Britain and Her Competitors*. New York: Berg Publishers.

Scherer, F.M. 1970. *Industrial Market Structures and Economic Performance*. Chicago: Rand McNally.

Schneiberg, Marc, and Rogers Hollingsworth. 1989. "Transaction Cost Economics and Trade Associations." In Masahiko Aoki, Bo Gustafsson, and Oliver Williamson, eds., *The Firm as a Nexus of Treaties*. Beverly Hills, CA: Sage.

Sorge, Arndt, and Wolfgang Streeck. 1987. "Industrial Relations and Technical Change: The Case for an Extended Perspective." Discussion paper No. 87–1. International Institute of Management, Wissenschaftszentrum Berlin.

Smircich, Linda. 1983. "Concepts of Culture and Organizational Analysis." *Administrative Science Quarterly* 28, 3:339–58.

Stevenson, Rodney. 1987. "Institutional Economics and the Theory of Production." *Journal of Economic Issues* 21, 4:1471–93.

Stinchcombe, Arthur. 1983. *Economic Sociology*. New York: Academic Press.

Stone, Katherine. 1981. "The Origins of Job Structures in the Steel Industry." In Mary Zey-Ferrell and Michael Aiken, eds., *Complex Organizations: Critical Perspectives*. Glenview, IL: Scott Foresman.

Streeck, Wolfgang. 1983. "Between Pluralism and Corporatism: German Business Associations and the State." *Journal of Public Policy* 3, 3:265–83.

———. 1989. "On the Social and Political Conditions of Diversified Quality Production." Paper presented at the International Conference, "No Way to Full Employment?" Wissenschaftszentrum Berlin für Socialforschung, Berlin, July 5–7.

Streeck, Wolfgang, and Philippe Schmitter. 1985. "Community, Market, State—and Associations? The Prospective Contribution of Interest Governance to Social Order." In Wolfgang Streeck and Philippe Schmitter, eds., *Private Interest Government: Beyond Market and State*. Beverly Hills, CA: Sage.

Swedberg, Richard. 1991. "Socioeconomics and the New Methodenstreit: On the Paradigmatic Struggle in Contemporary Economics." In Amitai Etzioni, ed., *Socio-Economics: Toward A New Synthesis*. Armonk, NY: M.E. Sharpe.

Torstendahl, Rolf. 1984. "Technology in the Development of Society, 1850–1980: Four Phases of Industrial Capitalism in Western Europe." *History and Technology* 1, 2:157–74.

Useem, Michael. 1984. *The Inner Circle: Large Corporations and the Rise of Business Political Activity in the U.S. and U.K.* New York: Oxford University Press.

Weiss, Linda. 1988. *Creating Capitalism: The State and Small Business since 1945*. New York: Basil Blackwell.

Williamson, Oliver. 1975. *Markets and Hierarchies: Analysis and Antitrust Implications*. New York: Free Press.

———. 1981. "The Economics of Organization: The Transaction Cost Approach." *American Journal of Sociology* 87, 3:548–77.

———. 1985. *The Economic Institutions of Capitalism*. New York: Free Press.

Young, Oran R. 1989. *International Cooperation: Building Regimes for Natural Resources and the Environment*. Ithaca, NY: Cornell University Press.

15

JERALD HAGE AND CATHERINE ALTER

Interorganizational Network Systems: A New Institution and Governance Mechanism

During the late 1960s and early 1970s, the United States federal government funded a number of demonstration projects that attempted to stimulate the creation of new programs for various clients and encourage cooperation between agencies. There was considerable concern about case coordination and following clients through the largely fragmented system of health and welfare found in most local communities. Many of these demonstration projects foundered on problems of agency competition and inadequate funding, and most demonstrated considerable amounts of conflict over who should do what to which clients and for what reasons.

Now, in the late 1980s and early 1990s—only two decades later—one finds a considerable change in the delivery of services in many U.S. communities. Not only is there much more coordination among agencies providing services for the mentally retarded, delinquent youth, and the chronically mentally ill, but delivery systems for previously unrecognized clients have also emerged, and not necessarily because of federally mandated programs. Recent efforts at coordinated care, for example Community Support Programs (CSP) for chronic mental patients (Turner and TenHoor, 1978), Primary Health Care–Community Mental Health Center linkage projects (Goldman, Gattozzi, and Taube, 1981) and Service Systems for Seriously Emotionally Ill Children and Youth (Stroul and Friedman, 1986) have involved very modest levels of support. A large amount of voluntary effort to establish delivery systems has been provided. Perhaps the most dramatic examples are services for victims of family violence including rape and child abuse and hospice services for the dying.

This paper has been condensed from Catherine Alter and Jerald Hage, *Organizations Working Together: Coordination in Interorganizational Networks* (forthcoming).

This change in the matter of a short decade, and coming at a time many predicted in the early 1970s that cooperative behavior between competing agencies was impossible, suggests a number of interesting questions: Why are agencies now more cooperative than they appeared to be some two decades ago? What changes in our society explain this evolution? Has it been primarily the influence of federal programs or are there more fundamental reasons?

We propose to answer these questions by developing a theory about cooperative behavior between organizations and the conditions that make for more effective coordination in this new governance mechanism: interorganizational network systems. One definition of such a system is that a group of organizations enters into a permanent, enduring relationship to produce goods or services that they could not achieve on their own and yet in areas that are central to organizational objectives and in which resources are allocated, a division of labor is created, and member behavior is controlled. It is these last three characteristics that make it a systemic network (Morrissey, Taussig, and Lindsey, 1984).

The distinctive characteristic of interorganizational networks is that they represent a much more complex form of coordination than either markets (economic exchanges) or hierarchies (organizations) represent, that is, a single authority organization, because they involve two or more organizations attempting in various ways attempting to produce a product or a service. Usually both a moral commitment as well as rational calculation are involved. We anticipate that increasing this new institutional form of governance will replace both markets and hierarchies (Williamson, 1975) as a governance mechanism.

Theoretical Framework

An interorganizational network system has coordination neither by exchanges in the market place nor by the determination of those at the top of the authority structure. Rather than let customers/clients put together their own package of products/services, or attempt to aggregate all of the needed products/services in one organization (Aiken et al., 1975), firms/agencies unite to form the package, whether in a joint venture, joint program, or a more complex combination of firms and agencies that we will call a systemic network. A true network requires give and take and mutual adjustment among its members. It is this quality that makes networks much more complex than either markets or hierarchies and therefore much more interesting.

Historically, interorganizational network systems represent a relatively new institutional form, as fundamental a change as the development of the large corporation (Chandler, 1977) or the public bureaucracy (Weber, 1946). For organizational theorists, interorganizational network systems pose a number of intellectual challenges. This new governance mechanism demands much higher levels of cooperation between public sector agencies or private sector firms than previously was thought possible in either organizational or economic theory. Conventional wisdom assumed that public organizations would attempt to maximize autonomy just as private organizations attempt to maximize profit (Gouldner, 1960; and see the interorganizational relations literature, for example, Hall et al., 1977; Aldrich, 1979; Benson, 1975; Whetten, 1981; by the mid-1980s, however, this assumption began to be challenged somewhat: see Lincoln, 1985) . The complexity involved in coordinating a number of disparate organizations necessitates new skills and capabilities on the part of managers, administrators, case workers, researchers, and other professionals involved in these complex governance mechanisms.

There are so many sources (Laumann and Marsden, 1982; Burt, 1980; Morrissey, Tausig, and Lindsey, 1984) explaining what network analysis is, and even in the area of organizational analysis, there are so many empirical examples, that little introduction would appear necessary. Yet in all this intellectual richness lies considerable conceptual confusion. In particular, different kinds of networks have not been analytically separated and, as a consequence, the need for different theories for different kinds of networks has been lost to view.

We need to perceive that within the large range of studies involving organizations, there are at best four distinct kinds of networks:

1. Information networks.
2. Resource networks of customers/clients, funds, and power.
3. Action sets, where organizations cooperate in tangential areas to achieve some common, but superordinate, goal, but do not coordinate or pool significant resources.
4. Network systems, where organizations cooperate in central areas, allocate personnel and funds to various members of the action network, attempt to coordinate their work, and control the behavior of the various members of the system.

The major differences lie between the third and fourth type of network. Recently, the action set has been extensively discussed in the business literature (Frazier, 1983). There are, for example, multispatial systems that purchase supplies together (Provan, 1984). These reflect action sets because the superordinate objective is not central to patient care. Quite different are multihospital systems in the same community that reorganize wards so that one hospital takes all pediatric cases, another all geriatric, another all cardiovascular, etc. When the central goal of the hospital is involved, extensive coordination is occurring, and a system with a division of labor has emerged. Many of the industry trade associations are also examples of action sets: business organizations delegate their lobby and information activities to a new unit. But again, these activities are not central to the specific production of products in the organization and there is little coordination involving the allocation of resources.

The order in which these kinds of networks are listed is important theoretically because it represents one way in which interorganizational delivery systems can emerge. Boundary spanners from organizations first share information about the problems of particular clients, make inquiries, and exchange news about new treatments. Then, as trust develops across time, two organizations might begin to create some joint programs (Aiken and Hage, 1968), and what is known in the business world as a joint venture. Gradually, as organizations learn that perhaps the benefits outweigh the costs of cooperative behavior (Axlerod, 1984), they become willing to engage in more complex arrangements such as inter-organizational network systems. Finally, the problem of administrative coordination is confronted, not always successfully. Interorganizational network systems can also be constructed from the top down, via administrative fiat in what are called mandated systems (Whetten, 1981).

A Theory of Interorganizational Network Systems

Our objective is to develop a theory about the choice of a form of systemic network. Just as hierarchies or organizations are coordinated in different ways (see Mintzberg, 1979; Hage, 1980; Aldrich and Muller, 1982), so is the new institutional governance mechanism of systemic networks.

While there is no best way to categorize systemic network systems, we have chosen to start building a contingency theory of coordination in network systems by selecting eight environmentally determined dimensions that appear to be the most basic. There are three external control or power variables: (1) resource dependency; (2) regulation; and (3) voluntary/nonvoluntary work. There are five technological variables: (1) task scope; (2) task uncertainty; (3) task intensity; (4) task duration; and (5) task volume. This theoretical framework has the advantage of integrating an important literature on the political economy of organizations, namely, resource dependency theory, with a task or technological approach to organizations (see Hage, 1980).

External Controls

Considerable attention has been paid to the issue of the external control of networks, especially action and service delivery networks in the nonprofit sector where political influence is an important consideration. It is possible to conceptualize interorganizational networks vis-à-vis their environment in more or less the same terms in which contingency theory conceptualizes single organizations vis-à-vis their environments. The question is, of course, to what degree does the organizational or interorganizational unit have the freedom to define its own future? To tackle this question we consider three different aspects of external control: resource dependency, regulation, and voluntary/involuntary work.

Our definition of resource dependency is straightforward: it is the degree to which a network of organizations requires external resources for survival and goal achievement. Probably the single most popular perspective on inter-organizational relationships has been the resource dependency approach (Benson, 1975; Pfeffer and Salancik, 1978), which asserts that all interorganizational interactions—communication as well as joint activity—are ultimately and fully dependent on resource acquisition (Yuchtman and Seashore, 1967). Organizational decision makers' primary focus is on finding and defending an adequate supply of resources, and this orientation dominates the system and determines its superstructure. "Such an orientation becomes, for decision makers," writes Benson, "an operational definition of the purposes of the organization and thus of their responsibilities as decision makers" (1975, p. 231). In sum, political economists argue that networks may be functional or dysfunctional—ineffective and/or effective—because of the political and economic forces that affect them, and the ability of members to change these dynamics and outcomes can be successful only within limits (Wildavsky, 1979). The amount of coordination and the choice of methods is, in this view, a direct result of the patterns of these external controls.

The definition of the network regulation variable is also straightforward: it is the degree to which a network is constrained in its ability to be self-governing, as opposed to being autonomous. There has been much confusion about this aspect of interorganizational networks. Most interorganizational relations (IOR) researchers have conceptualized the presence of constraint on decision making as resource dependency and thus treated constraint as the opposite end of the dependency continuum; or, resource dependency and autonomy are viewed as separate dimensions but ones that are negatively related. Pfeffer and Salancik (1978), for example, asserted that reliance on external sources for resources means a constraint on autonomy, and that as autonomy decreases, interorganizational conflict increases and cooperation decreases.

Each of these conceptualizations may be true in certain circumstances. We believe, however, that at this theory-building stage, resource dependency and regulation should be thought of as separate variables. The reason is that if dependency is conceptualized as the degree to which interorganizational networks must rely on external resources, then it is logical to conceptualize its absence as self-sufficiency, not autonomy. If autonomy is conceptualized as the freedom for stakeholders to make democratic decisions concerning the goals and operations of their network, then the absence of this freedom is regulation, not dependency. What is important is that constraint does not necessarily derive exclusively from resource dependency or characteristics of the economy, but can emanate from laws and regulations or other political or altruistic decisions made by the state or some other governance structure.

Another way in which external forces influence network structure and process is by controlling the inputs, or "work status," of the system, which we define as follows: Work status refers to the degree to which the inputs of a network system are mandated rather than voluntarily agreed to by participants. In the public sector one measure of mandated work in networks is the proportion of clients who are involuntary, who are ordered into the system by a legal authority. In the

Table 15.1

Typology of Resource Dependency and Network Regulation as Independent Concepts

	Resource Dependency	
	Low	High
Low	Self-sufficiency with Autonomy e.g., an action network or well-endowed private foundations	Dependency with Autonomy e.g., a production network of firms and universities engaged in high-tech research
Regulation		
High	Self-sufficiency with Constraint e.g., an exchange network of hospitals that allocate organs for transplant	Dependency with Constraint e.g., a production network of public and private family service agencies charged with child protection

private sector one measure of mandated work in networks is the proportion of the funded products for which there are detailed input specifications.

This aspect of external control has been given little theoretical attention in the IOR literature, even though it is a major issue in the social welfare literature. In service systems, many categories of "raw materials" are involuntary: felons, abusive parents, juvenile delinquents, and the chronic mentally ill are only a few of the clients who are under court jurisdiction or are otherwise effectively pressured into a service delivery system. In private sector networks an analogous situation exists whenever external forces establish the materials and technologies to be used by the network.

The Impact of External Controls on the Choice of Coordination and Integration Methods

The central theme and debate during the past decade has been the necessity of reducing government spending. Given this general political atmosphere and the perceived need to cut back funds for human services, there have been many pressures to contain costs. Cost containment measures are, of course, one form of external control.

It is commonly accepted wisdom in the organizational literature that greater efficiency is achieved through the routinizing of work, which is achieved, in turn, by the bureaucratization of structure (Thompson, 1967). These factors lead to the choice of efficient processes—impersonal methods of administrative coordination and sequential task integration. Further, if this is the case, then we might expect that, in contrast, when interorganizational network systems are self-sufficient, there will be a greater emphasis on the quality of work. Under these conditions administrators will choose effective processes—group methods of administrative coordination and team task integration. The hypothesis is:

> *Hypothesis 1:* The greater the dependency on vertical sources for needed resources, the more likely impersonal methods of coordination will be used and the work flow will be arranged in a sequential pattern; the less the dependency on vertical sources for needed resources, the more likely group methods of coordination will be used and the work flow will be arranged in a team pattern.

In spite of our insistence on the conceptual independence of resource dependency and regulation, it is illogical to generalize that the impact of regulation, if driven by an efficiency motive, would be any different for the two external controls. Therefore:

> *Hypothesis 2:* The greater the regulation of networks, the more likely impersonal methods of coordination will be used and the work flow will be arranged in a sequential pattern; the less the regulation of networks, the more likely group methods of coordination will be used and the work flow will be arranged in a team pattern.

In networks where inputs or throughputs are involuntarily established, the major objective of the external force is, of course, control of the output. When human service systems must treat involuntary clients, for example, these clients are resistive, the therapeutic relationship is difficult to establish, and therapeutic objectives are much more difficult to achieve. When research and development networks must undertake projects with firmly specified objectives and methods, the nature of the throughput processes will be affected. This variable, then, also has impact on the choice of coordinative and integrative methods and is an important dimension affecting the shape and configuration of the network itself (Alter, 1988b). The hypothesis is:

> *Hypothesis 3:* The less choice in the nature of the work (a large proportion of involuntary clients, for example), the more likely impersonal methods of coordination will be used and the work flow will be sequential; the more choice in the nature of the work (a small proportion of involuntary clients, for example), the more likely group methods of coordination will be used and the work flow will be arranged in a team pattern.

Technology: The Task Dimensions

It is not far-fetched to assume that the nature of the technology used within a network would be an important aspect in any interorganizational analysis, yet this has not been the case. During the 1960s the study of technology enjoyed a certain vogue, but by the mid-1970s most researchers had lost interest. Partially responsible was the proliferation of a large number of variables that frequently only tapped a minor aspect rather than the whole production system (see Collins, Hage, and Hull, 1988, for a critique and the need for a new perspective). Another problem was the difficulty of finding dimensions that applied to both manufacturing and service organizations. More recently, there has been renewed interest (Alexander and Randolph, 1985; Collins, Hage, and Hull, 1988; also see various issues of *Management Science* and the *Academy of Management Review* and *Journal*), but technology has been largely ignored in research on interorganizational relationship (exceptions are Gillespie and Mileti, 1979; and Provan, 1984). We believe that network systems cannot be fully understood without taking into account the nature of the technology being used. There are five task dimensions that are particularly important: scope, uncertainty, intensity, volume, and duration.

The first dimension, scope, is a major variable, referring to the complexity of the technology of the production or throughput process. It may be defined as the degree to which tasks are variable and require a multidisciplinary or multidimensional approach. The degree to which the problem to be solved must be examined from many different perspectives, or the degree to which human services must take in the whole biological space of patients and clients, is one measure of task scope (Lefton and Rosengren, 1966; Lefton, 1970; Rosengren, 1968).

As knowledge has grown, our perceptions of human behavior have become more complex. The knowledge base of the various professions has broadened and each today is exhorted to engage in interdisciplinary research and practice in order to improve the quality of their work through a broadened perspective. The growth of knowledge is an evolutionary process, and can be captured by the variable we term task scope (Rosengren, 1968), which we use to refer to the degree to which administrators and workers view their consumers in comprehensive ways. Network systems that have broad task scope are composed of organizations that use detailed theoretical frameworks for diagnosis or problem assessment, and who have workers that assume numerous roles during the throughput process.

The concept of task uncertainty has been a factor in organizational theory for many years (Burns and Stalker, 1961; Thompson, 1967), but like scope, uncertainty is seldom used in the study of interorganizational networks. It may be defined as the extent to which task processes or interventions have knowable outcomes.

Organizational theorists (Duncan, 1972) have shown that some kinds of work involve tasks that are difficult because they cannot be preprogrammed, and therefore each case requires an individualized approach (also see Perrow, 1967). When work has this characteristic, outcomes are difficult to predict and it often takes a long time before they are known (Lefton and Rosengren, 1966; Lawrence and Lorsch, 1967). The assumption is that as the amount of time needed for feedback increases, so does task uncertainty. The difficulty of choosing the best intervention or method is related to the length of time before one receives feedback: if we don't know what works, it's hard to decide what to do!

Tasks also vary in the amount of time devoted to them. This dimension, task intensity, is the amount of time spent on, or on behalf of, one client or work unit during a specific period of time. Intensity is the degree to which workers have time to devote their energy, talent, and experience to a single case or unit of work. When intensity is low, the process is receiving a small portion of the worker's skill. When intensity increases, the process comes closer to receiving all the worker has to offer. This concept is illustrated by the simple observation that it takes 1,120 times longer to produce a Waterford crystal goblet than to mass-produce a jelly jar. This concept is an indicator of effective and high-quality outcomes, and often covaries with task scope. For example, Dewar and Hage (1978) found that task intensity was strongly associated with the utilization of a variety of occupations.

In service delivery, the intensity of services can vary greatly from community to community. Drug treatment programs for juveniles, for example, can range from those that require the adolescent to see a counselor for a half-hour once a week to residential treatment programs with high staff ratios. The first service represents a very minimal investment while the second indicates a community's willingness to invest in high-quality treatment programs for their adolescents. Of course, there are situations where low task intensity can be more effective than high, and intensity certainly does not guarantee effectiveness. But, in general, we believe that high intensity is associated with high quality.

Another dimension of technology that uses time as a measure is task duration, which is the total length of time it takes to produce or process one unit of output. There are interorganizational projects that take years to complete (e.g., putting people on the moon), and there are those that take minutes. Duration differs from intensity in that it is concerned with how long it takes to complete a unit from beginning to end. In the work of Lefton and Rosengren (1966) this was labeled the "lateral dimension." As with intensity, as duration increases, the resource investment also increases.

In human services task duration is analogous to long-term care. Clients or patients may be "treated" or "reformed" by one organization, and may be referred at discharge to another for ongoing aftercare. The offender released to a probation worker and the elderly man discharged from the hospital and linked to a homemaker have something in common: they experience duration and continuity of care because there is a network of organizations that takes an indeterminate rather than a truncated interest in them. In doing network research, however, a distinction should be made between how long the task takes and how long it should take in a normative sense. In our Fulton and Farnam study (described briefly below, and more fully in Alter and Hage, forthcoming), some clients were discharged because of lack of funds rather than because they had successfully completed a treatment program. Related to task duration is the degree to which a worker can devote exclusive attention to a case or unit: task volume is the average number of units that must be processed simultaneously by a worker. When systems have to produce large numbers of units or manage large client loads, the total amount of resources required grows geometrically (Lefton and Rosengren, 1966). This is especially true if the process is of long duration, such as in community support systems (CSS) for the chronic mentally ill. It can also be an important factor, however, even with brief processes, if they are intensive, as in residential treatment facilities.

By itself, however, task volume is not an adequate measure of the size of the operation and its cost. The total scale of a system is determined by combining intensity, duration, and volume. A number of models have been developed for specific manufacturing sectors and industries, most for use in cost-benefit analysis, but in general they combine only two of these dimensions into a scale dimension.

All of these ideas about technology can be applied to collaborative efforts of private or public organizations, or to partnerships between the two. The basic idea is that the complexity of the problem and the scale with which it must be handled determine to a large degree the forms and processes of interorganizational networks, especially when they involve collaborative work. One reason why most of our examples of interorganizational relationships among business firms are of research efforts is that they are high in task scope—i.e., they require inputs from different kinds of organizations—and they are large-scale—i.e., they involve intense effort of long duration requiring many tasks. And in business organizations the uncertainty of outcome is a well-understood concept (see Lawrence and Lorsch, 1967; Duncan, 1972; and for criticisms of this idea, see Aldrich, 1979; and Hage, 1980).

The Impact of Technology on Choice of
Coordination and Integration Methods

The importance of understanding task dimensions rests on the assumption that as technology increases or decreases, pressure on organizations to interact covaries with it (Alter, 1988c). Our central thesis is that as the complexity of technology increases, there is increasing pressure toward coordination and integration. Three of our task variables influence interorganizational networks in this direction: scope, uncertainty, and intensity. Conversely, while volume and duration may also encourage entry into a network system, their pressure has the opposite impact on the choice of coordination mechanisms. What, then, is the impact of the complexity of the work on the choice of administrative coordination and task integration methods? Three task dimensions are indicators of complexity and they push networks toward using collective methods of coordination and integration and their absence tends to decrease the use of these methods.

Hypothesis 4: The narrower the task scope, the more likely impersonal methods of coordination and sequential work flow will be used; the broader the task scope, the more likely group methods of administrative coordination and team work flow will be used.

Hypothesis 5: The less the uncertainty of the task, the more likely impersonal methods of coordination and sequential work flow will be used; the greater the uncertainty of the task, the more likely group methods of administrative coordination and team work flow will be used.

Hypothesis 6: The less the intensity of the task, the more likely impersonal methods of coordination and sequential work flow will be used; the greater the intensity of the task, the more likely group methods of coordination and team methods of work flow will be used.

As we noted above, there are two other ways in addition to task intensity that the scale of work can increase: the number of work units can be large and/or the total length of time required to process a unit can be very long. Task intensity, volume, or duration can each increase scale by themselves, but when two or even all three increase, then the scale of the operation grows geometrically.

We wish to speculate that as research accumulates about networks, the nature of task intensity will be shown to be fundamentally different from both task volume and duration, that when very intense effort is devoted to a project or program, the motivation is to achieve a very high quality result. When, on the other hand, very large numbers of units must be produced or serviced, or when the duration of time they are in the system is very long, then the process must be efficient. This is a simplistic analysis, of course, because different levels for each of the three variables will relate in different ways to both performance standards. Until we have studied a large number of different kinds of networks we cannot speculate about multivariate models of scale.

In the nonprofit sector the question of task scale is really an issue of public policy. Where services are a form of public utility, choices are made by politicians and administrators concerning levels of intensity, duration, and volume, and it is only in the last few years that different models have been used for different client population. Research, for example, has shown that treatment services for abusive parents are more effective if they are highly intensive and brief (Nelson, Landsman, and Deutelbaum, 1990). On the other hand, for populations for which there is no "cure," maintenance requires much less intensity but much longer duration.

If task volume or duration increases, then the scale of service increases, but if both volume and duration increase simultaneously, then the scale increases dramatically. In service delivery systems, as case loads grow, whether due to new cases or the failure to close old cases, there are strong pressures to rationalize the system in order to contain costs and maintain control. In this situation the system becomes increasingly dependent on external sources for resources and they mandate cost control obtained via written rules, procedures, and by avoiding the heavy resource investments required by case conferences, interagency teams, and case management (Alter, 1988a). The hypotheses are, therefore, straightforward:

> *Hypothesis 7:* The longer the task duration, the more likely impersonal methods of coordination and sequential work flow will be used; the shorter the task duration, the more likely group methods of coordination and team methods of work flow will be used.

> *Hypothesis 8:* The larger the task volume, the more likely impersonal methods of coordination and sequential work flow will be used; the smaller the task volume, the more likely group methods of coordination and team work flows will be used.

Findings

While space limitations prevent us from describing at length the sample (see Alter and Hage, forthcoming), the central point is that there are fifteen network systems in two counties of two adjacent states and thus different political jurisdictions. Of these fifteen network systems, seven are matched in the two counties that are part of the same metropolitan area. They have been deliberately selected to reflect considerable ranges in scope, duration, resource dependency, and the like. We labeled these counties *Fulton* and *Farnam.*

External Control and Coordination

In the first three hypotheses above we said that there is a relationship between external controls and work processes. Cast in yet more theoretical language, we said that the control structure under which networks operate determines to some degree the choice of how they are internally coordinated and integrated. Since most interorganizational network systems are complex, and, therefore, may potentially employ all three methods of administrative coordination and task integration, we asked each respondent to report the proportion of decisions handled by each method of coordination in their service delivery system and the proportion of clients treated by each mode of task integration in their service delivery system. Table 15.2 reports the zero-order correlations between each of the external controls with each of the coordination and integration methods.

We made the argument in the first three hypotheses that external controls lead to a greater emphasis on impersonal coordination and sequential task integration. To our surprise we found that the Farnam and Fulton data *do not* support this reasoning. Only one of the nine correlation coefficients between external controls and administrative decision making was statistically significant; that is, the correlations were at least 0.50. Further, all of the nine coefficients were in the opposite direction of what we predicted; that is, vertical funding was weakly but negatively associated with impersonal administrative methods ($r = -0.31$) and

Table 15.2

Relationships among Methods of Coordination and Task Integration and External Controls of Network Systems ($N = 15$)

| | Methods of Administrative Coordination | | | | | | | | Methods of Task Integration | | | |
| | Impersonal | | Personal | | Group | | Sequential | | Reciprocal | | Team | |
	r	beta	r	beta	r	beta	r	beta	r	beta	r	beta
Vertical Dependency	-0.31	-0.66	0.00		0.24		-0.69**	-0.88	0.43	0.69	0.50	0.50
Regulation	-0.07		0.28		0.15		-0.51*		0.27		0.41	
Involuntary Client Status	0.19		-0.27		-0.51*		-0.22	0.32	-0.02	-0.44	0.29	
Adj. R²		0.20						0.46		0.19		0.19
F		2.71						6.97		2.60		4.37
p <		0.10						0.00		0.10		0.05

*$p \le 0.05$
**$p \le 0.01$

involuntary client status had a strong positive relationship with group coordination methods. The correlation coefficients between the external controls and methods of task integration were somewhat stronger; that is, three of the nine were above 0.50, but the direction of these correlations also contradicted the prediction. Specifically, vertical dependency led to a reduction in sequential task integration ($r = -0.69$), but an increase in reciprocal ($r = 0.43$) and team methods ($r = 0.50$). The other two external controls followed the same pattern.

Why this reversal of the signs? There are two good reasons—qualifications and contingencies—that should be added to any resource dependency or political-economy approach to network analysis. We now believe that to predict coordination, we must know who is controlling the resources and what their performance objectives are, e.g., efficiency versus quality. In the case of Fulton and Farnam counties, the systems chosen for study were to a large extent dependent on federal funds, which for these programs meant more resources than would have been available locally, but also meant higher expectations regarding quality. Where governance was by the participant organizations acting as a group, and where workers from different agencies had treatment plans made jointly and implemented jointly, it was to some measurable extent because federal funds made this possible. And therein lies an interesting finding.

Resource dependency is not necessarily undesirable, as much of the resource dependency literature implies. Similarly, freedom from regulation at the local level does not necessarily lead to effective service networks. If we believe, given highly complex work, that coordination and integration are necessary to produce high quality, then both adequate funding *and* the use of group governance and teaming are necessary (the implementation of which may be mandated by vertical funding sources or adopted voluntarily by community participants). We have here in our findings the internal existential dilemma about the tradeoffs between money and power, both of which may be used for either ineffective or effective ends. Organizations may go it alone or surrender autonomy in exchange for more resources, and in both cases the effectiveness of results will depend on the aims and values of those making the decision, wherever they may be.

By combining the effects of the external controls we can tell which have the strongest effect on coordination and integration. Table 15.2 shows the results of regression analysis combining the effects of the two most useful variables on each of the coordination and integration methods. Because of our small sample size ($N = 15$), we were limited to only two independent variables when using this type of statistical analysis. The results do give us, however, some interesting clues about the effects of external controls in Fulton and Farnam counties.

Overall, the six regression equations accounted for a significant amount of variance in coordination and integration. In particular, external controls affected the use of impersonal coordination (Adj. $R^2 = 0.20$, F = 2.71, $p < 0.10$), as well as the use of all of the task integration methods: sequential (Adj. $R^2 = 0.46$, F = 6.97, $p < 0.00$), reciprocal (Adj. $R^2 = 0.19$, F = 2.60, $p <$

0.10), and team (Adj. R^2 = 0.19, F = 4.27, p < 0.05). In Table 15.1 it is also clear that of the external control variables included in this study, vertical dependency was the most useful for predicting coordination and integration. Again, however, the signs were not as we hypothesized: the standardized coefficients for vertical dependency on impersonal coordination (β = –0.66) and on sequential task integration (β = –0.88) were negative, while they were positive for reciprocal task integration (β = 0.69) and team task integration (β = 0.50). These results, of course, are consistent with the correlations. It should be noted that involuntary client status also had a weak effect on sequential task integration (β = 0.32) and reciprocal task integration (β = 0.44). It is logical to generalize from this finding (if we can generalize at all from fifteen cases) that court-ordered clients are for the most part referred in very structured and sequenced ways.

Technology and Coordination

Analysis of the relationships between the external control variables and the technology variables shows that the correlation coefficients between the external control variables had a high and positive pattern, while those between the task characteristics are consistently weak. Task scope and task intensity were positively related (r = 0.36) and task volume and task duration were also positively related (r = 0.48), but neither is statistically significant. These findings suggest that we should anticipate parallel impacts on the choice of coordination and integration methods.

The story is told in Table 15.3. Starting with the zero-order correlations, we note that only three task variables were strongly related to choice of coordination methods. Task scope, which was measured by an index containing the number of diagnostic categories and intervention roles used by respondents, was weakly related to impersonal coordination (r = –0.50) but strongly related to group coordination (r = 0.71). The importance of this finding is the pattern of the signs: the associations shifted from negative to positive across the three coordination methods. We therefore identify the following linear relationship as evidence for our fourth hypothesis: decreases in the scope of service are generally associated with increases in the use of impersonal coordination methods and increases in scope are associated with the use of group methods.

The same pattern occurred with task uncertainty, evidence for the fifth hypothesis, although overall, the coefficients were not as strong. This finding is noteworthy because task scope and uncertainty have been viewed in the management literature as substitutes for each other, while organizational theorists have been critical of the use of uncertainty (Aldrich, 1979; Hage, 1980). Here is empirical evidence that this is an important variable.

The findings concerning task integration methods in Table 15.3 are somewhat stronger. There are five statistically significant coefficients involving task integration (p < 0.05), in contrast to only three involving administrative coordination.

Table 15.3

Relationships between Coordination and Integration Methods and the Characteristics of Tasks in Network Systems

| | Methods of Administrative Coordination | | | | | | Methods of Task Integration | | | | | |
| | Impersonal | | Personal | | Group | | Sequential | | Reciprocal | | Team | |
	r	beta	r	beta	r	beta	r	beta	r	beta	r	beta
Task Scope	−0.50	−0.39	−0.27		0.71**	0.63	−0.69**	−0.60	−0.03		0.83***	0.83
Task Uncertainty	−0.53*	−0.43	0.17		0.49	0.33	−0.39		0.26		0.25	
Task Intensity	−0.01		−0.32		0.10		−0.60*	−0.76	0.28		0.49	
Task Duration	−0.01		−0.25	−0.54	−0.19		0.00		0.05		−0.01	
Task Volume	−0.21		0.34	0.60	−0.11		0.09		0.59	0.59	−0.34	
Adj. R^2	0.32		0.23		0.54		0.64		0.29		0.66	
F	4.36		3.10		9.32		13.28		6.80		28.55	
$p <$	0.03		0.08		0.00		0.02		0.00		0.00	

$*p \leq 0.05$
$**p \leq 0.01$
$***p \leq 0.001$

The three complexity variables show the same pattern of signs, with task scope being the clearest: its association with sequential integration is negative ($r = -0.69$), but its association with teaming is positive ($r = 0.83$). Task intensity also fits this pattern: negatively related to sequential integration ($r = -0.60$) and positively related to teaming ($r = 0.50$). And although the signs for task uncertainty also fit the pattern, its coefficients are not statistically significant. This is consistent with the management literature that argues that uncertainty creates more problems for administrators than difficulty at the product level.

That the coefficients for task volume were not higher was disappointing; we found no evidence for our seventh hypothesis, in spite of the fact that many organizational theorists believe that this variable is one of the two most important factors shaping organizational structure (Blau, 1970, 1972, 1973; Hall et al., 1977; Mintzberg, 1979; Hage, 1980). The coefficients for task duration are also insignificant, providing no evidence for the eighth hypothesis. An examination of the raw score shows that there is very little variation in the length of time clients spend in these systems in Fulton and Farnam.

Table 15.3 also gives the results of regressing the five task characteristics on the methods of administrative coordination and task integration. As a whole, these variables did a better job of accounting for variance than did the external control variables, ranging from team methods with the highest variance (Adj. $R^2 = 0.66$; F = 28.55; $p < 0.00$) to personal coordination having the lowest (Adj. $R^2 = 0.23$; F = 3.10; $p < 0.08$). Given the correlation coefficients in Table 15.3, it was not unexpected that the first three technology variables (scope, uncertainty, and intensity) dominated the two extremes of impersonal and group, sequential and team), and the second two technology variables (duration and volume) dominated (either alone or together) the middle (personal and reciprocal). The regression coefficients of task scope and task uncertainty on impersonal methods were negative ($\beta = -0.39$ and $\beta = -0.43$, respectively), but were positive on group methods ($\beta = 0.63$ and $\beta = 0.33$, respectively). Likewise, task uncertainty and intensity on impersonal methods were negative ($\beta = -0.60$ and $\beta = -0.76$, respectively) and scope was highly predictive of high levels of team task integration ($\beta = 0.83$).

The regression coefficients for the middle values of coordination were also consistent and, again, disconfirm our hypothesis. It was very apparent that when there were large volumes of clients, both administrators and workers tended to use personal and most direct methods of coordinating ($\beta = 0.60$) and integrating ($\beta = 0.59$).

External Controls and Task Characteristics Together

Which is the dominant set of determinants—external controls or task characteristics? We point out in passing that the line separating these two sets of variables is not as sharp as it appears. Task scope, intensity, volume, and duration are all

Table 15.4

Regression of Methods of Coordination and Integration in Network Systems on Measures of External Control and Technology ($N = 15$)

	Methods of Administrative Coordination			Methods of Task Integration		
	Impersonal beta	Personal beta	Group beta	Sequential beta	Reciprocal beta	Team beta
Vertical Dependency Regulation	−0.66			−0.54	0.40	0.30
Involuntary Client Status	0.58					
Task Scope			0.63			0.75
Task Uncertainty			0.33	−0.55		
Task Intensity						
Task Duration		−0.54				
Task Volume		0.60			0.37	
Adj. R^2	0.22	0.23	0.54	0.71	0.40	0.73
F	5.02	3.10	9.32	18.10	5.57	20.21
$p <$	0.03	0.08	0.00	0.00	0.01	0.00

political decisions, not just technological givens. Their values represent choices made by the policies of their political and cultural environments.

The relative impact of the political economy and the technological perspectives is reported in Table 15.4 where the two most significant variables for each method of administrative coordination and task integration are reported (again, we can have only two variables in each equation). The results shown in Table 15.4 are robust despite the limitations of small size, and in fact, we experimented with three variables and found no improvement in the F statistic.

Table 15.4 puts it all together and a consistent story emerges. Vertical dependency is the most useful external control variable because it enters four of the equations and the signs are consistent with a revision of our first hypothesis. Not surprisingly, involuntary client status is also predictive of impersonal administrative coordination. Among the task characteristics, task scope is the most useful in its ability to predict high levels of coordination and task integration. High volume and short duration are both predictive of personal administrative methods.

The most successful models are those for group coordination (Adj. $R^2 = -0.54$; F = 9.32; $p < 0.00$), sequential task integration (Adj. $R^2 = 0.71$; F = 18.10; $p < 0.00$), and teaming (Adj. $R^2 = 0.73$; F = 20.21; $p < 0.00$). This result leads us to conclude that vertical dependency and task scope are the two most useful dimensions for understanding network systems, especially when the focus is on the opposite poles of the coordination and integration continuum.

Conclusions

Systemic networks do exist and are becoming an important kind of governance mechanism. However, they occur in more than one form of coordination. We have advanced a theory that combines resource dependency and technology theory. Contrary to our hypotheses, resource dependency as such pushes organizations towards group-administered coordination and especially towards team integration, presumably because of concerns about quality. In contrast, one dimension of external control, involuntary status or mandated systems, leads to the selection of impersonal or bureaucratic mechanisms. Task scope and uncertainty, as we had hypothesized, also push systemic networks towards the choice of group administrative coordination and team task integration.

References

Aiken, Michael, and Jerald Hage. 1968. "Organizational Interdependence and Intra-organizational Structure." *American Sociological Review* 33:912–31.
Aiken, Michael, R. Dewar, N. DiTomaso, Jerald Hage, and G. Zeitz. 1975. *Coordinating Human Services.* San Francisco: Jossey-Bass.
Aldrich, Howard E. 1979. *Organizations and Environments.* Englewood Cliffs, NJ: Prentice Hall.
Aldrich, H., and S. Muller. 1982. "The Evolution of Organizational Forms: Technology,

Coordination and Control." *Research in Organizational Behavior* 4:33–87.

Alexander, J., and W.A. Randolph. 1985. "The Fit between Technology and Structure as a Predictor of Performance in Nursing Subunits." *Academy of Management Journal* 28, 4:844–59.

Alter, C. 1988a. "The Changing Structure of Elderly Service Delivery Systems." *The Gerontologist* 28:91–98.

———. 1988b. "Form, Function, and Change of Juvenile Justice Systems." *Children and Youth Services Review* 10, 2:148–65.

———. 1988c. "Integration in Interorganizational Hospice Care Systems." *The Hospice Journal* 3:11–32.

Alter, C., and Jerald Hage. Forthcoming. *Organizations Working Together: Coordination in Interorganizational Networks.* Lexington, MA: D.C. Heath.

Axlerod, R. 1984. *The Evolution of Cooperation.* New York: Basic Books.

Benson, J. 1975. "The Interorganizational Network as a Political Economy." *Administrative Science Quarterly* 20, 2:229–49.

Blau, Peter. 1970. "A Formal Theory of Differentiation in Organizations." *American Sociological Review* 35:210–18.

———. 1972. "Interdependence and Hierarchy in Organizations." *Social Science Research* 1:2–24.

———. 1973. *The Organization of Academic Work.* New York: John Wiley & Sons.

Burns, T., and G.M. Stalker. 1961. *The Management of Innovation.* London: Tavistock Publications.

Burt, R. 1980. "Models of Network Structure." *Annual Review of Sociology* 6:79–91.

Chandler, Alfred. 1977. *The Visible Hand: The Managerial Revolution in American Business.* Cambridge, MA: Harvard University Press.

Collins, Paul, Jerald Hage, and Frank Hull. 1988. "Organizational and Technological Predictors of Change in Automaticity." *Academy of Management Journal* 31, 3:512–43.

Dewar, Robert, and Jerald Hage. 1978. "Size, Technology and Structural Differentiation: Toward a Theoretical Synthesis." *Administrative Science Quarterly* 23:111–36.

Duncan, R.B. 1972. "Characteristics of Organizational Environments and Perceived Environmental Uncertainty." *Administrative Science Quarterly* 17:313–27.

Frazier, G. 1983. "Interorganizational Exchange Behavior in Marketing Channels: A Broadened Perspective." *Journal of Marketing* 47:68–78.

Gillespie, D., and D. Mileti. 1979. *Technostructures and Interorganizational Behavior.* Lexington, MA: Lexington Books.

Goldman, H.H., A.A. Gattozzi, and C.A. Taube. 1981. "Defining and Counting the Chronically Mentally Ill." *Hospital and Community Psychiatry* 32, 1:21–27.

Gouldner, A. 1960. "The Norm of Reciprocity." *American Sociological Review* 25, 2:161–78.

Hage, Jerald. 1980. *Theories of Organizations: Form, Process, and Transformation.* New York: Wiley-Interscience.

Hall, R., J.P. Clark, P.C. Giordano, P.V. Johnson, and M. Van Roekel. 1977. "Patterns of Interorganizational Relationships." *Administrative Science Quarterly* 22, 3:457–74.

Laumann, E., and P. Marsden. 1982. "Microstructural Analysis in Interorganizational Systems." *Social Networks* 4:329–48.

Lawrence, Paul R., and Jay W. Lorsch. 1967. "Differentiation and Integration in Complex Organizations." *Administrative Science Quarterly* 12:1–47.

Lefton, M. 1970. "Client Characteristics and Structural Outcomes." In W. Rosengren and M. Lefton, eds., *Organizations and Clients.* Columbus, OH: Charles E. Merrill.

Lefton, M., and W. Rosengren. 1966. "Organizations and Clients: Lateral and Longitudinal Dimensions." *American Sociological Review* 31, 6:802–10.

Lincoln, Y., ed. 1985. *Organizational Theory and Inquiry: The Paradigm Revolution.* Beverly Hills, CA: Sage.

Mintzberg, Henry. 1979. *The Structuring of Organizations.* Englewood Cliffs, NJ: Prentice Hall.

Morrissey, J.P., R.H. Hall, and M.L. Lindsey. 1982. *Interorganizational Relations: A Sourcebook of Measures for Mental Health Programs.* Washington, DC: National Institute of Mental Health, Series BN No. 2, DHHS Pub. No. ADM 82–1187.

Morrissey, J.P., M. Tausig, and M.L. Lindsey. 1984. *Interorganizational Networks in Mental Health Systems: Assessing Community Support Programs for the Chronically Mentally Ill.* Washington, DC, September 17–18: Community Support Rehabilitation Branch, Division of Mental Health Service Programs.

Nelson, K., M. Landsman, and W. Deutelbaum. 1990. "Three Models of Family-centered Placement Prevention Services." *Child Welfare* 54, 1:3–21.

Perrow, Charles. 1967. "A Framework for the Comparative Analysis of Organizations." *American Sociological Review* 32:194–208.

Pfeffer, Jeffrey, and Gerald Salancik. 1978. *The External Control of Organizations: A Resource Dependence Perspective.* New York: Harper & Row.

Provan, K.G. 1984. "Interorganizational Cooperation and Decision Making Autonomy in a Consortium Multihospital System." *Academy of Management Review* 9, 3:494–504.

Rosengren, W. 1968. "Organizational Age, Structure, and Orientations toward Clients." *Social Forces* 46, 1:1–11.

Stroul, B.A., and R.M. Friedman. 1986. *A System of Care for Severely Emotionally Disturbed Children and Youth.* Washington, DC: Georgetown University Child Development Center, Child and Adolescent Service System Program (CASSP) Technical Assistance Center.

Thompson, J.D. 1967. *Organizations in Action.* New York: McGraw-Hill.

Turner, J.C., and W.J. TenHoor, 1978. "NIMH Community Support Program: Pilot Approach to a Needed Social Reform." *Schizophrenia Bulletin* 4, 3:319–34.

Weber, M. 1946. "Bureaucracy." In H. Gerth and C.W. Mills, eds., *From Max Weber: Essays in Sociology.* New York: Oxford University Press.

Whetten, D.A. 1981. "Interorganizational Relations: A Review of the Field." *Journal of Higher Education* 52, 1:1–28.

Wildavsky, A. 1979. *Speaking Truth to Power: The Art and Craft of Policy Analysis.* Boston: Little, Brown.

Williamson, O.E. 1975. *Markets and Hierarchies, Analysis and Antitrust Implication: A Study in the Economics of Internal Organizations.* New York: Free Press.

Yuchtman, E., and S.E. Seashore. 1967. "System Resource Approach to Organizational Effectiveness." *American Sociological Review* 32:891–903.

16

JEROME M. SEGAL

Alternative Conceptions of the Economic Realm

Private and public action in the economic realm cannot be reasonably grounded unless it is placed within a larger understanding of human existence. This includes views of the nature of man, the nature of the good life, the point or purpose of human life, the existence and nature of God, and the nature of the broader human project.

Our civilization (at least since the late eighteenth century) has sharply tended not to think of the economic realm in this way. This is reflected in our view that economics is a science, that there are those who are experts in this science, and that decision making might best be left to those experts.

To illustrate the critical relevance of external questions, let us take seriously for a moment the following propositions:

1. The life of each individual is followed by an afterlife.

2. In the afterlife, one goes to either Heaven or Hell.

3. The duration and the intensity of the pleasures and pains in the afterlife are of such magnitude that they reduce earthly experiences to close to irrelevance.

4. Assignment to these conditions depends upon behavior while on the earth.

5. Behaviors for which one is condemned to Hell include charging interest and setting prices that maximize profits.

For much of Western history, many people believed these five propositions. Certainly, in determining what is rational economic behavior and what are rational economic institutions, their truth or falsity is critical.

The key difference between our world, where these considerations are not part of our approach to the economic realm, and a world where they are a vital part of decision making, is not that today no one believes these propositions or anything analogous to them, but rather that the big questions are in principle excluded from decision making.

Part of my intention in this paper is to develop an awareness that most of us believe some analogous, equally powerful propositions, and yet we, as a civilization, suspend such beliefs. We bracket our deepest concerns and carry on with economic life as though they were irrelevant. And this is irrational.

My approach is one of intellectual history. I will take a quick look at how the economic realm was perceived by Aristotle, by Seneca, in the Middle Ages, during the Reformation, and finally by Mandeville. This quick survey, which stops a full seventy-five years before Adam Smith, is adequate to take us from ancient times into the modern era, as most of the modern orientation can be found in Mandeville.

How We Think about the Economic Realm

Today to a very large extent, economic matters are a distinct sphere; intellectually, they are the province of the economists. We judge our economies in terms of three main criteria: the unemployment rate, the inflation rate, and the growth rate.

The two main performance criteria, the unemployment rate and the growth rate, are not themselves ultimate economic desiderata. Rather, higher levels of growth are valued because they lead to higher levels of income, and lower levels of unemployment are valued because employment is typically a necessary condition for receiving a share of the income pie, and secondly because the failure to utilize productive resources fully causes lower total levels of income. Thus, at bottom, the mainstream framework of economic thought rests on matters of income and its distribution (largely through employment). In turn, the concern with income itself emerges from a concern with well-being. How this connection is understood within mainstream doctrine is captured in the familiar equation:

$$U = f(C)$$

This equation simply asserts that utility is a function of the level of consumption. Typically, a further assumption is made—namely, that a person's utility is independent from that of others.

While economists have articulated and formalized this way of thinking about economic life, they did not invent it. They played a role, and they fostered it, but what is at issue is really a vast cultural orientation, how an entire society, not a mere limited body of professionals, thinks about economic life.[1]

There is nothing natural about this way of thinking about economic life. Even in the Western tradition, it has only had a firm hold for roughly two hundred years. But economic thought and indeed some forms of economic policy and regulation go back at least three thousand years.[2]

Aristotle

Three elements of Aristotle's thought are important for us here: (1) his vision of the good life; (2) his view of the place of economic activity in the good life; and (3) his account of slavery.

The Good Life

Aristotle makes clear that happiness is not a specific kind of experience, it is not for instance, pleasure. Rather, to be happy is to live a certain kind of life. It is not that a certain kind of life causes someone to "feel happy" as if this feeling were the objective, and could in principle be caused by a variety of different factors. Rather, happiness, or "living well" (which is probably a better translation of the Aristotelian concept) is itself a certain kind of living. It is among other things, a way of living that is undertaken for its own sake, not because it is instrumental to anything else, including sensations, and feelings.

Aristotle tells us that "the good of man is an activity of the soul in conformity with excellence or virtue" (Aristotle, 1962, p. 17). This formulation will not be so strange sounding to our ears if we make some adjustments. For instance, within this Aristotelian spirit, we might say: To live well is to live a life which emerges from the deepest part of oneself and which achieves the highest standards which are appropriate to the activities of that life. Essentially, the good life is one in which a person most fully, and at the highest level of excellence, fulfills his deepest nature. In yet more contemporary terms, one might speak of a life in which there is a flourishing of one's truest self.

There were in Aristotle's day alternative visions of the nature of human happiness. And these "misconceptions" with respect to the nature of happiness carried with them powerful implications with respect to economic life. One of these "confused" doctrines was that human happiness consists in pleasure. Aristotle addresses this issue and identifies the source of the error:

> Pleasant amusements, too [are desirable for their own sake]. We do not choose them for the sake of something else. . . . But most of those who are considered happy find an escape in pastimes of this sort, and this is why people who are well versed in such pastimes find favor at the courts of tyrants; they make themselves pleasant by providing what the tyrants are after, and what they want is amusement. Accordingly, such amusements are regarded as being conducive to happiness, because men who are in positions of power devote their leisure to them. . . .

> . . . happiness does not consist in amusement. In fact, it would be strange if our end were amusement, and if we were to labor and suffer hardships all our life long merely to amuse ourselves. . . . amusement is a form of rest, and since we cannot work continuously, we need rest. Thus rest is not an end, for we take it for the sake of [further] activity. The happy life is regarded as a life in conformity with virtue. It is a life which involves effort and is not spent in amusement. [Aristotle, 1962, pp. 287–88]

Living well, for Aristotle, then, is not a matter of the utility derived from consumption activities. The economic realm is necessary to the good life, but only indirectly so.

The Role of Economic Activity

Book VII of Aristotle's *Politics* opens with a focus on the role of external goods in the good life. By "external goods," he means wealth, property, power, and reputation. He contrasts them with the goods of the soul (i.e., fortitude, temperance, justice, and wisdom), and tells us:

> External goods, like all other instruments, have a necessary limit of size. Indeed all things of utility [including the goods of the body as well as external goods] are of this character; and any excessive amount of such things must either cause its possessor some injury, or at any rate, bring him no benefit. [It is the opposite with the goods of the soul.] The greater the amount of each of the goods of the soul, the greater is its utility — if indeed it is proper to predicate "utility" at all here, and we ought not simply to predicate "value." [Aristotle, 1961]

This passage, which has been ignored by historians of economics, could be judged to be the first statement of the principle of diminishing marginal utility. Aristotle suggests that with all external goods, we find that the more we have, the less utility we receive from each additional amount, and that at some point "any excessive amount" does us no good.

Actually, Aristotle's view of the utility curve is quite radical. Not only does the total utility level fail to rise beyond an upper bound (as in classical presentations of the diminishing character of marginal utility), but the total utility level may actually diminish, implying that the marginal utility attached to excessive amounts of external goods diminishes beyond the zero level, and actually becomes negative. If we assume a fixed realm of goods and translate this into a thesis about the marginal utility of money, the implication is that additional increments of money beyond a given level are not only useless, but negative in their effect. Translated to the society at large, the thesis emerges as one about the desirable limits to growth: economic growth beyond a given point is actually harmful to human happiness.

Aristotle focuses his attention on the core issue: property and the art of acquisition. He starts with the observation that there are a variety of different modes of subsistence, and that this gives rise to a variety of different ways of life. This is as true among animals as it is among humans. Some animals live in herds, and others live in isolation. Some eat plants; others eat meat. Among human beings he identifies five ways of life: the pastoral, the farming, fishing, hunting, and piracy. What he calls "true wealth" is acquired through these activities and consists of the amount of household property that suffices for the good life. This he regards as a limited amount.

In distinction to these modes of acquisition which supply the household with its needs, there is a second form of the art of acquisition. Aristotle tells us that while the first is natural, the second form of acquisition is not:

The [natural] art of acquisition is connected with the management of the household [which in turn is connected with the general acquisition of all the resources needed for its life] but the other form is a matter only of retail trade, and it is concerned only with getting a fund of money, and that only by the method of conducting the exchange of commodities.

. . . the acquisition of wealth by the art of household management (as contrasted with the art of acquisition in its retail form) has a limit; and the object of that art is not an unlimited amount of wealth. [1961, p. 25]

Aristotle then goes on to analyze the pathology of this unnatural process. His account is powerful and acute. The problem is not merely of the sort described by Galbraith (1958); that is, man on a squirrel wheel fruitlessly expending time and resources and not getting anywhere. For Aristotle the issue is more serious. The pursuit of higher and higher levels of income results in a distortion of the personality:

as what they seek appears to depend on the activity of acquisition, they are thus led to occupy themselves wholly in the making of money. . . . and if they cannot get what they want by the use of that art—i.e. the art of acquisition—they attempt to do so by other means, using each and every capacity in a way not consonant with its nature. [1961, p. 26]

The result is a distortion of human capacities. Consider how thoroughly Aristotle is echoed by Marx (1966, p. 165):

The properties of money are my own (the possessor's) properties and faculties. What I am and can do is, therefore, not at all determined by my individuality. I am ugly, but I can buy the most beautiful woman for myself. Consequently I am not ugly for the effect of ugliness, its power to repel is annulled by money. . . . I am a detestable, dishonorable, unscrupulous and stupid man but money is honored and so also is its possessor. Money is the highest good, and so its possessor is good. . . . I who can have through the power of money, everything for which the human heart longs, do I not possess all human abilities? Does not my money, therefore, transform all my incapacities into their opposites?

Who wrote the next paragraph, Marx or Aristotle?

The proper function of courage, for example, is not to produce money but to give confidence. The same is true of military and medical ability: neither has the function of producing money: the one has the function of producing victory, and the other that of producing health. But those of whom we are speaking turn all such capacities into forms of the art of acquisition, as though to make money were the one aim and everything else must contribute to that aim.

It was Aristotle (1961, p. 27), and the criticism that is made here is as fundamental as is possible within the Aristotelian framework. First, it should be clear that when Aristotle is criticizing this second form of the art of acquisition, he is criticizing not merely certain economic activities but an outlook and a form of life. Insofar as this becomes dominant, the object of criticism is then the entire form of social life. Thus, Aristotle has generated the framework in terms of which commercial civilizations, be they capitalist or precapitalist, are to be condemned.

In the passage just quoted, Aristotle articulates what is really behind his characterization of the "art of acquisition" as "unnatural": it produces a distortion of our nature. As he describes it, every human capacity gets placed at the service of obtaining money, essentially we ourselves are distorted. Within the Aristotelian framework, to say that our capacities—that is, our selves—are separated from their proper function is to say that we are thus denied self-actualization. It is also to say that we are thus denied the possibility of living well for to live well, as we have been told, is to express virtue at high levels of excellence. In short, Aristotle has articulated the most basic condemnation that is possible within his framework.

It is easy to miss the full significance of this, as his style is elevated and devoid of any obvious passion. Yet to see the full force of Aristotle and to appreciate the extent to which he laid the groundwork for the Christian tradition in this respect, all we have to do is shift the language a bit. Retaining his condemnation, simply replace his reference to the unbridled "art of acquisition" with the term "vice of acquisitiveness" and replace his reference to using our capacities "in a way not consonant with their nature" with "loss of our soul" and we have the much more powerful-sounding medieval condemnation of avarice as a mortal sin.

In formal terms, what the Aristotelian tradition illustrates is an approach to economic life that is rooted in a larger conception of human life and fulfillment. It refuses to treat economic life as a separate realm to be judged only in terms of limited objectives (e.g., production, consumption) and thus subject only to a limited range of criteria (e.g., the efficiency of the productive process, the justness of the distribution of income).

When seen from the Aristotelian framework, the very framework within which the science of economics poses its problems is the expression of a perversion of the intellect—or one that mirrors in the intellectual life the distortions induced by the one-sided specialization Aristotle finds in the life of acquisition.[3]

Slavery

Aristotle's views on slavery implicitly underlie his view of the economy. He tells us that there are those who

> regard the control of slaves by a master as contrary to nature. In their view the distinction of master and slave is due to law or convention; there is no natural

difference between them: the relation of master and slave is based on force, and being so based has no warrant in justice. [1961, p. 9]

Aristotle rejects this view. First, he defines a natural slave as "anyone who by his nature is not his own man, but another's" (1961, p. 11). And then he proceeds to investigate whether or not such persons exist. To his satisfaction, he concludes that they do, and notes that

> it is nature's intention also to erect a physical difference between the body of the freeman and that of the slave, giving the latter strength for the menial duties of life, but making the former upright in carriage and (though useless for physical labor) useful for the various purposes of civic life. [1961, p. 13]

He further points out that sometimes things go astray, and freemen by nature end up with the bodies of slaves, and natural slaves with the bodies of freemen. Further, he agrees with those who criticize the enslavement of conquered people, as this would mean that *mere power* was the basis for the distinction between slave and freeman. So while he admits that there may be injustice in specific cases of enslavement, the institution itself is just and natural and for the good of both parties.

Thus, mankind can be sorted out into higher and lower classes of human beings based on some principle of nobility, much as we make such distinctions between types of animal life. And these differences are inherent characteristics. They are given by nature; they are not the result of having been born into free and slave environments; they are not the result of education and upbringing. In short, for Aristotle, there is no great transcendent potential to be found in all of mankind.

That Aristotle comes to this conclusion is of great importance for the entire tenor of his thought about political life and economics.[4] His acceptance of the naturalness of slavery allows Aristotle to accept mass poverty as a natural and appropriate condition. The concept of household slavery is particularly suited to this, since the household slave is attached to the household unit and as part of it, is supposed to achieve whatever level of development he is capable of achieving.

With this presupposition, the socioeconomic framework of the polis can be fit neatly into a theory of human development. The polis can be viewed as the environment within which human fulfillment occurs, because the situation of the vast majority of persons simply falls by the wayside. Indeed, it is really not until the eighteenth century that the claims of the masses to achieve the highest levels of human development are embedded within the structures of political ideology and action.

On this basis, Aristotle is able to proceed without ever having to face the issue of mass poverty. Had he reasoned differently, he would have been forced to conclude that the world as he knew it, the world of the Greek polis, did not provide for the full development of mankind. It did so for a limited class at best.

Because this is not his perception, the issue of developing the economic basis to provide for fuller development for larger segments of the population did not arise for him. And thus, nowhere in his discussion of economic life is there any discussion of sustained economic growth. Given his assumptions, such growth is unnecessary. It is only in Marx's writings, over two thousand years later, that we have a synthesis of Aristotle's view of the role of the economic in human life and the historical problem of mass transcendence and economic growth.

Seneca

The Roman philosopher Seneca, a contemporary of Christ, is quite despairing about human virtue and happiness. While he was one of the first to articulate a belief in the continued progress of knowledge, he does not see this as leading to increasing human well-being.

Seneca makes a critical distinction among kinds of knowledge, distinguishing wisdom and philosophy from ingenuity (roughly what we mean by applied knowledge or technology). It appears that Seneca did not see the close link between knowledge and technological advance—and one might imagine that this is why he did not connect the indefinite expansion of human knowledge with an increase in human happiness. But that is exactly not the reason. Had Seneca understood how advances in pure knowledge would themselves lead to technological progress, his despair would have only been greater.

He writes:

> Posidonius says: "When men were scattered over the earth, protected by caves or by the dug-out shelter of a cliff or by the trunk of a hollow tree, it was philosophy that taught them to build houses." But I, for my part, do not hold that philosophy devised these shrewdly-contrived dwellings of ours which rise story upon story, where city crowds against city, any more than that she invented fish preserves, that are enclosed for the purposes of saving men's gluttony from having to run the risk of storms and in order that, no matter how wildly the sea is raging, luxury may have its safe harbors in which to fatten fancy breeds of fish. . . . Was it not enough for man to provide himself a roof of any chance covering and to contrive for himself some natural retreat without the help of art and without trouble? Believe me that was a happy age, before the days of architects, before the days of builders! All this sort of thing was born when luxury was being born.
>
> . . . The things that are indispensable require no elaborate pains for their acquisition; it is only the luxuries that call for labor. Follow nature, and you will need no skilled craftsmen. [1947, pp. 95–96]

Invention, mechanical skill, ingenuity, labor, or to call it what it is, economic growth—all of this emerges from human vice and foolishness. The path of wisdom and happiness lies elsewhere.

In his very severe way, Seneca is an advocate of a basic needs notion of development. He tells us:

> Houses, shelter, creature comforts, food, and all that has now become the source of vast trouble, were ready at hand, free to all, and obtainable for trifling pains. For the limit everywhere corresponded to the *need*; it is we that have made all other things valuable, we that have made them admired, we that have caused them to be sought for by extensive and manifold devices. . . that moderation which nature prescribes, which limits our desires by resources restricted to our *needs*, has abandoned the field. [1947, p. 98]

Seneca's views can be thought of an extension of Aristotle. Both elevate the pursuit of pure knowledge. And both have a sharp sense of the corrupting influence of unbridled absorption in worldly goods. With respect to the question, "how much is enough?" Aristotle gives the perspective of moderation—essentially enough to run a decent Athenian household replete with household slaves. For Seneca (who was vastly wealthy) enough is the barest minimum that sustains life.

Like Aristotle, Seneca saw no problem of mass poverty, but for a different reason. For Aristotle the masses were not by nature free persons and thus were not in need of the requirements of aristocratic life. Indeed, within the well-ordered household, household servants would achieve the fullest degree of self-realization that they were capable of achieving. The stoic philosophers, on the other hand, had a universalist vision of human nature that distinguished no classes of natural slaves. For Seneca, no problem of mass poverty arose because the required level of income for living the highest form of life was extraordinarily little. It would only have been in the face of mass starvation that the issue of inadequate economic resources would have arisen for Seneca.

The vast realm of economic activity above this minimal level not only represents a waste of time and energy (as it contributes nothing to human happiness), but is worse; as with Aristotle, it expresses a faulty understanding of the good life and is itself corrupting of human character.

The Middle Ages and the Reformation

The discussion in this section is the briefest sketch and is really a short summary of R. H. Tawney's classic work, *Religion and the Rise of Capitalism* (1938).

In the Middle Ages, Tawney tells us, the basic vision was that "the economic interests are subordinate to the real business of life, which is salvation, and that economic conduct is one aspect of personal conduct, upon which, as in other parts of it, the rules of morality are binding" (1938, p. 44). Further,

> The medieval theorist condemned as a sin precisely that effort to achieve a continuous and unlimited increase in material wealth which modern societies applaud as meritorious and the vices for which he reserved his most merciless

denunciation were the more refined and subtle of the economic virtues. "He who has enough to satisfy his wants" wrote a Schoolman of the fourteenth century, "and nevertheless ceaselessly labors to acquire riches, either in order to obtain a higher social position, that subsequently he may have enough to live without labor, or that his sones may become men of wealth and importance—all such are incited by a damnable avarice, sensuality or pride." [p. 48][5]

The medieval understanding of the economic realm broke down not in response to a theoretical challenge, but under the sustained impact of economic growth. The Reformation, which emerged in the sixteenth century, was a reaction against this collapse.

With respect to economics, the Reformation was marked by two very different strands of thought: one, represented by Luther, sought a full reversal, a turning back of the clock towards a more purified period:

> Luther thought that the most admirable life was that of the peasant, for it was least touched by the corroding spirit of commercial calculation. [Tawney, 1938, p. 96]

The contrast with Calvin was stark:

> Calvin, with all his rigor, accepted the main institutions of a commercial civilization, and supplied a creed to the classes which were to dominate the future. [1938, p. 97]

Yet the Calvinists were not endorsing unbridled avarice and the pursuit of wealth. Even Calvin's acceptance of some (but not *any*) level of interest rates, is not to be understood as a partial loosening of restrictions—along a progression that has Luther at one end and modern economic thought on the other. Rather, the Calvinist orientation towards economic life was part of a still more intensified and more integrated religious orientation.

In the Calvinist economic vision there was no acceptance of the "laws of the market place"—no vision of the desirability of allowing the impersonal forces of supply and demand to regulate prices. Following the trial of one Robert Keane, who was judged to have charged his customers excessively, the minister of Boston enumerated in his sermon the set of false principles that led the poor man astray:

> 1. That a man might sell as dear as he can, and buy as cheap as he can.
> 2. If a man lose by casualty of sea etc., in some of his commodities, he may raise the price of the rest.
> 3. That he may sell as he bought, though he paid too dear . . .
> 4. That, as a man may take the advantage of his own skills or ability, so he may of another's ignorance or necessity. [Tawney, 1938, p. 126]

The Puritan ethic that developed was a work ethic—a devotion to one's calling now understood as one's productive economic activity. It was not done for the sake of consumption. It was not a utilitarian orientation towards economic life. Rather it was in the work activity that the virtues were expressed. The Puritans thus focused sharply on the issues of virtue and vice. Economic life was a stage upon which our inner being was revealed, and in that revelation, a clue to our destiny in the hereafter. But the substance of Christian virtues shifted from that of the medieval period. Covetousness was not as serious a sin as sloth.[6]

It is going too far to say that there was a complete reversal of virtues, that what was vice became virtue and what was virtue became vice. There is some of this, to be sure; for instance, a life of religious withdrawal and contemplation was condemned. But there was also a shifting of emphasis. The virtues of diligence, moderation, sobriety, thrift emerged as factors that insure advantage. Vice was not defined as that which is ruinous of earthly success, but that is its effect.

Most basically, the economic realm is a place within which one's essential identity and fate are revealed. Thus, who one is, both in the eyes of the community and in the eyes of God, is revealed through economic life. Thus, while the establishment of personal and social identity is not the conscious objective of economic activity, economic life is most essentially the process whereby such identity is created. Thus, an anthropologist of puritanism might say that the Puritans produced not in order to consume, but in order to *be*.

Mandeville's Fable of the Bees

In 1705, halfway between the 150 years that separate the landing of the Puritans in the New World and the publication of Adam Smith's *Wealth of Nations*, Bernard Mandeville published a twenty-six-page poem called *The Grumbling Hive: or Knaves Turned Honest*. In 1714, the poem reappeared as part of a much larger work entitled *The Fable of the Bees: or, Private Vices, Publick Benefits* (Mandeville, 1966).

The basic poem appears to be a simple tale. It is the story of a flourishing hive of bees that, not having the sense to leave well enough alone, prayed to the God Jove that they be made virtuous. He answered their prayer, but virtue proved their ruin. My primary concern is less with Mandeville's novel empirical thesis (that vice is beneficial), than it is with the values, attitudes, and orientation implicit in Mandeville's thought.

Stripped to its essentials, Mandeville's poem is telling us that a thriving prosperous economy is what is important, regardless of whether prosperity requires behavior and character that violate religious, moral, or spiritual ideals. Mandeville is the voice of the great separation of economic life from any project of human transcendence.

Like many others, his tale is of The Fall. But it is not a fall from grace, innocence, or purity. Mandeville's Eden has a very particular character. Consider the happy state in which his bees originally find themselves:

> A Spacious Hive well stockt with Bees,
> That liv'd in *Luxury and Ease;*
> And yet as fam'd for Laws and Arms,
> As yielding large and early Swarms;
> Was counted the great Nursery
> Of Sciences and Industry. [p. 17]

The Hive represents not just man's social life, it is life within the nation-state. It is life under a particular government "fam'd for Laws and Arms." The central accomplishment is the life of ease and luxury. It is this that will be lost, not the spiritual innocence commonly ascribed to Paradise. The bees in Paradise are far from innocent.

> All Trades and Places knew some Cheat,
> No Calling was without Deceit. [p. 20]

Mandeville describes, profession by profession, this deceit:

> The Lawyers, . . .
> They kept off Hearings wilfully,
> To finger the refreshing fee;
> And to defend a wicked Cause,
> Examin'd and survey'd the Laws,
> As Burglars Shops and Houses do,
> To find out where they'd best break through.
>
> Physicians valu'd Fame and Wealth
> Above the drooping Patient's Health,
> Or their own Skill: The greatest Part
> Study'd, instead of Rules of Art,
> Grave pensive Looks and dull Behavior,
> To gain th' Apothecary's Favour; [p. 20]

Of the "Priests of Jove," he tells us

> Yet all pass'd Muster that could hide
> Their Sloth, Lust, Avarice and Pride; [p. 21]

Mandeville paints a picture of *an entire society that is untrue to the values inherent in their social roles,* a picture of decadence and corruption, but of a very particular kind: it is a corruption in the economic sphere.

Having painted the picture, he takes his novel turn:

> Thus every Part was full of Vice,
> Yet the whole Mass a Paradise;
> Flatter'd in Peace, and fear'd in Wars,
> They were th' Esteem of Foreigners, [p. 24]

He then proceeds to sketch how this worked: each vice, it seems, produced some benefit. Thus,

> The Root of Evil, Avarice,
> That damne'd ill-natur'd baneful Vice,
> Was Slave to Prodigality,
> That nouble Sin; whilst Luxury
> Employ'd a Million of the Poor,
> And odious Pride a Million more:
> Envy it self, and Vanity,
> Were Ministers of Industry;
> Their darling Folly, Fickleness,
> In Diet, Furniture and Dress,
> That strange ridic'lous Vice, was made
> The very Wheel that turn'd the Trade. [p. 25]

His vision of "modern" life found its echoes in Veblen and Galbraith. He zeroes right in on the issue of consumption; he looks at what lies behind the demand curve, and he finds vice and folly, vanity and envy and the fashion industry! Yet he embraces it all.

And what is the central benefit he cites? Employment. Jobs for millions. In particular the poor. And not just jobs, but higher incomes:

> Thus, Vice nurs'd Ingenuity,
> Which join'd with Time and Industry,
> Had carry'd Life's Conveniencies
> Its real Pleasures, Comforts, Ease,
> To such a Height, the very Poor
> Liv'd better than the Rich before,
> And nothing could be added more. [p. 26]

Thus, we have it. Since Mandeville first stated it, it has been repeated a thousand times. It is of course, a major strand in the celebration of capitalism. Jobs and income; employment and higher per-capita GNP. That is the bottom line.

The tale continues. Vanity, it appears, was the bees' undoing, in particular a vanity that concerns itself with the inner state. "How Vain is Mortal Happiness!" They failed to recognize "the Bounds of Bliss." They called out for honesty, and Jove, in anger, "rid the bawling Hive of Fraud."

Bit by bit, disaster sets in. With a change in motivation and appetite, market demand is altered. "The Price of Land and houses falls"; "The building Trade is quite destroyed, Artificers are not employ'd"—

> The slight and fickle Age is past;
> And Clothes, as well as Fashions, last.
> Weavers, that join'd rich Silk with Plate,
> And all the Trades subordinate,
> Are gone . . . [p. 34]

> As Pride and Luxury decrease,
> So by degrees they leave the Seas,
> Not Merchants now, but Companies
> Remove whole Manufactories.
> All Arts and Craft neglected lie;
> Content, the Bane of Industry,
> Makes 'em admire their homely Store,
> And neither seek nor covet more. [p. 35]

Ultimately, they are attacked by external foes, they fight, and are forced to retreat. Many die, and the survivors—

> They flew into a hollow Tree,
> Blest with Content and Honesty. [p. 35]

The poem concludes:

> Then leave Complaints: Fools only strive
> To make a Great an Honest Hive
> T' enjoy the World's conveniencies,
> Be famed in War, yet live in Ease,
> Without great Vices, is a vain
> Eutopia seated in the Brain. [p. 35]

Implicit in the poem is an emphasis on and an argument for being a powerful nation. The pre-Fall Hive is "fam'd for Law and Arms" and the ultimate denouement of the virtuous Hive occurs because they are attacked from without. Thus, *the economy must be thought of as within a violent competitive international arena.* National defense issues are central to issues of economic life. Mandeville [1966, p. 104] brings this out more directly in "Remark K":

> Abundance of moderate Men I know that are Enemies to Extremes will tell me, that Frugality might happily supply the Place of the two Vices I speak of [avarice and prodigality], that, if Men had not so many profuse ways of spending Wealth, they would not be tempted to so many evil Practices to scrape it together, and consequently that the same Number of men by equally avoiding both Extremes, might render themselves more happy, and be less vicious without than they could with them, Whoever argues thus shews himself a better Man than he is a Politician. Frugality is like Honesty, a mean starving Virtue, that is only fit for small Societies of good peaceable Men, who are contented to be poor so they may be easy; but in a large stirring Nation you may have soon enough of it.

In this way of thinking about economic life, in terms of what is required to be a powerful nation, Mandeville falls in with the Mercantilist tradition. On policy specifics, he was an advocate of laissez faire.

Mandeville's approach to vice does not follow of itself from his empirical thesis that the vices are necessary conditions for human happiness. It is one thing to argue that economic well-being depends on certain modes of behavior or traits of character commonly understood to be vices. It is quite different to conclude that we are therefore foolish to seek to reduce or eliminate those vices. A Puritan who accepted Mandeville's empirical thesis would reach a rather different, shattering conclusion. The Puritan, of course, would not readily accept the empirical claim. He would affirm something quite different, that virtue, indeed, Puritan virtue, is at the root of economic prosperity. But the important point is that if the Puritan was brought around to accepting Mandeville's thesis, he would reject prosperity, not virtue. Put in different terms, Mandeville is soft on vice. He is willing to accommodate to it on economic grounds. These attitudes rest on something more basic: *he is thoroughly divorced from the religious world view that characterized both the Reformation and the medieval world.* It goes almost without saying that he does not take seriously the proposition that a life of vice is ultimately contrary to self-interest because it imperils one's salvation.

But more fundamentally, Mandeville is close to amoral with respect to questions of character. As a diagnostician he is seized by the issue of character. And the central categories he is concerned with are those of the Christian tradition: avarice, envy, vanity, pride, etc. But he simply is untroubled by finding that such characteristics and motives pervade human life. It is not merely that he doubts that much progress can be made in the elimination of such motives, but further that he is not even attracted to such transformations. If anything, he is amused by the human spectacle. Moreover, it is not that there is some other set of characteristics or virtues that he is concerned about (e.g., Nietzschean vitality), he simply is not seized by the project of our becoming very different than we are. For Mandeville, all that matters is simply that we be better off.

A second, and somewhat paradoxical, feature of Mandeville's orientation is how he understands what it is for a person to be better off. In the poem we read,

> Thus Vice nurs'd Ingenuity,
> Which join'd with Time and Industry,
> Had carry'd Life's Conveniencies
> It's real Pleasures, Comforts, Ease,
> To such a Height, the very Poor
> Liv'd better than the Rich before,
> And nothing could be added more. [p. 26]

In "Remarks O" and "P," Mandeville explicates the thought behind this passage. First he explains his use of the term "real Pleasures." He says that he is of the "Opinion, that whether men be good or bad, what they take delight in is their pleasure ... we ought to dispute no more about Men's Pleasures than their Tastes" (p. 148).

The question of what it is really to be better off is central to economics. Certainly, one major criterion for the evaluation of economic circumstances and alternative economic systems is whether or not the population, or any representative individual, is better off in one or the other system. Mandeville tells us that "The very Poor Liv'd better than the Rich before" and we look to his explication to reveal his understanding of what it is to "live better":

> If we trace the most flourishing Nations in their Origin, we shall find that in the remote Beginnings of every Society, the richest and most considerable Men among them were a great while destitute of a great many Comforts of Life that are now enjoy'd by the meanest and most humble Wretches. [p. 169]

His answer appears to be quite simple. One lives better insofar as one has more of "the Comforts of Life." In the contemporary idiom, this might be called an opulence notion of standard of living.[7]

Mandeville goes on to explain how our notion of what constitutes a luxury is constantly changing:

> many things which were once look'd upon as the Invention of Luxury, are now allow'd even to those that are so miserably poor as to become the Objects of publick Charity, nay counted so necessary, that we think no Human Creature ought to want them. [p. 169]

He then goes on to identify some of the remarkable luxuries that are now available to all. He calls our attention to "the most ordinary Yorkshire Cloth," saying—

> What depth of Thought and Ingenuity, what Toil and Labor, and what length of Time must it have cost, before Man could learn from a Seed to raise and prepare so useful a Product as Linen. [p. 170]

And further:

> The Arts of Brewing, and making Bread, have by slow degrees been brought to the Perfection they now are in, but to have invented them at once, and a priori, would have required more Knowledge and a deeper Insight into the Nature of Fermentation, than the greatest Philosopher has hitherto been endowed with; yet the Fruits of both are now enjoy'ed by the meanest of our Species, and a starving Wretch knows not how to make a more humble, or a more modest Petition, than by asking for a Bit of Bread, or a Draught of Small Beer. . . .

> From Caves, Huts, Hovels, Tents and Barracks, with which Mankind took up at first we are come to warm and well-wrought Houses, and the meanest habitations to be seen in Cities, are regular Buildings contriv'd by Persons skill'd in Proportions and Architecture. If the Ancient Britons and Gauls

should come out of their Graves, with what Amazement wou'd they gaze on the mighty Structures everywhere rais'd for the Poor! [p. 171]

Compare this to the passage from Seneca considered above. All that Mandeville celebrates, Seneca condemned, on grounds of its effect on both character and human happiness.

It is remarkable to discover in Mandeville so much of the way in which we presently think about economic life. The central elements of his outlook are:

1. A lack of concern with respect to vice and virtue.

2. A view of the economic realm as a free-standing realm to be evaluated on its own terms (e.g., levels of employment, income, production, consumption).

3. A view that all classes gain as a result of economic growth.

4. An underlying identification of "living well" with living at a high level of material consumption.

5. A refusal to base policy judgments on any judgment of what yields true happiness other than those found within the actual behavior of economic agents (i.e., demand fulfillment as the criterion).

6. Situating economic policy within the world of national security and inter-state competition, with these areas providing central criteria for policymaking.

7. A concern with the possibility of economic collapse and unemployment, and a focus on the importance of high levels of consumer demand as necessary for economic vitality.

Articulated in Mandeville is the most dramatic break with the way the Western world had theretofore thought of the economic realm.[8]

Conclusion

Many alternative ways of thinking about the economic realm are not only possible, but in fact have long traditions within Western civilization. In somewhat simplified form, the range of perspectives includes:

1. *Instrumental consumptionism:* Basically, the economic realm impacts on human well-being through the production and distribution of goods and services. The higher the level of consumption, the better off any individual person is. Societies that have higher levels of consumption are better off than those with lower levels.

2. *International supremacism:* The cost of weakness in the international realm is overwhelming. The benefits of being on top are an extra feature; the great thing is to be able to impose rather than to be imposed upon. We attain freedom both through defense and through identification with the state/culture, which itself exercises power in the international/intercultural realm. The central function of the economy is to maintain the international position of the state.

3. *Economic liberalism:* There is no single conception of the good. The point of the economy is to enable the widest possible group of people to pursue their

own conceptions of the good. Market economies are largely neutral with respect to these conceptions and in their actual impact on the individual.

4. *Noble enablism* (Aristotle): Human happiness does not emerge from consumption. It is not something that can be attained through leisure time and recreational spending. Human well-being consists of activity in accord with our highest qualities and potentials. The pursuit of ever higher levels of income results in a distortion of the personality: a misuse of capacities and harm to the character.

5. *Universal minimal enablism* (Stoicism): The central outcome of most economic life is the manufacture of desire. This is the destruction of freedom and the perversion of the personality. It necessitates labor and labor is a curse. The economic realm should be reduced to almost nothing, or as close to nothing as possible. Almost all technology is harmful.

6. *Mass enablism* (one strand in Marx): Aristotle is basically correct with respect to the human good, but men are of equal dignity and the good life can only be attained on a mass basis through the development of vast technological means; thus, the economic realm is a necessary evil to be passed through historically so that most of mankind can live the good life outside that realm.

7. *Extratemporal instrumentalism* (medieval): Extratemporal rewards and punishments are based on behavior within the economic realm. Economic interactions are to be governed by the will of the creator, who has laid down what we should do and not do.

8. *Extratemporal dramatism* (Calvin): Economic behavior does not cause extratemporal rewards but manifests one's character within that drama. Virtue and vice are displayed. The character one manifests reveals where one is situated within that drama. It reveals and displays identity and destiny. The point of the economic realm is not consumption, but identity.

9. *Human transactionism* (a second strand of Marxism): Human happiness does not emerge from consumption, but is also not something largely divorced from or outside of the realms of production and exchange. The human good emerges from activities that enrich the lives and being of other people. The basic objective of the economy is to create these kinds of roles. An economy should be judged not in terms of the level of income but in terms of its ability to provide meaningful and transformative social roles to the population. Market relationships and demand creation are distorting. The great story of each life is the creation of one's own self, the achievement of something that is authentically one's own. Absorption with economic life is typically a distorting factor as we are pulled away from ourselves.

10. *Scientific and aesthetic progressivism* (Renaissance): Human progress is to be measured against standards of achievement in the aesthetic and scientific realms. What happens to specific individuals is irrelevant. The economic realm is positive insofar as it advances mankind in this drama and negative insofar as it retards.

This is not an exhaustive listing of alternative ways of viewing the economic realm, but it covers a good deal of the terrain. My reading of our own culture is that it is largely governed by the first two of these conceptions, instrumental consumption and international supremacism with some intellectual assent and/or lip service to the third—economic liberalism.

Notes

1. I am not denying that the problems of economics, or even the definition of efficiency, can be specified in sufficiently abstract terms such that almost any notion of the good can be fit within the framework. Rather, I am concerned with the actual cultural substance of how we think about the economy, and with the dominant notion of the good, as we find it. Thus, in principle, formal economics can accept the idea that man's most basic good is his gaining access to Heaven and his most basic evil is his suffering admission to Hell. But to connect these "empirical" assumptions to the formalism of economics would be to transform in almost every detail the actual substance of the modern orientation to economic life.

2. For instance, our earliest legislation with respect to labor laws, and with which we have a continuous history, was laid down in the commandment to keep the Sabbath. This injunction prohibiting seven days of labor was not just a matter for the individual believer. It applied as well to the slave and to the farm animals. Similarly, throughout the Old Testament we find an abundance of thought on economic life. Even within the Ten Commandments there is a second and somewhat startling injunction, "Thou shalt not covet thy neighbor's house." Putting aside the question of coveting thy neighbor's wife, the injunction against coveting his possessions goes against the heart of much of contemporary economic life, the desire for possessions based upon an awareness of the possessions of the neighbor. The emphasis in the commandment should not be placed upon the fact that the possessions belong to the neighbor, but rather on the coveting of them. This injunction is a prohibition against a certain kind of desire or preference. The idea that preferences or desires should be ruled inadmissible rather than satisfied and fulfilled, of course, runs counter to the bottom-line framework of modern economic thought.

3. Following this penetrating criticism of the art of acquisition Aristotle offers an explanation of why the trade of the petty usurer is hated most: "it makes a profit from currency itself, instead of making it from the process [i.e., of exchange] which currency was meant to serve. . . . [O]f all mode of acquisition, usury is the most unnatural." [1961, p. 29]. Aristotle's explanation is lacking in power, as are all such attacks on lending with interest that merely talk of the unnaturalness of trying to make money "breed" money. The real issue is what effect does the practice of money lending have on the people involved. It is not clear that the acquisitive instincts unleashed are more powerful in the case of money lending than in any other commercial ventures.

4. This is not because the issue of slavery plays any explicit role throughout his thought. Indeed, there is no extended discussion of it in his work other than in the few pages at the opening of the Politics.

5. The fourteenth-century "Schoolman" quote is from Henry of Langenstein.

6. Indeed, it was even affirmed that God desires us to choose the more profitable occupation: "If God show you a way in which you may lawfully get more than in another way (without wrong to your soul or to any other) if you refuse this, and choose the less gainful way, you cross one of the ends of your Calling, and you refuse to be God's steward" (in Tawney, 1938, p. 218). This quote is especially remarkable for it makes the maximization of profits a religious duty as well as the index to God's will. In a world

seized by the issue of salvation, this is nothing less than the metaphysical foundation of economic rationality, an overdetermination of reasons. Here Tawney is quoting an unidentified source, which appears from his notes to be from Richard Steele's *The Tradesman's Calling* (1684).

7. This distinction between an opulence notion of the standard of living and other conceptions has been explored by Amartya Sen.

8. I have noted the modern ring to Mandeville's concern with employment and incomes. We should not make the mistake, however, of assuming that he is the forerunner of conceptions of equitable development, or growth with equity. Mandeville's many commentators often overlook the fact that not all bees partook equally of that luxury and ease of the Hive before the Fall.

References

Aristotle. 1961. *Politics*. Trans. Ernest Barker. New York: Oxford University Press.

———. 1962. *Nichomachean Ethics*. Trans. Martin Ostwald. Indianapolis: Bobbs Merrill.

Galbraith, John Kenneth. 1958. *The Affluent Society*. Boston: Houghton Mifflin.

Mandeville, Bernard. 1966. *The Fable of the Bees*, ed. F.B. Kaye. Oxford: Oxford University Press.

Marx, Karl. 1966. "Economic and Philosophical Manuscripts." In Erich Fromm, ed., *Marx's Concept of Man*. New York: Ungar Books.

Seneca. 1947. "Epistulae Morales." In Frederick Teggart, ed., *The Idea of Progress*. Berkeley: University of California Press.

Tawney, R.H. (1938). *Religion and the Rise of Capitalism*. Harmondsworth, UK: Pelican Books.

Socio-Economics of Work and the Workplace

17

PATRICK MICHAEL ROONEY

Employee Ownership in the United States: Intentions, Perceptions, and Reality

As the title of this paper suggests, the goal of this essay is to summarize and analyze: (1) the intention(s) the presidents of firms responding to a mail survey had in choosing to adopt employee ownership; (2) their perceptions of the effects employee ownership on their firms; and (3) how their perceptions correlate with reality as measured by observable data. We will also examine whether the person who initiated the process to adopt employee ownership makes a difference.

After an initial discussion of what we mean by intentions and the problems in examining them, the second section briefly summarizes the theoretical advantages and disadvantages of surplus sharing of various forms, including employee ownership as well as the role for employee ownership as a mediating mechanism in a social economy. The third section delineates the methodology employed in this research project. The results are presented in the fourth section. We conclude with a brief summary and implications in the fifth section.

The moral philosopher Alasdair MacIntyre (1981) elucidates that we cannot characterize behavior independently of its intentions; nor can we characterize intentions independently of the settings that make those intentions intelligible both to the agents themselves and to others. Furthermore, the setting itself has a history. According to MacIntyre, intentions need to be ordered both causally and temporally; both orderings will make references to the relevant settings. Thus, MacIntyre concludes that there is no such thing as "behavior" to be identified prior to and independently of intentions, beliefs, and settings.

Given this reasoning, we must accept that without conducting extensive case studies of each firm, we cannot say too much about either the setting or the

The author would like to thank Michael McCully and the editor, Richard Coughlin, for helpful comments. Any remaining errors are, of course, my own.

history of each of these firms. This study has sacrificed much of the individual detail available from case studies in order to look at a relatively large number of firms. We must also accept that ultimately we cannot measure what the respondents' true intentions are or were; yet, we can try to discern them both by asking the individuals anonymously to convey their intentions—thereby protecting them from any possible backlash or embarrassment—and by comparing these intentions to the outcomes or reality as we can measure it.

Assuming that this process yields an acceptable proxy for the respondents' intentions, we must allow for the possibility of: (1) measurement error; (2) nonresponse bias; and (3) incorrect completion of the survey instrument, whether intentional or accidental. Finally, we should recognize that even if a president of a firm truly revealed his or her intentions, there may be a divergence between intentions, perceptions, and reality for any of several reasons.

First, the respondent's intentions may have been unrealistic or unobtainable. Second, market forces may have changed enough to swamp the effects of adopting employee ownership, hence masking the relationship between intentions, perceptions, and reality. Likewise, changes in market forces may have produced results that, while desirable, were not part of the original set of intentions. Third, most people view themselves as being consistent; hence, "cognitive dissonance" will prevent most people from maintaining two contradictory ideas (Akerlof and Dickens, 1982).

Employee Ownership

In association with the productivity decline in the 1970s and 1980s, worker participation and employee ownership have generated much interest not as ends in themselves—such as an alternative to wage labor or the self-actualization of workers—but rather as a means to a different end, namely, increased labor productivity and improved labor relations. The history of employee ownership and worker participation in the United States suggests that economic and political conditions of the time can play an important role in the development as well as the hindrance of these phenomena (see Curl, 1980; Jones, 1979; Rosen, Klein, and Young, 1986). This remains true today. The passage of an array of preferential tax laws for employee-owned firms on both the federal and state levels reflects the concern among legislators that something must be done. In 1974, when the first favorable federal legislation was passed, there were approximately 300 Employee Stock Ownership Plans (ESOPs). A decade later, there were over 7,000 ESOPs and a few thousand more firms with other employee ownership plans (Rosen, Klein, and Young, 1986).

Employee ownership is not simply a dichotomous variable. Rather, we do better to treat it as a continuous variable with an obvious lower boundary—zero—but more nebulous upper boundaries, as well as an undefined middle ground of "some" employee ownership. For example, in most employee-owned firms in the

United States, the levels of worker participation are quite low, even in the majority-owned firms (see Rooney, 1988a). So, even for firms that are nominally "worker-owned," there may be very little worker influence, much less control. While firms with even a very small amount of employee ownership may be referred to as "employee owned," the traditional attributes of ownership may or may not be conveyed upon the employee owners.

This distinction between employee ownership and control is important because it is often ignored in the literature. However, it is not always clear which benefits in an idealized labor-managed firm result from the employee-ownership aspect and which arise from the aspects of labor self-management or worker participation. For example, Vanek (1970) suggests that labor-managed firms will obtain greater effort as a result of self-governing activities, participation, and the full allocation of value-added to the members. Vanek maintains that there is greater goal identification with the labor-managed enterprise and its goals. This generates a team spirit of production or "production-mindedness" as workers internalize the goals of the firm. As the degree of goal convergence increases, greater effort is contributed by the members. As this production-mindedness takes over members' attitudes and as solidarity increases, there is less need for supervisors, as self- and group policing increase or internal and horizontal monitoring supplant vertical monitoring.

Vanek also hypothesizes that there will be production gains from diminished worker conflict with management. Since workers want to maximize their net income, they will be less resistant to technological change than they are in a profit-maximizing firm where they might fear job loss. Also, as members have a direct or indirect voice in management, one would expect a disappearance of labor-management conflict, thereby rendering decision making more flexible and less fractious. And, there should be some production gains in a labor-managed firm from a lack of industrial conflict, especially strikes.

According to Cable and Fitzroy (1980a, 1980b), workers, faced with immobility due to job-specific skills, will naturally collude to restrict output either formally in collective bargaining agreements or informally in tacit agreements to punish "rate busters" under piecework schemes. When workers participate in the decision-making process, however, they are given an alternative to both negative collusion and to exit. They can counter employers' opportunism without negative collusion. Cable and Fitzroy conclude that "when decisions are in some sense taken jointly, they are more likely to be regarded as fair" (1980, p. 144). Hence, these decisions are more likely to be more acceptable to the workers, and, consequently, more likely to be implemented rather than circumvented. This acceptability, to some extent, supplants positive collusion for the traditional negative collusion. Therefore, participatory firms can produce better outcomes than traditional profit-maximizing firms, especially since the costs of labor turnover are high to both the employer and the employee.[1]

Cable and Fitzroy's argument continues where many leave off. They contend that workers will not maximize joint wealth if some portion of that wealth accrues entirely to others (i.e., profits). Profits depend, in large part, on both the effort yielded and the decisions made. Workers feel that they deserve a share in the profits that arose from their effort and decisions. They maintain that workers are much more willing to maximize joint wealth in a firm in which they both participate in decision making and share in the residual of the firm.

Conversely, workers who participate in ownership, yet are not included in decision making in some way—at least on key issues—may become frustrated, particularly when these employees own an appreciable share of the firm. Lack of shareholder power runs contrary to the conditions specified by Alchian and Demsetz (1972) in their delineation of how a corporation ought to be structured for highest efficiency. More importantly, it is contrary to the social custom and well-established bundle of property rights that accompanies share ownership in the United States. Some evidence for employee-owner frustration when there is little or no worker participation can be found in interviews with workers and case studies.[2]

When we make comparisons between traditional firms and firms with profit sharing, it should be understood that the same arguments in favor of profit sharing would favor employee ownership even more strongly. That profit sharing is simply a special case of employee ownership can be easily seen.

With profit sharing, as with employee ownership, profits are shared with employees; yet, in a profit-sharing plan, the distribution of the residual to employees is irrespective of ownership rights and is strictly an incentive proffered by the owner or manager. Like other "gifts" from management, profit sharing can be unilaterally amended or abrogated by management, whereas the accrual of profits to *shareholders* is a well-established property right. It is this distinction that sets employee ownership apart from other incentive plans and/or fringe benefits. Hence, in an employee-owned firm, employee owners' claim to a share in the residual is indisputable, just as are the shareholders' claims in any corporation. The employee owners are protected from arbitrary discontinuation of the plan by management—unless the structuring of the employee-ownership plan gives top management either majority ownership or control over the nonvested shares. While this is often the case, it is not always or necessarily the case.

Steinherr (1977) suggests that worker participation in decision making and in profits may have a variety of both positive and negative effects on the productivity of both managers and workers. Managers may view worker participation positively to the extent that they perceive that it raises productivity and/or it satisfies their sense of justice. Furthermore, managers may "enjoy seeing labor act more responsibly" (Steinherr, 1977, p. 547). On the other hand, to the extent that managers perceive that worker involvement in management diminishes the independence and/or status of managers, managers' perception of the value of participation may fall.

According to Steinherr, the costs of increased participation, such as increased resource requirements due to greater "information processing, meetings, and extensive discussion" (p. 548), may be offset by the diminished conflict arising from increased goal congruence. Although we must recognize that the marginal cost of increased participation is likely to increase as firm size increases, Steinherr hypothesizes that, on balance, worker participation may: lower the level of conflict within the firm; lower monitoring costs; reduce managerial shirking; and increase the productivity of labor. Steinherr demonstrates that if worker participation is a public good (see also Dreze, 1976), the optimal degree of participation is always strictly positive. Furthermore, he shows that if profit sharing generates an initial increase in efficiency, then a positive degree of profit sharing will always be optimal.

Using a principal-agent framework, Varian (1989) shows that agents may be able to monitor each other better than a principal could. He also demonstrates that we can reasonably expect agents to respond more favorably to "carrots" rather than "sticks." This suggests that both employee ownership and participatory management should yield preferable outcomes.

Fitzroy and Kraft (1987) discuss the possibility that profit sharing and horizontal monitoring should motivate cooperation since the joint production effort yields positive externalities to coworkers when there is surplus-sharing. Although workers may have an incentive to overstate the difficulty and/or disutility of a task in a nonsurplus-sharing arrangement, those same social sanctions can be used to increase output to generate positive externalities in production. They contend that efficient cooperation may be stabilized by repeated plays of the surplus-sharing game (Axelrod, 1984).

Of course, surplus-sharing and participatory management are not without their critics. All of the critics emphasize that any gains from an individual's additional or marginal effort are not captured entirely by that individual. Rather, they are shared by all of the employees (if the surplus-sharing is egalitarian). Consequently, as the number of employees grows, the return to any one individual to his or her increased effort falls until it approaches zero. In addition, Meade (1972, 1974) discusses the "perverse labor-supply response" first brought up by Vanek (1970) and the fact that inefficiencies from imperfect competition arising in traditional capitalist economies are exacerbated in a labor-managed economy, which is dependent upon the creation of new firms to maintain efficient outcomes.

Alchian and Demsetz (1972) stress the notion that employees get to keep only a portion of the extra revenue they generate from additional effort, but they consume all of the leisure they generate from on-the-job shirking. They also contend that surplus-sharing will diminish the owner/monitor's incentives to such a large degree that the cost of team (firm) production will increase. Jensen and Meckling (1979) maintain that if codetermination and other participatory schemes are such good ideas, there would be no need to mandate them legislatively. Similarly, if workers thought they were such good ideas, they would just pay firms for the right to participate.[3]

In a radical critique, Fantasia et al. (1988) argue that managers give just enough participation "to increase productivity, but not enough to spawn demands for autonomous workers' control" (p. 485). Russell (1988) claims that the most important forms of employee participation, which he considers to be employee board representation and employee ownership of entire companies, are numerically trivial. Yet, the most pervasive forms of employee participation, such as quality circles and minority Employee Stock Ownership Plans (ESOPs), Russell believes, have trivial effects on the employees and, presumably, their firms.

It is clear that employee ownership tends to blend the roles of owners and workers, thereby blurring the distinctions between the central monitor or residual claimant and the other factor inputs. Continuing the analogy from Alchian and Demsetz, shareholders, who, in employee-ownership firms, are also employees, are like shareholders in any other corporation in that they are probably better off if they do not participate in all of the managerial decisions. It is important, however, that they do have some leverage over management to reduce managerial shirking and that they have control over important decisions. This assumes, of course, that the employees are, collectively, the majority, if not the exclusive, shareholder in the firm.

With respect to the effects of worker participation on job satisfaction, Flanagan, Strauss, and Ulman (1974) hypothesize that workers will try to alter the mix between pecuniary and nonpecuniary rewards from the job to maximize their utility. If they were dissatisfied with the existing mix of rewards, their dissatisfaction might manifest itself in one of the following forms: increased strikes, especially wildcats; higher rates of absenteeism and/or quits; or a decline in the rate of growth of productivity. Empirically, they found that job dissatisfaction was not associated with a slowdown in productivity or increases in absenteeism or strikes. They did find that those with high levels of job dissatisfaction were 15 percent more likely to quit.

Using regression analysis, Long (1978b, 1982) found that job satisfaction was a function of worker participation but was unrelated to employee ownership. Rosen et al. (1986) also found that employee ownership did not significantly affect job satisfaction; but both management's and labor's perception of the level of worker participation was positively and significantly related to job satisfaction. Rooney (1988c) found that worker participation significantly enhanced job satisfaction but employee ownership had either a negative or an insignificant effect on various empirical proxies of job satisfaction. Gurdon (1980), Long (1982), and Sockell (1985) demonstrate that employee owners, may have unmet expectations with respect to participation.

This blurred role between employees as owners and employees as workers has a potentially important role of mediating conflict in the encapsulated competition delineated by Etzioni (1988). While Etzioni does not advocate employee ownership, it is a likely candidate as a social mechanism for reducing X-inefficiency (Leibenstein, 1973). For example, as discussed above, employee ownership may generate: (1) a convergence of goals between the employees as workers and the firm; (2) lower levels of labor-management conflict, including the costliest form, namely, strikes; (3) improvements in the balance of power between capital and labor by giving labor some additional legal and moral rights associated with ownership; (4) enhanced social efficiency by giving workers an alternative to exit, especially if the employee ownership provides for some worker participation, thereby reducing turnover and the costs of search, hiring, and training; this would tend to raise the average tenure at firms, which would improve the firm-specific human capital, which should increase productivity; and (5) higher levels of job satisfaction and morale, which may be considered desirable whether or not they increase productivity. This form has the additional advantage of relying primarily on normative and social mechanisms with little, if any, necessary direct governmental involvement.

Methodology

The data used in the present study are from an original data set compiled by the author using mail questionnaires. The targeted population included a census of all majority-employee-owned firms, as well as nonemployee-owned firms matched by four-digit SIC code and number of employees.[4] Dillman's (1978) "Total Design Method" was used; it includes up to three follow-up mailings to nonrespondents.

A matched sample is desirable, because it helps to control for any biases inherent in the survey instrument. It also facilitates comparisons between employee-owned firms and nonemployee-owned firms. The matched survey data also permits controls for several factors, such as capital intensity and changes in technology. Furthermore, the matched sample permits greater control in isolating the effects of employee ownership by more accurately controlling for such factors as the business cycle, the rate of inflation in that industry, and the level of competition in that industry.

Of the surveys sent to employee-owned firms, 56 percent were returned, and 15 percent of the surveys sent to the matched nonemployee-owned firms were completed. While these response rates fall short of those obtained on average by Dillman and others using his method, they are much higher than most of the previous attempts in the United States to obtain such data. Dillman suggests that it is more difficult to generate a response with mail surveys, because the potential respondent can examine the entire questionnaire at his or her leisure. Given the proprietary nature of the requested information, the response rate from the employee-owned firms is excellent. The difference in response rates between the employee-owned and nonemployee-owned is somewhat troubling, but the nonemployee-owned firms can be understandably less interested in participating in a project focused on the incentive effects of employee ownership. Also, while a five-wave approach was utilized for the employee-owned firms, the nonemployee-owned firms received only four waves (i.e., no telephone calls were made to nonrespondents). The difference in response rates does not appear to be due to any systematic bias.

Intentions are measured on a scale from "not a factor at all," which was given a value of one (1), to "a somewhat important factor," which was given a value of three (3), to "a very important factor," which was given the maximum value of five (5). Respondents were asked to rate the importance of each of the following factors in their firm's decision to adopt employee ownership:

1. To allow existing (or previous) owner to transfer ownership to employees.

2. The owners'/shareholders' philosophical commitment to employee ownership.

3. To improve the productivity of employees.

4. To improve labor relations.

5. To avoid a merger.

6. To avoid a shutdown.

7. To take advantage of current tax incentives for ESOPs.

8. To provide a retirement program.

9. To startup a firm.

10. In exchange for wage concessions.

The factors evaluated were selected because of their intuitive appeal and/or evidence from earlier case study or survey-empirical research suggested their relevance.

Perceptions were measured on a scale that ranged from "very negative influence," which was given a value of one (1), to "no influence," which was given a value of three (3), to "very positive influence," which was given the maximum value of five (5). The president of the firm was asked to rate, separately, the influence he or she believed employee ownership has had on each of the following items.

1. Cooperation among employees.

2. Productivity of employees.

3. Employee suggestions.

4. Employee morale.

5. Employee loyalty to the firm.

These "perceptions" and "intentions" will be compared to the "reality" as measured by the following variables.

Productivity is measured as value-added per employee.[5] This adjusts for differences in the amount of raw materials and intermediate inputs between firms and industries.[6] Shirking is measured as the total overhead costs per employee. While shirking is an imperfect measure of the costs of monitoring, the greater the need for vertical monitoring, the greater the firm's overhead costs, holding everything else constant. Adjusting the measure for firm size via the number of employees is better for this measure than would be an adjustment for dollars of sales since there may be far more employees per dollar of sales depending on the industry as well as the stage of production within any given industry.

This study utilizes two proxies for job satisfaction or, more accurately, job dissatisfaction. The first is the average number of quits between 1981 and 1985. Because quitting can be very costly to the employee as well as the employer, this variable is the most direct measure of job dissatisfaction.

The second measure of job dissatisfaction is the average number of days absent between 1981 and 1985. It would be preferable to have information for absences for reasons other than health; however, most firms did not keep or did not want to release data on absenteeism, much less the reason for the absences.[7] If an employee is dissatisfied, absenteeism is a less dramatic expression of dissatisfaction than is quitting, but it may give the employee the feeling of having some power; it also permits the employee to force the employer to pay the employee for the ultimate form of shirking—time away from the job.

Results

The results are presented in four subsections, each coinciding with the elements of the title. The first subsection discusses various measures of the extent of employee ownership. The other subsections discuss the intentions, perceptions, and reality of employee ownership in these firms respectively.

Employee Ownership

Primary and Secondary Plans

The most prevalent type of plan in the sample was an Employee Stock Ownership Plan (ESOP). Of the firms responding, eighty-five (49 percent) had ESOPs as their major plan; two more firms utilized ESOPs as their secondary plans. Sixteen firms (9 percent) utilized direct stock purchase plans as their primary plan, and five more firms had direct stock purchase plans as a secondary option. Producer cooperatives constituted 10 percent of the sample ($N = 17$). While only seventeen firms instituted profit sharing as their primary plan (10 percent), another thirty-four firms used profit sharing as a supplement to their primary plans. Three firms (2 percent) indicated "other" as their primary plan; these were 401K's. Finally, thirty-four firms (20 percent) had no plan with which to share ownership of the firm with the employees.

Percent of Firm Stock Owned by the Employees

On average, employees owned 46.6 percent of the firm's stock (standard deviation = 42.3). However, this figure increases to 66.8 percent when the fifty-two firms (30 percent) with *no* employee ownership are removed from the mean.

Another fourteen firms (8 percent) have up to 10 percent of the stock owned by the employees. Thirty firms (18 percent) have between 11 and 50 percent of the stock owned by the employees. The remaining seventy-six firms are majority employee-owned (44 percent) with forty-five of these (26 percent) being 100 percent employee-owned firms. The median percentage of employee ownership for the entire sample is 40 percent; however, when the nonemployee-ownership firms are removed, the median percentage doubles to 80 percent.

Percent of Firm Stock That is Vested

Of the employee ownership firms, 62.8 percent of the firm's stock was vested in the employees' accounts (standard deviation = 36.6). The median percent vested was 70. Sixty-seven percent of the firms had 50 percent or more of the firm's stock vested, including 31 percent that were 100 percent vested.

Percent of Firm Stock That is Owned by Salaried versus Non-salaried Employees

Of the eighty-five firms providing this information, the percentages of the stock held by the employee-ownership plan in the accounts of salaried and nonsalaried employees were nearly equal. Salaried personnel held, on average, 51.2 percent of the stock owned by all employees (standard deviation = 35.7), and nonsalaried employees averaged 45.7 percent (standard deviation = 34.8). The median holdings were 50 percent for salaried and 47.5 percent for nonsalaried employees. The biggest difference between the two groups is that in 18 of these firms (21 percent of those reporting this information), the salaried employees own 100 percent of the stock held by the employee-ownership plan, whereas the nonsalaried employees are the exclusive owners in only six cases.

Another key difference is that while hourly employees comprised at least 60 percent,[8] on average, of the firm's total number of all employees, they received less than half of the stock. This is attributable to the allocation formulas used. The allocations are predominately based on annual earnings.

Employee Ownership Intentions

As discussed in the methodology section, this study used a scale from (1) "not a factor at all," to (5) "a very important factor" in order to gauge the intensity of various factors in the firms' decisions to adopt employee ownership. The option selected most often as an important factor was "The owners'/shareholders' philosophical commitment to employee ownership." This may be a true reflection of the underlying reasons for adopting employee ownership or may represent a reaction to cognitive dissonance. That is, the president who decides to institute employee ownership for whatever reason(s) may feel philosophically committed

Table 17.1

Intentions: Why Firms Initiated Employee Ownership

	Not a Factor At All		A Some-what Important Factor		A Very Important factor	Mean Score	Standard Deviation
	1	2	3	4	5		
Transfer of ownership	38%	2%	11%	9%	40%	3.1	1.8
Philosophical commitment	27	6	14	14	40	3.3	1.4
Improve productivity	23	10	27	25	16	3.0	1.4
Improve labor relations	46	9	21	11	13	2.4	1.5
Avoid a merger	79	6	3	5	6	1.5	1.2
Avoid a shutdown	79	4	3	3	11	1.6	1.3
Tax incentives	47	6	14	16	17	2.5	1.6
Retirement benefit	41	9	14	15	21	2.6	1.6
Start up firm	78	2	6	2	13	1.7	1.4
Exchange for wage concessions	86	2	4	3	5	1.4	1.1

Note: Percentages may not sum to 100 due to rounding.

to employee ownership in order to avoid utilizing a strategy inconsistent with his or her philosophy. The other reasons were ranked in order of their frequency as follows (see Table 17.1):

2. To allow the existing (or previous) owner to transfer ownership to the employees.

3. To improve the productivity of the employees.

4. To provide a retirement plan.

5. To take advantage of current tax incentives for ESOPs.

6. To improve labor relations.

7. To start up a firm.

8. To avoid a shutdown.

9. To avoid a merger.

10. In exchange for wage concessions.

Despite the fact that press coverage of ESOPs has focused primarily on the dramatic buyouts of failing firms and/or those where workers have been asked to give wage concessions in exchange for employee ownership, these are, in reality, among the least important factors given by respondents in this sample. As Table 17.1 demonstrates, there is a large drop in the mean scores of the top three intentions and the next three, and a larger drop still between the middle group and the bottom four intentions, including avoiding a shutdown and in exchange for wage concessions. This, coalesced with the fact that 79 percent of the respondents stated that avoiding a shutdown was not a factor at all and 86 percent said that wage concessions were not a factor at all, suggests that the media distort the relative importance and the norms for the implementation of employee ownership when they portray employee ownership as a form of lemon socialism or last-ditch method to try to save failing firms.

Some of the reasons are positively and significantly correlated with one another such that four groupings emerge. The first grouping is based on property rights and consists of transfer of ownership, avoiding a merger, and avoiding a shutdown. The second possible grouping concerns the philosophical commitment to employee ownership and includes startups as well. The third grouping centers on labor (or, negatively, labor problems) and includes the desire to improve the productivity of employees, to improve labor relations, and employee ownership in exchange for wage concessions. The final grouping is focused on the tax incentives for ESOPs and includes the desire to provide a retirement program (see Table 17.2).

In an effort to better discern intentions, this study asked who initiated employee ownership as well as why employee ownership was adopted. Possible selections were: the owner, management, union leaders, workers, or other. Correlation analysis was utilized to discern any patterns between the group or person who initiated employee ownership and the reasons employee ownership was adopted.

Correlation analysis found that when plans were initiated by the owner, there is a strong positive correlation with adopting employee ownership to allow the existing owner to transfer ownership to employees and with provision of retirement programs. Owner-initiated plans are significantly negatively correlated with startups and avoiding mergers. Managers were most likely to initiate employee ownership to avoid a merger. Conversely, they were least likely to initiate employee ownership in startups or for philosophical reasons—both of which had strong negative correlations with management-led plans. Union leadership was not significantly positively related to any of the reasons for adopting employee ownership, but was negatively related to the transfer of ownership from the existing owner to the employees and the provision of a retirement plan. Note that these two reasons had the opposite sign for owner-initiated plans. Finally, worker-initiated plans were significantly positively related to startups and philosophical commitment to employee ownership. Worker-initiated plans were strongly negatively correlated with tax incentives, retirement programs, and the transference of ownership from the owner to the employees (see Table 17.3).

Employee Ownership Perceptions

In order to gauge the perceptions of the effects of employee ownership, the firms' presidents were asked to rate what influence employee ownership has had on cooperation, productivity, suggestions, morale, and loyalty. The ratings

Table 17.2

Importance of Factors to Adopt Employee Ownership: Correlation Matrix among Factors

Factor	1	2	3	4	5	6	7	8	9	10
1 Transfer of ownership	1.0 (0)									
2 Philosophical commitment	.01 (.82)	1.0 (0)								
3 Improve productivity	-.06 (.48)	.34*** (.0001)	1.0 (0)							
4 Improve labor relations	.07 (.44)	.19** (.03)	.66*** (.0001)	1.0 (0)						
5 Avoid a merger	.29*** (.0001)	-.03 (.75)	-.06 (.50)	.12 (.19)	1.0 (0)					
6 Avoid a shutdown	.18** (.05)	-.23*** (.009)	-.03 (.71)	.10 (.28)	.26*** (.003)	1.0 (0)				
7 Tax incentives	.22*** (.01)	.02 (.80)	.28*** (.001)	.24*** (.006)	.17* (.06)	-.05 (.54)	1.0 (0)			
8 Retirement benefit	.004 (.96)	.05 (.55)	.43*** (.0001)	.36*** (.0001)	.05 (.57)	-.05 (.55)	.37*** (.0001)	1.0 (0)		
9 Start up firm	-.31*** (.0001)	.21** (.02)	.10 (.28)	.12 (.17)	-.06 (.53)	.04 (.69)	-.14 (.13)	-.14 (.12)	1.0 (0)	
10 Exchange for wage concessions	-.02 (.81)	.13 (.14)	.23*** (.01)	.29*** (.001)	.11 (.24)	.38*** (.0001)	.02 (.80)	.10 (.25)	.16* (.07)	1.0 (0)

Note: The top number in each element is the Pearson correlation coefficient.
The value in parentheses is the probability that the coefficient is actually equal to zero (0).
$* p \leq 0.10; ** p \leq 0.05; *** p \leq 0.01$

Table 17.3

Correlations between Who Initiated Employee Ownership and the Reason Employee Ownership Was Adopted

	Initiator			
	Owner	Management	Union	Workers
Transfer of ownership	.20** (.02)	.04 (.68)	−.20** (.03)	−.25*** (.004)
Philosophical commitment	.14 (.12)	−.20** (.03)	−.09 (.32)	.16 (.06)
Improve productivity	.06 (.51)	.003 (.97)	−.08 (.35)	−.10 (.27)
Improve labor relations	.04 (.63)	.02 (.86)	.60 (.60)	−.10 (.27)
Avoid a merger	−.17** (.05)	.30*** (.001)	−.10 (.26)	−.06 (.48)
Avoid a shutdown	−.11 (.20)	.08 (.38)	.12 (.18)	−.16 (.50)
Tax incentives	.10 (.26)	.12 (.17)	−.14 (.12)	.28*** (.001)
Retirement benefit	.19** (.03)	.07 (.42)	−.16* (.08)	−.29*** (.001)
Start up firm	−.17* (.06)	−.20** (.02)	.07 (.42)	.47*** (.0001)
Exchange for wage concessions	−.03 (.71)	−.07 (.42)	.05 (.54)	.02 (.84)

Note: The top number in each element is the Pearson correlation coefficient.
The value in parentheses is the probability that the coefficient is actually equal to zero (0).

* $p \le .10$
** $p \le .05$
*** $p \le .01$

ranged from "very negative influence" (1), to "no influence" (3), to "very positive influence" (5). As can be seen in Table 17.4, the presidents perceived that employee ownership has had, for the most part, either a positive or a very positive influence on each of the items evaluated. For example, 6 percent or less believed that employee ownership has had a negative or very negative influence

Table 17.4

Perceptions: Effects of Employee Ownership

	Very Negative Influence		No Influence		Very Positive Influence	Mean Score	Standard Deviation
	1	2	3	4	5		
Cooperation	0	2	14	60	24	4.0	0.7
Productivity	0	2	19	56	24	4.0	0.8
Suggestions	1	5	30	43	21	3.7	0.9
Morale	1	5	16	50	29	4.0	0.8
Loyalty	0	3	14	49	33	4.1	0.8

Note: Percentages may not sum to 100 due to rounding.

on any of the items. Conversely, 64 percent or more of the firms responding perceived that the influence of employee ownership was either a positive or a very positive influence on each item.

In fact, approximately 80 percent of the respondents felt that the effects of employee ownership had a positive or very positive influence on cooperation, productivity, morale, and loyalty. Likewise, the mean score for cooperation, productivity, morale, and loyalty is 4.0 or higher, implying that, on average, employee ownership has had a positive effect on each of these factors. Only employee suggestions lagged behind the other items, averaging 3.7, which still suggests a positive influence from employee ownership.

Finally, if we examine the correlation matrix between perceptions and intentions (see Table 17.5), we see a fairly consistent pattern. Namely, the largest correlation coefficients and those with the greatest probability of statistical significance are those associated with, for the most part, intentions that could be characterized as more positive in tone. For example, philosophical commitment to employee ownership, the desire to improve productivity, the desire to improve labor relations had much larger correlation coefficients and had the smallest probability of actually being not significantly different from zero than the rest of the intentions for establishing employee ownership plans. What makes this more notable is the fact that the intention of transferring ownership was not significantly correlated with any of the perception items, yet it was the second most important intention for establishing employee ownership given by the respondents.

A reasonable explanation for this pattern can be found in the desire by most individuals to be consistent psychologically (Akerloff and Dickens, 1982). Those who adopt employee ownership for "positive" reasons may have a need to see their positive intentions have positive actual outcomes. Hence, their perceptions may be focusing in on the positive effects and filtering out any discordant information about negative effects. This simply bolsters our claim, however, that it is

Table 17.5

Employee Ownership: Perceptions and Intentions

	Coopera-tion	Productivity	Sugges-tions	Morale	Loyalty
Transfer of ownership	.01	−.04	−.03	−.03	.02
	(.80)	(.27)	(.46)	(.42)	(.53)
Philosophical commitment	.34***	.25***	.25***	.20***	.25***
	(.0001)	(.0001)	(.0001)	(.0001)	(.0001)
Improve productivity	.31***	.26***	.24***	.31***	.24***
	(.0001)	(.0001)	(.0001)	(.0001)	(.0001)
Improve labor relations	.23***	.29***	.23***	.23***	.18***
	(.0001)	(.0001)	(.0001)	(.0001)	(.0001)
Avoid a merger	.09**	−.04	−.02	.09**	.03
	(.02)	(.33)	(.54)	(.02)	(.48)
Avoid a shutdown	.09**	.10***	.12***	.07*	.09**
	(.02)	(.01)	(.003)	(.09)	(.03)
Tax incentives	.07*	.02	.12***	.13***	.03
	(.09)	(.59)	(.002)	(.0001)	(.40)
Retirement benefit	.10***	.01	.09**	.15***	.01
	(.01)	(.72)	(.02)	(.0001)	(.80)
Start up firm	.08**	.18***	.20***	.05	.11***
	(.03)	(.0001)	(.0001)	(.21)	(.0003)
Exchange for wage concessions	.26***	.24***	.19***	.15***	.13***
	(.0001)	(.0001)	(.0001)	(.0001)	(.01)

Note: The top number in each element is the Pearson correlation coefficient.
The value in parentheses is the probability that the coefficient is actually equal to zero (0).

$* p < 0.10$
$** p < 0.05$
$*** p < 0.01$

important to examine not only the intentions, the perceptions, and the reality in isolation, but also to delineate their interrelationships.

The only exception to this pattern is the fact that the intention of establishing employee ownership in exchange for wage concessions had a positive and significant correlation with all five of the perception variables. It is certainly hard to argue that wage concessions could be viewed as a positive factor in deciding to adopt employee ownership. It is more likely a reflection of the correlation among all of the labor variables. That is, the firms that are searching for ways to make wage concessions more tolerable to their workers are also likely to be very interested in improving labor relations and increasing labor productivity.

Reality

Let us first examine the relationship between the intentions for establishing employee ownership and the available empirical proxies. Recall that value-added and shirking are used as proxies for productivity, cooperation, and employee suggestions. We would hypothesize a positive relationship with value-added and a negative relationship with shirking as they are measured in this study. Likewise, we are using absenteeism and quits as proxies for morale and loyalty. However, with these proxies, we would expect an inverse relationship.

As may be seen in Table 17.6, neither the desire to transfer ownership to employees nor the philosophical commitment to employee ownership has any significant correlation with value-added, yet both are significantly correlated with lowered shirking. The desire to increase productivity, improve labor relations, avoid a merger, avoid a shutdown, take advantage of tax incentives, provide a retirement program, and in exchange for wage concessions all have positive correlations with value-added. Paradoxically, of these, the desire to improve labor relations as well as to avoid a shutdown are both correlated with increases in shirking, which is contrary to our expectations. Subsequently, all of the intentions have at least some of the desired effects with respect to our measures of productivity, with the exception of startups. This may be due to the difficulty of starting up and attaining sufficient capitalization for any type of firm, especially one with an alternative ownership structure.

With respect to job satisfaction, we find the somewhat surprising result that virtually all of the intentions are either not significantly correlated with our proxies for job satisfaction, or they are in fact positively associated with absenteeism or quits.[9] This suggests one of two possibilities: either the intentions to establish employee ownership were, across the board, much more closely related to concerns about productivity than they were about job satisfaction, or employee ownership does not have much of an effect on job satisfaction as measured by these variables. This latter claim can be made because only the firms that had established employee ownership plans would have answered the questions regarding their intentions to establish such a plan.[10]

Consistent with this pattern is the fact that managers' perceptions of the effects of employee ownership in all five areas (cooperation, productivity, suggestions, morale, and loyalty) are positively correlated with value-added; yet only the perceptions of the effects of employee ownership on suggestions has a significant correlation with either of the job satisfaction proxies. The good news is that there is a positive correlation both between managers' intention to im-

Table 17.6

Employee Ownership: Intentions versus Reality

	Value-added	Shirking	Absenteeism	Quits
Transfer of ownership	−.03 (.60)	−.16** (.04)	−.18 (.19)	.01 (.90)
Philosophical commitment	.07 (.22)	−.23*** (.004)	.25* (.07)	.19** (.03)
Improve productivity	.33*** (.0001)	.08 (.31)	.25* (.07)	.21** (.02)
Improve labor relations	.40*** (.001)	.16** (.05)	.28** (.05)	.29*** (.001)
Avoid a merger	.24*** (.0001)	−.007 (.94)	−.11 (.43)	.12 (.16)
Avoid a shutdown	.18*** (.004)	.17** (.03)	−.12 (.40)	−.15* (.08)
Tax incentives	.16*** (.009)	−.005 (.95)	.24* (.08)	.24*** (.007)
Retirement benefit	.15** (.02)	−.07 (.35)	.22 (.12)	.35*** (.0001)
Start-up firm	.03 (.58)	−.02 (.78)	−.04 (.77)	−.07 (.44)
Exchange for wage concessions	.17*** (.004)	.06 (.42)	−.07 (.62)	−.11 (.21)

Note: The top number in each element is the Pearson correlation coefficient.
The value in parentheses is the probability that the coefficient is actually equal to zero (0).

$* p \leq 0.10$
$** p \leq 0.05$
$*** p \leq 0.01$

prove productivity and their perception that productivity has improved and between the managers' perception that productivity has increased and our empirical proxy for productivity (see Table 17.7).

Conclusion

This paper has summarized responses from one of the most comprehensive surveys of employee-owned firms in the United States with respect to the intentions

Table 17.7

Employee Ownership: Perceptions versus Reality

	Value-added	Shirking	Absenteeism	Quits
Cooperation	.37***	−.009	.12	.10
	(.0001)	(.91)	(.88)	(.24)
Productivity	.23***	−.16**	.03	−.005
	(.0001)	(.05)	(.85)	(.96)
Suggestions	.13**	−.22***	−.07	−.15*
	(.03)	(.006)	(.61)	(.10)
Morale	.28***	−.02	.08	.005
	(.0001)	(.78)	(.59)	(.95)
Loyalty	.27***	−.06	.05	.04
	(.0001)	(.48)	(.71)	(.67)

Note: The top number in each element is the Pearson correlation coefficient.
The value in parentheses is the probability that the coefficient is actually equal to zero (0).

   * $p \leq 0.10$
  ** $p \leq 0.05$
 *** $p \leq 0.01$

for adopting employee ownership and the perceptions of their effects. In addition, comparisons were made between both the intentions and the perceptions to reality as measured by observable data. In general, we can conclude that while managers' perceptions are not a perfect proxy for measuring reality, there is a positive correlation between their perceptions of the effects of both employee ownership and our best empirical proxies.

More specifically, we found that the owners' philosophical commitment to employee ownership was the most important intention and avoiding a shutdown and/or in exchange for wage concessions were among the least important intentions for adopting employee ownership. Intentions were also correlated with which agent initiated the plan in a somewhat predictable pattern. Owners initiating employee ownership indicated that they were primarily interested in it as a method for transferring ownership to the employees or to establish a retirement benefit. Managers intended to avoid a merger (which could cause increased job insecurity), and were not interested in the philosophical aspects of employee ownership, or in starting up employee-owned firms. Conversely, workers who initiated employee-ownership plans were very much interested in both the philosophical commitment to employee ownership and the desire to start up employee-owned firms. These patterns seem consistent with utility-maximizing choices for each of the respective groups.

As suggested by Etzioni (1988), utility maximization can be disaggregated into two sets of factors that affect individuals' behavior: pleasure/economic factors and moral duty. The survey data and correlation analysis presented here suggest the moral dimension certainly affects the intentions of the owners and managers. However, when we disaggregate who initiated the plan, it becomes clear from the discussion above that the behavior of the initiators seemed to be influenced by their pleasure/economic factors pole more than their moral duty pole. This is clearly reflected by the fact that the primary intention for adopting employee ownership was the philosophical commitment to employee ownership, yet only management initiation was significantly correlated with the philosophical commitment—and they were negatively correlated. Conversely, workers were most interested in start ups and least interested in employee ownership as a retirement benefit. Owners, on the other hand, were most interested in employee ownership to facilitate the transfer of ownership and to provide retirement benefits and least interested in employee ownership as a vehicle to start up new firms or to avoid a merger.

The firm manager at the responding firms perceived that employee ownership had a positive effect in all areas. These perceptions of the effects of employee ownership and a proxy for productivity were positively correlated, as were managers' intention to increase productivity and their perception that productivity has increased.

These results suggest that the managers are not entirely self-deceiving. They are at least accurate in appraising the sign of change. Nor should they be entirely disappointed with their firms' productivity effects from employee ownership. We must restrict ourselves to this relatively cautious appraisal in that the correlation analysis did not indicate anywhere near perfect correlations. In addition, correlation analysis cannot indicate causality, nor does it control for other factors that may also have a significant intervening effect between employee ownership and productivity and/or job satisfaction.

Notes

1. For example, the firm faces costs such as recruiting, screening, hiring, and training. The individual has lost earnings, which can never be replaced, time spent in job search, and the stress associated with unemployment.

2. See Rosen, Klein, and Young (1986); Sockell (1985); Rooney (1983–84); Long (1978a, 1978b, 1980, 1982); Gurdon (1980); and Zwerdling (1980).

3. Obviously, the points raised by both Alchian and Demsetz (1972) and Jensen and Meckling (1979) should involve empirical testing. Several authors have measured the effects of alternative ownership and participatory arrangements on shirking as measured by various criteria of efficiency, including profitability, productivity, and growth. The literature suggests that these types of alternative compensation and participatory management have either no effect or a positive effect on effort. See Bellas (1972); Berman (1967); Conte and Tannenbaum (1978); Marsh and McAllister (1981); Tannenbaum, Cook, and Lohmann (1984); Wagner (1984); Quarrey (1986); Blumberg (1968); U.S.

Department of Health, Education, and Welfare (1973); Espinosa and Zimbalist (1978); Jones and Bakus (1977); Brown and Medoff (1978); Schuster (1983, 1984); Freeman and Medoff (1984); General Accounting Office (1986, 1987); Estrin and Jones (1988); Conte and Svejnar (1981, 1988); Cable and Fitzroy (1980a, 1980b); Defourney, Estrin, and Jones (1985); Drago (1986, 1988); Jones and Svejnar (1985, 1987); Fitzroy and Kraft (1987); Svejnar (1981, 1982); Jones (1987); Berman and Berman (1989); Cable and Wilson (1989); Katz, Kochan, and Gobeille (1983); Cooke (1989); Delaney, Ichniowski, and Lewin (1988); and especially, Rooney (1988a, 1988b) for a more complete discussion and refutation of these issues.

4. The present project revolves around the creation of two data sets, which are merged into one for econometric analyses. The first consists of survey responses sent to approximately 200 majority employee-owned firms. Of these firms, roughly fifty surveyed are producer cooperatives. Firms' names and addresses were obtained from the National Center for Employee Ownership (NCEO)—an information clearinghouse and research organization for employee-ownership issues. A second data set was created to serve as a control group. This data set consists of survey responses sent to approximately 500 nonemployee-owned firms that were matched to the employee-owned survey respondents by Standard Industrial Classification codes (SIC codes) and firm size as measured by number of employees in 1985. These firms were selected from *Disclosure*, the *Electronic Yellow Pages*, and *Dun and Bradstreet Million Dollar Directory* computer files available at the University of Notre Dame. In this study, the sample was obtained from the National Center for Employee Ownership's (NCEO) employee-ownership list of majority employee-owned firms in America. Their list is a census of all known majority employee-owned firms. Yet, there may be a bias, because there may be some majority employee-owned firms that are not currently on the NCEO employee-ownership list. Given that NCEO's employee-ownership list is largely generated from newspaper articles on employee ownership and consultants in this area, there may be a bias oversampling the more dramatic buyouts of failing firms or of larger firms that implement employee ownership, in general, and, correspondingly, understating smaller, less publicized firms with employee ownership. However, the NCEO employee-ownership list is consistent with the preliminary results from the General Accounting Office (GAO) study using Internal Revenue Service data and survey results. In a telephone conversation with the author, GAO Project Director, Patrick Grasse, stated that the NCEO list was more or less a census of majority employee-owned firms in the United States, and, to the extent that it was not a census, it did not seem to differ in a biased fashion.

5. A disadvantage of value-added per employee is that using the number of employees rather than the number of hours worked may introduce some distortions. For example, differences in vacation, sick days, and personal leave policies as well as differences in paid clean-up time or "coffee breaks" may show up in differences in productivity, even though two firms' employees may exert the same effort while working. This study does not attempt to correct for this potential distortion for three reasons. First, it is likely that the distortions are small. Second, the companies' policy differences that cause these differences in hours worked may generate greater effort while the employees are "on the clock"; hence, not counting those hours would actually bias the results. Third, hours worked is not readily available and is not reported by the government for comparisons.

6. Virtually all measures of productivity diverge from the economist's conception of how efficiency ought to be measured. Economists prefer to discuss either the marginal physical product of labor (MPPL) or the value of the marginal product of labor (VMPL). Theoretically, a profit-maximizing firm will continue to hire workers until the cost of adding an additional worker, which is the market wage rate in competitive labor markets, is just below or equal to the value of the marginal increment that the worker adds to the

total product of the firm (wage = VMPL). The problem, even if we ignore the simultaneity problem of wage determination, is finding the proverbial marginal worker. Real-world productivity measures are equivalent to the economist's average product of labor (APL), which is simply the ratio of the total product (TP) to a measure of the quantity of labor (L), measured in either hours or number of employees (e.g., APL = TP/L).

7. See, for example, Allen (1981), who found, using a utility-maximizing framework, that "Absenteeism is significantly higher among workers who are young, receive low wages, report unhealthy or dangerous working conditions, work the same hours each day and claim to be in poor health" (p. 82).

8. This figure probably understates the true average because a number of firms call all of their employees "associates" or something besides hourly or nonsalaried employees. Consequently, these firms listed zero hourly employees.

9. The exception to this is that the desire to avoid a shutdown is negatively correlated with quits. However, one could argue that in the case of a firm trying to avoid a shutdown, there probably have been significant layoffs already. Thus, those who remain are either those who are least able to leave or who have the most to lose by leaving. Hence, we would expect fewer quits among firms that are trying to avoid a shutdown.

10. This is supported by regression analysis done for another paper (Rooney, 1988c).

References

Akerlof, George, and William Dickens. 1982. "The Economic Consequences of Cognitive Dissonance." *American Economic Review* 72:307–19.

Alchian, Armen, and Harold Demsetz. 1972. "Production, Information Costs and Economic Organization." *American Economic Review* 62:777–95.

Allen, Steven. 1981. "An Empirical Model of Work Attendance." *Review of Economics and Statistics* 63:77–88.

Axelrod, Robert. 1984. *The Evolution of Cooperation.* New York: Basic Books.

Bellas, C.J. 1972. *Industrial Democracy and the Worker-Owned Firm: A Study of Twenty-one Plywood Companies in the Pacific Northwest.* New York: Praeger.

Berman, K. 1967. *Worker-Owned Plywood Companies: An Economic Analysis.* Pullman, WA: Washington State University Press.

Berman, Katrina V., and Matthew D. Berman. 1989. "An Empirical Test of the Theory of the Labor-Managed Firm." *Journal of Comparative Economics* 13:281–300.

Blumberg, Paul. 1968. *Industrial Democracy.* London: Constable.

Brown, C., and J Medoff. 1978. "Trade Unions in the Productive Process." *Journal of Political Economy* 86:355–78.

Cable, John, and Felix Fitzroy. 1980a. "Cooperation and Productivity: Some Evidence from the West German Experience." In Alasdair Clayre, ed., *The Political Economy of Cooperation and Participation.* Oxford: Oxford University Press.

———. 1980b. "Productive Efficiency, Incentives and Employee Participation: Some Preliminary Results for West Germany." *Kyklos* 33:100–21.

Cable, John, and Nicholas Wilson. 1989. "Profit-Sharing and Productivity: An Analysis of UK Engineering Firms." *Economic Journal* 99 (June): 366–75.

Conte, Michael. 1982. "Participation and Performance in U.S. Labor-Managed Firms." In Derek Jones and Jan Svejnar, eds., *Participatory and Self-Managed Firms: Evaluating Economic Performance.* Lexington, MA: D.C. Heath.

Conte, Michael, and Arnold Tannenbaum. 1978. "Employee Owned Companies: Is the Difference Measurable?" *Monthly Labor Review* 101 (July): 23–28.

Conte, Michael, and Jan Svejnar. 1981. "Measuring the Productivity Effects of Worker Participation and Ownership." Unpublished paper.

———. 1988. "Productivity Effects of Worker Participation in Management, Profit-Sharing, Worker Ownership of Assets and Unionization in U.S. Firms." *International Journal of Industrial Organization* 6:139–51.

Cooke, William N. 1989. "Improving Productivity and Quality Through Collaboration." *Industrial Relations* 28:299–319.

Curl, John. 1980. *History of Work Cooperation in America.* Berkeley, CA: Homeward Press.

Defourney, Jacques, Saul Estrin, and Derek Jones. 1985. "The Effects of Workers' Participation on Enterprise Performance: Empirical Evidence from French Cooperatives." *International Journal of Industrial Organization* 3:197–217.

Delaney, John Thomas, Casey Ichniowski, and David Lewin. 1988. "The Effects of IR and HR Policies and Practices on Organizational Performance." In Barbara D. Dennis, ed., *Industrial Relations Research Association Series: Proceedings of the Forty-First Annual Meeting,* New York, December 28–30.

Dillman, Don A. 1978. *Mail and Telephone Surveys: The Total Design Method.* New York: Wiley.

Drago, Robert. 1986. "Participatory Management in Capitalist Firms: An Analysis of 'Quality Circles.' " *Economic Analysis and Workers' Management* 20:233–49.

———. 1988. "Quality Circle Survival: An Exploratory Analysis." *Industrial Relations* 27:336–51.

Dreze, J.H. 1976. "Some Theories of Labor-Management and Participation." *Econometrica* 44:1125–39.

Espinosa, J.G., and A.S. Zimbalist, 1978. *Economic Democracy: Workers' Participation in Chilean Industry, 1970–73.* New York: Academic Press.

Estrin, Saul, and Derek Jones. 1988. "Workers' Participation, Employee Ownership and Productivity: Results from French Producer Cooperatives." Working Paper Series, #87/10, Department of Economics, Hamilton College, Clinton, NY.

Etzioni, Amitai. 1988. *The Moral Dimension: Toward a New Economics.* New York: Free Press.

Fantasia, Rick, Dan Clawson, and Gregory Graham. 1988. "A Critical View of Worker Participation in American Industry." *Work and Occupations* 15:468–88.

Fitzroy, Felix, and Kornelius Kraft. 1987. "Cooperation, Productivity, and Profit Sharing." *Quarterly Journal of Economics* CII:23–35.

Flanagan, R., G. Strauss, and L. Ulman. 1974. "Worker Discontent and Workplace Behavior." *Industrial Relations* 13:101–23.

Freeman, Richard, and James Medoff. 1984. *What Do Unions Do?* New York: Basic Books.

General Accounting Office. 1986. *Employee Stock Ownership Plans: Interim Report on a Survey and Related Trends.* Washington, DC: U.S. General Accounting Office, February.

———. 1987. *Employee Stock Ownership Plans: Little Evidence of Effects on Corporate Performance.* Washington, DC: U.S. General Accounting Office, October.

Gurdon, Michael. 1980. "An American Approach to Self-Management." In Hem Jain, ed., *Worker Participation: Success and Problems.* New York: Praeger.

Jensen, Michael, and William Meckling. 1979. "Rights and Production Functions: An Application to Labor-Managed Firms and Codetermination." *Journal of Business* 52:469–506.

Jones, Derek. 1979. "U.S. Producer Cooperatives: The Record to Date." *Industrial Relations* 8:342–56.

———. 1987. "The Productivity Effects of Worker Directors and Financial Participation by Employees in the Firm: The Case of British Retail Cooperatives." *Industrial and Labor Relations Review* 41:79–92.

Jones, Derek, and D. Backus. 1977. "British Producer Cooperatives in the Footwear Industry: An Empirical Test of the Theory of Financing." *Economic Journal* 87:488–510.

Jones, Derek, and Jan Svejnar. 1985. "Participation, Profit-Sharing, Worker Ownership and Efficiency in Italian Producer Cooperatives." *Economica* 52:449–65.

————. 1987. "Workers' Control, Profitsharing and Capital Ownership: A Partial Survey and Policy Implications." Unpublished paper, December.

————, eds. 1982. *Participatory and Self-managed Firms.* Lexington, MA: Lexington Books.

Katz, Harry C., Thomas A. Kochan, and Kenneth R. Gobeille. 1983. "Industrial Relations Performance, Economic Performance, and QWL Programs: An Interplant Analysis." *Industrial and Labor Relations Review* 37 (October): 3–17.

Leibenstein, Harvey. 1973. "Competition and X-Efficiency." *Journal of Political Economy* 81 (May): 765–77.

Long, Richard. 1978a. "The Effect of Employee Ownership on Organizational Identification, Employee Job Attitudes, and Organizational Performance: A Tentative Framework and Empirical Findings." *Human Relations* 31:29–48.

————. 1978b. "The Relative Effects of Share Ownership vs. Control on Job Attitudes in an Employee-Owned Company." *Human Relations* 31:753–63.

————. 1980. "Job Attitudes and Organizational Performance under Employee Ownership." *Academy of Management Journal*, 23:726–37.

————. 1982. "Worker Ownership and Job Attitudes: A Field Study." *Industrial Relations* 21:196–215.

MacIntyre, Alasdair. N.D. "The Relationship of Theory to Narrative in Social Scientific Understanding." Unpublished paper prepared for The College of Wooster Symposium.

————. 1981. *After Virtue.* Notre Dame, IN: University of Notre Dame Press.

Marsh, Thomas, and Dale McAllister. 1981. "ESOPs: A Survey of Companies with Employee Stock Ownership Plans." *Journal of Corporation Law* 6:552–620.

Meade, J.E. 1972. "The Theory of Labor-Managed Firms and of Profit-Sharing." *Economic Journal* 32:402–38.

————. 1974. "Labour-Managed Firms in Conditions of Imperfect Competition." *Economic Journal* 84:817–25.

Quarrey, Michael. 1986. "Research Report: Employee Ownership and Corporate Performance." Unpublished paper, Arlington, VA: National Center for Employee Ownership.

Rooney, Patrick Michael. 1983–84. "Worker Control: Greater Productivity and Job Satisfaction." *Economic Forum* 14 (Winter): 97–123.

————. 1988a. Worker Participation in Employee-Owned Firms." *Journal of Economic Issues* 22 (June): 451–58.

————. 1988b. "Employee Ownership and Worker Participation: Effects on Firm-Level Productivity in the U.S." Association for Comparative Economic Systems' Annual Meetings, New York, December.

————. 1988c. "Employee Ownership and Worker Participation: Effects on Job Satisfaction." American Economic Association's Annual Meetings, New York.

————. 1989a. "Principals, Agents, Property Rights, and Employee Ownership." Association for Evolutionary Economics Annual Meetings, Atlanta, December.

————. 1989b. "On the Theory of the Firm: Shirking vs. Horizontal and Internal Monitoring." Association for Comparative Economic Studies Annual Meetings, Atlanta, December.

Rosen, Corey, Katherine J. Klein, and Karen M. Young. 1986. *Employee Ownership in America: The Equity Solution.* Lexington, MA: Lexington Books.

Russell, Raymond. 1988. "Forms and Extent of Employee Participation in the Contemporary United States." *Work and Occupations* 15:374–95.

Schuster, Michael. 1983. "Impact of Union-Management Cooperation and Employment." *Industrial and Labor Relations Review* 36:415–30.

———. 1984. *Union-Management Cooperation: Structure, Process, Impact.* Kalamazoo, MI: W.E. Upjohn Institute for Employment Research.

Sockell, D. 1985. "Attitudes, Behavior, and Employee Ownership: Some Preliminary Data." *Industrial Relations* 24 (Winter): 130–38.

Steinherr, Alfred. 1977. "On the Efficiency of Profit Sharing and Labor Participation in Management." *Bell Journal of Economics* 8:545–55.

Svejnar, Jan. 1981. "Relative Wage Effects of Unions, Dictatorship and Codetermination: Econometric Evidence from Germany." *Review of Economics and Statistics* 63:188–97.

———. 1982. "Codetermination and Productivity: Empirical Evidence from the Federal Republic of West Germany." In Derek Jones and Jan Svejnar, eds., *Participatory and Self-Managed Firms: Evaluating Economic Performance.* Lexington, MA: D.C. Heath.

Tannenbaum, Arnold, Harold Cook, and Jack Lohmann. 1984. *The Relationship of Employee Ownership to the Technological Adaptiveness and Performance of Companies.* Unpublished paper, Ann Arbor, MI: Institute for Social Research.

U.S. Department of Health, Education and Welfare. 1973. *Work in America.* Cambridge, MA: MIT Press.

Vanek, Jaroslav. 1970. *The General Theory of Labor-Managed Market Economies.* Ithaca, NY: Cornell University Press.

Varian, Hal. 1989. "Monitoring Agents with Other Agents." CREST Working Paper, Center for Research on Economic and Social Theory, University of Michigan, Ann Arbor.

Wagner, Ira. 1984. "Report to the New York Stock Exchange on the Performance of Publicly Traded Companies with Employee Ownership Plans." Unpublished paper, Arlington, VA: National Center for Employee Ownership.

Zwerdling, Daniel. 1980. *Workplace Democracy.* New York: Harper & Row.

18

Howard S. Schwartz

Narcissism Project and Corporate Decay: The Case of General Motors

When I left graduate school and began teaching organizational behavior courses, I was struck by the irrelevance of what I had learned to the actual organizational experience of my students.

My students experienced and understood organizational life as a kind of "vanity fair," in which individuals who were interested in "getting ahead" could do so by playing to the vanity of their superiors. One needed to do this in two respects. One needed to flatter the superior as an individual and as an occupant of the superior role. This latter process tended to trail off into an adulation of the organization in general.

Work either fit into this process of adulation, in which case it made sense; or it did not fit in, in which case it did not make sense. Work that did not make sense in this way, my students felt, was best left to the suckers who hadn't figured out yet how to get ahead and who deserved whatever torment this system led them to inherit. If, through this process, important, valid information was lost to the system by being withheld or simply unappreciated, that was not their concern. Through luck or guile, the consequences would, or could be made to, occur on somebody else's watch.

At first glance, my students' attitude looked to me like cynicism. But closer analysis suggested that although they had a great deal of cynicism in them, they were not simply being cynical, for they believed in the righteousness of what they were doing.

For them, getting ahead was a moral imperative, which justified any means necessary for its accomplishment. But more than this, the system itself which called upon subordinates to idealize it was held morally sacrosanct. A person who refused to go along with the system was seen as not only stupid and naive, but as morally inferior. And this was so even if the individual in question was offering a point of view that was essential for the organization to do its work effectively and efficiently.

It thus seemed to me that, for my students, the organization's processes were held to define moral value. As defined by its processes, the organization seemed to exist in a moral world of its own, which served to justify anything done on its behalf, and which did not require justification on any grounds outside of itself. This view was inconsistent with a view of the organization as an instrument to do work. For my students, the organization did not exist in order to do work; it did work in order to exist.

Yet even while holding this point of view, many of my students did not appear to have a deep loyalty to the organizations that they so supported. On the contrary, for the most part they were willing to change organizations with no regrets or guilt. Their loyalty, if that is what it was, seemed to be to an abstract idea of organization, an idea of the organization as a vehicle for the revelation of their own grandiosity. Ultimately, therefore, their loyalty appeared to be directed at themselves.

Over time, trying to be a good empiricist, I came to take their stories about organizational life increasingly seriously. I made the assumption that organizational life was just what my students, whom I came to consider my research subjects, and sometimes informants, appeared to be living. Relegating what I had learned in graduate school to the status of a fantasy, I tried to fashion a theoretical conception that would explain this organizational reality. Following Shorris (1981), I called the syndrome "organizational totalitarianism" (Schwartz, 1987a).

I first understood organizational totalitarianism in moral terms, in terms of the psychological damage done to the individuals involved (Schwartz, 1987a). But as time went by it became more and more clear to me that the processes I was coming to understand must have practical consequences as well—consequences for the effective functioning, the efficiency, the profitability, the competitiveness of organizations. In a word, it did not seem to me that organizations as I understood them could possibly be successful even in terms of the narrowest economic criteria, without regard to the moral costs involved. So it was that when American industry seemed to be incapable of competing with foreign enterprises, I did not find myself at all surprised.

Getting beyond my students' accounts to gain evidence of the systemic effects of the process, however, proved to be a problem. There is a kind of "uncertainty principle" that applies here. Organizational participants who are in a position to be able to describe these systemic effects have typically given up the moral autonomy that would have enabled them to perceive them. Participants who insist on retaining their moral autonomy are typically excluded from important positions in the system precisely because of that insistence. Thus, the closer one is to the data, the less likely one is to be able to see it.

Accordingly, in the present paper I am going to rely heavily on one of the very few accounts that I know of by a highly positioned insider who became alienated from the system and reported on its processes to the outside. This is a book by John Z. De Lorean, co-written by J. Patrick Wright and published by the latter under his own name, called *On A Clear Day You Can See General Motors* (1979).

There are problems with using De Lorean's testimony, arising primarily from his subsequent problems with the law and from the apparent mismanagement of his own car company. Fortunately, therefore, there is a more recent account of GM by Maryann Keller (1989), which bears none of his taint. I will be using her work to lend secondary support to my case.

Organizational Totalitarianism and the Theory of the Organization Ideal

The theory I shall use to discuss organizational totalitarianism begins with the premise that, for people like my students, the idea of the organization represents an ego ideal—a symbol of the person one ought to become such that, if one were to become that person, one would again be the center of a loving world as one experienced oneself as a child. The ego ideal represents a return to narcissism (Freud, 1955, 1957; Chasseguet-Smirgel, 1985, 1986). It represents an end to the anxiety that entered our lives when we experienced ourselves as separate from our apparently all-powerful mothers.

With regard to organizations, this means that individuals redefine themselves as part of an organization, which is conceived as perfect. Thus, the image of such an organization is one in which members are perfectly integrated into a collectivity that is perfectly adapted to its environment. An image of an organization serving as an ego ideal may be called an "organization ideal" (Schwartz, 1987a, 1987b, 1987c). The organization ideal, thus, represents a project for the return to narcissism.

The problem with the organization ideal, like any ego ideal, is that it can never be attained. It represents a denial of our separation, finitude, vulnerability, and mortality; but these remain with us by virtue of our existence as concrete individual human beings (Becker, 1973, Chasseguet-Smirgel, 1985, Schwartz, 1987b).

Given the importance of maintaining belief in the possibility of attaining the ego ideal, organizations often attempt to generate a way of preserving the illusion of the organization ideal in the face of the failure of the organization to exemplify it. The attempt to manage an organization by imposing this illusion is what I call "organizational totalitarianism."

Organizations attempt this imposition in a number of ways. As Klein and Ritti

(1984) observe, they give and withhold information to create a myth of the organization as more effective than it really is. They impose patterns of speech and behavior on participants that make them seem more integrated than they really are. They promote the attribution that their problems are due to forces that do not belong in the world, which is to say to "bad" forces. And they generate an image of a gradient of Being, an "ontological differentiation," in the organization (Schwartz, 1987b; also see Sievers, 1987, and Schwartz, 1987d) which idealizes the higher figures in the organization (Klein and Ritti, 1984, pp. 170–72) as individuals who have fulfilled the project of the return to narcissism and become centers of a loving world. This provides the drive to climb the hierarchy that my students experience as the central spirit in their moral world (Schwartz, 1987a). Moreover, it delegitimates those who are farther down (Sennett and Cobb, 1973). This makes it possible for organizations to maintain the idea of the perfection of the organization's core and blame its imperfections on peripheral elements.

Organizational Decay

The problem is that such symbolic manipulation places falsehood right at the core of organizational functioning and therefore cannot help but lead to a loss of rationality. For the return to narcissism is impossible, short of psychosis (Chasseguet-Smirgel, 1985), and therefore organizational totalitarianism means the superimposition of a psychosis upon organizational functioning. Ultimately, whatever the gains in motivation, such a loss of rationality leads to generalized and systemic organizational ineffectiveness.

Moreover, I suggest that this condition of generalized and systemic ineffectiveness has a unity to it, and therefore represents something like an organizational disease. I would like to give it the name "organizational decay," in order to convey the impression of an internal process of rot, not occasioned by outside forces; and of a holistic process, not taking place in isolated parts of the organization but typically and increasingly sapping the vitality of the organization as a whole. This decay eventually may manifest itself in any of a number of ways. I shall discuss a few of them, relying on De Lorean's and Keller's books about General Motors to provide illustrations.

Some Causes of Decay

Commitment to Bad Decisions

Perhaps the most obvious symptom of organizational decay is the commitment to bad decisions. Staw (1980) has noted that the tendency to justify past actions can be a powerful motivation behind organizational behavior and can often run counter to rationality. As he notes, the justification process leads to escalating commitment. When mistaken actions cannot be seen as mistaken actions, the principle on which they are made is not seen as being mistaken. Worse, our feeling that it is a valid principle becomes enhanced through our need to defend our decision and further decisions are made on the basis of it.

This process must be especially lethal in the case of the totalitarian organization, where the idea of the perfection of the organization provides the organization's very motivational base. Here, the assumption of the identity of the individual decision maker and his or her organizational role turns the tendency to justify past actions from a defensive tendency on the part of individuals to a core organizational process—a central element of the organization's culture.

The case of the Corvair illustrates the process of commitment to bad decisions. Modeled after the Porsche, the Corvair was powered by a rear engine and had an independent, swing-axle suspension system. According to De Lorean, any car so powered and so suspended is going to have serious problems—problems that were well known and documented by GM's engineering staff long before the Corvair was offered for sale.

> The questionable safety of the car caused a massive internal fight among GM's engineers.... On one side of the argument was Chevrolet's then General Manager, Ed Cole.... On the other side was a wide assortment of top-flight engineers....
>
> ... One top corporate engineer told me that he showed his test results to Cole but by then, he said, "Cole's mind was made up...." Management not only went along with Cole, it also told dissenters in effect to "stop these objections. Get on the team, or you can find someplace else to work." The ill fated Corvair was launched in the fall of 1959.
>
> The results were disastrous. [Wright, 1979, pp. 65–66]

De Lorean then goes on to note that it was not until the 1964 model that GM added the $15 stabilizer bar that was needed to solve the problem. He adds:

> To date, millions of dollars have been spent in legal expenses and out-of-court settlements in compensation for those killed or maimed in the Corvair. The corporation steadfastly defends the car's safety, despite the internal engineering records which indicated it was not safe, and the ghastly toll in deaths and injury it recorded. [p. 67]

Advancement of Participants Who Detach Themselves from Reality and Discouragement of Reality-oriented Participants Who Are Committed to Their Work

When core organizational process becomes the dramatization of the organization and its high officials as ideal, the evaluation of individuals for promotion and even for continued inclusion comes to be made on the basis of how much they contribute to this dramatization. This means that, increasingly, promotion criteria shift from achievement and competence to ideology and politics.[1] De Lorean describes the process this way:

> ... as I grew in General Motors it became apparent that objective criteria were not always used to evaluate an executive's performance. Many times the work record of a man who was promoted was far inferior to the records of others around him who were not promoted. It was quite obvious that something different than job performance was being used to rate these men.
>
> That something different was a very subjective criterion which encompassed style, appearance, personality and, most importantly, personal loyalty to the man (or men) who was the promoter, and to the system which brought this all about. There were rules of this fraternity of management at GM. Those pledges willing to obey the rules were promoted. In the vernacular, they were the company's "team players." Those who didn't fit into the mold of a manager, who didn't adhere to the rules because they thought they were silly, generally weren't promoted. "He's not a team player," was the frequent, and many times only, objection to an executive in line for promotion. It didn't mean he was doing a poor job. It meant he didn't fit neatly into a stereotype of style, appearance and manner. He didn't display blind loyalty to the system of management, to the man or men doing the promoting. He rocked the boat. He took unpopular stands on products or policy which contradicted the prevailing attitude of top management. [p. 40]

Keller (1989) adumbrates this point in a number of places; for example:

> Elitism within the system was inevitable. Over the years it has become easy for executives to buy staff loyalty; everyone knows that's how you get on the fast-track—in GM lingo that's called being a HI-POT, a high-potential employee. At General Motors, the road to the corporate dining room is paved with occasions of looking the other way, of saying yes, of supporting the team, of keeping one's opinions to oneself. Those chosen few—about four thousand in number—who have achieved bonus-eligible status continue to be yessayers, their huge bonus earnings buying their loyalty. [p. 33]

One result of this will be that those individuals who are retained and promoted will be those who will know very well how things are *supposed to look*, according to the viewpoint of the dominant coalition, but who will be less and less attached to reality insofar as it conflicts with, or simply is independent of, this viewpoint. The problem is, of course, that since no organization is, or can be, the organization ideal, this means that those individuals who are retained and promoted will be those who can cut themselves loose from discrepant reality.

Another result of this sort of selection must be that realistic and concerned persons must lose the belief that the organization's real purpose is productive work and come to the conclusion that its real purpose is self-promotion. They then are likely to see their work as being alien to the purposes of the organization and must find doing good work increasingly depressing and useless.

De Lorean puts it this way:

> . . . in any system where inexperience and even incompetence exists in the upper reaches of management, lower-echelon executives become demoralized and dissatisfied. They see a system which impedes rather than enhances decision making. Their own jobs become frustrating. Divisional managers reporting to a group executive who is uneducated in their businesses must literally try to teach the business to him before getting decisions from him on their proposals. We often waltzed our bosses on the Fourteenth Floor through a step-by-step explanation of each program proposal—what it meant, how it related to the rest of the business and what it would do for the company. Even after this, their judgment most often was based on what GM had done before. [p. 255]

And gives this example of the clash between the incompetent who have been promoted and their competent but discouraged subordinates:

> Increasingly, group and upper managers seemed to look upon their jobs in such narrow terms that it was impossible to competently direct broad corporate policy. Often misplaced, unprepared or simply undertalented, these executives filled their days and our committee meetings with minutiae. After one particularly frustrating meeting of the Administrative Committee, John Beltz and I were picking up our notes when he looked down at the far end of the conference table at the corporate management and said to me, "I wouldn't let one of those guys run a gas station for me." It was a bitter and sad indictment of our top management by one of the then young, truly bright lights of General Motors management. [p. 256]

A third effect, obvious by this point, is that higher management is effectively isolated from criticism, or even serious discussion, of its thought and actions. De Lorean gives this account:

> This system quickly shut top management off from the real world because it surrounded itself in many cases with "yes" men. There soon became no real vehicle for adequate outside input. Lower executives, eager to please the boss and rise up the corporate ladder, worked hard to learn what he wanted or how he thought on a particular subject. They then either fed the boss exactly what he wanted to know, or they modified their own proposals to suit his preferences.
>
> Original ideas were often sacrificed in deference to what the boss wanted. Committee meetings no longer were forums for open discourse, but rather either soliloquies by the top man, or conversations between a few top men with the rest of the meeting looking on. [p. 47]

Indeed, as organizational promotion and retention criteria shift toward the dramatization of the perfection of the organization, this shapes the very job of the subordinate into what Janis (1972) calls "mindguarding"—the suppression of criticism.[2]

Keller (1989, p. 34) also comments on the conflict between what one needs to do to get promoted and the quality of one's work:

> One retired executive rails against a system that creates vertical thinkers and cautious leaders. "The whole system stinks once you're in it. You continue to want to make vertical decisions: 'What is it that I should decide that will be good for me. Never make a horizontal decision based on what is good for the company. I want to get promoted.'
>
> "So you get promoted because you're sponsored by someone; you get promoted before they catch up with you. I can go through a litany of those clowns. They go from this plant to that complex and then, all of a sudden, they've got plaques all over the walls that say how great they've done—but the plant's falling apart and the division's falling apart."

The Creation of the Organizational Jungle

The more successful the organization is at projecting the image of itself as the organization ideal, the more deeply must committed participants experience anxiety. For the image projected, the image of the individual as perfectly a part of the perfect organization, is only an image; and the more perfect it is, the more acute the discrepancy between the *role* and the *role player*. Given the importance of the organization ideal in the individual's self-concept, some way must be found in which the individual can reconcile the discrepancy between the centrality in a loving world he or she is supposed to be experiencing and the wretchedness he or she in fact feels. As we have seen above, the typical way is to attempt to deepen the identity of self and organization by rising in the organization's hierarchy and by fighting off what are perceived as threats to the organizational identity one has attained—perceived threats that are often projections of one's own self-doubts.

The result of this is that individuals become obsessed with organizational rank. They become compelled to beat down anyone who threatens or competes with them in their pursuit of higher rank or who is perceived as threatening the rank they have already acquired. Thus, ironically, behind the display of the organization ideal, of everyone working together to realize shared values, the real motivational process becomes a Hobbesian battle of narcissism project against narcissism project.[3] The consequences of this for coordination, cooperation, and motivation are clear enough. De Lorean says:

> Not only is the system perpetuating itself, but in the act of perpetuating itself the system has fostered several destructive practices which are harmful to executive morale. They developed from the psychological need, as I see it, of less competent managers to affirm in their own minds a logical right to their positions, even though the basis for their promotions was illogical by any business-performance standard. Once in a position of power, a manager who was promoted by the system is insecure because, consciously or not, he knows

that it was something other than his ability to manage and his knowledge of the business that put him in his position. . . . He thus looks for methods and defense mechanisms to ward off threats to his power. [p. 49]

Isolation of Management and Rupture of Communications

A related problem is that the greater the success of the totalitarian manager, the more the manager is isolated from his or her subordinates. The world that the subordinates live in is the world of the organization ideal as created by the totalitarian manager. The world that the totalitarian manager lives in is the world of the *construction of the image of* the organization ideal. These two worlds are incommensurable and it cannot help but happen that communication and trust must break down between them. For communication and trust mean two different things to these groups. Indeed, for totalitarian management, communication to subordinates is not communication at all—it is deception. To conceal the fact of this deception, the fact that the presentation is a presentation must be covered up. And then the coverup must be covered up, and so on, in the manner that Argyris and Schön (1974) have described.

Development of Hostile Orientation toward the Environment

If the totalitarian manager is successful, as we have seen, organizational participants take the organization as an organization ideal. It must follow, in their thinking, that such an organization will be successful in its dealings with the world. This poses a difficulty of interpretation for the necessarily problematic relationships between the organization and its environment.

Thus, in the nature of things (Katz and Kahn, 1966) the environment places constant demands on the organization. Failure to meet them will result in the organization's death. But from the standpoint of the totalitarian manager committed to portraying the organization as the organization ideal, this sort of reasoning cannot be acknowledged. From this point of view it is the organization that is the criterion of worth. The environment is not conceived to exist as an independent environment at all; it exists only in order to support the organization. From this standpoint the demands of the environment must be presented as hostile actions on the part of bad external forces—hostile actions to which a legitimate response is equally hostile action.

The General Motors Corporation, in response to Ralph Nader's (1965) book about the Corvair, *Unsafe At Any Speed,* hired private detectives to find ways to discredit him. De Lorean remembers it this way:

> When Nader's book threatened the Corvair's sales and profits, he became an enemy of the system. Instead of trying to attack his credentials or the factual basis of his arguments, the company sought to attack him personally. [p. 64]

Sending private detectives to find out the dirty details of Nader's private life suggests something about their attitude toward him. It suggests that they expected to find something to show that he was a bad person. He had to be a bad person: he had attacked GM, hadn't he?

Again:

> Criticism from the outside is generally viewed as ill-informed. General Motors management thinks what it is doing is right, because it is GM that is doing it and the outside world is wrong. It is always "they" versus "us." [p. 257]

Thus, the picture of the organization as organization ideal leads to an orientation toward the world that can best be described as paranoid. It is clear enough that such a conception must degrade the relationships with the environment that ultimately the organization requires for its survival.

The Transposition of Work and Ritual

When work, the productive process, becomes display, its meaning becomes lost. Its performance as part of the organizational drama becomes the only meaning that it has. Accordingly, the parts it plays in the organization's transactions with the world become irrelevant. When this happens, it loses its adaptive function and becomes mere ritual.

At the same time, those rituals that serve to express the individual's identification with the organization ideal, especially those connected with rank, come to be infused with significance for the individual. They become sacred. Thus, reality and appearance trade places. The energy that once went into the production of goods and services of value to others is channeled into the dramatization of a narcissistic fantasy in which the organization's environment is merely a stage setting.

Consider how this shows up in the matter of dress. One can easily make a case that patterns of dress among organizational participants often have some functionality. But when the issue comes to be invested with great meaning, one must suspect that ritual has supplanted function. De Lorean gives some examples:

> At General Motors, good appearance meant conservative dress. In my first meeting as a GM employee in 1956 at Pontiac, half the session was taken up in discussion about some vice-president downtown at headquarters who was sent home that morning for wearing a brown suit. Only blue or black suits were tolerated then. I remember thinking that was silly. But in those days I followed the rules closely. [pp. 40–41]

Later on, when he was less inclined to follow the rules just because they were the rules, De Lorean found out what violation of them meant:

I made a habit of widening my circle of friends and broadening my tastes. This awareness precipitated a seemingly endless chain of personality conflicts, the most difficult of which was with Roger Keyes, who was my boss while I was running Pontiac and Chevrolet divisions. He made life unbearable for me, and he was dedicated to getting me fired; he told me so, many times. Fortunately, I had the protection of my ability as I ran those two divisions to fend off Keyes. But I remember vividly my conflicts with him, especially when he was irritated by my style of dress. The corporate rule was dark suits, light shirts and muted ties. I followed the rule to the letter, only I wore stylish Italian-cut suits, wide collared off-white shirts and wide ties.

"Goddamit, John," he'd yell. "Can't you dress like a businessman? And get your hair cut, too."

My hair was ear length with sideburns. [pp. 9–10]

The dynamics of the ways in which ritual comes to assume the importance work should have help to explain the dynamics of the ritualization of work. For the willingness to allow one's behavior to be determined by meaningless rituals comes to be justified by an idealization of the organization that elevates its customs above, and discredits, one's values—one's sense of what is important. This willingness to subordinate and delegitimate, in a word to repress, one's own sense of what is important, even about matters that should be within the competence of anyone's judgment, must have its consequences magnified when the matters in question become more abstruse and difficult to make judgments about, as is the case with real executive work. Then the repression of one's values deprives one of any basis for making such judgments, and leads naturally to a superimposition of the rituals with which one is familiar, even where, patently, they do not belong. This is what gives the horror to De Lorean's story about what he found when he was elevated to the Fourteenth Floor, GM's executive suite, as group executive in charge of the domestic Car and Truck Group:

> . . . When I finally moved upstairs. . . I saw that the job. . . often consisted only of . . . little, stupid, make-work kinds of assignments, things which I thought should have been decided further down the line.
>
> Some of these things, which had little or no impact on the business, were an insult to a person's intelligence. . . As I recall, [for example, my boss] asked me to catalogue service parts numbers and to prepare reports on the size of parts inventories.
>
> . . . "This is supposed to be a planning job," I remember thinking, "but I feel like a file clerk. I've spent many years learning to be a good executive. Now I can't use that knowledge."
>
> . . . I set up a meeting with Vice-Chairman Tom Murphy, to whom I had reported when he held the job I now held. . . .
>
> "Tom, I think I know what has to be done for the long-term health of GM. But I don't get any time to work on it. I just don't get any time to plan my days because of this array of meetings, inane assignments and tons of endless paperwork."

He responded, "Hell, John, when I had that job I never got to plan one minute. It was completely planned for me. The job just drags you from place to place. You don't have time to plan. It is not that kind of a job. . . ."

"Well that's exactly what's happening to me, and I don't consider it satisfactory," I said. "The system is deciding what I should be working on and what is important; I'm not. I'm not doing any planning of the direction of the company, and this is a planning job. No one else seems to be planning either. We're in for trouble. . . ."

Murphy didn't say much further. I suddenly realized that what I felt was a weakness of life on the Fourteenth Floor, he and others thought was "business as usual." They were quite happy to let their jobs drag them from one place to the next, trying to solve problems as they came up, but not getting into the kind of long-range planning that Fourteenth Floor executives were supposed to be doing[4] . . . . I later mentioned my frustration to [President Ed] Cole and he told me: "You've got to go through the steps. This job is part of the process." That process didn't seem very attractive and fulfilling to me.

So I quit doing the things I thought weren't worthwhile to the job. . . .

It quickly evolved that I wasn't a "member of the team." [pp. 26–34]

De Lorean explains the matter this way:

A promotional system which stressed "loyalty to the boss" more than performance put into top management executives who, while hard-working, nevertheless lacked the experience, and in some cases the ability to manage capably or guide the business. The preoccupation on The Fourteenth Floor with the appearance of working—putting in long hours, going through the motions of the job, occupying time with minutiae—is a direct result of management's inability to grasp the scope of its job and grapple with the problems that arise. [p. 250]

Loss of Creativity

The delegitimation of one's sense of what is important gives rise to a special case of the ritualization of work—the loss of creativity. Thus, Schein (1983) describes the condition of "conformity" which follows from an insistence by the organization that all of its norms be accepted as being equally important. Under that condition, the individual

. . . can tune in so completely on what he sees to be the way others are handling themselves that he becomes a carbon-copy and sometimes a caricature of them. . . . The conforming individual curbs his creativity and thereby moves the organization toward a sterile form of bureaucracy. [p. 197]

Maslow (1970) gives us insight into the psychodynamics of this when he observes that creativity is characteristic of both ends of the continuum of personality development, but not of the stages in the middle (pp. 170–71). Creativity, this suggests, is a function of spontaneity, a function of taking seriously our actual affects and interacting in the world in consideration of our spontaneous feelings. But as the self comes to be dominated by a concern for how things appear to others, which is characteristic of the middle stages of personality development (Schwartz, 1983), creativity disappears as a mode of interacting with the world. As the organization requires that the individual subordinate his or her spontaneous perception to an uncritical acceptance of the organization's preferred vision of itself, it thus determines that the affective basis of creativity will be repressed.

The lack of creativity, since it is a lack of something, cannot be positively demonstrated. As an experience, it makes itself known as a feeling of missing something different that has not occurred, even though one does not what the different element would have been. Thus, De Lorean found himself introducing a "new" crop of Chevrolets that were not really new at all:

> This whole show is nothing but a replay of last year's show, and the year before that and the year before that. The speech I just gave was the same speech I gave last year, written by the same guy in public relations about the same superficial product improvements as previous years. . . . Almost nothing has changed. . . . there was nothing new and revolutionary in car development and there hadn't been for years. [pp.60–1]

In benign times, one may experience boredom: the consciousness of a sameness, a lack of originality. When circumstances are harsh, partly as a result of the lack of creativity that the organization needed if it was to have adapted, one may simply experience the intractability of the situation. Adding up the figures in the usual way simply shows one, again and again, how hopeless the situation is. One may then experience the loss of creativity as a wish for a savior who will make the organization's problems disappear.

In the hard times, I suspect, one rarely comes to recognize that the ideas that the organization needed in order to have avoided its present hopeless state may have been upon the scene a long time ago. But the individuals who had them might have been passed over for promotion because they were not "team players," or perhaps they were made to feel uncomfortable because they did not fit it in, or maybe they were scapegoated whenever the organization needed a victim. Indeed, ironically, the very ideas that were needed might have been laughed at or ignored because they were not "the way we do things around here."

Dominance of the Financial Staff

Another hypothesis may be used to account for the emergent dominance of the financial function of the corporation that De Lorean finds in General Motors and that others, for example Halberstam (1986), have partly blamed for the decline of American industry.

As envisioned by Alfred Sloan, the financial function and the operations side of the corporation were both supposed to be represented strongly at the top level of the corporation. But, as De Lorean notes, over time, and specifically through the rise of Frederick Donner, the financial side came to dominate the corporation. Why?

I propose that finance, rather than operations, offers the greater narcissistic possibilities. As Nader and Taylor (1986) note, operations, the productive process, tends to temper grandiosity. The recalcitrance of matter, so to speak, exerts a humbling influence. Not so with finance. Seen through a kind of latter-day pythagoreanism, the world, as mere instantiation of number, imposes no bounds on the imagination's flights concerning the self. In the cut and thrust of executive competition, where humility can act as a brake on appetite, can we not suppose that the humble might be surpassed? When the matter comes to competitive elevation of the organization ideal, who can do it better, who can represent it better, than the officer whose bonds to earthly substance are the lightest? Who better than the specialist in finance?

Keller's analysis is similar:

> Financial people operate in a rarefied environment. For them, solving a problem means successfully juggling the numbers on financial statements. What happens when the numbers determine every major investment and product initiative? Reality gets distorted. [1989, pp. 26–27]

And she observes that the more skillful financial executives are at this sort of manipulation, the more they are blessed with promotion (p. 28).

Cynicism and Corruption or Self-Deception and the Narcissistic Loss of Reality

Referring to the ways people are related to their own presentations, Goffman (1959, pp. 17–18) notes that one can either be taken in by one's own performance or not taken in by it, using it only "to guide the conviction of his audience . . . as a means to other ends." In the latter case we refer to the individual as a cynic. Such persons disassociate themselves from discrepant information consciously and through deception. In the former case, the individual "comes to be performer and observer of the same show." Goffman adds:

> It will have been necessary for the individual in his performing capacity to conceal from himself in his audience capacity the discreditable facts that he has had to learn about the performance; in everyday terms, there will be things he knows, or has known, that he will not be able to tell himself. [p. 81]

Goffman notes that these persons cut themselves loose from discrepant information through repression and disassociation, a point that corresponds perfectly with psychoanalytic theory concerning the maintenance of the ego ideal.

We may refer to such individuals as self-deceptive. Thus, in the totalitarian organization, no matter what its espoused values, promotion and even continued inclusion will tend to go to deceptive cynics whose moral involvement in their organizational activity is attenuated, or to self-deceptive persons whose involvement in reality is attenuated.

Of the two, it is difficult to say which is to be preferred. Cynics at least know what is going on around them; and if their moral involvement in their organizational role is attenuated, that does not seem inappropriate in an organization as deceptive as one that is managed by totalitarian means. Indeed, in organizations that have seriously degenerated as a result of these processes, it is often only the cynics who can get anything done at all.

Nonetheless, there is no doubt that cynicism tends toward corruption. Corruption does not play a major role in De Lorean's picture of General Motors, although he notes its presence (p. 83). Our analysis leads us to suspect that, as time goes by, if GM continues to deteriorate, it will become increasingly difficult for even minimally functioning individuals to idealize it. Then, corruption will increasingly become a problem.

For the present, I think the more serious problem comes in with those who deceive themselves and distance themselves from reality. For as the processes I have described operate, and as the organization degenerates accordingly, it becomes increasingly difficult to see it as the ideal, and individuals who are able to do so must become increasingly self-deceptive. A point must come when such individuals may not be said to be psychologically living in the same world that the real organization is in. What makes this even worse is that, since this capacity for self-deception is an important advantage in the race for promotion, the total disassociation of the individual from organizational reality is likely to be correlated with the individual's position in the hierarchy. Then the most important processes within the organization come to be under the authority of people who are not operating in the real world as far as the organization's requirements are concerned.

Keller hints at this:

> During the 1970's, a writer for *Fortune* magazine set out on a quest for dissenting views at General Motors, and found it hard "to find a top executive at GM who does not evidence enthusiasm for what he or the company is doing." One view might hold that GM had achieved a state of management consensus that would be the envy of any company. But more likely, the lack of dissension was motivated by self-interest. It was managerial suicide to be the person who got labeled a naysayer. There was also an element of denial; in the same way that children of alcoholics often refuse to accept their parents' addiction, GM employees refused to admit the truth about their corporate parent. They didn't want to believe. [pp. 65–66]

Overcentralization

The narcissistic loss of reality among those at the top of the corporation may be a major cause of overcentralization of operational decision making. De Lorean found this overcentralization to characterize General Motors, and with it the tendency to provide simplistic answers to complex questions. The idea that, having risen to the top of the corporation, individuals would hold themselves as bearing all of its knowledge and virtues follows immediately from what we have been saying.

From this would follow the tendency of top management to believe themselves more capable than anyone else of providing answers to any questions that arise. Having no command of specific details beyond those in their imaginations, the answers that they give, and that would come to bind the rest of the corporation, would necessarily be simplistic and inappropriate. Moreover, as the decay process continues, and as the competence of top management declines accordingly, both their tendency to impose simple answers to complex problems, and the specific inadequacy even of the simplistic answers they propose, would tend to increase. Moreover, the capacity of the system to correct itself would tend to decrease, since the increasing power of the higher echelons of the corporation, and their increasing narcissism, would tend toward an attribution of blame to the lower levels of the organization. This would delegitimate those whose judgment would be necessary to reverse the decay process.

De Lorean provides a number of examples of this. This one will serve our purpose:

> . . . the corporate program for maximum standardization of parts across product lines was a knee-jerk cost-cutting reaction to the incredible proliferation of models, engines and parts which took place in the uncontrolled and unplanned boom of the 1960's. However, the program was not intelligently thought out. It was not thoroughly analyzed for its actual effect on the company. On paper the concept looked good and seemed like a sure way to save money. In reality it wasted money. The car divisions rebelled at various stages of the standardization program. Their cries were unanswered. When Chevrolet rebelled against using the new corporate U-joint. . . Keyes told me, "Use the corporate one or I'll get someone in Chevy who will."
>
> We used it, at an investment of about $16 million in tooling, and our costs rose $1.40 per car. In addition, the corporate design failed in use and Chevy paid out about $5 million extra in warranty claims.
>
> Instead of saving money, the standardization program at GM wound up costing the corporation about $300 million extra per year. . . .
>
> The last straw came in 1972, however, when management asked us: "Why is the cost of building a Chevrolet $70 closer to Oldsmobile today than it was in 1964?" The question from the top was offered in the usual "you aren't doing your job" manner. The irony was incredible. [pp. 252–53]

Keller offers numerous observations of this sort of narcissistic inflation leading to overcentralization. Considerations of space, however, preclude examination of them at this point.

An Overview

Before I conclude this discussion of the practical consequences of totalitarian management, it is worthwhile to note a characteristic that the consequences mentioned have in common: they are all cumulative and interactive with each other. They all tend to build within the system and, interacting with each other, take over the system bit by bit. This is the way in which the ineffectiveness characteristic of the decadent organization becomes systemic and generalized. Thus, for example, the accumulation of bad decisions taken within the system suggests that those who manifest belief in it as an organization ideal must increasingly be self-deceptive or cynical, which in turn decreases the retention of realism and concern for work, which leads to a further increase in bad decisions, further degradation of the relationship with the environment, and so on.

The result of this is that the *rate* of decay will tend to accelerate. On the basis of this the fact that GM's market share took six years to decline from 46 percent to 41 percent, but only three more years to go to 35 percent (*Wall Street Journal*, December 14, 1989, p. 1), comes to make a certain chilling sense.

Conclusion: On Averting Organizational Decay

There is no doubt that fantasy plays an important part in our mental lives. To say this one does not need either to approve of fantasy or to regret its inroads into the psyche. Fantasy simply *is*. So it is with the ego ideal, which is a particularly central fantasy in our lives.

But the same cannot be said for organizational totalitarianism and organizational decay. These are neither necessary nor inevitable features of organizational life. They become features of organizational life when the *desire* to be the center of a loving world becomes a *demand* and when the *power* is available to turn this demand into a program of action.

What this suggests is that (1) organizational totalitarianism and organizational decay, which first appear as systemic problems that concern the organization, are at their root existential, moral, even spiritual, problems that concern the individual; and (2) these problems at the individual level become systemic problems for the organization when organizational power is used to effect this transformation.

Putting the matter this way enables us to perceive a continuity between our analysis of organizational decay, on one hand; and the Greek conception of tragedy, on the other. What we see in both cases is the horror that comes from the claims of powerful mortals to be more than mortal. The Greeks called this *hubris* and they knew that the gods, whom we might refer to as reality, do not stand for it. They demand humility.

Notes

1. Note the connection here with the findings of Luthans, Hodgetts, and Rosenkrantz (1988) on the unrelatedness of competence and advancement. From the point of view of the theory of organizational decay, the further intriguing possibility presents itself that Luthans et al. have managed to capture only a phase of the decay process. On the basis of the considerations adduced here, one would expect to find that as the organization decayed further, the correlation between competence and advancement would become negative. In organizations of this sort, bad management drives out good.

2. The reader will note that a number of the processes I describe here are similar to those Janis called "groupthink." The advantage my approach offers is that it reveals the underlying psychodynamics of the syndrome and shows how it is manifested in a wide range of organizational functions, rather than just in decision making.

3. Note here the obvious connection to Argyris and Schön's (1974) distinction between "espoused theory" and "theory-in-use."

4. De Lorean's account here is in accordance with Mintzberg's (1973) observations of managerial work. It is tempting to speculate that much of what Mintzberg was observing was not managerial work, as such, but rather a decadent form of it.

References

Argyris, C., and D.A. Schön. 1974. *Theory in Practice*. San Francisco: Jossey-Bass.

Becker, E. 1973. *The Denial of Death*. New York: Free Press.

Chasseguet-Smirgel, Janine. 1985. *The Ego Ideal: A Psychoanalytic Essay on the Malady of the Ideal*, first American ed., trans. by P. Barrows. New York: Norton.

———. 1986. *Sexuality and Mind: The Role of the Father and the Mother in the Psyche*. New York: New York University Press.

Freud, Sigmund. 1955. *Group Psychology and the Analysis of the Ego*, stand. ed., vol. 18. London: Hogarth.

———. 1957. *On Narcissism: An Introduction*, stand. ed., vol. 14. London: Hogarth.

Goffman, Erving. 1959. *The Presentation of Self in Everyday Life*. New York: Doubleday Anchor.

Halberstam, David. 1986. *The Reckoning*. New York: William Morrow.

Janis, I.L. 1972. *Victims of Groupthink*. Boston: Houghton Mifflin.

Katz, Daniel, and Robert L. Kahn. 1966. *The Social Psychology of Organizations*. New York: Wiley.

Keller, Maryann. 1989. *Rude Awakening: The Rise, Fall, and Struggle for Recovery of General Motors*. New York: William Morrow.

Kets de Vries, M.F.R., and D. Miller. 1984. *The Neurotic Organization*. San Francisco: Jossey-Bass.

Klein, Stuart M., and R. Richard Ritti. 1984. *Understanding Organizational Behavior*, 2nd ed. Boston: Kent.

Luthans, Fred, Roger M. Hodgetts, and Stuart A. Rosenkrantz. 1988. *Real Managers*. Cambridge, MA: Ballinger.

Maslow, Abraham H. 1970. *Motivation and Personality*, 2nd ed. New York: Harper and Row.

Mintzberg, Henry. 1973. *The Nature of Managerial Work*. New York: Harper & Row.

Nader, Ralph. 1965. *Unsafe at Any Speed*. New York: Grossman.

Nader, Ralph, and William Taylor. 1986. *The Big Boys: Power and Position in American Business*. New York: Pantheon.

Schein, Edgar H. 1983. "Organizational Socialization and the Profession of Management." In B.M. Staw, ed., *Psychological Foundations of Organizational Behavior*, 2nd ed. Glenview, IL: Scott, Foresman.

Schwartz, Howard S. 1983. "Maslow and the Hierarchical Enactment of Organizational Reality," *Human Relations* 36:10.

———. 1987a. "On the Psychodynamics of Organizational Totalitarianism," *Journal of Management* 13, 1:38–51.

———. 1987b. "Antisocial Actions of Committed Organizational Participants: An Existential Psychoanalytic Perpective," *Organization Studies* 8, 4:327–40.

———. 1987c. "On the Psychodynamics of Organizational Disaster: The Case of the Space Shuttle Challenger," *Columbia Journal of World Business* 22, 1:59–67.

———. 1987d. "Rousseau's *Discourse on Inequality* Revisited: Psychology of Work at the Public Esteem Stage of Maslow's Hierarchy." *International Journal of Management* 4, 2:180–93.

———. 1988. "The Symbol of the Space Shuttle and the Degeneration of the American Dream." *Journal of Organizational Change Management* 1, 2:5–20.

Sennett, R., and J. Cobb. 1973. *The Hidden Injuries of Class*. New York: Vintage.

Shorris, E. 1981. *The Oppressed Middle: Politics of Middle Management/Scenes from Corporate Life*. Garden City, NY: Anchor/Doubleday.

Sievers, Burkard. 1987. "Beyond the Surrogate of Motivation." *Organization Studies* 7, 4:335–51.

Staw, B.M. 1980. "Rationality and Justification in Organization Life." In B.M. Staw and L.L. Cummings, eds., *Research in Organizational Behavior* vol. 2. Greenwich, CT: JAI Press.

Wright, J. Patrick. 1979. *On a Clear Day You Can See General Motors: John Z. De Lorean's Look inside the Automotive Giant*. New York: Avon.

19

SUSAN HELPER

An Exit-Voice Analysis
of Supplier Relations

Two decades ago, musings on deterioration of service by the Nigerian state railway led Albert O. Hirschman to formulate a theory of "responses to decline in firms, organizations, and states." He postulated two types of responses to such problems: "exit" to a better alternative, or "voice," defined as "any attempt at all to change, rather than to escape from, an objectionable state of affairs" (Hirschman, 1970, p. 30).

This theory has been extended beyond even its original wide boundaries to institutions such as labor unions and the family.[1] In this paper, I propose a further extension: beyond individual consumers' responses to deterioration of quality to include responses to problems of various types that arise between customer and supplier firms.

In this situation, agents' choice of exit or voice as a method of problem resolution turns out to be an important strategic decision, one that has implications for all parts of the organization, not just the purchasing function. Requirements for implementing exit and voice supplier relations strategies are discussed in the first section of the paper. The second section looks at the social welfare implications of a firm's choice of supplier relations strategy, and shows conditions that generate a tradeoff between customer bargaining power and industry technical change. The third section looks at the relationship between exit and voice strategies and shows that the use of one of the strategies can undermine the effectiveness of the other. The fourth section looks at the theoretical implications of the foregoing analysis. It shows that incorporation of exit/voice concepts can enrich Williamson's (1975, 1985) transaction cost framework, by freeing it from his assumptions that the "environmental conditions" and "human factors" leading to transaction costs are exogenous, and that economic agents

The author would like to thank Albert O. Hirschman and David I. Levine for their helpful comments.

always act in a socially efficient manner. The paper concludes by summarizing the contributions of the analysis to our understanding of the exit/voice paradigm in general and of supplier relations in particular.

Exit and Voice in Supplier Relations

Many problems can arise in a relationship between customer and supplier.[2] For example, suppose one party wants the other party to undertake a specific action (lower its price, improve its quality), but the other party refuses, either because it lacks the capability (decision makers in the firm do not know how to implement the proposed changes), or because it lacks the incentive (decision makers have other, more profitable, courses of action open to them).[3] Another possibility is that one party may feel that there is a problem (the customer may find that its products aren't selling as well as it would like), and may believe that changed behavior by the other party would contribute to its solution, but is not able to propose a specific course of action.

I will concentrate here on responses to problems arising in a particular type of customer-supplier relationship, one in which the customer can make take-it-or-leave-it offers to suppliers. These offers include not only the price of the input, but also the length of the (implicit or explicit) contract, and the nature of the task that the supplier is to perform (amount of design work, subassembly, etc.). Because a powerful agent can change conditions (such as the design of components, the number of suppliers, and their skills) that another agent might have to take as given, examining the case of a powerful agent allows us to look more fully at the differential implications of exit and voice strategies. For evidence, I draw on my previous work on supplier relations in the automotive industry (Helper, 1987, 1990b, 1991).

Borrowing Hirschman's terminology, we can identify two types of responses to problems arising in a customer-supplier relationship: (1) exit, where the customer firm's response to problems with a supplier is to find a new supplier; and (2) voice, where the customer's response is to work with the original supplier until the problem is corrected.

In Hirschman's original conception, "a random lapse in efficiency" leads to a decline in product quality; the dissatisfied party is an individual consumer or member of an organization, and voice is usually characterized as a sharp message of protest. Whereas "exit requires nothing but a clearcut either-or decision," voice requires a great deal of creativity and hard work to find effective ways to get the message across (1970, p. 43). Since the quality decline that leads to the choice of exit or voice "results from a random lapse in efficiency, rather than from a calculated attempt, on the part of the firm, to reduce costs by skimping on quality" (1970, p. 23), the solution to the problem seems to lie in a renewed attention to detail. The organization is induced to provide such attention in the case of exit by the threat of lost profits; the motivation for listening to consumer voice is less clear, but seems to be based on a desire to avoid the hassle of public protest.

Applying Hirschman's framework to the case of a customer/supplier relationship calls for different assumptions with respect to many of the above features. In contrast to an individual consumer, a customer firm such as General Motors is likely to procure the same items repeatedly, and to have the power to have more than a marginal impact on the nature of what it is supplied.

To the extent that such a customer maximizes profits, it will be interested in obtaining systematic improvements from its suppliers, as well as in avoiding random lapses in quality. Achieving these improvements may require not just increased work effort, but also large, irreversible investments in physical, human, and organizational capital. Therefore, voice may well take the form not just of isolated complaints, but of ongoing dialog between the two organizations. Use of the exit option requires the continued availability of suppliers who are close substitutes.

Under these conditions, effective use of either an exit or a voice problem-solving mechanism requires a great deal of effort and investment. All parts of the customer's organization, not just the purchasing department, are affected. Therefore, a firm's choice of mechanism for solving problems with suppliers is a strategic one, since such a choice carries with it (implicitly or explicitly) a set of policies that have a significant influence on the way an organization marshals resources to achieve its goals (see Helper and Leone, 1989).

The key to the exit strategy is making credible the customer's threat to leave if its demands are not met. Therefore, the customer must have access to many interchangeable suppliers, and/or the ability to tool up quickly for in-house production. For a customer who demands components that are made to order, establishing and maintaining such access requires active intervention. For example, in the decades before the import wave began in the 1970s, U.S. automakers *created* a fiercely competitive components industry. They did this by reducing barriers to entry through such mechanisms as taking complex functions like engineering and R&D almost completely in house. They employed several (six to eight) competing suppliers for each part, offered only short-term (one-year) contracts, and required suppliers to license major innovations. They also divided up parts into small, easy-to-produce pieces, and hired managers to coordinate the assembly of these parts centrally.

In contrast, the key to the voice strategy is setting up a communication system that will allow the rich flow of information that is essential to the "let's work things out" approach of the voice strategy. Where the exit strategy secures compliance by use of the "stick" of threats to withdraw from the relationship, the voice strategy relies on the "carrot" of increased profits for both parties due to improved products.[4]

We can summarize the differences in supplier relations strategies along two dimensions: the degree of administrative coordination and the nature of incentive systems used by the customer and its suppliers.

"Administrative coordination" describes the nature and amount of information that flows between producing units. At the lowest level of administrative coordination, the only information exchanged is price information, as in the "market" described in economics textbooks. At intermediate levels, information about finances, or characteristics of plant and equipment may be transferred. At the highest levels of administrative coordination the information flow is characterized by "feedback" between the customer and supplier; suggestions for improvement can be initiated by either party.

"Incentive systems" are the mechanisms (both explicit and implicit) used by a customer and a supplier to elicit desired behavior from the other party. An important type of incentive for obtaining desired behavior over time is the granting or withholding of commitments to undertake particular actions in the future.

A supplier has a commitment from a customer when the supplier knows that the customer will continue to purchase its products for some length of time. This assurance can be provided in several ways, including financial ties such as equity investment or long-term loans, long-term contracts, and parties' concern for their reputations for fair dealing. Commitment can also be provided involuntarily, as when a customer faces an oligopolistic supplier industry. That is, if a firm can obtain an input from only a few vendors, the firm's ability to exit from a relationship with them is very weak.

Another important commitment mechanism, analyzed extensively by Hirschman (1970), is loyalty. Loyalty has been conspicuously absent from the U.S. auto industry in recent decades (see below). However, loyalty has been a powerful force for promoting voice-based supplier relations in Japan.[5]

Contrary to the implicit assumption of much of the literature on vertical integration,[6] equity investment in a downstream process (i.e., a decision to "make" rather than "buy") is neither necessary nor sufficient for administrative coordination; for example, a financially independent customer and supplier who have had long-term dealings may have closer administrative relations than would two divisions of the same holding company. As shown below, the key determinant of the quantity and type of information exchanged by a customer and supplier is not the existence of a financial connection, but rather the strength of the commitment between them.

Figure 19.1 shows four regions of supplier relations strategies. The voice and exit methods of problem resolution outlined above each require a different combination of administrative coordination and commitment.

To implement the voice-based strategy, the customer needs a high degree of administrative coordination with its suppliers. Maintaining this degree of information flow both requires and engenders a high degree of commitment to the relationship, for three reasons. First, it is costly to establish and maintain extensive communication systems with more than one supplier. Second, there is a need for trust when exchanging proprietary information. Finally, customers and suppliers can reap substantial benefits from knowledge of each other's products

Figure 19.1. **Dimensions of Supplier Relations**

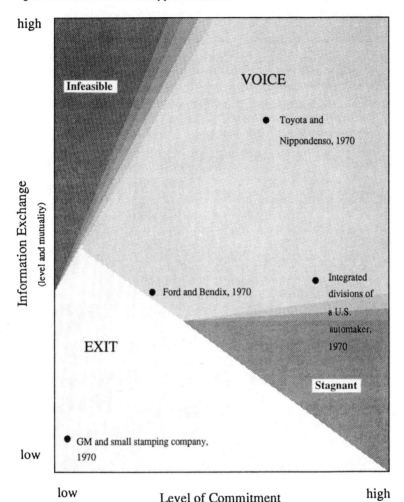

and processes gained by working together over time.

In contrast, an exit-based strategy requires low commitment, so as to maintain the credibility of the customer's threat to leave. Therefore, administrative coordination must also be low.

Since high administrative coordination requires high commitment, the high administrative coordination/low commitment area of Figure 19.1 is marked "infeasible."

Conversely, the low administrative coordination/high commitment region is labeled "stagnant," since the customer has few tools for problem resolution available; it has neither the threat of exit, nor the channels through which to exercise voice. That is, there are not two but three classes of responses to problems: exit, voice, and "do nothing." For example, employees of the Fisher Body Division of General Motors tended to describe themselves as "working for Fisher", not for GM; in one incident, Fisher responded to complaints about its product design by saying, "If you want this car to have some doors, you'll do it our way."[7]

Choosing Exit and Voice Strategies: What Difference Does It Make?

The customer's choice of method of problem resolution is important, because it affects both (1) the customer's and the supplier's relative bargaining power, and (2) their propensity to introduce new technologies of various types.

It is straightforward to see that the exit strategy gives the customer a great deal of bargaining power because it has little commitment to any one supplier. Conversely, the voice strategy reduces the customer's bargaining power by increasing its cost of switching between suppliers.[8]

On the other hand, most types of technical change[9] require moderate to high levels of both commitment and administrative coordination, thus favoring the voice-based strategy.

Commitment and Technical Change

The theoretical arguments about the importance of commitment for technical progress are basically Schumpeterian:[10]

First, uncertainty increases when markets are competitive (i.e., when the customer has low commitment to any one supplier). That is, there exist some projects whose net present value would be positive if performed by a firm that was an oligopolist, but negative if the firm was a perfect competitor, since added to technical uncertainty would be uncertainty about whether a given firm will be the winner of the patent race.[11]

Second, capital markets are imperfect where technical change is concerned, so the innovating firm must rely on internally generated funds for research and development. Since innovation in mature industries requires the coordinated efforts of many people and a long gestation period, these funds must be available over a long period of time. Unless the innovating firm has some sort of commitment from its customers, it will not be able to accumulate these funds.[12]

Results of a 1989 survey of automotive suppliers conducted for MIT's International Motor Vehicle Program indicate that high commitment (as measured by contract length and degree of trust in the customer) is significantly related to investment in automation.[13] Figure 19.2 shows how markedly use of computer numerically controlled (CNC) machine tools increases as contracts lengthen. For each contract length, the left bar of each pair shows the percentage of firms who say CNC is applicable to their operations but have *not* adopted the technology.

Figure 19.2. **Use of Computer Numerically Controlled (CNC) Machine Tools**

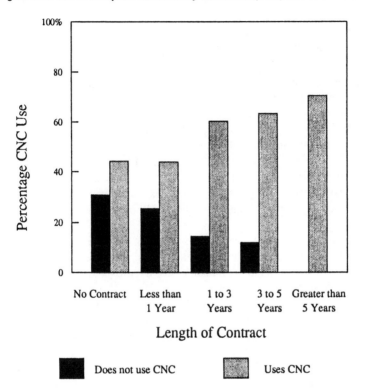

This percentage steadily falls from 41 percent for firms with no contract all the way to zero for firms with contracts longer than five years. Similar graphs could be shown for computer-aided design (CAD) and manufacturing cells. The rationale for the connection with contract length is that before they make large investments, firms want to have some assurance that they will have enough work to cover their additional fixed costs.[14]

However, auto industry evidence also indicates that *too much* commitment can reduce innovative activity by increasing fixed costs and thereby giving the parties too much security. Particularly problematic for high-commitment systems are "radical" innovations, which make obsolete a large body of industry knowledge. An example would be the substitution of electronic fuel injection for mechanical carburetors. In this case, automakers who were vertically integrated into carburetor manufacture (i.e., had a strong commitment to the existing technology) have been slower to change over than those who were not (Porter, 1983).

Because of this disincentive (as well as more traditional managerial-diseconomy effects), vertical integration is not a panacea that allows the customer to maintain always and everywhere both high bargaining power and fast technical progress.[15]

Administrative Coordination and Technical Change

Administrative coordination as well as commitment is important when introduction of new technology requires interdependent actions by customer and supplier. Interdependence is particularly likely in the case of a mature industry, since firms have over time built up a great deal of organizational and physical capital in current production techniques. Without extensive consultation, it would be highly unlikely that an outside firm could come up with a new product or process for a customer in a mature industry that either fit right into the existing process, or was sufficiently superior to existing techniques that it justified the expenditure of the millions (sometimes billions) of dollars required to start fresh.[16]

Failure to understand the above point has cost U.S. automakers dearly in recent years. For example, consider their attempts to adopt computer-integrated manufacturing (CIM). Only the automakers have detailed knowledge about desired attributes of automotive products and processes, but only the CIM manufacturers have a deep understanding of the capabilities of their equipment. Thus, in order for CIM to be successfully introduced, customer and supplier must work closely together, making changes in both the customer's designs and the supplier's materials. These complex tradeoffs cannot be resolved quickly by use of an arm's length market; a significant amount of detailed process information (not just data on product price and quantity) must cross firm boundaries.

Instead of investing in such administrative coordination, however,

> many early CIM implementors—automakers among them—were desperate to achieve the triple-digit efficiency and quality jumps promised by CIM vendors and their proponents. So they bit off more than they could chew with huge investments in computerized hardware and software that weren't adequately planned or installed and didn't mesh properly. [*Ward's Auto World*, 1986, p. 9]

Can Exit and Voice Coexist?

The previous section showed that while the exit strategy maximizes customer bargaining power, the voice strategy maximizes most types of technical change. Therefore, there is a tradeoff between customer bargaining power and industry technical change.

One of Hirschman's main concerns is the effect of the use of one strategy on the fortunes of the other strategy. That is, what is the impact of the use of a problem-solving mechanism in one part of exit/voice space on the choices available at other times and to other parties? In *Exit, Voice, and Loyalty*, Hirschman emphasized the negative interaction between exit and voice; in particular, he stated, "the presence of the exit alternative can . . . *tend to atrophy the development of the art of voice*" (1970, p. 43).

While some access to exit is helpful in encouraging suppliers to "listen" to voice and otherwise avoid stagnation, too much exit has a negative impact both on voice and on system performance, for three reasons.

First, there is the demand-side effect that Hirschman emphasized: if those most able to change a situation are also those most able to escape from it, easy access to exit can preclude efforts to remedy inferior performance. For example, Hirschman pointed out that rich, education-oriented parents are often the first to remove their children from public schools when they deteriorate, leaving behind families who are less able to use either voice or exit; the schools may never recover.

An analogous situation occurs in the auto industry. The automakers are the agents most capable both of changing the situation of low-quality suppliers *and* of escaping from it, either by buying from firms nurtured under a voice system abroad (such as Japanese suppliers in the United States or overseas), or by abandoning production altogether and importing whole cars from Korea and Japan. Meanwhile, supplier firms, workers, and their communities are left to cope with the consequences of dislocation.[17]

The second reason that too much exit is bad for voice is that the presence of suppliers practicing what might be called "exit-based competition" (acceptance of low margins and little investment in building technological or organizational capability) can drive out suppliers who wish to practice voice-based competition. The need to compete with low-overhead suppliers of existing products (who continue to produce as long as price exceeds marginal cost) hinders the ability of other firms to invest in creating new products. In gasket production, for example, large firms such as Goodyear and General Tire were hindered in the amount they could invest in creating new (but nonpatentable) rubber compounds by the need to match the low prices of small firms who simply copied the big firms' designs. (interview with large rubber producer, November 1984).

Finally, because of the different organizational structures required, it is difficult for any one firm to practice both voice and exit on a large scale. Basically, the exit-based strategy requires the customer to invest a lot in design engineers and not much in internal communications, while the voice strategy requires expensive communication and evaluation systems and not many design engineers. The investments required are sufficiently large that it is not profitable for the customer to hedge its bets by maintaining the capability to use both exit and voice strategies simultaneously.

In many cases, U.S. automakers are moving toward adopting a voice strategy with their suppliers.[18] This transition from exit to voice is not without cost for automakers or suppliers. In order to achieve their newfound goal of increased technical progress, the Big Three must do more than just change the relative prices of innovation and other desired supplier actions. They must also change a *relationship*—incentive structures, expectations, and capabilities that have become "embedded" in the system over decades.[19]

To the extent that U.S. automakers adopt a voice strategy, they must dismantle many of the structures that kept barriers to entry low in their supplier industries. In order to make it administratively feasible to maintain a rich flow of information with suppliers, they are drastically reducing their supplier base; Ford cut the number of its suppliers from 5,000 in 1982 to 2,300 in July 1987.[20] Meanwhile, automakers are allowing some of their engineering capability to "atrophy"(as a Ford executive put it) in order to reduce fixed costs and take advantage of the quality improvements that result from having a supplier both design and produce a component.

Suppliers must develop new capabilities in order both to provide information to customers and to respond to customers' voice. In addition to participating in the design of their products and coordinating their subassembly, suppliers are expected to adopt statistical process control and just-in-time inventory techniques, both of which are manager-intensive innovations. Since for most suppliers in the past the incentives for innovative activity were few, they did not bother to develop innovative capability. This situation is not remedied overnight.[21]

A powerful incentive to participate in voice is a share of the joint profits that result from performance improvements. However, since many of the payoffs to voice are long-term and difficult to observe, trust is a prerequisite to making the necessary investments.

Unfortunately, decades of using the exit strategy means that U.S. automakers face a legacy of mistrust, due to their years of "cutting the legs out from under our suppliers," as one Ford executive put it (Interview at Ford Motor Company, World Headquarters, Dearborn, MI, August, 1985). One supplier executive, after citing several instances in which his firm had made investments in R&D on its products only to see another firm awarded the contract using his firm's design, described one of the auto companies in this way:

> They're nasty, abusive, and ugly. They would take a dime from a starving grandmother. They steal our innovations; they make uneconomic demands, like "follow us around the globe, and build plants near ours. We need good suppliers like you—but if you can't do it, we'll find somebody else."[22]

Interestingly, Japanese automakers operating in the United States face a challenge opposite to that faced by the U.S. Big Three. The Japanese must learn some of the skills developed by the exit strategy in order to transfer product designs to their American suppliers. Because Japanese suppliers have so much responsibility for continuous improvement of the product and process, Japanese automakers often can provide only vague specifications to their new U.S. suppliers. Several suppliers I interviewed during the summer of 1989 reported instances in which their Japanese customers admitted that their components met the specifications provided, but still wanted changes because they "didn't feel right."

Exit, Voice, and Transaction Costs

Oliver Williamson has developed a theory of organization form that "advance[s] the proposition that the economic institutions of capitalism have the main purpose and effect of economizing on transaction costs" (Williamson, 1985, p. 17).

Transaction-cost theory rests explicitly on the assumption that "in the beginning there were markets"; the only reason that this exit-based mechanism does not always suffice is the intervention of the "human factors" (H) of bounded rationality and opportunism and the "environmental conditions" (E) of uncertainty/complexity and asset specificity. The presence of these factors favors the "adaptive sequential decision making" allowed by vertical integration and some hybrid forms of organization (Williamson, 1975, 1985). Williamson's general model of the customer-firm's problem may be stated as follows:

$$\min_{O, X} C\,(T, X) + G\,(H\,(T), E\,(T), O, X)$$

That is, the firm's problem is to minimize the sum of production costs, C (which are a function of technology, T and output, X), and transaction costs, G which are a function of H, E, and organization form, O. Its only choice variables are O, organization form, and X, level of output.[23] Under these conditions, there is no incentive for the firm to act in an anti-social manner.

Changing organization form changes the level of transaction costs both directly and indirectly. Williamson looks only at the direct effects. That is, he assumes that levels of H and E are given, and then notes that a particular choice of O leads to a particular level of transaction costs. For example, a customer may face uncertainty about whether a supplier will deliver as scheduled. Transaction-cost analysis would suggest that one should take as given the probability that the supplier would not deliver on time, and then choose a form of organization (such as multiple suppliers) that would minimize the cost of this given level of uncertainty. Using similar logic, U.S. automakers were careful to avoid dependence on a sole source.

However, the choice of O also affects the level of transaction costs indirectly, by affecting H and E. Making H and E endogenous means that dominant firms can do both better and worse with respect to the social optimum as specified by transaction-cost economists. For example, Toyota managers faced with delivery problems tried to *reduce* the level of uncertainty—not to take this level as given—by working with suppliers to improve reliability. This strategy led to a different choice of organization form: sole (or nearly so) sourcing with extensive technical assistance.[24]

On the other hand, U.S. automakers chose an exit strategy that *created* transaction costs so as to minimize their suppliers' bargaining power. Dominant firms can exercise their power not only by directly giving orders to subordinates (as in a hierarchy), but also by structuring markets so as to affect the levels of H and E faced by upstream and downstream firms.

This paper has presented several such examples. One is that automakers created uncertainty about their future commitments to suppliers, so as to minimize their profit margins, even though this uncertainty also reduced supplier investment. In another example, automakers integrated difficult functions such as engineering and product design, so as to reduce barriers to entry in their supplier industries, despite the increase in bounded rationality entailed by this separation between design and execution.[25]

Williamson is willing to admit that socially nonoptimal forms of organization might exist. He insists, however, that efficiency is the "main case" (1986a, 1986b), and does not attempt to incorporate the exceptional cases into his theory. Instead, he invites opponents of this view to answer two questions: (1) under what conditions will inefficient forms of organization be selected, and (2) "Can a remedy be fashioned which yields net social gains?" (1986b, pp. 9, 15).

I believe that the exit/voice analysis presented above helps answer both questions. By relaxing the assumption that the determinants of transaction costs are exogenous, we can see that where performance improvements require large irreversible investments, powerful customers face a tradeoff between promoting technical change and maintaining bargaining power with their suppliers. We have looked at two determinants of this choice: (1) customer final-product market power, and (2) past supplier relations decisions.

If a firm is a member of a tight oligopoly (such as Detroit's Big Three), then the profits lost due to foregone technical change are small relative to those available by maintaining bargaining power. If the oligopoly is loose, then technical change will be favored, as in the automotive industries of postwar Europe and Japan, the United States before the 1920s,[26] and the global industry of today. The reason is that these firms have enough market power to give them the capability of making commitments to suppliers and establishing a rich flow of information, yet not so much that they lose the incentive to do so.[27]

Another determinant of a powerful customer's supplier relations strategy is its past decisions. As the previous section showed, there are high costs of switching strategies, because both customer and supplier must develop different capabilities and change their expectations about the other party's behavior.

It is well and good to find evidence of inefficiency; however, as Williamson points out, "Unless the condition can be remedied with net social gains, the distortion is (as an operational matter) simply a regrettable state of affairs" (1986b, p. 9).

On the basis of the above analysis, several policies can be recommended. Both exit and voice can be useful.

As argued above, the automakers' excessive market power led to reduced social welfare; effective antitrust action in the 1950s and 1960s might have prevented some of today's painful upheaval. Also, where large and irreversible investments are not necessary either to communicate the existence of a problem or to solve it, exit is a fine remedy. (This is often the case with radical innovations. For example, in recent years firms have solved their problem of lack of individual computing power by exiting from IBM mainframes in favor of personal computers from Apple.)

Voice, however, provides an opportunity to *reduce*, not just live with, the levels of bounded rationality, uncertainty, and opportunism that lead to transaction costs. Setting up mechanisms for voice-based supplier relationships both improves the flow of information, and reduces the need for explicit information transfer, by promoting trust and mutually familiar ways of doing things. Policies to promote "the development of the art of voice" include encouraging the development of regional networks of firms (Piore and Sabel, 1984) and reducing costs of switching from an exit system by providing assistance in such areas as electronic data interchange, just-in-time production techniques, statistical quality control, and value analysis/value engineering.[28]

One implication of the views described above is that industrial policy needs to be concerned with transforming the way that firms work internally, not just with picking winning industries or changing the broad parameters within which industries function. The networks of information and technological capability[29] that exist between firms (and among different divisions of large firms) are an important type of infrastructure, one that is just as crucial to economic development (and that has been just as neglected) as are roads, sewers, and bridges.

Conclusion

This paper has applied Hirschman's exit/voice framework to relationships between customer and supplier firms. This case is likely to be different in two ways from those analyzed by Hirschman, which largely involved individual consumers' responses to quality deterioration in firms and other organizations: (1) investment may well be required to achieve performance improvements, and (2) in many instances, customers are likely to be powerful relative to suppliers. This approach yields two contributions toward what might be called a general theory of exit and voice:

1. Where large irreversible investment is required to make performance improvements, a powerful customer will face a tradeoff between maximizing technical change and maintaining bargaining power with suppliers.

2. Exit and voice can be the cause, as well as the effect, of substandard performance. As discussed above, under the exit strategy, supplier investment

may well be too low. But parties who continue to use voice when they should exit will also run into trouble; an example would be a relationship that has focused on incremental improvements, that continues despite the availability of radically better techniques.

Exit/voice analysis also makes some contributions to the study of supplier relations:

First, it provides a classification scheme for modes of supplier relationships that allows for more than the extremes of "make" and "buy." The classification is based on the nature of problem solving rather than on financial considerations; the new criterion turns out to be more useful in predicting the effects of supplier relationships on the nature and rate of technical change.

Second, the exit/voice approach highlights the role of strategy in supplier relations decisions. A customer with final-product market power does not have to take as given the structure of its input markets. A powerful customer can choose to make profits by adopting a voice-based supplier relations strategy, which gives it a relatively small share of a pie made large through technical change, or an exit-based strategy, which gives the customer a large share at the expense of a small pie. That is, there is a conflict between *selecting* suppliers who offer the best deal at any given point in time (a strategy that requires a high ability to exit from current relationships) and *developing* vendors with improved capabilities (a strategy that requires a long-term commitment and the development of mechanisms for technical assistance and other types of administrative coordination).

Finally, by recognizing the endogeneity of the factors determining transaction costs and by showing conditions under which there is a tradeoff between bargaining power and innovation, exit/voice analysis provides a remedy for two of the serious weaknesses of the transaction-cost framework.

Notes

1. For citations from the "expanding sphere of influence" of exit/voice analysis, see Hirschman (1981, 1986).

2. I use the term "supplier" to encompass both financially independent downstream firms and vertically integrated downstream divisions. The analysis in this paper, however, focuses on the case of independent firms; for more on the case of vertical integration, see Helper (1987).

3. On the distinction between incentives and capabilities, see Lazonick (1990).

4. For more detail on the impact of supplier relations strategy on the internal organization of and relationships between customers and suppliers in the U.S. auto industry, see Helper (1987, 1990b).

5. Loyalty is not necessarily in conflict with our emphasis here on behavior that is profit maximizing, at least in outcome. Dore (1983) argues that a culturally based loyalty is key to Japanese economic success; in essence he says that commitment is more profit maximizing in effect when it is less profit maximizing in intent.

6. See, for example, Williamson (1975, 1985) and the articles cited in Kaserman (1978).

7. *Automotive News,* August 15, 1984, p. 3; interviews with James Meehan, Department of Economics, Colby College, April 1986 and with staff of former Fisher plants, November 1990. This example illustrates that the ability of a vertically integrated firm to "effect internal adaptations by fiat" (Williamson, 1985, p. 75) is not automatic; incentive systems must be carefully established and maintained.

8. In fact, during the heyday of the exit-based supplier relations system (1935–70), the automakers were quite successful at protecting their oligopoly rents from their suppliers; while the Big Three's returns on total assets were substantially above the manufacturing average. their suppliers' returns were not. Conversely, the UAW's sit-down strikes dramatically reduced the automakers' ability to exit from their suppliers of labor. Not surprisingly, auto workers *have* shared in their employers' good fortune, in the sense that automotive wages have consistently been higher than the manufacturing average (see Helper, 1990b).

9. I use the term "technical change" very broadly; I mean it to encompass invention, innovation, and diffusion of products and processes by both supplier and customer firms. I specifically wish to include organization innovations such as just-in-time production techniques and statistical quality control.

10. Schumpeter (1950) focused on only one type of commitment—that provided by market power. His analysis, however, extends more broadly.

11. See Lazonick (1990); Dasgupta and Stiglitz (1980).

12. On capital-market imperfections, see Stiglitz and Weiss (1981); on the expense of innovation in mature industries, see Abernathy (1978), Schumpeter (1950), and Galbraith (1967).

13. For a description of the survey methodology, see Helper (1991). The survey instrument was mailed to firms and divisions that account for almost all direct purchases in the United States by U.S.-owned automotive assemblers; 47 percent (453 firms) responded—an unusually high rate for a postal survey of firms.

14. An alternative interpretation is that long-term contracts are *the result of* investment; they don't cause it. That is, "good" or "skilled" firms seize upon investment opportunities and are rewarded for their performance with long-term contracts. However, research in progress using logistic regression shows that contract length remains a significant determinant (at the 0.01 level) of CNC use, even when one controls for such variables as (self-rated) skill at manufacturing engineering, incremental process improvement, and entirely new process introduction. That is, there are firms that are technically ready to make the investment (in the sense that they have the skills to use the technology), but do not do so because of institutional barriers.

15. Theoretically, a firm could act as a holding company for its vertically integrated divisions, but this seems impossible in practice. See Helper (1990b); Williamson (1985, p. 161); Hirschman (1986).

16. Of course, some technical changes (for example, the invention of the personal computer) require neither very much capital nor very much buyer-specific information exchange. However, these types of technical changes are less likely to be practical in a mature industry such as automobiles, in which huge investments in physical and organizational capital specific to a particular way of doing things have been built up over time. See Abernathy and Wayne (1974); Abernathy and Clark (1985); and Clark (1985a).

17. On autoworkers' attempts to avoid and cope with dislocation, see Helper (1990a).

18. The rationale behind this change is explored in Helper (1990b): Before the import challenge of the 1970s, three firms (General Motors, Ford, and Chrysler) shared control of the U.S. auto industry, so they were free to choose a supplier relations strategy at the high buyer bargaining power/low technical change end of the tradeoff. With the entry of the Japanese and European automakers producing high-quality, innovative products, U.S.

automakers no longer were able to make profits by minimizing supplier bargaining power at the expense of quality and innovation. This analysis thus attributes the change in supplier relations not to the rectification of errors caused by past bad management, but rather to a change in the strategy that maximized profits.

19. On "embeddedness," see Granovetter (1985).

20. *Chemical Week,* November 11, 1987, p. 10; *Wall Street Journal,* February 23, 1988, p. 22. Similar figures could be cited for General Motors and Chrysler.

21. On the difficulties of the transition, see Helper (1987, chap. 5; 1990b, and 1991).

22. While the above is an extreme view, only 7 percent of the 1989 survey respondents reported that their "customer always treats us fairly." The average was 3.1, squarely in the middle of a scale where 1 was "can't depend on customer to treat us fairly" and 5 was "customer always treats us fairly." Both of these perceptions were unchanged from five years ago (Helper, 1991).

23. Riordan and Williamson (1985) allow the level of asset specificity to be set endogenously, but continue to assume that it is set efficiently.

24. On the development of just-in-time production philosophy at Toyota, see Cusumano (1985).

25. One blatant example was the automakers' common practice when a supplier designed a part of recopying it onto their paper and then releasing the design back to the same supplier. This process strengthened the automakers' claim to the design, but in the days of hand copying, often introduced mistakes into the drawing and certainly increased cost (Flynn, 1986).

26. On voice relationships in Europe, see Shapiro (1985) and Lamming (1989); in Japan, see Asanuma (1985), Smitka (1989), Nishiguchi (1990), and Odaka, Ono, and Adachi (1988); in the early U.S. auto industry, see Helper (1990c).

27. The story for other types of market structure and other types of institutions is more complicated. I am currently investigating these issues with Bernard Elbaum of the University of Santa Cruz.

28. Value analysis/value engineering is a technique that can lead to significant cost reductions and performance improvements through careful consideration of the cost and functionality of detailed aspects of a part's design. For greatest effectiveness, it requires extensive sharing of information between the supplier, who has expertise in producing the part, and the customer, who understands how the part fits into the product as a whole. See Dobler, Lee, and Burt (1984, chap. 15) for more on value analysis, and Asanuma (1985) for detailed discussion of its application in the Japanese auto industry.

29. That is, the "backward and forward linkages," to use another bit of Hirschman terminology.

References

Abernathy, W. 1978. *The Productivity Dilemma.* Baltimore: Johns Hopkins University Press.

Abernathy, W., and K. Clark. 1985. "Mapping the Winds of Creative Destruction." *Research Policy* 14 (February): 3–22.

Abernathy, W., K. Clark, and A. Kantrow. 1983. *Industrial Renaissance.* New York: Basic Books.

Abernathy, W., and K. Wayne. 1974. "The Limits of the Learning Curve." *Harvard Business Review* 52 (September–October): 109–19.

Andrea, David, Mark Everett, and Dan Luria. 1988. "Automobile Company Parts Sourcing: Implications for Michigan Suppliers." Ann Arbor, MI: Industrial Technology Institute. Xerox.

Asanuma, B. 1985. "The Organization of Parts Purchases in the Japanese Automotive Industry." *Japanese Economic Studies* 13 (Summer): 32–53.

Clark, K. 1985. "Managing Technology in International Competition: The Case of Product Development in Response to Foreign Entry." Harvard Business School Working Paper, Boston, MA.

Cusumano, M. 1985. *The Japanese Automobile Industry*. Cambridge, MA: Harvard University Press.

Dasgupta, P., and A. Stiglitz. 1980. "Uncertainty, Industrial Structure, and the Speed of R&D." Bell *Journal of Economics* 11:128–41.

Dobler, D., L. Lee, and D. Burt. 1984. *Purchasing and Materials Management*, 2nd ed. New York: McGraw-Hill.

Dore, R. 1983. "Goodwill and the Spirit of Market Capitalism." *British Journal of Sociology* 34, 4:459–82.

Flynn, M. 1986. "Engineering Outsourcing." *AIM Newsletter* 2 (November): 5–7.

Galbraith, J.K. 1967. *The New Industrial State*. Boston: Houghton Mifflin.

Granovetter, M. 1985. "Economic Action and Social Structure: A Theory of Embeddedness." *American Journal of Sociology* 91 (November): 481–510.

Helper, S. 1987. "Supplier Relations and Technical Change: Theory and Application to the U.S. Auto Industry." Ph.D. dissertation, Department of Economics, Harvard University.

———. 1990a. "Responses to Subcontracting: Innovative Labor Strategies" *Labor Research Review* #15 (April): 89–99.

———. 1990b. "Strategy and Irreversibility in Supplier Relations: The Case of the U.S. Automobile Industry." *Business History Review*, forthcoming.

———. 1990c. "Comparative Supplier Relations in the U.S. and Japanese Automobile Industries." Business History Conference, Johns Hopkins University, Baltimore, March.

———. 1991. "Supplier Relations at a Crossroads: Results of Survey Research in the U.S. Automobile Industry." *Sloan Management Review* (forthcoming).

Helper, S., and R. Leone. 1989. "Strategic Procurement: Using an Administrative Function for Strategic Advantage." Boston University. Photocopy.

Hirschman, A. 1970. *Exit, Voice, and Loyalty*. Cambridge, MA: Harvard University Press.

———. 1981. *Essays in Trespassing: Economics to Politics and Beyond*. Cambridge: Cambridge University Press.

———. 1986. *Rival Views of Market Society and Other Recent Essays*. New York: Viking.

Kaserman, D. 1978. "Theories of Vertical Integration: Implications for Antitrust Policy." *Antitrust Bulletin* 23 (Fall): 483–510.

Klein, B., R. Crawford, and A. Alchian. "Vertical Integration, Appropriable Quasi-Rents, and the Competitive Contracting Process." *Journal of Law and Economics* 297.

Lamming, R. 1989. "The Causes and Effects of Structural Change in the European Automotive Components Industry." Working Paper, International Motor Vehicle Program, Massachusetts Institute of Technology, Cambridge, MA.

Lazonick, W. 1990. *The Myth of the Market Economy*. Cambridge: Cambridge University Press.

Nishiguchi, Toshihiro. 1990. "Japanese Subcontracting: The Evolution Towards Flexibility." D.Phil. thesis, University of Oxford.

Odaka, K., K. Ono, F. Adachi. 1988. *The Automobile Industry in Japan: A Study of Ancillary Firm Development*. Oxford: Oxford University Press.

Piore, M., and C. Sabel. 1984. *The Second Industrial Divide*. New York: Basic Books.

Porter, M. 1983. *Cases in Competitive Strategy.* New York: Free Press.

Riordan, M., and O. Williamson. 1985. "Asset Specificity and Economic Organization." *International Journal of Industrial Organization* 3: 365–78.

Scherer, F. 1980. *Industrial Market Structure and Economic Performance.* Chicago: Rand McNally.

Schumpeter, J. 1950. *Capitalism, Socialism, and Democracy.* New York: Harper & Row.

Shapiro, R. 1985. "Toward Effective Vendor Management: International Comparisons." Harvard Business School Working Paper.

Smitka, M. 1989. "Competitive Ties: Subcontracting in the Japanese Automobile Industry." Ph.D. dissertation, Department of Economics, Yale University, New Haven, CT.

Stiglitz, J., and A. Weiss. 1981. "Credit Rationing in Markets with Imperfect Information." *American Economics Review* 71:393–410.

Ward's Auto World. 1986. "CIM Falls Short" (August): 8–9.

Williamson, O. 1975. *Markets and Hierarchies.* New York: Free Press.

———. 1976. "The Economics of Internal Organization: Exit and Voice in Relation to Markets and Hierarchies." *American Economic Review* 66 (May): 369–77.

———. 1985. *The Economic Institutions of Capitalism.* New York: Free Press.

———. 1986a. "Economics and Sociology: Promoting a Dialog." Yale University Working Paper, Series D, #25.

———. 1986b. "Transaction Cost Economics: The Comparative Contracting Perspective." Yale University Working Paper, Series D, #29.

7

Policy Analysis

20

AMITAI ETZIONI

The Moral Dimension
in Policy Analysis

A policy analyst suggested that in order to reduce the incidence of skin cancer in the United States, blacks ought to be asked to occupy the seats on the sunny side of sports arenas (blacks are supposed to be biologically less sensitive to the sun rays). The analyst added that he recognizes such a policy would encounter "some social difficulty in implementation." From an efficiency perspective alone (or, narrow utilitarianism), it is difficult to fault the suggested policy. It would clearly raise the total well-being of society at a low cost. Some would argue that policies should be designed in such a way that they improve the well-being of some, but only as long as they do not reduce the well-being of any. This is a possibly worthy rule, but it is practically always impossible to follow. Attempts to fault the proposal on grounds of inefficiency (the policy may lead to riots and hence to high costs) fail because the estimated probability of such riots is undetermined or low. Instead, most would reject the policy on the basis of our first reaction, our moral intuition; it *sounds* outrageous. On examination, we would reject it because it is unfair to ask those who have suffered long and still do, to take on yet one more burden (a disproportionately small but yet additional amount of skin cancer), in order to help a group that has historically imposed many disadvantages on the targeted minority, the blacks. Many also oppose policies that deliberately impose an illness on a specific group of people, especially one defined by racial criteria. The suggested policy is therefore judged morally inappropriate even if it is efficient.

Another policy option highlighting the same points is the suggestion to hang each year, at random, one hundred drug dealers in order to reduce the sale of illegal drugs (Kleiman, 1988, pp. 14, 16). When this policy idea was discussed at a seminar on values and public policy at the John F. Kennedy School of Govern-

---

This article grew out of an extensive dialogue with Mark Kleiman. The author is indebted to Judith Lurie for editorial assistance.

ment, a professor of ethics suggested, to further point out the moral unacceptability of such a proposal, that since drug dealers are hardened souls, they already accept the risk of death as part of their trade—hanging drug *users* would cut even more drug sales and would therefore be more efficient.

Both of these proposals conflict with the values most Americans adhere to, which suggest that we not hang people because of transactional crimes (as distinct from those directly and deliberately involved with the taking of life). Furthermore, these values reject (as a matter of principle) deliberately meting out harsher punishments to those chosen at random, compared to the others who committed the same crime. For the same reason, most Americans oppose shooting *young*, likely recidivistic offenders, which would be much less costly than paying for their jail terms, even though from a narrow efficiency perspective, with jail terms costing $20,000 per year or more per offender, the younger the offender, the higher the saving that would result from executions.

These policy proposals are extreme, perverse products of a thinking that extols efficiency and leaves moral judgments to individuals who, it is assumed, express their preferences through the market, an approach that forswears moral consideration. True, most—indeed, practically all—neoclassical economists and other neoclassicists would be quick to reject these policy proposals. Nevertheless, it is not accidental that those few who explore them are neoclassicists; the extolling of efficiency *über alles* points in this direction of narrow utilitarianism and consequentialism.

We strive to significantly correct this way of thinking with a paradigm based on a deontological ethic, one that sees individuals as responding to moral and social values, in *addition* to rational drives toward maximizing utility, and one that encompasses moral examination in its framework. A new discipline, socio-economics, combines analysis of economics and efficiency with factors of social and moral values. By viewing human motivations as *co*determined (by a quest for economy or efficiency and by moral\social factors), socio-economics seeks to improve the descriptive and normative bases of policy analysis.

We turn below to the many questions that come to mind. Where does one find these moral factors? Why have they been missing from policy analysis? What, more specifically, do they represent? According to *whose* moral values should one evaluate and design policy? Once the applicable moral values are located, how are their conflicting claims to be balanced? How can one reach one policy conclusion when the validity of two criteria—efficiency and morality—are recognized?

Omnipresence of the Moral Dimension

For the policy proposals discussed so far, the relevance of the moral dimension seems quite evident. When the moral intuition reacts rather strongly, it is not very taxing to explicate, nor is it difficult to provide its basis in careful reasoning and established moral principles. Normally, though, the moral dimension is not as obvious, nor is the moral judgment. Nevertheless, rarely, if ever, is the moral dimension absent, and furthermore, it requires a separate mode of analysis above and beyond the evaluation of efficiency. True, some proposals are highly technical, such as whether we should paint highway dividing lines white or yellow; and they seem to lack a moral dimension. These are, however, implementing decisions, not true *policy* proposals. In effect, we cannot come up with a single genuine policy proposal in which the moral dimension is not present. For instance, as a rule, changes in economic policy affect some groups differently than others, as illustrated by inflation, an often cited example, which hurts pensioners (because of their inflexible incomes) more than workers (whose pay tends to rise with prices). Hence, economists regularly make equity decisions that have moral implications: Should we hurt groups X, Y, and Z to advance groups A, B, and C ? Similarly, many policies affect the environment (often considered a "public" good): Should we allow it to be diminished? By how much? How fast? Also related are labor policies, such as giving employees decision-making opportunities, which have the potential to raise human dignity and self-esteem.

A typical example of the presence of the moral dimension is the policy debate over whether or not to raise the speed limit on highways. In part, the question is one of cost-benefit analysis of efficiency. The more time we spend on the road, due to slower driving, the higher the costs of the policy because we "waste" people's valuable time and spend more money in truckers' wages (Kamerud, 1988, pp. 343, 346). In part, it is a question of moral judgment: should we deliberately reset a public policy that saves lives to one that saves fewer lives?

Reductionism

Throughout human thought, from the Cynics to Karl Marx to Gary Becker, attempts have been made to deny the significance or autonomy of the moral dimension. In the neoclassical tradition little to no room is left for authentic altruism or other "pure" moral motivations. At every step utilitarian thinking imputes some calculating motive and hence, diminishes the moral dimension; every action is depicted as a result of self-interest. An early tale captures the approach: when Thomas Hobbes was asked why he gave money to a beggar, and whether this was not due to Christian ethics, he responded that he did so, "with the sole intent of relieving his own misery at the sight of the beggar" (Losco, 1986, p. 323).

Neoclassical policy analysts do not normally deny the presence of the moral dimension, but they often argue that we need not study moral and social values as a *separate* category because they are already reflected in the preferences; and one need not study what "lurks" behind these preferences. "In the usual neoclassical formulation, a person is simply a bundle of preferences, and his moral ideals, if they enter the analysis at all, enter simply as some among his preferences—his taste for honesty being on a par with his taste for peanut-butter" (McPherson, 1984, p. 243). Hence, when the utilitarian model heaps all preferences and desires into one pile and attributes them to self-interest, it, in effect, absorbs the moral dimension and loses it in the shuffle.

Moreover, these attempts to reduce moral motivations into self-interested efficiency drives break down both in the face of much evidence to the contrary (Mansbridge, forthcoming) and everyday examples. A poignant example: by standard exchange theory, the husband or wife of an ailing Alzheimer's patient has no reason to stay with his or her mate; they get nothing in return. Victims of Alzheimer's (a disease without as much as a dim hope for a cure) slowly lose their memory, first of events and names of simple objects, until finally they cannot recognize even those members of their own family who care for them. Eventually, they require constant care, and become incontinent and abusive. This means spouses of these patients labor and nurse with no promise of reciprocal care, no thanks, or even worse, with abuse in return. Nevertheless, nearly all husbands and wives of Alzheimer's patients stay with their spouses throughout their illness. Exchange theorists may try to explain this behavior by arguing that they stay rather than endure the neighbors' gossip. Yet weighed against all of the hardships endured in caring for an Alzheimer's patient, this argument seems quite unconvincing. People seem to stay mainly because it is the right thing to do. That is, certain courses of action present themselves to these individuals as morally necessary (see Fried, 1964).

Voting behavior serves as further evidence. Neoclassicists argue that normally there is little reason for people to vote because they get nothing in exchange; they cannot reasonably expect that their vote will make a difference. They may vote, therefore, only when the election is close, when they feel their individual vote will make a difference. There is, however, only weak evidence in support of this correlation between voter turnout and closeness of the election. And, obviously, many millions vote when the elections are not close. *The* explanatory and predicting factor, on the contrary, turns out to be a moral commitment: people vote because they feel it is their "civic duty" (Barry, 1978, p. 17).

The Multiple Self

Utilitarian neoclassical psychology, with its view of individuals as orderly and rational bundles of preferences and desires, is similarly reductionistic. These psychologists assume that people are unitary, that they are driven by one overriding preference (usually for "pleasure" or some other monistic "utile"). Deontological psychology, on the other hand, recognizes that, like policy proposals, people also have a moral dimension. It is increasingly realized that humans, unlike animals, are constituted of "multiple selves" (Elster, 1985): Their behavior is controlled by two layers of preferences, one (the meta-preference) used to evaluate the other (the regular preference), and that when these two come into conflict, a typical struggle ensues. The simple statement, "I would *like* to go to a movie, but I *ought* to visit my friend in the hospital," captures the common tension. Moral values are the most important source of these scrutinizing meta-preferences.

While it is possible to study the forces behind the two levels of preferences systematically, the outcome of the struggle rarely lands on one side or the other. Rather, human behavior is frequently conflicting and not consolidated; choices are multifaceted events. If the friend is neglected, guilt nags; if the movie is skipped today it may appeal more strongly the next time a duty calls. Typically the presence of the moral dimension is reflected in terms of "ought" statements and thoughts (although not all "ought" statements are morally based). For example, the testimony, "I would like to spend more money now (say, on a car) but ought to save so as not to be dependent on the government or my children," reflects its influence. Policy analysis, to be accurate and normatively effective, ought to encompass this conflict. Policies should be designed to appeal to moral values; and policies ought to be evaluated in terms of their moral standing (in addition to the efficiency factors). For example, the government may appeal to the public's obligation to future generations to encourage saving, a policy that generates no immediate pleasure. Relying only on economic factors—say, tax deductions for those who save in IRAs—is both limited in appeal and costly, if a sense of obligation can carry part of the policy load. Since two major kinds of factors affect people, policies should encompass both.

What Belongs in the Moral Dimension?

If a major source of meta-preferences is moral, how does one distinguish between moral and other voices? Despite many hundreds of years of difficult labor, philosophers have still not produced a fully satisfactory definition of what is moral. Many, though, agree that statements are to be viewed as moral if they meet the following four criteria: first, persons who act on the basis of moral meta-preferences sense that they "must" behave in the prescribed way. Their moral acts are experienced as "*imperatives,*" things they must do because they are obligated, duty-bound. Most of us are familiar introspectively with this experience, doing something because it is right, as distinguished from doing it because it is enjoyable.

The notion of an imperative is supported by the observation that people set aside certain realms as commanding a special, compelling status. Durkheim (1947) points to the fact that people treat certain acts as "sacred" (which need not mean religious). Such sacred moral principles characteristically repudiate the instrumental rationality that includes cost-benefit analysis: for example, people feel obligated to save a life or donate blood without calculating the potential payoffs (Goodin, 1980).

The need for additional criteria to characterize moral acts arises out of the fact that there can also be nonmoral imperatives, for example, obsessions with a forlorn love or even with an object, such as an illegal drug or a fetish. The addition of a second and third criterion helps here to separate moral imperatives from others (Childress, 1977).

Second, individuals who act morally are *able to generalize* their behavior—they are able to justify an act to others and to themselves by pointing to general rules. Statements such as "because I want it" or "I need it badly" do not meet this criterion because no generalization is entailed. "Do unto others as you wish others to do unto you," on the other hand, is a prime example of a generalized rule.

Third, moral preferences must be *symmetrical* in that there must be a willingness to accord other comparable people, under comparable circumstances, the same standing or right. (Otherwise, the moral dictum is rendered arbitrary. Such an arbitrary rule would state, "This rule applies to Jane but not to Jim although there is no relevant difference between them.") Racist ideologies, although they otherwise have the appearance of moral systems, in that they are compelling (to their believers) and possibly generalizable, fail to qualify as moral by this test.

Finally, moral preferences *affirm or express a commitment,* rather than involve the consumption of a good or a service. Therefore, they are intrinsically motivated and not subject to means-end analysis (Dyke, 1981, p. 11). (The fact that there are nonmoral acts that are intrinsically motivated does not invalidate this criterion. It only shows that the universe of such acts is larger than that of moral acts, and hence, as was already indicated, this criterion is necessary but not sufficient in itself.) As for the argument that moral acts themselves are not impulsive acts but reflect deliberations and judgments (especially evident when one must sort out what course to follow when one is subject to conflicting moral claims), these deliberations are not of the same kind as a means-end considerations; they require judgments among moral ends.

Whose Morals?

These criteria are useful in excluding some claims on moral appropriateness, for example, authoritarian statements like "I did it because the president ordered" are rejected because they are not symmetrical. Also, those claims derived from some version of humanistic psychology, "Because it feels right," can properly be excluded because they are not generalizable. This still leaves open the question: according to whose morals should policy alternatives be evaluated?

Combining the above-described criteria with a coherent moral theory discriminates the field of applicable moral judgments one step further. The result, though, depends on which moral theory one embraces. One theory, not widely shared in the contemporary United States, holds that there is an *absolute* set of values (sometimes referred to as "natural") by which we all must abide. Some religious thinkers, for example, may insist that the Ten Commandments are an absolute moral code, applicable to all people in all circumstances. In secular circles, absolute moral codes have been embodied in France's revolutionary Declaration of the Rights of Man and later in the American Declaration of Independence in the belief in the "natural" equality of all men and their consequent rights to freedom, security, and the pursuit of happiness (McDonald, 1984, p. 27). Contemporary libertarians extrapolate individual rights from these fundamental doctrines—basic laws considered valid "natural facts" irrespective of their societal context and despite the fact that they cannot be verified.

Another position, and one that takes its lead from empirical data rather than from dogmatic reasoning, asserts that there is a *universal* set of values that all people reaffirm. Those include the value of life, health, human dignity, even comfort. Inkeles and Smith (1974), for instance, found that people in very different cultures wanted basically the same things. After an extensive empirical study of the impact of modernity on six Third World countries, they conclude that:

> These separate cultures may give the individual personalities in each distinctive context, but we believe those cultures do not alter the basic principles which govern the structuring of personality in all men. We believe certain pan-human patterns of response persist in the face of variability in culture content. These transcultural similarities in the psychic properties of individuals provide the basis for a common response to common stimuli. [p. 12]

Various attempts have been made to construct lists of these basic human needs. Some of those traits may be the universal desire for affection (solidarity, love); recognition (self-esteem, approval); context (orientation, meaning); and repeated gratification (the length of time varies, but all people seem to demand rewards for their activities) (Maslow, 1954; Etzioni, 1968, pp. 623–26).

Many hold that values are relative to particular cultures and periods. Still, they are not without guidance; they can draw on a procedural position. They use the consensus in the community for which the policy is intended as their guide to what is morally appropriate. Accordingly, for most issues, if the legislature enacted a law—after proper deliberations and a vote—we normally owe it allegiance even if we disagree with its content. The consensus method encompasses not only shared values, but also a recognition of the right to differ on certain matters (e.g., it leaves room for conscientious objections even if the war is declared legitimate)—even to engage in civil disobedience. Still, on most matters, for most people, at most times, consensus forms the moral standard.

In addition, when the relevant community cannot reach a consensus, policy analysts may turn to *moral reasoning* to help form a consensus or serve as guidance in its absence. This branch of ethics provides guidance on how to sort out what is morally appropriate when there are conflicting moral claims. Typically, moral reasoning draws on competing ethical theories (act and rule utilitarianism; act and rule deontology, and so on; see Beauchamp, 1982). One may use one or a mix of those competing theories to sort out which position to follow.

Granted, this might be difficult to accomplish because it leaves open to justification choosing the general moral principle from which the reasoning takes off. The Harvard Business School uses a Braniff "case," in which a new CEO was brought in to rescue Braniff (close to bankruptcy). A potential customer called and asked whether the airline would be in operation for months hence. The CEO responded that he was not quite sure. Some students in the class wondered whether the CEO should not have lied, should have said boldly that Braniff will indeed continue to fly. This question led to a 1988–89 faculty seminar on Truth Telling with Harvard's Dennis Thompson, Tom Schelling, Sissela Bok, and twenty others (including the author) participating. In this seminar, utilitarians argued that the CEO should have told the truth only if a "calculus" of harm would indicate that it would cause less harm than telling a lie. In the case at hand, because his statement was likely to hurt employees, stock and bond holders, and the community (and benefit "only" the consumers), lies seemed justified. On the other hand, deontologists (the author included) sided with Kant, and argued that the CEO should not have lied. He might have stated that he would do his very best to keep the airline flying, without violating a binding duty to be truthful. In short, as the case illustrates, which ethical theory one embraces will color one's ethical reasoning and policy conclusions.

A different form of moral reasoning seems more suitable. One can start off with a well-established principle and use it to sort out conflicting claims. Goodin (1989, pp. 574–624) provides an important example when he asks, whose rights should prevail, those of the smoker or of the nonsmoker? The issue is, of course, relevant to the formulation of such policies as prohibition of smoking in public facilities (offices, schools, buses, trains, and planes) as well as public support of antismoking messages (banning ads, stronger Surgeon General warnings). Goodin suggests that the rights of nonsmokers should take precedence; his reasoning takes off from the moral position that one's liberty does not entail a freedom to violate another's. He quotes the popular expression: "My right to stretch out my fist ends at your nose." Therefore, since the conduct of the nonsmoker does not violate the smoker, but that of the smoker does violate the nonsmoker (literally enters his or her nose), Goodin concludes sovereignty should be given to the rights of the nonsmoker.

To the extent that a policy proposal promotes some value already endorsed by the community, its acceptance is "homefree." When such a consensus is absent, however, values cannot simply be inserted into the population in order to foster approval of the policy; the moral principles must come first, followed by policies that build on them. Or the policy analyst may draw on his or her own values and promote a policy based explicitly on his or her opinion, without attempting to legitimize it through consensus. Finally, policies may be presented on a menu of options, each in accord with respective moral standards. For example, to promote

public health, a policy analyst may suggest that either the industry should introduce voluntary warning labels about the dangers to fetuses of pregnant women
consuming alcohol, or the government should impose such labels.

Moral Appropriateness and Efficiency

Our discussion so far has focused on the moral dimension because it is often
neglected. This is not to suggest, however, that it ought to replace considerations
of efficiency, or that the latter are inappropriate. Rather, the point is that policy
analysis ought to encompass both kinds of considerations. Thus, when cost-
benefit analysis points to opportunities for significant economies, and there are
no moral hindrances, this factor surely should guide policy.

Consider as an example the findings on the lives saved by expenditures on
encouraging citizens to wear seat belts compared with lives saved by expenditures on improving drivers' skills. The Public Health Service estimated that its
program to encourage seat belt use, which cost $2 million from 1968 to 1972,
averted nearly 23,000 deaths over that period, resulting in a "cost-per-death-
averted" of $87; in contrast, driver education programs, which ran $750.5 million over the same period, were estimated to have prevented a little over 8,500
deaths, or $88,000 per death averted (Drew, 1967, p. 16). As long as we agree
that education to use seat belts voluntarily is not morally inferior to other modes
of driver education, seat belts are clearly to be preferred.

We argue that analysis ought to proceed on two levels: considerations of costs
and benefits or other indications of efficiency, and of moral appropriateness. For
example, a recent study on the costs of smoking and drinking approached the
problem from both perspectives (Manning et al., 1989). From a narrow efficiency viewpoint, the study found that taxes on cigarettes are high enough because they more than pay for their harms (the external costs to society are $0.15
per pack, but taxes are set at $0.37 per pack) because a pack of cigarettes
increases medical costs but reduces life expectancy by 137 minutes, lowering the
amount of pension payments collected. But when the study broadened its pur-
view to encompass moral criteria, it found reasons that might support raising the
taxes on cigarettes. One argument is that even if one accepts uncritically that one
ought not to interfere in private choices, there is still some room to consider it
morally appropriate to act to discourage smoking. The authors point out that the
young, when they "choose" to smoke—and become addicted—often are not
fully informed about the consequences of their choice; hence, to help them stop
smoking is, in effect, to act according to their latent preference (our terminology,
not theirs). Second, the fact that many smokers try to quit signals their "true"
desire. It would be quite a different matter to, say, impose chastity upon them,
since there is little indication that this is what they desire.

There is no reason to argue that it is logically necessary or productive to
assume that there are only two main sources of evaluation and no others may be

considered. For example, aesthetic satisfaction might be another criterion (something might be efficient, moral, and—ugly). The main question, though, is not whether one can discern a third (or fourth, or fifth) utility in addition to efficiency and moral values, but whether one can keep the *number small*, to avoid overdetermination, to preserve parsimony. And one must ask for *the criteria* for introducing into one's paradigm new utilities versus subsuming an observed motive, drive, or preference in a utility that is already a member of one's paradigm or theory.

In part, the question is pragmatic. Criteria of evaluation are not found in nature or on location in the brain; they are concepts we introduce to organize our thinking and the evidence we generate. The question, hence, is in part a matter of what "works," what is productive. No attempt is made here to formulate a list of evaluative concepts. It is sufficient to establish that a multiple but small number is preferable to one, and to a larger list. (For additional discussion, see Etzioni, 1988, chaps. 2 and 3). Here we limit the discussion to two, although the procedures for three or four are not basically different.

The question arises: once each analysis is completed in its own track, so to speak, how does one proceed? To the extent that a particular policy proposal is both more efficient and morally appropriate than another (or than an existing policy in place)—say, one enables people to get off welfare and to gain meaningful and well-paying work, without neglecting their children—there is obviously no difficulty. To the extent that a policy is both morally unacceptable and inefficient (compared to some others), again, the choice (assuming all other things being equal) is easy.

In cases when the two criteria are pointing in opposite directions, however, when one is very strong and the other weak, the stronger will tend to, and often ought to, carry. For example, few would favor retaining a profit-making corporation to arrange for executions (Donahue, 1989).

In other situations the moral and efficiency considerations collide head-on. A recent discussion in the *New York Times* (Mydans, 1989, p. A1) of new policies to combat drug abuse provides examples of both kinds. Among the drug enforcement policies considered by some to be relatively less offensive is the suggestion in Washington, DC, to ban loitering and gathering in a group of two or more in certain areas of the city. Among those policies considered by the author of the article to be "more extreme" is the proposal to allow public whippings.

When the two criteria strongly conflict, when what is much more efficient is significantly more morally dubious, or what is more morally preferred is significantly less efficient than some other policy, the typical result is a deadlock. For example, we do not expect the more extreme antidrug policy to be implemented. Temporary inaction is an intelligent policy conclusion under these circumstances. For example, the Supreme Court frequently defers hearing cases on issues not deemed ripe for consideration. Congress and other legislatures often "table" issues, bottle them up in committees, go through first and second but not final readings, etc. True, other purposes are served this way. However, clearly such a stance is neither unusual nor without merit. Policy analysts should recommend it more often.

In such cases, the first obligation of the policy analysts is to inform the client and/or community of the conflict and urge a quest for a third alternative or limited partial resolutions, which circumvent the problem. (Before abortion was legalized, it was allowed in certain states for women under unusual stress.) In the meantime, an effort is made to evolve consensus, push for new technological development (e.g., the French pill), change economic conditions, or alter some other major factor that will allow a resolution to the stalemate by enabling a policy option that is efficient and morally appropriate.

Conclusion

In conclusion, we agree with Hirshman (1984): there can be too much parsimony. Policy analysis surely suffers when only criteria of efficiency are introduced, and moral considerations are either ignored or lumped together with myriad other considerations. Specifically, we suggest that each policy ought to be examined from at least two distinct viewpoints: its efficiency and its moral appropriateness. This view draws on the recognition that human nature is best perceived not as a unitary bundle of preferences, but as a multiple self, one in which meta-preferences vie with preferences over who will control behavior. The most important sources of meta-preferences are moral and social values. While these do not always provide an unambiguous guideline, philosophers have developed criteria to distinguish what is moral from what is not, and have even found ways to deal with conflicting moral claims.

How is one to combine the two (often conflicting) criteria into one policy conclusion? When the two criteria are mutually enforcing (i.e., the action is both moral and efficient, or neither), it is rather easy (although additional considerations may intrude); when one provides a strong endorsement and the other a weak hindrance, the conclusion is still relatively evident. In those cases in which the two criterion clash head-on ("deadlock"), a search for other alternatives is called for.

References

Barry, Brian. 1978. *Sociologists, Economists, and Democracy.* Chicago: University of Chicago Press.

Beauchamp, Tom. 1982. *Philosophical Ethics: Introduction to Moral Philosophy.* New York: McGraw-Hill.

Childress, James F. 1977. "The Identification of Ethical Principles." *Journal of Religious Ethics* 5, 1:39–68.

Donahue, John. 1989. *The Privatization Decision: Public Ends, Private Means.* New York: Basic Books.

Drew, Elizabeth. 1967. "HEW Grapples with PBS." *Public Interest* 8:9–29.
Durkheim, Emile. 1947. *The Division of Labor in Society*. Glencoe, IL: Free Press.
Dyke, C. 1981. *Philosophy of Economics*. Engelwood Cliffs, NJ: Prentice Hall.
Elster, Jon. 1985. *The Multiple Self*. Cambridge: Cambridge University Press.
Etzioni, Amitai. 1968. *The Active Society*. New York: Free Press.
————. 1988. *The Moral Dimension: Toward a New Economics*. New York: Free Press.
Fried, Charles. 1964. "Moral Causation." *Harvard Law Review*. 77, 77 (May): 1258–70.
Goodin, Robert E. 1980. "Making Moral Incentives Pay." *Policy Sciences* 12 (August): 131–45.
————. 1989. "The Ethics of Smoking." *Ethics* 99:574–624.
Hirshman, Albert O. 1984. "Against Parsimony: Three Easy Ways of Complicating Some Categories of Economic Discourse." *Bulletin: The American Academy of Arts and Sciences* 37, 8 (May): 11–28.
Inkeles, Alex, and David H. Smith. 1974. *Becoming Modern: Individual Change in Six Developing Countries*. Cambridge, MA: Harvard University Press.
Kamerud, Dana. 1988. "Benefits and Costs of the 55 MPH Speed Limit: New Estimates and Their Implications." *Journal of Policy Analysis and Management* 7 (Winter): 341–52.
Kleiman, Mark. 1988. "Dead Wrong." *New Republic,* September 26, 1988, pp. 14, 16.
Losco, Joseph. 1986. "Understanding Altruism: A Critique and Proposal for Integrating Various Aproaches." *Political Psychology* 7, 2:323–48.
Manning, Willard G. et al. 1989. "The Taxes of Sin: Do Smokers and Drinkers Pay Their Way?" *Journal of the American Medical Association* 261, 11:1604–9.
Mansbridge, Jane. 1989. *Beyond Self-Interest*. Chicago: University of Chicago Press.
Maslow, Abraham H. 1954. *Motivation and Personality*. New York: Harper Press.
McDonald, Margaret. 1984. "Natural Rights." In Jeremy Waldron, ed., *Theories of Rights*. New York: Oxford University Press.
McPherson, Michael S. 1984. "On Shelling, Hirshman and Sen: Revising the Conception of the Self." *Partisan Review* 51, 2:236–47.
Mydans, Seth. 1989. "Powerful Arms of Drug War Arousing Concern for Rights." *New York Times,* October 16, 1989, pp. A1, B10.

21

ROBERT W. RYCROFT

The Socio-Economics of Environmental Risk: Comparing Air Quality, Acid Rain, and Global Change

Risk is the most common theme of public debate about science and technology in the late twentieth century. It plays an essential role as a reference point for empirical detail about the nature, severity, and importance of a range of social problems, the most significant of which have to do with environmental health and safety. For instance, risk underlies all discussion of toxic pollution. As such, risk links human activity and the biosphere and helps hold economic activity accountable for its costs of production (Ridley, 1989). Operationalized through risk analysis, it also serves to connect knowledge and action, by performing what has been termed a "science as method" function (Schmandt and Katz, 1986). Risk analysis takes some of its characteristics from science (quantitative data that can only be used according to specified rules), and some from policy (a focus on timely action and the need to accept uncertainty and inevitable imperfections). But because it has one foot in each camp, risk analysis is controversial for all parties-at-interest. The scientific community expresses concern about the dangers of politicized science. Thus, it proposes the insulation of risk analysis from the policy process—by making a distinction between scientific and management (the political determination of acceptable risk) aspects. Industry, as the major source of risky technologies, supports this formulation, and presses for the incorporation of cost-benefit or risk-benefit frameworks. Environmentalists, suspicious of both initiatives, fear that the current approach is not sufficiently action-forcing (National Research Council, 1983; Mazur, 1985; Hattis and Kennedy, 1986). These are not rhetorical debates. Each of the major protagonists understands that environmental threat is part of the "reality of events" they now confront, and that their latitude for action is to some degree constrained as a result. Physical phenomena, those things that it is physically possible to do, increasingly generate obstacles as well as provide opportunities for social systems. Dramatic discoveries and accidents place pressures on all actors, who find themselves as limited by what is physically possible as by what is socially attainable. This is what William Ruckelshaus (1989, p. 174), twice administrator of the U.S. Environmental Protection Agency, has in mind when he says that, to allow growth and development to take place within the limits set by ecological imperatives:

> [W]e shall have to redefine our concepts of political and economic feasibility. These concepts are, after all, simply human constructs; they were different in the past, and they will surely change in the future. But the earth is real, and we are obliged by the fact of our utter dependence on it to listen more closely than we have to its messages.

This chapter is about how the "earth's messages," communicated in the language of environmental risk, contribute to redefining political, social, and economic "human constructs."

There is substantial bias against considering physical facts in much social analysis. Yet we recognize that inappropriate fit between the natural world and our policy systems often is a major source of crisis. American energy policy in the early 1970s is perhaps the clearest example of how a misfit between politics and the natural order (policy based on assumptions of abundant, cheap, domestic sources while reality imposed expensive, import dependency) can create chaos (Kash and Rycroft, 1985). Changing physical circumstances do matter.

The focus here is on three contentious U.S. environmental conflicts: air quality, acid rain, and global change. They are compared in order to illustrate how environmental threats themselves play a role in the structuring and defining of social conflicts. This is not to say that environmental events do not have social causes, or acquire social meanings, but that their dynamics do not reduce to the social. Any analysis that minimizes the importance of physical facts by over-emphasizing the cultural, for example, is likely to be off target (Dietz and Rycroft, 1987). A useful starting point, therefore, is the perspective developed by Dietz, Stern, and Rycroft (1989, p. 53):

> Our position is not that of pure social constructionists. Although we believe societies and individuals can label things and activities as clean or polluting more or less as they choose, the freedom to socially construct reality is constrained by the reality of environmental threats. A selection process ultimately links the reality of events to their social constructions: A society that treats as clean a water supply with high concentrations of typhoid bacteria, pesticides, or heavy metals will suffer a high toll of illness and death; a society that sees an implacable enemy as benign is likely to fall victim in war. So a construction discrepant with reality may prove costly.
>
> Also, reality sometimes constrains social construction because technological limits, physical laws, and natural processes make some things impossible.

For instance, although it is possible to consider the earth's climate as an economic good, it is not possible for individuals to buy their way out of global climatic changes. Global climate is a nearly public good and, unless it becomes possible to escape to other habitable worlds, it would be a sophistry to treat it as a commodity.

Within the limits established by physical "things in the world," societies can be said to divide human activities into three domains: economic, political, and scientific-technical activity. Each of these has boundaries subject to constant redefinition, but each is marked by a particular set of actors, rules, resources, and values. It matters where the boundaries are placed because defining an event or dispute in a particular domain benefits those actors who play by the accepted rules and who are viewed as pursuing their interests in a legitimate manner (Stern, 1990). Thus, defining energy as a commodity benefits energy-producing corporations, while defining it as an ecological threat benefits environmentalists and everyone who breathes polluted air. Similarly, if energy is a matter for research and development (R&D), then the beneficiaries are the members of the scientific community.

The thesis of this chapter is that the physical reality of environmental risk has been a significant constraint on the social construction of conflict in the air quality, acid rain, and global change debates. In the sections that follow, it is argued that the current placement of air quality in the political, acid rain in the economic, and global change in the scientific-technical domain is in large part a function of fundamental differences in physical reality.

Because standard disciplinary approaches to this question have not been satisfactory, this paper turns to the new field of socio-economics for a view of boundary setting between knowledge, the market, and governance. Especially attractive is the notion of socio-economics that new models of decision making are needed in order to take into account the role of community (Etzioni, 1990). Throughout the following sections the ideas of community values and standards of fairness and obligation are central.

Air Quality

The U.S. approach to all science and technology policy, including the protection of the environment, is designed to take advantage of the highly pluralistic nature of American society as well as the decentralized character of the scientific enterprise. The result is a "messy" system, but one that has the advantages of being flexible, adaptive, and redundant. Air quality policy is typical: power is dispersed throughout the federal government and shared with states and localities; interest groups proliferate and build coalitions more often based on shared opposition to proposals rather than on any coherent idea of how to attain goals; general public support for clean air has been high, but backing for any specific

Table 21.1

Risk Characteristics of Air Quality, Acid Rain, and Global Change Issues

	Air quality	Acid rain	Global change
Nature of threat	Damage to human health & welfare	Damage to natural resources	Damage to earth's atmosphere
Scope of threat	Local/regional	Regional	Global
Timing of threat	Short- to mid-term	Mid-term	Long-term
Pollutants	Criteria pollutants (sulfur dioxide, carbon monoxide, hydrocarbons, lead, nitrogen dioxide, total suspended particulates, ozone); Hazardous air pollutants	Sulfur dioxide, Nitrogen oxides, (Nitric oxide, nitrogen dioxide)	Greenhouse gasses (carbon dioxide, methane, nitrous oxide, tropospheric ozone, chlorofluorocarbons)
Known impacts	Damage to human respiratory and cardiovascular systems, increased susceptibility to infections, impaired visibility, toxic to plant and animal life, precursors to acid rain	Destruction of aquatic systems	Global-mean surface warming
Probable impacts	Neurobehavioral effects	Forest damage	Sea level rise, polar warming, reduction of sea ice, water quality deterioration
Possible impacts	Carcinogenic effects	Damage to materials, water quality, soil, human health	Continental drought, vegetation changes, reduction in biological diversity, increased frequency of unique weather patterns

Artificial sources	Combustion of fossil fuels, industrial processes	Combustion of fossil fuels, industrial processes	Combustion of fossil fuels, agriculture, chemical production, deforestation
Common knowledge	Much	Little	Almost none
Institutions involved	Domestic	International, bilateral	International, multilateral
Institutional risk culture	Egalitarian	Corporatist	Technocratic
Policy response	Removal, mitigation, monitoring and R&D	Monitoring and R&D	Monitoring and R&D

Sources: Fritzsche (1989); U.S. Environmental Protection Agency (1989); World Resources Institute (1988); National Research Council (1986).

initiative can be quite volatile and subject to intense conflict. It is a system that has been described as policy formulation and implementation by fragmentation (Rosenbaum, 1985, pp. 112–17).

The Air Quality Act of 1967 began the current approach to air pollution control, and Clean Air Act (CAA) amendments were passed in 1970 and 1977. The basic approach was to limit the amount of pollution emitted by any source and the maximum concentration of certain pollutants that could be present at ground level. The air quality issue that generated the CAA legislation and subsequent conflict has some important risk characteristics outlined in Table 21.1.

As Table 21.1 shows, the U.S. ambient air quality issue is complex, yet a good deal is known about the pollutants, their impacts, and their sources. Action has been taken toward the prevention and clean-up of certain effects and there are ongoing efforts to learn about potential consequences. By most accounts, there has been meaningful progress on a number of fronts. Urban air pollution monitoring data, for example, show improvements in emissions levels of sulfur dioxide (an 18 percent reduction), suspended particulate matter (down 34 percent), carbon monoxide (reduced some 23 percent), and lead (decreased by a spectacular 74 percent) between 1974 and 1984 (United Nations Environment Programme and World Health Organization, 1989).

This is not to say that the problem has gone away. Nothing could be further from the truth. Little has been done about emissions of nitrogen oxides, for instance, and newer problems, such as those presented by toxic air pollutants, have complicated the issue. Conflict continues to take place at every step of the way. Perhaps the best indicator of how contentious the air quality debate has been is the fact that CAA reauthorization, scheduled to take place in 1981, could not put together a winning political coalition for nine years. Only in November 1990 was a breakthrough possible.

The conventional wisdom regarding American air quality conflicts in the 1970s suggests that lofty environmental protection values and goals triumphed in the absence of empirical data from physics, chemistry, engineering, public health, and economics—knowledge that would have tempered the early optimism that air pollution problems could be solved quickly and at low cost. According to this line of thought, the environmental movement succeeded by gaining societal acceptance for a definition of the air quality debate as a battle between value differences (a public good, clean air, versus private profits). Social equity became the central concern and air quality was placed in the political domain. Had there been "good science," then control of air pollution could have been made more cost-effective and efficient (Lave and Omenn, 1981). In other words, the issue would have been placed in the economic domain had we done our scientific homework.

Why wasn't air quality initially defined as a scientific-technical activity? Three factors are usually mentioned: the widespread perception of ecological crisis, the strong moral appeal of environmental equity arguments such as the "polluter pays" principle, and the declining trust in scientific and technical expertise. Action was and continues to be a higher priority for members of the environmental community than is science (Rycroft, 1990a). But there was something else. The physical reality of the risks of air pollution had a key role in defining air quality in political, rather than scientific-technical or economic, terms.

Deteriorating air quality manifested itself in ways that were very compatible with American democracy. It harmed individual health in dramatic ways, over a relatively short period of time, and was a local phenomenon with substantial common knowledge. The last two points are critical. Urban air pollution as a local concern dates at least as far back as 1273, when a series of royal decrees were issued barring the combustion of coal. The Industrial Revolution put enough pressure on England's air quality that in 1819 Parliament undertook several studies of pollution abatement measures. In the United States, contemporary air pollution problems first emerged in the 1920s, and by the 1940s serious local health crises had been experienced in Los Angeles and Donora, Pennsylvania (Cowling, 1982). Over time, we developed a good deal of "traditional" or "folk" knowledge of the phenomenon, and it resided in the locality. This was one of the basic reasons why air pollution control in this country was a municipal government responsibility until the mid-1950s, and, as noted above, even subsequent federal legislation has continued to share power with state governments and localities. This represents a clear recognition of the physical reality of risks of declining ambient air quality. And it dovetailed nicely with the grassroots political strength of environmental groups and their value system favoring broad citizen involvement. It also helped that both the costs and benefits of urban air pollution control accrued to essentially the same community. Electric power production from coal-fired power plants or gasoline consumption in automobiles generated sulfur dioxide, suspended particulates, or ozone for many of the same people who captured the benefits. The substantial overlap among beneficiaries and cost bearers, when combined with the common knowledge of the hazards of local air pollution, made the negotiation of equity simpler and to some extent also reduced the pressure for any formal economic benefit-cost calculus. Thus, the CAA bases its standards solely on health protection, and does not permit an evaluation of the costs relative to achieving some desired reduction in risks (Regens, Dietz, and Rycroft, 1983).

Risk management, in these circumstances, could be extremely "egalitarian," operating according to values emphasizing cooperation, consensus building, and public debate (Rayner, 1984). Even the Environmental Protection Agency in the early 1970s, captured as it was by environmentalists, internalized many of these norms. A convergence of the social organization of risk institutions and the nature of the risks themselves determined the policy process. All this was to change, however, as the very different physical reality of acid rain altered the definition of conflict and of community.

Acid Rain

The CAA said nothing about long-range, transboundary pollution. Thus, when acid rain first surfaced as a policy issue in the early 1970s, it presented a significant dilemma. Unlike ambient air quality, acid rain is a process by which emissions of sulfur dioxide and nitrogen compounds are transported through the atmosphere, often extremely long distances, and are transformed by atmospheric chemistry, then deposited back again on earth in either a wet or dry form, causing damage to lakes and streams, and most likely posing risks for forests as well. The dilemma was whether to address this new problem in the context of CAA reauthorization or through separate acid rain legislation. The former path ultimately was successful, but not without one of the most contentious debates imaginable.

The reasons for the difficulty in linking acid rain to air quality are outlined in Table 21.1. On most dimensions, the problem of acid rain is clearly differentiated from that of air quality. Yet, because of two key commonalities, overlap in the pollutants addressed and the sources of those pollutants, they have been linked. Unfortunately, this gridlocked the policy system, because subordinating the acid rain debate to the clean air reauthorization conflict only served to make the latter more complex. The physical reality of acid rain risks—their greater scientific uncertainty and lower level of common knowledge, international, longer-term, and natural resource effects (rather than health), and multiplicity of management institutions dealing with a bilateral problem—made it difficult to incorporate the issue into the existing air quality management system.

Common experience with and knowledge of acid rain has been less than with ambient air quality. For example, public opinion polls have shown that in 1980 few Americans identified it as a policy problem, while two-thirds of Canadians did so. Awareness has increased dramatically since then, but experience has not. Very few Americans will ever experience both the costs and benefits of acid rain, unless it is shown to be a national rather than a regional problem. Similarly, the absence of demonstrated human health impacts has decreased the salience of the acid rain issue for many groups and individuals. Fish kills and possible forest destruction simply do not carry the same weight.

The most important result of all this is that the acid rain conflict has not been placed in the political domain. Instead, it has gone though a transition from scientific-technical to economic. The "good science" rationale dominated the definition of acid rain for almost a decade in the late 1970s and early 1980s. Manifested in R&D efforts such as the National Acid Precipitation Assessment Program, science was the only policy acceptable to all actors. This began to change as new knowledge demonstrated damage to aquatic systems, but unlike air quality, advocates of acid rain controls have been unable to translate evidence of risk into a debate about values. Rather, the conflict has come to be defined as one between vested interests. Because most sulfur dioxide emissions linked to the acid rain problem originate in the midwestern states, and most damage is in the Northeast and in Canada, demonstrably high costs are concentrated, while uncertain benefits are distributed (to many non-Americans). Thus, the conflict has come to be seen as one between potential winners and losers, and balancing economic costs, risks, and benefits has become the focus. A concise statement of the vested interest definition was put forth by John Sununu (1985, p. 60), former governor of New Hampshire and current chief of staff in the Bush White House, who framed the controversy in terms of economic sectors and geographic regions:

> The uneven distribution of the costs and benefits of control has pitted region against region in the debate over acid rain. Each constituency has distinct perceptions of the problem and of the equitable allocation of costs. Some favor a straight "polluter pays" approach; others think the costs should be widely shared through such mechanisms as a tax on electricity use or emissions, which could then be used to defray some of the capital and operating expenses of control.

Several factors are offered as an explanation for this trend toward more explicit specifications of economic cost bearers and beneficiaries: less sense of ecological crisis than in the case of ambient air quality; changed economic conditions, in which more limited resources make costs more important; lowered incremental benefits that risk regulation can attain; and improved political bargaining position for industry, with ideological allies in both the Reagan and Bush administrations. Again, however, this omits consideration that a quite different set of environmental risks is presented by the physical reality of acid deposition than was the case with urban air pollution.

A transboundary, intergenerational, multimedia (air, water, land use) phenomenon like acid rain challenges regulation and other standard mechanisms of pollution control. In the face of such complexity, industry argues, it is more effective to allow a greater role for market forces. Thus, "corporatist" risk management has become more attractive. This emphasizes risk as a legitimate and often necessary cost of economic growth, the use of pollution rights and other indirect economic tools as alternatives to CAA-type controls, and reliance on cost-effectiveness as the criterion for action. The Office of Management and Budget in the White House has become an influential promoter of this kind of institutional culture (Morall, 1986). Even the EPA, captured by industry in the 1980s, has become to some extent an advocate of corporatist risk management (Dietz and Rycroft, 1987).

The counterattack by environmentalists and their allies has argued that acid rain migration cannot be reduced to an argument about return on investment. They attack risk-benefit and cost-benefit analysis as interest-severing tools of polluters and criticize market-based options as ways to avoid internalizing the costs of environmental protection. The vested interest definition of conflict is perceived by these groups as a way to disguise the basic value differences by appealing to the "rationality" of economic analysis. They attempt to put formal cost-benefit assessments on the same level with admittedly value-based environmental protection arguments by arguing that since policy choices always involve tradeoffs and uncertainties, value systems are the only basis of conflict resolution. The inescapable fact of this debate is that unregulated acid rain arena produces certain benefits for industry and uncertain costs for society, while regulation promises certain costs for industry but uncertain benefits for society. This imbalance has made it extremely difficult to move acid rain into the political domain.

In a democratic society, it is important to identify what must be foregone to achieve various goals and who will be affected for better and for worse. The physical reality of acid rain has made such an identification itself a major source of economic conflict. Thus, debates over acid rain legislation have, on any number of occasions, come unhinged because of disagreement about who the winners and losers are likely to be and whether and how the former ought to compensate the latter (Regens and Rycroft, 1988). This in effect pitted New York recreational interests against West Virginia coal mining and Michigan automotive interests and it was very destructive of the notion of community. Add to this the stake held by Canadian tourism and forestry interests and international good will became a casualty as well. The resolution of the economic gridlock was only possible when a tradeoff was made balancing levels of pollution reduction with the use of market incentives, such as pollution rights.

Global Change

If acid rain stressed the traditional air quality system, then global change has overwhelmed it. Another look at Table 21.1 shows why. The issue of global change, or the "greenhouse effect," expands every dimension of environmental risk, in most instances quite dramatically. Simply stated, the problem is as follows: the earth's atmosphere is transparent to incoming solar radiation, but absorbs lower-energy radiation reradiated by the earth—the extra energy remaining warms like a greenhouse. The nature, scope, and timing of this threat, its range of pollutants and impacts, and the variety of institutions involved are much more broadly defined than in the case of acid rain, to say nothing of air quality. Taken together, the resolution of this problem appears to require nothing less than what one scientist has called "adaptive planetary management." Obviously, the issue has been assigned to the scientific-technical domain, and there would be no conflict except for one critical point: global change underscores, in a way the more limited air quality and acid rain issues could never do, the significance of the fossil fuel combustion "crosscut." The only linkage between the three issues, as demonstrated again in Table 21.1, is the production and consumption of energy. This is a key physical characteristic of many environmental problems:

they are interrelated through their physics, chemistry, and biology, and have common causes, chief among them the generation and utilization of energy (White, 1989). Because the risks posed by local air pollution and acid rain are linked to global change by fossil fuel combustion, at first glance it would seem that the short-term significance of the greenhouse effect might have been to justify action to reduce acid rain pollutants. This has not been the case because, as shown in Table 21.1, the acid rain ''culprits,'' sulfur dioxide and nitrogen dioxide, are not greenhouse gases. Reducing the precursors of acid rain helps with local air quality (due to reductions in sulfur dioxide), but does nothing for global change. What does make a difference for all three problems is reduced combustion of fossil fuels (Graedel and Crutzen, 1989). So while it is true that global change holds the potential to alter the definition of conflict in the air quality and acid rain arenas, it does so only indirectly.

The longer-term consequence of the emergence of global change may be to force greater integration of all these conflicts. There is some evidence that the threat of global change already is causing decision makers to recognize the interrelatedness of heretofore discrete concerns, to develop coherent language, analysis, and policy. The physical cycle of global change itself could become both a conceptual framework and a policy mechanism for integration. The Bush administration's new Global Change Research Strategy shows some signs of this in the funding priorities for scientific fields such as ''biogeochemical dynamics'' and ''solid earth processes'' (Rycroft, 1990b).

Even if integration is not on the horizon, new forms of interaction may be required to address the risks posed by global change. At a minimum, members of environmental groups and their allies may be obliged to bring their values to the center of the economy, rather than continue their pattern of standing on the periphery because it constitutes the moral ''high ground.'' Continued advocacy of expensive technology-forcing and command-and-control regulatory systems does not hold much hope of success in the case of global change. In part, this is because the greenhouse effect seems likely to lead to subtle, perhaps even irreversible consequences, yet may never manifest itself in the form of a tangible crisis. Also, even if the United States is able to mobilize in the traditional manner, global change requires multilateral responses, involving the Third World. Our old ways of implementing costly technological fixes cannot be transferred to these less developed nations (Brundtland, 1989).

A better way to link environmental values to the economy has been suggested by the authors of a recent National Academy of Engineering study. They argue that the same industrial economy that has brought about environmental disruption is also the main route to environmental quality in the future. The key is to shift the structure of economic incentives from negative to positive reinforcement and to reduce dispute resolution costs. This might be done by adopting any one of a number of new frameworks of analysis. For example, defining environmental problems in terms of ''industrial metabolism'' might unify consideration of both production and consumption in useful ways. Although patterns of production may continue to be industrial and local, there is ample evidence that consumption will be dispersed, global, and thus a problem for everyone (Ausubel, Frosch, and Herman, 1989). Global change brings this home clearly for anyone who examines the case of chlorofluorocarbons (CFCs), which are not only a greenhouse gas but a serious problem for depletion of the ozone layer. The production of CFCs is very concentrated, dominated by U.S. multinational chemical firms, while consumption is highly decentralized, with processes ranging from aerosols and refrigeration to solvents and fire extinguishers. The Montreal Protocol on Substances that Deplete the Ozone Layer set a new precedent for regulation at the international level, but this simply won't work with other greenhouse gases such as carbon dioxide (Doniger, 1988).

There are some promising signs that environmental values are now being brought to bear in the process of technological innovation. Global change has reinvigorated research into safer, more environmentally benign nuclear reactors, for instance. But it needs to be more systematic and comprehensive. Waste minimization or pollution prevention practices are now used in a number of industrial sectors, and they appear to provide something of a model for the future. This is not something that can be forced through regulation, however. The answer is in the research and development process itself. Already, R&D on pulverized coal combustion technology has offered possibilities for reduced particulate emissions (Friedlander, 1989). This is designing risk reduction into technologies themselves, and it provides an effective way for environmental protection values to be made decisionable.

Conclusions

The three air pollution conflicts examined here have been defined quite differently. Ambient air quality was debated and to some extent resolved in terms of political values. Acid rain was and is fought in terms of vested economic interests. Global change is a scientific-technological activity that may be exerting enough pressure to redefine the other two somewhat. Numerous factors help explain these different definitions, but physical phenomena have played a major role. This role, particularly the function played by environmental risks, has been underestimated in much of the literature, particularly that part concerned with social construction of conflict. Indeed, the risks posed by phenomena such as global change may be forcing an interdependence between ecology and economy that could not have been brought about by knowledge, values, or vested interest alone.

References

Ausubel, Jesse H., Robert A. Frosch, and Robert Herman. 1989. "Technology and Environment: An Overview." In Jesse H. Ausubel and Hedy E. Sladovich, eds., *Technology and Environment*. Washington, DC: National Academy Press.

Brundtland, Gro H. 1989. "Global Change and Our Common Future." *Environment* 31 (June): 16–20, 40–43.

Cowling, E.B. 1982. "Acid Rain Precipitation in Historical Perspective." *Environmental Science and Technology* 16 (February): 110A–23A.

Dietz, Thomas M., and Robert W. Rycroft. 1987. *The Risk Professionals*. New York: Russell Sage Foundation.

Dietz, Thomas M., Paul C. Stern, and Robert W. Rycroft. 1989. "Definitions of Conflict and the Legitimation of Resources: The Case of Environmental Risk." *Sociological Forum* 4 (March): 47–70.

Doniger, David D. 1988. "Politics of the Ozone Layer." *Issues in Science and Technology* 4 (Spring): 86–92.

Etzioni, Amitai. 1990. "A New Kind of Socioeconomics." *Challenge* 33 (January/February): 31–32.

Friedlander, Sheldon K. 1989. "Pollution Prevention: Implications for Engineering Design, Research, and Education." *Environment* 31 (May): 10–15, 36–38.

Fritzsche, Andrew F. 1989. "The Health Risks of Energy Production." *Risk Analysis* 9 (December): 566–77.

Graedel, Thomas E., and Paul J. Crutzen. 1989. "The Changing Atmosphere." *Scientific American* 261 (September): 58–68.

Hattis, Dale, and Donald Kennedy. 1986. "Assessing Risks from Health Hazards: An Imperfect Science." *Technology Review* 89 (May/June): 61–71.

Kash, Don E., and Robert W. Rycroft. 1985. "Energy Policy: How Failure Was Snatched from the Jaws of Success." *Policy Studies Review* 4 (February): 433–444.

Lave, Lester B., and Gilbert S. Omenn. 1981. *Clearing the Air: Reforming the Clean Air Act*. Washington, DC: Brookings Institution.

Mazur, Allan. 1985. "Bias in Risk-Benefit Analysis." *Technology in Society* 7, 1:20–30.

Morrall, John F., III. 1986. "A Review of the Record." *Regulation* 10 (November–December): 25–34.

National Research Council. 1983. *Risk Assessment in the Federal Government: Managing the Process*. Washington, DC: National Academy Press.

———. 1986. *Acid Rain Deposition: Long-Term Trends*. Washington, DC: National Academy Press.

Rayner, Steve. 1984. "Disagreeing about Risk: The Institutional Cultures of Risk Management and Planning for Future Generations." In Susan G. Hadden, ed., *Risk Analysis, Institutions, and Public Policy*. New York: Associated Faculty Press.

Regens, James L., Thomas M. Dietz, and Robert W. Rycroft. 1983. "Risk Assessment in the Policy Making Process: Environmental Health and Safety Protection." *Public Administration Review* 43 (March/April): 137–46.

Regens, James L., and Robert W. Rycroft. 1988. *The Acid Rain Controversy*. Pittsburgh, PA: University of Pittsburgh Press.

Ridley, Matt. 1989. "The Pace and Complexity of Developments in Science: Social, Economic and Environmental Implications for Policy-Makers." Oxfordshire, UK: Ditchley Foundation.

Rosenbaum, Walter A. 1985. *Environmental Politics and Policy*. Washington, DC: Congressional Quarterly, Inc.

Ruckelshaus, William D. 1989. "Toward a Sustainable World." *Scientific American* 216 (September): 166–75.

Rycroft, Robert W. 1990a. "Environmentalism and Science." Paper presented at the Annual Meeting of the American Association for the Advancement of Science, New Orleans, February 18.

————. 1990b. "Acid Rain: Air Quality, Global Change, or What?" *National Forum* 70 (Winter): 40–42.

Schmandt, Jurgen, and James E. Katz. 1986. "The Scientific State: A Theory with Hypotheses." *Science, Technology, and Human Values* 11 (Winter): 40–52.

Stern, Paul C. 1990. "The Social Construction of the Economy." *Challenge* 33 (January/February): 38–45.

Sununu, John H. 1985. "Acid Rain: Sharing the Cost." *Issues in Science and Technology* 1 (Winter): 47–59.

United Nations Environment Programme and World Health Organization. 1989. "Monitoring the Global Environment: An Assessment of Urban Air Quality." *Environment* 31 (October): 6–13, 26–37.

U.S. Environmental Protection Agency. 1989. *The Potential Effects of Global Climate Change on the United States.* Washington, DC: Government Printing Office, December.

White, Robert M. 1989. "Greenhouse Policy and Climate Uncertainty." Presentation by the President, of the National Academy of Engineering to the National Academy of Sciences Annual Meeting, Washington, DC, April 24.

World Resources Institute. 1988. *World Resources 1988–89.* New York: Basic Books.

About the Contributors

Catherine Alter is Associate Professor of Social Work and Director of the School of Social Work at the University of Iowa. Her research interest is inter-organizational service delivery systems in the nonprofit sector.

Norman E. Bowie holds the Elmer L. Andersen Chair in Corporate Responsibility, Strategic Management, and Organization in the Curtis L. Carlson School of Management at the University of Minnesota, Twin Cities. He is the coauthor of *Business Ethics* and coeditor of *Ethical Theory and Business* and is currently working on a monograph on university-business partnerships.

John L. Campbell is Assistant Professor of Sociology at Harvard University. He is author of *Collapse of an Industry: Nuclear Power and the Contradictions of U.S. Policy* and is editor with Leon Lindberg and Rogers Hollingsworth of *Governance of the American Economy.* He is currently studying the political economy of U.S. tax policy and is continuing his work on economic governance.

Max B.E. Clarkson is Professor Emeritus of Management on the Faculty of Management, at the University of Toronto. After a successful career as a business executive in the United States, he returned to Canada as dean of the Faculty of Management. He has taught courses on strategy and corporate social responsibilities as well as required courses in business ethics. He is the founding director of the Center for Corporate Social Performance and Ethics.

Richard M. Coughlin is Professor and Chair of the Department of Sociology at the University of New Mexico, where he has taught since 1978. He received a Ph.D. in sociology from the University of California at Berkeley in 1977. He is the author of *Ideology, Public Opinion, and Welfare Policy* and editor of *Reforming Welfare.* His research interests include comparative social policy and public opinion in advanced industrialized societies.

Kenneth G. Dau-Schmidt is Professor of Law and Economics at the University of Cincinnati College of Law. He received his J.D. and his M.A. and Ph.D. in Economics from the University of Michigan. His academic work includes articles on labor economics, labor law, and the economic analysis of law. His contribution to this volume is an adaptation of his *Duke Law Journal* article entitled "An Economic Analysis of the Criminal Law as a Preference Shaping Policy."

Robyn M. Dawes received his Ph.D. in mathematical psychology with a content interest in behavioral decision making, social interaction, and attitude measurement. Currently he is Professor of Psychology in the Department of Social and Decision Sciences at Carnegie Mellon University. The author of over 100 journal articles and three books, Dawes has also served in numerous capacities outside the university, including over three years on the National Research Council's Committee on AIDS Research and the Behavioral, Social, and Statistical Sciences.

Chris de Neubourg studied economics and sociology at the University of Louvain and the University of Antwerp. He lectured at the University of Groningen and is currently Associate Professor of Economics at the University of Limburg, Maastricht in the Netherlands. His research focuses on labor market issues, including unemployment and labor utilization, studied in an international comparative context.

Peter B. Doeringer is Professor of Economics at Boston University and a Research Fellow at the Center for Business and Government, John F. Kennedy School of Government, Harvard University. He is a specialist on labor markets and industrial relations. His latest book, *Turbulence in the American Workplace*, looks at how recent economic change is affecting labor productivity and earnings.

John D. Donahue is Associate Professor at the John F. Kennedy School of Government at Harvard University where he teaches courses in public management, finance, and business-government relations. His publications include *New Deals: The Chrysler Revival and the American System* (with Robert B. Reich) **and** *The Privatization Decision: Public Ends, Private Means*.

Amitai Etzioni is the first University Professor of The George Washington University. In 1987–89, he served as the Thomas Henry Carroll Ford Foundation Professor at the Harvard Business School. He is the author of fourteen books, including *A Comparative Analysis of Complex Organizations*, *Modern Organizations*, *Political Unification*, *The Active Society*, *Genetic Fix*, *Social Problems*, and most recently, *An Immodest Agenda*, *Capital Corruption*, and *The Moral Dimension*.

Karen N. Gaertner is Associate Professor of Behavioral Sciences in the School of Business Administration at Georgetown University. She earned her Ph.D. at the University of Chicago Graduate School of Business. Her publications include articles and chapters on career patterns, performance appraisal and merit pay, employee commitment, and work-family relations. Currently she is conducting research on creating and maintaining ethical climates in organizations, and is completing work on the effects of internal labor markets on employee commitment and performance.

Jerald Hage is Professor of Sociology at the University of Maryland at College Park, where he also serves as Director of the Center for Innovation. The chapter in this volume, with Catherine Alter, is condensed from their forthcoming book, *Organizations Working Together: Coordination in Interorganizational Networks.*

Susan Helper is Assistant Professor of Economics at the Weatherhead School of Management, Case Western Reserve University. She previously taught operations management at Boston University, and is a research affiliate of the International Motor Vehicle Program at MIT. She holds a Ph.D. in economics from Harvard University.

Robert E. Lane is Eugene Meyer Professor of Political Science Emeritus at Yale University. He is a past president of the American Political Science Association, International Society of Political Psychology, and Policy Studies Organization. Among his published works are *The Regulation of Businessmen; Political Life; The Liberties of Wit; Political Ideology; Political Thinking and Consciousness; Political Man;* and numerous articles on market effects on persons and their experiences. The paper included in this volume is a modified version of a chapter in his forthcoming *The Market Experience*.

Leon N. Lindberg is Professor of Political Science at the University of Wisconsin-Madison. He has published widely on comparative and international political economy, including *The Politics of Inflation and Economic Stagnation, The Energy Syndrome, Stress and Contradiction in Modern Capitalism,* and *Europe's Would-Be Polity.* He is editor with John Campbell and Rogers Hollingsworth of *Governance of the American Economy.* He is currently working on a study of "Capital Movements, Financial Services, and the Politics of Monetary Policy in the European Community."

Klaus Nielsen is Associate Professor at the University of Roskilde and Research Director at the Center for Public Organization and Management in Copenhagen. His research has primarily been concerned with institutional economics, public finance, and economic policy.

Ove K. Pedersen is Associate Professor at the University of Roskilde and Research Director at the Center for Public Organization and Management in Copenhagen. His research has primarily been concerned with philosophy of science, industrial relations, institutional history, and organizational change in public administration in the Nordic countries.

Patrick Michael Rooney received his B.A., M.A., and Ph.D. from the University of Notre Dame. He has written extensively on employee ownership and worker participation including four papers that have won refereed national paper contests. He has published in *The Journal of Economic Issues, The Journal of Applied Business Research,* and *The Economic Forum.* He has an essay forthcoming in *The International Handbook of Participation in Organizations,* published by Oxford University Press.

Robert W. Rycroft is Associate Professor in the Center for International Science and Technology Policy, Elliott School of International Affairs, at George Washington University. He holds a Ph.D. from the University of Oklahoma. His research interests include science and technology policy, natural resources and environmental policy, policy evaluation, technology assessment, and risk analysis. He is coauthor of eight books, including *The Acid Rain Controversy; The Risk Professionals; U.S. Energy Policy: Crisis and Complacency;* and *Energy in the Global Arena.*

Howard S. Schwartz received his Bachelor's and Master's degrees in philosophy from Antioch College and the University of California, San Diego, respectively. His Ph.D. is in organizational behavior from Cornell. Since 1977, he has been teaching at Oakland University in Rochester, Michigan. The article appearing in this volume is from his book *Narcissistic Process and Corporate Decay: The Theory of the Organizational Ideal.*

Jerome M. Segal is a Research Scholar at the Institute for Philosophy and Public Policy, University of Maryland. He is the author of *Creating the Palestinian State,* and *Agency and Alienation.* Previously he was the Senior Advisor for Agency Planning at the Agency for International Development.

Lester C. Thurow is Dean of the Sloan School of Management at the Massachusetts Institute of Technology, where he has served on the faculty since 1968. He received his M.A. from Balliol College, Oxford, and Ph.D. in economics from Harvard. His numerous publications include *The Zero-Sum Society, Dangerous Currents,* and *The Zero-Sum Solution.*

John Oliver Wilson teaches in the Walter A. Haas School of Business and the Graduate School of Public Policy at the University of California at Berkeley. He is co-chair of the Berkeley Forum on Ethics and International Business. Active in business, he is Chief Economist at the Bank of America and serves on several corporate boards of directors.

Index